Items should be returned on or before the last date shown below. Items not already requested by other borrowers may be renewed in person, in writing or by telephone. To renew, please quote the number on the barcode label. To renew online a PIN is required. This can be requested at your local library.
Renew online @ **www.dublincitypubliclibraries.ie**
Fines charged for overdue items will include postage incurred in recovery. Damage to or loss of items will be charged to the borrower.

Leabharlanna Poiblí Chathair Bhaile Átha Cliath
Dublin City Public Libraries

Comhairle Cathrach
Bhaile Átha Cliath
Dublin City Council

Brainse Fhionnglaise   Finglas Library
T: (01) 8344906 E: finglaslibrary@dublincity.ie

In Back Office

Date Due	Date Due	Date Due
Brainse Fhionnglaise Finglas Library		
T: (01) 8344906 E: finglaslibrary@dublincity.ie		

The Rich Husband, by the Author of 'the Ruling Passion'

J. Billing, Printer and Stereotyper, Guildford, Surrey.

THE

RICH HUSBAND.

CHAPTER I.

A LONG time ago—at least, what we should
think such, were it snipped by fate's sharp relent-
less scissors out of a human life, though it can be
considered but as a very brief period, when compared with the duration of the world's great
history: a long, long time ago, speaking of
the lapse of years, as that lapse affects, not the
grey old earth itself, indeed, but the dwellers
thereupon; before omnibuses were, or cabs had
been christened, or the new police invented;
ere the electric telegraph had annihilated space,
or steam rendered distance a myth, and set, to

borrow an American expression, "all creation moving," when, in a dozen brief words, the past was the present, and the present the future;— a long, a very long time ago, in the ordinary sense of the phrase, it so chanced that Mr. Henry Bultin lodged, or (as the sentence is now constructed,) occupied apartments in, the house of a Mrs. Hilton, whose four-story mansion was known to her friends, the postman, the watchman, all general acquaintances, and her extensive business connexion, as Number 72, Great Crowland Street.

Having stated which facts for mine own especial purpose, I should proceed forthwith along the regular highroad of this veracious narrative, if at the very outset of the three-volume journey it did not seem better (in order to prevent future delays,) to stop short and politely satisfy the curiosity of an inquisitive reader, whom I prophetically hear demanding—

"And pray who was Mr. Henry Bultin?— and where is Great Crowland Street?"

The latter question, being a much more important one than the former, I may for once cast aside established rule, and proceed to bestow the order of publicity upon the locality once honoured by being made the abiding-place of Mr. Henry Bultin, rather than upon that gentleman himself,—at least, in the first instance.

Great Crowland Steet, dear reader, may then, to the best of my belief, be found to this day, in the very heart of that large indefinite neutral ground, which people living near the monument insist on calling the West End, and people dwelling within bowshot of the Duke of Wellington, (not the public-house, be it understood, but the statue) stigmatize as the East; wherefore, it may safely be pronounced a happy cross betwixt the two, since it is thus proved to be quite as far removed from the unspeakable vulgarity of the one region, as from the overpowering gentility of the other.

It is no business of mine to define more precisely the limits, and land-marks, and boundaries of this locality. I have not the slightest intention of making a martyr of myself, by stating for the edification of any one, the exact point where, losing sight of the "true blues," we find ourselves getting into a different sort of society—a shade removed from the genuine ultramarine of Tyburnia, walking through an atmosphere

redolent less of attar of roses than of rose water;
—a sphere well enough to do in its own way,
doubtless, and requiring, like every other sphere
about London, a vast deal of money to revolve
creditably in; yet still lying outside the fairy
ring, separated by an indefinable, although most
powerful something from the much-envied circle
of fashion; in short—I do not feel called upon
to bring censorious tongues upon this instructive
narrative, by endeavouring to state that whereof I
am wholly in ignorance myself,—namely: where
superlative gentility ceases; where comparative
gentility commences; where positive vulgarity
abides.   East and West!   Thank Heaven,
I am writing not in French, which acknow-
ledges no neuter gender, but in English, which
does, and can therefore, as before intimated,
take refuge in a something lying conveniently
betwixt the two: a vague, debateable, respectable, once aristocratic land, the mere fact of
dwelling in which, renders further reference to
either one or the other superfluous.   The people
nhabiting Great Crowland Street were called
West-End folks in Mark Lane, it is true, but
Grosvenor Square turned up its Roman nose
in their faces, and styled them Eastern barba-

rians, as though they had belonged to some of
the wild tribes of Tartary, yet still, notwithstanding these things, most of the estimable
individuals who had habitations in that locality,
were far too much occupied with their own
concerns to be either unduly exalted by the
first sentence of homage, or hopelessly abased
by the last most unfounded and illiberal
slander.

They lived there apart, separated only by a
few squares from regions where the nobility
drove ceaselessly backwards and forwards in
splendid carriages, rendered still more splendid
by the addition of a couple of hapless footmen
clinging on behind:—only divided by such a
little space from rank, fashion, beauty; the very
exotics of Albion's garden, the richest cream of
English society, and still, had the Libyan desert
yawned between, they could not have felt further removed from the "Great World," could
not have lived in more total and isolated seclusion;—a peculiar people, "zealous of good
works."

Well, as for the final portion of the foregoing sentence, it is to be hoped they were; at
all events, if they gave their thoughts to eternal

matters with one-tenth portion of the vigour
and hearty good-will wherewith they devoted
their energies to the great temporal affair of
making money, they must surely have found
heaps of incorruptible treasure awaiting their advent in a better world.   But whether this proved
so or not, it is impossible to tell; their good
works, worthy people, were hidden, as good
works ought to be, while their ostensible employment everybody was free to see and comment
upon, for it was that most laudable and common
one called " turning the penny," fifty times in
the course of the day when they could, and of
turning it each time moreover, if possible, to
greater advantage.

For their place of abode was a shop street, ay,
and for that matter is a shop street still, wherein
an inquisitive stranger, blessed at once with
patience inexhaustible, and legs untireable, and
a tongue unwearying, might, after painful re-
search and long walking, and frequent questioning, make purchases to his heart's content,
even to this present hour.   But at the remote
period of which this story treats, the glory o
important publicity still hung about the place.
It was then, indeed, a good and notable shop

street, in the very prime and vigour of life, without the faintest conception that time should ever arrive, which has now arrived, for it to be hustled by younger and healthier rivals into the corner of dreamy oblivion, where now in its old age it sleepily reposes.

Just as in our own day the last young beauty out forgets in the triumph of her first season that her hair must grow gray, and her eyes lose their brilliancy, and her cheeks be deprived of their roses; so Great Crowland Street, all radiant with bright red bricks, and fresh paint, and first-class shops, and unexceptionable sign-boards, fancied its day would last for ever, that the glory of morning could scarcely at eve depart from it.

It found out its mistake, however, years ago, when the house fronts grew of a dirty reddish black, when the paint peeled off its window sills, when grander *Magasin des modes*, and Pantechnethicas, and Heimatemporions, and monster bazaars, and endless dépots and milliners' show-rooms, springing into existence in more modern thoroughfares it was compelled, *bongré malgré*, to walk into the background, and stand in the shade for evermore. But Great Crowland Street

undoubtedly enjoyed its day of prosperous cele-
brity as the new comers enjoy theirs, and the
period when it had arrived at the very zenith
of its splendour was that of which I write—a
long time ago.

Next to the number and excellence of its
shops, the thing most noticeable about Great
Crowland Street was their arrangement. There
were two of every sort under the sun—I won't
say clean and unclean, but of every other species
and description. Two bakers, two butchers,
two jewellers, two grocers, two apothecaries, two
ironmongers, two upholsterers, two hair-dressers,
two fruiterers, and so on *ad infinitum*, or at least
so on to the last number in the street, which
was an even one.

But the reader must not imagine the spirit of
regularity was satisfied with this ingenious arrangement of pairs. Oh! no, it further divided the said pairs, and distributed them equally
at both sides of the thoroughfare. One of each
made up the row on one side, one of each
balanced them precisely on the other: not that
the rivals exactly faced—innovation herself dare
scarcely have suggested such a hostile procedure
—they merely, as stated above, balanced. Thus

No. 2 was a tobaconist, and No. 31, a long bias across the way, had a full-length Highlander over his entrance also.

The plan was at once a judicious and a successful one, since it brought two of a trade together, and yet still compelled them to agree; the last consummation most devoutly to be prayed for, being materially influenced by the etiquette of the street, which ordained it a point of honour that the north side should patronize the north solely and exclusively, whilst the south poured forth its favours on the south in like manner.

The consequence of which equitable arrangement was, that every man, woman, and child, dwelling in houses, 1 to 44, inclusive had his, her, and its hair cut and curled at No. 16, on their own side; and every soul inhabiting Nos. 45 to 88, bought bread from Mr. Hilton, who sold the same at No. 72. The northerns had their beer brought daily to their doors, by the pot-boy, from corner shop No. 1; whilst the southerners, ignoring its very existence, flocked unanimously to public-house No. 45.

How this singular fashion originally came to be adopted by the Great Crowlanders, it were

vain to conjecture ; for it was a genuine Cockney
locality, in which, to employ a phrase more expressive than grammatical, "Nobody knew nothing about nobody." Opposite neighbours had
children, but the events were never even· suspected by people over the way. People over the
way got husbands for pretty daughters, and
opposite neighbours remained in blessed ignorance of the portion of the bride, of the name
of the bridegroom. Men and women died from
time to time on both sides of the street, and
living men and women, old residents in the same
thoroughfare knew nothing about the matter
until the undertaker came to take the corpse
away, when they felt satisfied somebody must
have departed into the silent land ; but who, or
why, or by what means they never inquired—they
were never informed.

The shopkeepers, it is true, had a sort of
acquaintance with their customers, but it was .
purely a shop acquaintance. They knew who
bought from them ; had a tolerably accurate
idea to which numbers things were to be sent
home, and were quite certain as to the parties from
whom they were to request payment of their
little accounts ; but further than that there was

no intercourse. Nobody associated with anybody in Great Crowland Street : perhaps that
was the reason they agreed so well. They never
quarrelled ; there were no soft answers needed
amongst them to turn away wrath, for they never
spoke at all, except across their counters, and
very little then.

They were the strangest set of people that
ever lived—taciturn even for London, wrapt up
so exclusively in their own families, their own
affairs, their own friends, their own efforts to
" make off a livelihood" and amass wealth ; so
totally engrossed with what happened within
their own abodes, that they had not a second's
leisure to bestow a thought on next door, whilst
next door was fifty times too busy to think of
them.

Perhaps, dear country reader, you may con-
ceive this description to be a little overdone,
and declare it impossible such self-contained,
unexcitable, uninquisitive folks could ever, even
in remote periods, have existed anywhere on this
earth. But never believe it : human nature is
much the same one time as another; and as
such people played out their several parts
in London long years ago, such people are

playing out their distinctive parts in London
still.

If you doubt it, come and see.   If you want
to know what perfect independence is—to be able
to do precisely as you list, to be free from censorious observation, to escape the keen scrutiny
and malignant criticism of old women of both
sexes; if you desire to live in what style you
choose, to wear out shabby clothes without being
pointed at as poor; to disport the most fashionable garments without being called extravagant;
to be married without a living soul but the
curate, the clerk, and your wife being the wiser;
to be buried without a score of idle tongues
telegraphing the fact from house to house, and
calling the funeral stingy, and holding a coroner's
inquest with a special jury over your memory;—
come and live in the very heart of London, for
you will find yourself more alone there than
would be the case if you were standing in the
middle of a Scotch moor, without a human
habitation within a dozen miles of you.

Some people might speedily weary of the experiment; for, as we know there are a few who,
sooner than live alone, would live with persons
they hated, so there are thousands who would

prefer being spoken evil of, to not being talked about at all. Some might dislike London for that which others imagine to be its crowning beauty; but all this has little or nothing to do with Great Crowland Street, where nobody knew anything about anybody, with the exception of Mrs. Hilton, who ventured to break the rule of the street by having vegetables from her son-in-law over the way; who, to remedy this error, to square the circle, to make odd even, and crooked straight, had his bread from No. 72. There was an excuse, however, for Mrs. Hilton's backsliding, on the score of motherly affection and near relationship; and, therefore, though she broke so far across the line as both to trade and talk, the other householders never deserted her for going over to the northern enemy, but, shutting their eyes to her solitary *faux pas*, continued to deal with her as formerly, and accordingly she throve and prospered exceedingly, and reigned in solemn state at No. 72, whereof Mr. Henry Bultin occupied the second floor.

For it was another peculiarity of Great Crowland Street, that everybody therein took lodgers. Where the family lived in each four-story brick mansion, could only be dimly surmised; the following being the sole conjecture anent the domestic arrangements, warranted by appearances —to wit—

Underground dungeon, commonly styled basement, used as kitchen, and serving for the abode of damp and the maid-of-all-work by day; and of damp, the maid-of-all-work, black beetles, cockroaches, crickets, and various other beasts of prey by night.

Ground floor :—portioned off into hall, shop, and back parlour; in which latter apartment, eight feet by ten or so, meals were taken, visitors received, the family, when "at home," resided, and private business of all kinds was transacted.

First floor :—lodgers.

Second ditto :—more lodgers, and above heavenwards, the whole establishment, parents, children, guests, apprentices, slept, the gods alone knew where or how.

Every individual householder or householdress in Great Crowland Street paid his or her rent with the money of single or widowed ladies, city bachelors, or young brokers, who had taken the cares of matrimony on them all too early.

Somebody was eternally giving or taking

notice in Great Crowland Street; landladies were perpetually requiring references; respectable shopkeepers were for ever indignantly refusing offers of "a week in advance," as a substitute for "a name as somebody knowed."

"Furnished apartments" were hung up inside the fanlights above the hall doors; exhibited to public view amongst the apples on the fruiterer's stall—and stuck in moist sugar behind the glass panes of the grocers' windows.

Apartments——furnished and unfurnished rooms for single and double gentlemen: for ladies suffering from domestic bereavements—for ladies who had not yet knocked themselves down to anybody in the matrimonial market; for those who had held on their lots till too late in the sale; for those who had never had a high enough bid; for others who had perhaps never been bid for at all; for crape-veiled widows, and cat-loving spinsters, and anxious mothers, and prudent heads of families, and testy, elderly bachelors, and third-rate spruce young dandies: apartments furnished and unfurnished for these —first floors and second floors; bedrooms, with use of sitting-rooms; sitting-rooms with sofa bedstead; lodgings with attendance, and lodgings without; these announcements met the eye at every turn, and may be said to have constituted, with ledgers on week days, and prayer books on Sundays, the literature of Great Crowland Street, where lodgers were always coming, whence lodgers were always going.

Save perhaps from the house of Mrs. Hilton, whose "ladies and gentlemen," as she colloquially styled them, always stayed with her for years, for she was a shrewd, sensible woman, who after a trial would lower her terms to secure good payers, wisely considering that low cash settlements every Saturday morning, were preferable to greater nominal profits at more uncertain intervals. It was a favourite maxim of the acute widow, that she knew as well as any one "how many yards it took to make a gownd;" which proverb being freely translated into modern English, meant that she clearly understood what sort of lodgers made up her rent.

Not wandering stars and unsatisfactory birds of passage, who were in and out fifty times a day, and wore the stair-carpeting into holes, and burnt coals *ad libitum*, and left the linen in a dilapidated condition, and kept some one sitting up half the night for them ; not strangers who

came to see London, and to exhaust a servant's
constitution and a landlady's patience in a week;
—but quiet, respectable "limited people," (by
which rather obscure phrase Mrs. H. meant
persons of limited incomes) who were sure to
pay and stay.

To these Mrs. Hilton let her apartments
gladly, and in the second floor set thereof Mr.
Henry Bultin lived.

He was a young man of large stature and
small means; clerk in an attorney's office, regular
and peaceable enough in his conduct; by no
means clever, or likely to set either the Thames
or any other river in the kingdom on fire; he
had not the smallest leaning towards becoming
a member of what is called, in the recognised
slang of the present day, "the fast school;" he
was not handsome, nor remarkable in any way,
(save in his own opinion) excepting for a certain
kind of what may be termed "lazy ambition;"
a full share of masculine vanity, and a selfish
imagination, which he always kept at full work
—building interminable Chateaux en Espagne.
Truly there never was anybody more unlike an
Adonis, and yet he fancied he was a lady-killer,
and liked to walk about the most fashionable

streets; stare into the handsomest carriages, look at the "pretty girls," as he carelessly called them, who reclined therein, and spent whole evenings which might one would think have been better employed, in erecting particularly airy castles concerning his future, and inventing nice tales for his own edification, the heroes wherein were invariably Henry Bultin, and the heroines beautiful duchesses; whilst the plots usually were to the effect that heiress after heiress fell in love with him, which universal devotion of the female aristocracy he rewarded by eventually marrying one of the fairest of the lot, in St. George's, Hanover Square, and breaking the hearts of the others—the curtain finally dropping upon a presentation-scene at court, and the words " lived happily ever after."

It would take a volume to tell the number and variety of feats of heroism he performed sitting in Mrs. Hilton's second floor front, or walking to his employer's office in the city; the run-away horses he stopped, the ladies he rescued from drowning, the beautiful heiresses he discovered in beggary, and whom, through his legal knowledge, he was enabled to reinstate in their rightful position, he of course mounting fortune's ladder along with them. Sometimes papas were grateful for the salvation of their daughters; necks, and pressed their hands and dowries upon him in quite an unprecedented manner ; but more frequently the loving creatures had property in their own right, and when mamma frowned, and papa stormed, cut the gordian knot of true-love difficulty by driving off to Gretna and tying another knot there; which many a wife and husband has ere now confessed, with a sigh, can be tied too hastily.

It may seem ridiculous to state that any man not a lunatic should spend his leisure moments in concocting such absurdities as these, but like many another plodder on this earth, he was dissatisfied with his own condition, whilst unfitted to better it ; too common-place to rise, too poor to save, and too self-indulgent even to make the endeavour; he disliked labour, and wished to have clerks under him instead of being clerk under any one; he was lazily ambitious, as I have said before, and selfishly imaginative ; wherefore he sate in his shabbily furnished room, and fancied himself in lordly chambers ; just as an indolent pauper inclined to gluttony, might, instead of going out to earn enough to purchase

a feast, lie down in the sun, and dream of
Christmas turkeys and endless plum puddings
falling ready cooked into his mouth.

The vulgar Irish proverb, "There is a
power of brains outside his head," which certainly implies a great deal more than it actually
expresses, describes his intellectual possessions to
a nicety; but still he had a general idea he was
a neglected genius, undervalued by his employers, unrecognised by society; a person from
whom the world received a great number of
important services, for which the world never
returned him any adequate remuneration.

Excepting his vanity, and a certain common
shrewdness, exhibited not in acquiring money,
but in making the most of it when he had got
it, there was not much about him worth speaking
of; and having little or nothing to do with the
progress of this story, he would never have been
mentioned therein, had it not chanced that just
at the period of which I treat, the occupation of
looking out of window formed the business and
amusement of all his leisure moments.   Under
the circumstances in which he was placed, this
breach of street etiquette was certainly excusable, for of the female portion of creation—that

portion, in fact, to which he exclusively devoted his attention, there was nothing " worth while" in Mrs. Hilton's establishment.

That lady herself had a wig on her head, and crows' feet about her eyes, and though she was plump and active, time's finger was clearly busy tracing the score of at least sixty lustres across her brow; then her daughters were respectable matrons, and her spinster niece looked older than her aunt, whilst the maid-of-all-work squinted, and the "retired" gentlewoman who occupied the first floor, and of whom the niece afore-mentioned "took care," was room-ridden—if not bed-ridden—eighty, doting, troublesome, and unsociable. There was clearly nothing in-doors for Mr. Bultin to inflict tortures upon, or to make sentimental romances concerning; wherefore no alternative remained but for him to direct his gaze across the street—which alternative he accordingly adopted.

To explain what he saw there, it will be better to turn over the page and commence a new chapter.

CHAPTER II.

FROM the apartments which Mr. Henry Bultin occupied at reduced rates, upon condition (Mrs. Hilton always made endless conditions with her lodgers) that if a more eligible "party" offered, he would vacate the second floor front sitting-room, whereof he had the use; he could see right down into the windows of No. 72's *vis-à-vis*, No. 16; and the solitary individual who monopolized the genteel flat in that habitation, rivetted Mr. Bultin's attention, in a manner which may safely be pronounced unprecedented.

There was something "queer" about her. What in fact first induced him to notice the lady at all, was that he had seen her—yes, that very identical, melancholy-looking woman driving through the park in a beautiful carriage drawn by a pair of unexceptionable greys, accompanied by, and talking earnestly to, a very fashionably dressed personage, whose beauty, although on the wane, was still sufficient to entitle her to the appellation of "strikingly handsome."

There was a mournful expression on her face, too—a dissatisfied, crushed, blighted heart had traced its fretwork across her countenance. Sorrow on both their brows : grief written there in unmistakeable characters !

Who could they be? the one living in Great Crowland Street, the other apparently surrounded by every luxury. Who could they be? Mr. Bultin's curiosity was excited.

Many a day after that on which he first beheld his opposite neighbour in such a fashionable locality, when sent by his city employers to transact business at the other end of town, he walked a full mile out of his way in the hope of catching another glimpse of that carriage, of learning to whom it belonged, of having a little light thrown on the position of its occupants ; all in vain. Equipage, livery, crest, footmen, horses, never would cross his path ; he could hear nothing about their owner. She might be in the park every day for aught he knew to the contrary, only he never chanced to see her; so partly in pique, partly in despair, he took up the study of No. 16's first floor lodger, and watched her during every spare moment with the lynx-eyed vigilance of a cat.

He was the only person in Great Crowland Street who ever did stare into other folks' windows: but then he had long summer evenings on hand after he returned from the city; he had no ledgers to look at—no lodgers to attend to—no taste for literature—no talent for flute-playing; was not rich enough to be always with "other fellows;" and besides, who knew, the 'lady opposite might be a "good spec;" so, morning and evening, week day and Sunday, he devoted himself and a pocket telescope to her. Partially hidden by the window-curtains, he pursued his observations, but they also led to nothing. At the end of thirteen weeks, he found himself just as wise as he had been at starting.

"She was a curious creature!" that was the sum total of his discovery. "Curious and a puzzle."

"Poor," he thought, at first; "lots of money," he decided afterwards.

He watched her in the summer mornings at her unsocial breakfast, which consisted of a single cup of coffee, and a slice of thin toasted bread; when that meal was concluded, she watered her geraniums, drew down the blinds, flung up the windows, and so shut out the sun and let in the air, just as Mr. Henry Bultin departed for the city.

When he returned thence, the blinds were up again, and she was dining; and after the servant had removed the cloth, she drew a low ottoman near to the window, where, screened from all observation but his, she gazed alternately at the street with its many passers-by, its ceaseless traffic, its eternal human tide ebbing and flowing, flowing and ebbing for ever, and at the pages of some book she held in her hand: It was poetry, Mr. Bultin concluded—but perhaps he was mistaken.

For the spring-time of her life was past, and what had she to do with poetry? what had a woman of peculiar habits, of uncertain age, who had eaten of sorrow and quaffed of the deep cup of mortal grief, to do with poetry? What indeed?

Mr. Bultin, however, settled she was senti-

mental, and could be "got at," and accordingly
he never ceased marvelling about and forming
schemes concerning her.

As twilight stole on, she closed the volume,
and looked up at the sky, and thought—thought
of what?

Mr. Bultin most earnestly desired to know
that, but the book of the mind is the only one
no curious eye may ever read, except by permission of the owner. That volume is hardly
laid open once in a century by any mortal unto
his fellow—seldom, if ever perused from beginning to end by any save its possessor.

Always a sealed-up chapter or two; a few
pages so closely pasted together that a stranger
cannot notice the deception; lines erased,
altered, blotted; explanatory notes suppressed;
whole paragraphs omitted. Ah, me! who, on
the face of this round globe, hears all, tells all?
who amongst us is there that would suffer the
story of his life to be snatched out of his breast,
and read from the first to the last, from the
name on the title page to the closing scene,
through by any one?

How frankly a man appears to tell you all the
tale, and yet still how he really shrinks from

touching on painful passages; how he glosses over evil deeds; how he omits whole transactions, how he dwells on what redounds to his credit; how he hurries over what might militate against his honor: how he abridges, expands, prunes, alters, hides. Take down his story from his own lips—place that manuscript beside the scroll concealed in his heart, and compare the two. Then say would you know there was more than a dim likeness of one another? would you know they were the same?

Who hears all? who knows all? one has heard a bit—and another suspects an incident; and a third was present when such a scene was enacted; and a fourth was the confidante of a fearful trial, or overpowering temptation, and so the morsels are fitted together and the book made up of extracts—mere extracts—yet it pleases the world to call it an authentic volume, to think it a faithful and accurate reproduction —a simple reprint of a human existence. It satisfies mankind this imperfect sketch—never destined to be filled up by mortal fingers; and perhaps it is well for people thus to delude themselves and others—well—as it keeps one drawer locked—one chamber secret, one spring

sealed—one spot hallowed—and so long as men
and women continue to be constituted as they
are, the tongue which betrays all other secrets,
will never betray the secrets of the heart, never
shoot back the bolts of its one skeleton closet
or angel-chamber ; never permit the light or
the darkness dwelling within to be revealed unto
human eye.

Who knows all ? not the wife leaning on her
husband's breast; not the child folded to its
mother's heart ; not the brother who has walked
by his sister's side from boyhood ; not the friend
known and trusted and confided in for years : not
the girl clasped in her lover's arms ; not the
judge sitting on the bench ; not the jury listening to evidence ; not the priest hearkening in the
confessional : not the boon companion of wasted
hours ; not the fellow laborer in philanthropic
efforts, in scientific pursuits ; not the nearest, or
the dearest, or the cleverest : not one on the
wide earth is thorough master of any history,
save his own ; not the best loved, the most
honored, the longest cherished.   In life and in
death the volume remains closed, first by resolute, feverish, clutching, living fingers—last—
by the steady immoveable hand of a corpse.

While the tide of existence swells on, the great secret is preserved—when the grave yawns wide, and then closes as suddenly up, the story is buried for ever.

Who knows all ? ah, none on earth, but One in heaven. He who is the refuge of the weary and the broken heart, the Almighty friend of the friendless, and stay of the widow, and Father of the orphan.

He knows all—but none other; and so, because of this arrangement of Nature, which gives into the keeping of each of us a separate something, upon which no other mortal may ever look as we look; with pain, joy, terror, repentance, disgust, aversion, affection, regret; because of this a far wiser and cleverer man than Mr. Henry Bultin might have failed even faintly to trace what the lonely lady who sate in her window looking up so steadily at the little speck of sky visible between the house-tops—evening after evening was thinking about.

She knew, and Mr. Bultin wondered.

She was a lady—of that he felt quite sure. Independently of the park incidents, there was a certain style about her appearance, carriage, walk, which implied she had, as the brief sentence of melancholy import runs, " known better days."

Not far from thirty he decided, with traces still lingering about her of a beauty sorrow had done its utmost to obliterate altogether. No visitors ever entered her door, so far as he could discover; but many letters came to her, and she wrote apparently a great number of them, for after the candles were lighted he could see by the shadows on the window-blind that she was leaning over a desk; perhaps she had rich relatives in the country, or most probably was an eccentric individual, who, having plenty of money at her own disposal, preferred this secluded existence, and had flown from the world because of a love cross, or some other disagreeable trans-action in early—very early life.

In any case—

" She must have means," he finally decided; "she does not teach, nor paint, nor sew—she takes lodgings, instead of letting them; her clothes are really good, though plain. She lives—not expensively, it is true—but still she does live; she reads a good deal, and consequently must either buy books, or subscribe to a library. She has a gold watch, and some handsome rings ;

she must pay her rent, for the Great Crowland Street alternative is, I know, 'pay up, or pack up.' And—and what a first-rate thing it would be if she had a snug couple of thousand, which I could get hold of and start in business for myself upon;—that we were, in short, to join common stock, and go to the parish church and get married."

The fancy dowager duchesses, and beautiful young widowed marchionesses, and innumerable daughters of peers of the realm, gave place finally to this one fixed idea; for as Mr. Bultin was at once a vain imaginative, and a vain practical man, he did not permit his visions of presentations at court to interfere with a matter-of-fact opportunity like that thus offered to him of securing a capital.

Besides, had he not seen her in the park, and might she not be " an honorable " in disguise, or, at all events, have powerful connexions, who, if he were once settled in practice for himself, would appoint him solicitor to some government office? A hundred vague speculations occurred to him; the only distinct idea he preserved for two days together, being, that if he could only get a decent pretext for speaking to her, he would " push the affair on a-head "—perhaps eventually into

Sunday, when it came on a soaking pour, just
as the congregation was being played out, he
befriended her with an umbrella, and, what was
better, saw her safely home under the shelter of
it. And when they met on the church-steps
the week following, she returned his salutation,
and permitted him to open the pew door for
her, the sextoness being otherwise engaged, in
a manner which he considered to be at once
gracious and encouraging.

On Christmas Day, which fell that year on a
Saturday, she forgot her handkerchief in the
seat; and he had the opportunity of restoring it
to her; and the same afternoon, not having a
relative's house in London whither he could
repair, to make himself ill with turkey and
mince-pies—Mr. Bultin, being influenced by
the mutual loneliness of their position, and
desiring to bring matters finally to a point, took
courage, paper, pen and ink, and commenced
inditing such an epistle as might, he fondly
hoped, serve to " open the pleadings" in a satisfactory manner.

He recommended himself to her favourable
consideration in all sorts of ways; he modestly
praised himself and invited attention to his

various merits, as humbly stated by self; he represented he was a solicitor " in good practice," had a brother with " landed property" in Berks, and a sister married to a gentleman who held a " responsible post under government "

His admiration for Miss Ridsdale knew no bounds. From the moment he first beheld her, he felt himself irresistibly attracted towards her. He begged permission to pay his addresses to her; the impossibility of obtaining a formal introduction through mutual friends, alone induced him to approach so tender a subject with such abruptness. Might he occasionally visit her? might he, at least, be allowed one interview, to urge his suit in person? He was her most obedient, humble servant,

HENRY BULTIN.

The whole epistle ending with a thin, hair-stroke flourish, which formed a sort of glory about the name.

He thought she was religious, so refrained from forwarding the precious missive on a Sunday, and therefore contented himself with reading it over fifty times upon his return from church, where, however, she did not make her

appearance; but the hours lagged terribly until
Monday morning, when he left the note in person at No. 16, on his way to the City—that
city from the drudgery of which he trusted this
coup of romantic policy would emancipate him
for ever.

What an interminable day that seemed; he
bore its monotony till he could endure it no
longer, and obtained permission to leave an hour
earlier than usual, on the plea of illness. The
other clerks laughed slily, and made bad jokes
at his expense, about Christmas dinners and the
penalties of a jollification. He let them laugh,
and buttoning up his top-coat, ran back to Great
Crowland Street, at a pace which it was fortunate his employer never dreamed of—knocked
impatiently for admittance, and rushed up the
stairs, like one possessed. Yes, there it was—a
real, genuine letter lying for him on the table.
It was but the work of a moment to light a
candle, break the seal, and—behold his own
epistle drop out on the carpet.

Such a blow—Mr. Bultin stood staring at the
despised work of his hands and brain as if some
one had struck him; but by degrees he recovered
his self-possession, and observing some writing

on the envelope, addressed himself to its perusal. It ran as follows :—

" Miss Millicent Ridsdale presents her compliments to Mr. Bultin, and regrets extremely that in consequence of the enclosed being directed to a person of the same name, she should have read a letter evidently not intended for her. She, therefore, returns the note at once, assuring Mr. Bultin of her sorrow for the unfortunate mistake.

" 16, Great Crowland Street,
  27 December, 18—."

Mr. Bultin first crushed up the billet and swore, then he smoothed it out flat, and considered things were not so bad after all ; to these moods the reflective succeeded, of which the reader needs not to be told that walking up and down the room, thrusting the hands into unfathomable depths, knitting the brows, pursing up the lips, and pulling all sorts of hideous faces, are sure and certain signs.

" I will go over and call upon her," he at length exclaimed aloud, by way of a conclusive finish to his silent cogitations ; " I will, by Jupiter !" and having thumped his clenched

hand on the table, as if to seal the vow, he once
again seized his hat, and was about to sally forth,
when he bethought him he had better brush
himself up a little, oil his hair, put on a fresh
shirt and his Sunday clothes.

Alas ! for the shortsightedness of all men,
particularly of men in love either with women or
money. That thought of changing his garments, of humouring the weakness of a female's
nature so far as to render himself as fascinating
as possible, "of doing up" his exquisite person " in
the new," settled his matrimonial proposals for
ever in that quarter, or rather prevented his
making them at all.   If he had only gone as he
at first intended, he might, perchance, have obtained some sort of an audience with her.

As it was—

" I think I shall do now," thought Mr. Bultin,
after looking at his own reflection for the fiftieth
time in the mirror.   " I was a fool to write at
all, nothing like a personal interview, it does
more good than a ton of blotted letter paper ; why
should I not call, and why should I not succeed ?
nothing venture nothing have; faint heart never
won fair lady !" and muttering a string of similar
encouraging proverbs, *sotto voce*, Mr. Bultin

descended the stairs, flung open the hall-door,
stepped forth into the street, crossed it, and had
his hand actually upon No. 16's black knocker,
when a carriage and pair turned the corner and
appeared in Great Crowland Street, with the
rapidity of a flash of lightning.

There was a tremendous clatter and noise,
then the coachman pulled short up; the footman jumped off in a moment to let down the
steps and assist his lady to alight; and before
the dingy maid-of-all-work had got half-way
from the lower to the upper regions, Mr. Bultin
found himself leaving the way clear for the same
fashionably-dressed individual he had seen once
before to enter No. 16, the very moment the
door should be opened.

He heard a rapid inquiry for Miss Ridsdale,
beheld the lady hastily enter the house before
the servant had time to answer; but the next
minute the door was banged to, and he found
himself standing on the wrong side of it, staring
at the fat coachman and the smoking horses,
and the handsome carriage, and the powdered
footman.

" What is the name of that lady who has just
gone into No. 16 ?" he demanded of the last-

mentioned individual, after a pause, devoted to surprise and disappointment. "What is her name ?"

"What would you give to know ?" was the civil rejoinder.

"Thank you," said Mr. Bultin, whereupon the fellow burst out into a horse laugh, in which the coachman joined, exclaiming ironically, by way of a finish—" If you make the thank-you a golden one—he will, perhaps, tell you the first letter. A guinea would be neither here nor there to a gentleman like you."

"Perhaps not, for anything worth having," retorted Mr. Bultin, as he turned away disappointed, and walked down Great Crowland Street, determined to watch and wait till the equipage should drive away, when he would pay his visit to the lady of his choice, spite of fate.

Spite of fate! Ah! he did not know what scene was being enacted in the home of the lonely woman, who, the moment the carriage stopped at her door, hurriedly ran down stairs to meet her visitor. The latter flung her arms around her on the landing-place.

"Judith, what is the matter? What can have brought you here at this hour?"

"Oh! Milly, Lillian is dying;" and then came a torrent of tears—a wild burst of despairing, passionate grief.

It needed no prophet to tell that she was dying, too. The hurried breathing—the wasted hands, clasped across the panting bosom—the fit of coughing, which exhausted her so that she had to sit down for a few minutes on the stairs before she could ascend to Miss Ridsdale's drawing-room, told that consumption was busy with her; and with a sort of soul-sickening despair Millicent knelt down before the shadowy creature, and, burying her face in her hands, groaned in agony of spirit.

"Dying—our Lillian!" she began, at length, in a husky voice; and then came another burst of weeping from her sister, succeeded, as before, by that racking cough.

"Don't sit there, Judith," she exclaimed, starting suddenly up. "Try and calm yourself. Come to my room—and tell me—all—about her."

The last words were uttered with an effort, as she passed an arm round her visitor's waist, and assisted her in her ascent. Good heavens! what a cough that was! Millicent's heart seemed to stand still within her, when she heard it.

"You ought not to have come out to-night," she said. "You ought—"

"Oh! don't mind me—don't think of me. Go to her, Milly. I can't. Oh! Milly! Milly! do you remember?" and laying her head on her sister's shoulder, she finished the sentence with sobs.

"Judith, you are doing very wrong," said the other, smothering the outward expression of her own grief with a powerful effort. "Remember how ill you are!—think how precious your life is—to me—to your daughter—to—"

"Hush, Milly! I know all about myself. It is just a matter of time, as I told you yesterday—a few weeks more or less; but, Lillian, to think of her lying in that old Welsh house—so far from all of us—dying! Oh! Milly! Milly dear! go to her at once, and then come back to me. If I could but see her for a moment—if I could get there, too! Don't you think I might travel with you? I need say nothing to Sir John; and it would be such a comfort to speak even a word to her. Pack up a few things, and we will start at once together—post down there —and—"

" How many stages, Judith, could you travel?"
asked her sister, sadly, as she paused for breath.
" No—no—that—must not be. I will go, and,
perhaps, may not find matters so bad as you
fear. Tell me when you get the news, and
what they are. Tell me all about it, if you
can."

" Mr. Mazingford sent up a letter by his
servant to town, I received it this afternoon,
just as I was going out to drive, saying Mrs.
Renelle was dying, and that, as her husband
would not write to inform us of the fact, he did.
He did not know your address, or he would have
written to you instead. The doctor has given
her over."

" Still she may not die," said Miss Ridsdale.

" Yes, she will," exclaimed the other. " How
could she live?—how could she? Oh! Milly,
it was a hard, cruel, sinful thing to make her
marry him, she was so young and so gay!
and—what a curse beauty was to all of us !—
worst of all to her! What could she do but
die ?"

There was a dead pause for a few moments :
then Millicent Ridsdale answered :—

" Beauty was not our curse, Judith, and that

you know. Look fairly into the past, and see
who and what blasted our lives. You, and I,
and Eleanor, had we no hand in the shaping of
our destinies? As for poor Lillian—"

"She deserved the best, and she received the
worst of any," interposed the other vehemently;
"but what is the use of looking into the past or
the future now? Don't waste time talking to
me, Milly, but get ready to go to her. I believe
you are right. I could not live through the
journey; but you—How will you travel?"

"By the night coach," answered her sister,
rising. "It will be nearly as rapid as posting—"

"No—it will not—you must post," interposed the other. "See—I brought enough
money with me: not much, but enough; and I
will drive you to wherever you start from."

"You must return straight home," said Millicent, "and I will send for a chaise. Your
footman can order one."

"Well, then, I will wait to see you off,"
was the reply, uttered as she wearily stretched
herself on the sofa. A soft, loving hand flung
a shawl over her feet, removed her bonnet, and
arranged a pillow for her head.

"Oh! Milly," said the poor invalid, "if we

could always be together; if you could have
lived with me as my sister; if I might even have
come to see you as yours; if heaven had sent
me a husband, not a master; but—but—you
will come back in time—won't you?"

"In time—for what?" asked her sister.

There was no audible answer; but a rain of
tears, falling on her hand, conveyed a fearfully
distinct reply to her heart.

"Judith, do be calm," she said, in a voice
which would shake, spite of all her efforts at
self-control. "Do not say such things—do not
be so foolish."

"I cannot help it," said the lady; and a fit
of coughing here cutting short the conversation,
if such it could be called, she did not afterwards
resume it, but laying her head down on the pillow, remained there alone with the flickering
firelight, whilst her sister was packing up in the
adjoining room a few articles needful for her
hurried journey.

Half an hour passed by, and still Mr. Bultin
beheld the carriage standing in Great Crowland
Street. At the expiration of that period, a post-
chaise rattled up to the door of No. 16.

"Why, what can be in the wind now?" he

thought; but no satisfactory solution of the enigma presented itself, until Miss Ridsdale and her guest appeared on the side-path.

"Hang it!" he muttered, "I shan't get speaking to her to-night. Still I may as well watch the end of this." .

"Now send for your doctor, Judith, the moment you reach home," said Miss Ridsdale, as she folded the cloaks and shawls around her sister. "Will you promise me?"

"Yes, yes, and, Milly—you'll be sure, quite sure to be back in time."

"I will," said the other.

"Good bye, then, for a little; and tell Lillian all I bade you, and don't forget—and come back—and—and—"

The full heart grew too full to utter more; but a long, tearful kiss completed the unfinished sentence.

"I won't go till I see you in the chaise and off. Good bye."

Mr. Bultin saw Miss Ridsdale enter the other vehicle: the postillion cracked his whip, and the horses started at a gallop down Great Crowland Street. .

"Home," said the strange lady; and in another instant her equipage had turned the opposite corner, and was whirling away towards St. James'.

Mr. Bultin stood alone in the unfashionable shop-street, marvelling much concerning both of them—whilst she, leaning back in her luxurious carriage, looked vacantly forth at the dimly-lighted streets, and thought of the single word she had spoken to the footman.

Home!—it was a solemn thing for her to remember, to what home she was really travelling — to that only quiet home mortal ever reaches on this side heaven—that dark, silent, narrow, lonely one—the grave!

CHAPTER III.

ONE dreary January night, about a fortnight after the events related in the last chapter, an awful storm was raging around a mansion in North Wales.

Where the mountains of that land are the loftiest, its valleys the richest, its streams the deepest, its waterfalls the grandest, its scenery the wildest—that lonely dwelling, half castle half hall, stood—pleasant to contemplate, romantic to live in, spite of 'the utter isolation of its position, the total human desolation of hill, and dale, and forest which surrounded it.

Placed about one-third up one of the acclivities, the windows of the old pile commanded a view far down a gorge in the mountains, which opened out at about three hundred yards distance from the house into a broad valley, that gave place in its turn to a still wider prospect beyond, of fields, trees, villages and slender spires. A line of hills, with mountains towering above, bounded, at the furthest point to which the eye could reach, the whole landscape, into a panorama of varied loveliness and majestic sublimity; for whilst the scattered hamlets, the white farm-houses, the abundant plantations, and the grey church-towers spoke of peace, civilization, and repose, the rugged mountain-peaks, rising to and blending with the skies—and the darker and nearer hills below gave a grandeur to the scene —formed an appropriate back-ground to such a picture!

Where the life, and charm, and restlessness of water were not wanting altogether either. They were supplied to the eye that turns instinctively to seek them everywhere by a brawling torrent, which, after leaping out of a crevice in the rocks above, first dashed downwards to the gorge, encountering and surmounting many an obstacle on its way, and then went fretting and fuming on its course, through creepers around huge stones, over smaller ones, under the trunks of prostrate trees, out into the

more open country beyond—there it subsided
into a wide, peaceable stream, and meeting with
numerous companions, which swelled its importance, finally became a very respectable, well-to-do
river, that pursued a devious, glittering, yet withal
useful and steady course, to the far-off sea, and
merged, when its appointed mission was fulfilled
on the land, a part and portion of the mighty ocean!

Thus the little mountain rivulet, that at its
outset merely formed sprayey waterfalls, springing lightly from ledge to ledge, and wore tiny
basins in the bosoms of dark rocks, prospered on
its course, and speeded through its existence; and
from the casements of the old Welsh mansion,
half-curtained with ivy though they were, you
could follow its track for miles; and if you
were poetically inclined, bless it as you did so,
for the grace and animation, and verdure it conferred, while wandering thus gently away—for
bestowing still another charm on a prospect,
which scarcely seemed, as you gazed upon it, to
require another touch from the pencil of Nature
to make it perfect.

But the great soul of man seems never satisfied, save when it can gaze away and away, without restraint or hindrance, through the valleys,

over the mountains, across the mighty deep—
farther than the shadowy sea-line, into the indefinite distance lying beyond! As his mental
sense will not be impeded by earth's obstacles as
it chafes against Time's boundaries, and feels it
must keep ever looking off into the great eternity whither it is bound, so his bodily eye likes
to glance out towards that vague point where
the real and the ideal meet, where the sky appears to touch the water, where the blue of
heaven mingles with the blue of the ocean,
where lies a region of dreams and phantoms,
to which the dark orb of the visionary instinctively turns—for, when standing on the sands
of the sea-shore, the mind and the body both
look freely forth, the latter into space, the former
into infinity.

And accordingly there was one want in the
landscape, wherefore it never satisfied, though
it always soothed; the terrestrial boundary of
mountains it had, but the glory of the trackless
sea, fading off like life into heaven, it lacked;
and so, after awhile, the soul pined for liberty,
and, wearying of its perpetual imprisonment,
grew sick, for want of a boundless highway
along which it might wander out into the un-

pressive, even in their bald and rugged simplicity
—still there was a want, which the roar of the
sea, the dashing of the foaming billows on some
iron-bound coast, the rippling of the waves
stealing in on the smooth sandy cove—the sound
of the waters fretting in underground caverns,
the sight of the white-winged vessels cleaving
their way to distant ports, and above all, the
perception of that distant ocean line, where the
dark horizon dropping a shadowy pall upon
further material objects, permits the bodily eye
to rest, while the mental one takes up and per-
forms with eager anxiety the unfinished task,
which these things, the attributes of the mighty
deep, could alone have satisfied—which they ever
do satisfy.

Apart, however, from the strange yearning of
humanity after the indefinite—casting aside old
thoughts of the sublime Atlantic, and forgetting
that there is a solitude which never seems desolation—a look that varies as the mood is on us,
a voice which speaks in every tone, a beauty
that tires not, a music which never wearies—
the Welsh landscape, visible from the windows
of Llandyl Hall, might safely have been pronounced perfect. The seasons brought variety,

the river gave animation, the distant villages
cheerfulness to it; and for one who desired at
once a retired abode, and the possibility not
merely of obtaining a telescopic sight of his
species, but of also holding occasional communication with them, no fitter dwelling-place
could have been conceived than Llandyl Hall,
the home of Henry Renelle, the impoverished
descendant of no mortal knew how many hundred ancestors, whose guineas were reported to
be as scarce and hard to get at, as his progenitors
were numerous and easy to find.

He was a poor, proud, miserly man of family,
who, having speculated in London to no purpose, save to lose, and tried business but to fail,
and asked for a government appointment solely
to be refused, had come back to spend the remainder of his days in Llandyl Hall, the last
vestige he still retained of once broad territories
that were portioned out as crown appenages—
so ran the genealogical legend—for the especial
benefit of the Renelles, they being appointed
rulers of the kingdom, shortly after the subsi-
dence of the deluge—by whom never accurately
transpired, but it is to be presumed by Noah.
Whatever ill-natured people may hint as to the

probability of this portion of the family chro-
nicle, all the world may rest assured that it is
a fact the Renelles did once own large tracts of
valley and mountain land, and receive great
revenues therefrom. Time had been, when the
name was one of as much local importance as that
of any city millionaire of the nineteenth century,
any duke in the peerage : time had been ; but it
was now passed away for ever ; the acres
had diminished and the rents with them ; then
the glory faded from the old familiar places where
it had shone for centuries ; ruin came to an ancient house. Misfortunes we know leave a train,
and long enough, assuredly, was the train that
swept across the Welsh mountains, to the home
of the proud Renelles. One by one their possessions departed from them; gradually their
woods were cut down, their various manors sold ;
their rights of water, minerals, coals, forests,
disposed of, to meet some pressing necessity,
some urgent claim ; the men scattered to seek
their fortunes abroad, the women married lower
than it had formerly been conceived Renelles
would stoop to mate ;—so an old house crumbled
to decay, while mushrooms grew up out of,
and flourished marvellously upon the ruins ;

and thus in the ordinary course of every-day events, Henry, the last male descendant of the Renelle family, the inheritor of more than its pristine arrogance, and its latest misfortunes, found himself, in the prime of life, just so much better than a beggar: that he had a shelter, albeit it was a very dilapidated one; some hundred acres of land, presenting to the eye the agreeable variety of rocks, weeds, and brambles; a flower garden, where roses trailed over fallen urns and broken balustrades, and bloomed amidst a wilderness of nettles and thistles, and all unlovely cumberers of the ground: a kitchen garden, that supplied the household with parsley and cabbage; and a wood of considerable extent, which, commencing at the back of the mansion and only ending at the very summit of the hill where Llandyl Hall was placed, gave an air of ancient respectability to the last possession of the Renelles, rescued the estate from oblivion, and made it so principal a feature in the scene, that every traveller passing along the valley below, drew bridle to gaze at the fine old pile, and to enquire who lived there, "up yonder in that large dwelling m ongst the trees."

From a distance the place, indeed, looked so imposing, that many strangers concluded it must be the abode of some great lord or baronet ; but a nearer view dispelled the illusion, for the hand of ruin was busy with the house, as it had been with the race.   Poverty was stamped upon its exterior, as palpably as it was written on the face of its owner, as it was revealed in his threadbare dress.

And it was around this lonely mansion in North Wales—this, the beautiful, romantic, ruinous home of the last of a haughty race—that the winter winds were raging one dreary January night—a long time ago.

It was a fearful night everywhere; in English baronial halls, sheltered by oaks, that had been growing for centuries ; on the bosom of the great ocean, where the stateliest ships were tossed about like playthings in the strong arms of the elements; in towns, along the streets whereof men hurried, staggering even as they ran ; in cities, where chimneys were hurled to the ground, and slates and tiles came flying thick as hailstones from the roofs ; in desolate country places, where old buildings were levelled with their foundations, and sheds were

carried off bodily through the air ; and the beech,
and the ash, and the chestnut, were rooted up
as instantaneously as though a giant had lifted
them out of the earth, solely for the pleasure of
laying them on it to die. In castle, cabin,
manor, on the lonely hill side, in the usually
peaceful, quiet valley, on the broad, open, unprotected plain ; in the city, on the moor, on the
water, on the land—it was a fearful night
everywhere.

Nowhere more fearful, however, than amid
the Welsh mountains ; the wind came howling
down amongst them with the force and impetuosity almost of a hurricane ; it roared
through the gorges and passes of that strangely
wild and beautiful land ; it lashed the waterfalls
into foamy fury, hastened the seaward progress
of the swollen rivers, snapped the branches of
the tough old pines, and tore at their roots,
muttering savagely, and threatening, whilst circling and eddying round the spot, to separate the
tree of the hills from its birth-place.

For a brief period, with broken crest and
shattered limbs it still remained unconquered ;
but at length the vindictive blast shaking a
strong hand in disappointed hate over that

dauntless enemy, detached a huge fragment of
rock from its position, and sent, with a loud
mocking yell of triumph, tree and support, child
and parent, pine and all, crashing down into the
valley beneath.   Then the storm rushed onward to Llandyl Hall, as if it had business to
do there, which might not longer be delayed;
and around that house it howled, and whistled,
and screamed, as though there was a mysterious
something about the lonely pile which chained
its swift footsteps there for a space, and arrested
it, hurrying with such frantic speed as had been
its pace before, away and away to the far-off
boiling ocean.

Down the wide chimneys, along the desolate
corridors, across lofty chambers and silent halls,
and dark passages and secret hiding-places, it
flew, as if seeking a lost companion or a concealed foe; it rattled furiously at the casements,
clamouring loudly to be permitted ingress, ere
it burst them open in its impatient efforts for
admittance; it extinguished candles, it fanned
blazing fires into greater brilliancy, it laughed at
locks and disarranged drapery, and as it leapt up
the outer walls, twisted its long fingers through
the ivy, and stripping that verdant covering off

the ancient pile, struck its angry palms in impotent rage against the unprotected surface of the old grey stones.

Outside or inside the house there was scarce a corner free from its violence, safe from its encroachments, whilst high above all arose the fearful din the spirits of the air, carried on that night around the dwelling, striving, laughing, struggling, yelling, gasping, destroying; it seemed, indeed, as though every storm-demon had sped from his home, and were out, enjoying the scene of frantic confusion, adding his tribute of noise to the loud voice of the hurricane, the roar, and power, and terror and majesty, of the tempest.

Around and above that lonely dwelling they paused, ere hurrying forward, something held them there.

Could that something be the unusual stillness of human passions, contrasting so forcibly with the war of the elements—the hush, and sorrow, and silence that had fallen on mortal hearts that night, when the storm-spirits held jubilee together?

It might, for in the same hour a life had been given—a life had been taken, and the awe-struck quietude which invariably succeeds the first shock of a great tragedy reigned in the house whence a soul had departed, where a soul had come.

Which was the tragedy, the being born into life, or the being removed from it—the being laid, as one of old hath said, so briefly into the arms of death, or the being delivered over to the mercies of the world? Which was the tragedy—who can tell?

Dear reader, unto you I leave the answer, which you will give according to your character, your experiences, your prejudices; one thing is certain, that whether you hold life or death to be the tragedy unto the actors or survivors, with whatever eyes you have gazed at the vast scheme of creation, whether your reading of the story of existence have proved beneficial unto you or not —no matter as what sort of performers on the world's boards you regard yourself and your fellow-mortals — a piece out of a not strange play had been enacted that night, which proved a tragedy unto some in the desolate pile.

It could not be unto her, whose heart had ceased throbbing for ever; who had gone away tired and broken-spirited, out of the world. It

could scarce be called such, to one who was
thankful for the long, untroubled sleep that
knows no waking; who, had the choice been
given to her of a throne or the grave, would unhesitatingly have selected the latter; but it was unto
the man whom she had left a widower—for with
such love as he was capable of bestowing upon
mortal, he had loved her. Selfish, jealous, in-
considerate, though his attachment might be
deemed, it had still been an intense passion—a
something, which had grown so for years, and
become so entirely a part and parcel of his stern,
reserved nature, that it was like having a portion
of his own being torn rudely away, this sudden
separation, this fearful leap, of the only creature
he had ever really cared for, from the known
shore of time, across the gulf of death, beyond,
into eternity. And yet, excepting for the name
of husband, he had never been anything unto
her; and this he knew: her heart and her soul
had always loathed the yoke, simple and light
to look upon as it was, of her golden wedding-
ring. He remembered once having seen her
take it off, and fling it from her with a gesture
and a cry which had never left his sight nor
his ear afterwards. He knew that the appren-

ticeship of years had never made the position of
his wife bearable unto her—time worked no
wonders in their case, it made her hate him, and
him want her love more. He had first striven with
all his might to reconcile her to the union, but
nothing could close the breach between them,
and so he, being of a strange, proud, jealous
nature, gradually changed from slave to master,
from serf to lord. He had been unable to win
her affections—he would take them, or, at least,
he would try a different plan from the one heretofore adopted; let it prove successful, or the
reverse, it was one more in accordance with his
original character, one of grinding tyranny and
no confidence, with occasional bursts of love,
that came just often enough to show his wife
what a woman possessed of craft, or the ability
to care for such an one, might have made of
him. But the marriage had been none of her
seeking; she had entered her protest against it,
to father, bridegroom, friends, but unavailingly:
it was, in fine, a choice between him and home
persecution, or rather, no choice at all was
offered her, and the older she grew, the more
she hated him, and the more she hated him,
the greater cause he gave her for doing so; and

thus matters got worse and worse—pecuniary difficulties daily increased, and poverty proved no softener of Mr. Renelle's temper, and she had little comfort in her children, and her health grew daily more precarious, and her step slower and her voice more subdued, and her eye dimmer, and the doctor said she was dying, and then Henry Renelle poured out a new tide of affection upon her, and still she could not care for him; but turning away her head from him, even in the last agony, laid it on her sister's shoulder and died.

A light in his heart was extinguished at the moment;—faint, and feeble, and insufficient, it had always surely been to irradiate even a portion of a man's nature, and yet he, feeling how much better it was than none, wept like one distracted when he beheld it go out for ever.

Then he kissed the lips and brow, and hands and cheeks of the departed; then he almost shrieked out frantic entreaties for her to return; then he flung himself on his knees beside the couch, and poured forth such words of love and devotion, and regret, and self-reproach into ears incapable of hearing another earthly sound, that Millicent Ridsdale's tears flowed in pity for him as she took his hand gently in hers, and led him away from the death-chamber into one of the lower apartments.

So dropped the dead woman's sister the curtain on one scene, ere raising it thoughtfully and sadly upon another.

CHAPTER IV.

THE history of a life—the histories of many lives passed through the lady's mind, as with hands clasped together across her bosom, she walked mournfully from the dining-room (where she had left her brother-in-law in company with a guest whose society, bad as it was, yet seemed to the widower better than none at all), along a corridor leading to another spacious apartment, which had, for the sake of convenience, been appropriated to the uses of a nursery during the latter portion of Mrs. Renelle's existence.

Miss Ridsdale, however, did not at once enter this chamber, but remained for a little time outside the door, gazing through one of the ivy-curtained, gallery windows, unconsciously, into the darkness of the night, consciously into the darkness of the past.

Leaning against the window sill, she hearkened to the howling tempest, to the noise and clamour and uproar of the storm; standing there with the loosened branches of the ivy flapping incessantly against the diamond panes, she thought, in the deep loneliness of the winter's night, of the dead, and looked with a despairing glance, for once straightforwardly, over the scroll of that departed one's life's story.

What a huge volume the future appears to the eye of youth, filled with bright scenes and great successes and high deeds, and much happiness; how deceitfully it lies, or has lain in the sight of each of us, with its golden clasps, and delusive title, and false table of contents, and unreal glitter. How the eyes of youth brighten as they gaze upon it—how the hands of youth tremble with eagerness to snatch and read it through—through from beginning to end.

What a huge volume it seems; and yet, when we have perused it from the first page to the concluding one—when what was once the future has become the past, into how small a compass may not all the bitter truths and weary lessons

we have gathered out of it, be condensed. A
volume for the one, a paragraph for the other—
pages of promise—a sentence of fulfilment —
threescore years and ten to gather the diffuse
contents of the first ; an hour or less of sorrowful recollection to master the events of the last.

What may be, expands so interminably before
the eye of imagination, that the mind, bewildered at the extent of the prospect ever opening and widening, can only survey a portion of
the possible at once. What has been, com-
presses itself into such narrow limits, that memory can grasp the facts of half a century in an
instant. The former is all vague, shadowy, indistinct, speculative, varying every moment in
form, colour, character ; shifting like the scenes
in a panorama, from point to point, chameleon
in hue, fairy-like in beauty, changeable in its
aspects ; whilst the latter is all incident, fact
—hard, dry, uncompromising reality.

Youth, like the man in the old eastern legend,
holds the phial of existence which contains within
itself what is to be the future, and which will
eventually become the receptacle of the past.
Eagerly he uncorks the magic bottle, and shadowy shapes and phantoms appear to him, out

of what, after all, is but the smoke of the Arabian tale; but gradually, as years roll on, substantial forms come forth out of the mist—the hard, cold forms of actual experience, the trials of manhood, the disappointments of life, that subsequently take possession of the empty phial, and usurp the place of all that was once so bright and gay and beautiful.

Age puts the stopper of silence in the flask, buries it, tries to forget its contents in vain! Man cannot banish from his recollection the memory of the young forms, and great hopes, and high aspirations, and noble purposes, that once he dreamed were to come forth from it; he cannot chase away from his brain the thought of all that lies within it now, and occasionally, when quite alone, he takes it out from the grave he had dug for it in his heart, and holding it up betwixt him and the light, looks at the actual events and sorrows, and dust and ashes it contains, thinking the while of the smoke he once saw issue from it; of the shapes, and the hopes, and the joys, and the happiness he had fancied he traced therein.

The universe cannot contain man's future—a nutshell suffices to enclose his past; but what

weary hours those are, when the nutshell is
opened and gazed into, when the various
events it entombs are turned over and considered.

Birth, life, death—all the incidents which had
occurred betwixt her sister's entrance into existence and her departure from out the world—
all that it had taken four-and-twenty years to
accomplish—passed with the rapidity of thought
through the mind of Millicent Ridsdale, and it
was but natural that at a moment, when she had
just seen "The End" written by the hand of
the mighty king of terrors, on the last leaf of a
human volume—when she had finished another
dreary chapter in the record of her own auto-
biography—she should pause to review the contents of both.

There is one book every individual in creation
is certain to print and publish; thousands upon
thousands are daily completed, thousands upon
thousands daily begun. Some are concluded so
quickly they seem but pamphlets; others, again,
are appalling in their drivelling, five-score year
extent; most are struck off merely for personal or
private circulation—a few are hawked about the
world and find favour or the reverse in the eyes

of men, as they prove good or evil, instructive
or pernicious, noble or base.

With life the work commences, with death
the work ends; and Lillian Renelle, having left
behind her work for ever, and gone away forth
that fearful night into eternity, Millicent, her
only unmarried sister, stayed for a few minutes
in the desolate corridor to look at the record the
departed one had left of her experiences of time.

Sad enough assuredly it was; so sad, that
finally Miss Ridsdale became unconscious of the
roar of the howling tempest, of the almost unprecedented fury of the storm, and remained
scanning with swimming eyes that story of a
life just concluded, until a blast more violent
even than its predecessor, burst the old-fashioned
casement by which she stood, open, and roused
the lady from her reverie.

To a consciousness of where she was, of whither
she had intended going, to a something beyond
a sickening memory of the corpse lying so
calmly in that distant chamber insensible to the
clamour of the elements, to a memory of life
and its duties—to a recollection that her work on
earth was not yet completed, that there was employment for her close at hand in the apartment

to which she had intended proceeding at once when she left her brother-in-law to the sympathy and companionship of one of about the most unsympathising men who ever existed — Mr. Mazingford to wit.

Still for an instant longer she lingered after she had fastened the window, looking out into the darkness in which, as the storm swept through it, she traced strange shapes and shadowy forms. There was music to her ear in the long sobs of the wind, as, during the brief lulls in the gale, it went wandering away through the woods, and the pine-tops, and the neighbouring ravines. Music, for it sounded like a wail for the dead; and Millicent's heart was touched and softened within her, and she wept because the melody of the exhausted blast was like that which was making mournful cadence in her own bosom.

But then the storm-fiends came rushing round the house again, and half terrified and whole awe-struck by the fearful din of the tempest, which had seemed an instant before falling away to sleep, Millicent hurriedly closed the shutters— by way of additional protection against the encroachments of the storm — and murmuring,

"Oh, Lillian, my sister, such a night!" in a tone that half implied she felt there could be no rest even for the dead, whilst that wild hurricane was raging—she turned away from the casement, and opening a door at the extreme end of the corridor, entered the apartment to which it gave ingress.

The noise caused by the howling of the tempest was so great, and that caused by her entrance so trivial, that the occupants of the room remained unconscious of the latter for some little time, during which Miss Ridsdale remained surveying the scene, and hearkening to the words of the speaking actors therein.

Once upon a time—in the days when the Renelles had wealth enough to maintain a position, and to exact consideration from all ranks and classes, the chamber had been a handsome reception-room, and a few chairs with faint traces of tarnished gilding and faded satin covers still remained, to tell the story of a magnificence that had been; of a glory which had departed; of a style and an importance that had ceased to be for ever.

A few portraits hung on the walls, vile daubs executed by unskilful hands, their very presence

sufficiently attesting their worthlessness, for
had they been of any value, had they
been possessed of sufficient merit to render
them saleable, these dingy relics of handsome
men and lovely women would have followed
the residue of a once goodly collection to the
auction-mart or the dealer's shop. It was because they were so bad they were permitted to
remain there, looking with faded, cracked faces,
out of blackened frames, at the carpetless floors,
the strangely furnished chamber, and the unwonted occupants that now tenanted it.

Ladies, hooped, powdered, jewelled, once sate
solemnly on antique settees in that very apartment, receiving the homage of lace-ruffled men,
who had seats assigned unto them in England's
highest places ; revelry had been held there ;
stately Welsh beauties had there trod minuets in
the days that were gone—song had been poured
forth—beauty admired—hearts won and lost—
mirrors once reflected smiling faces—lights once
blazed, where now all was gloom ; there had
formerly in that place been a hum of happy
human voices ; a profusion of (for that period)
handsome furniture, tapestry, paintings ; life, light,
cheerfulness, riches : and of these things what re-

mained, save a gloomy, desolate room—an ancient harpsichord, darkened by time, covered with dust, fast tumbling to pieces—a few old, tattered, chairs, a cracked mirror, the despised portraits of the dead and gone—these things filled up the catalogue of all that was left of the things which once had been.

And what supplied their place?—three bed-steads, two of them small and curtainless, the other large, and furnished with crimson velvet drapery—moth-eaten, stained, rotten, dropping to decay; these, together with a very scanty array of the commonest nursery furniture, served but to show the vast size of the chamber in com-parison with what it contained, and spoke more of poverty than the meanest hovel could possibly have done.

As she gazed around, into the dark corners, at the wrecks which on every side met her view, Millicent Ridsdale found herself pitying him on whose house such ruin had fallen—and forget-ting her own sorrows to think of his.

In the couch, which once had been a state bed, under the shade of the plumes of feathers, and the crimson curtains, and the white satin lining, an infant lay slumbering, and directly her

eye fell on the little unconscious being who had
been ushered into life under such circumstances,
the aunt's glance became fastened there—and
her attention riveted to the words of dismal prophecy an old Welsh woman was uttering over the
child.

"I tell you," she said almost vehemently, to
a middle-aged nurse who stood by her side vainly
striving to win from the wise one's lips, some
sentence of hopeful augury for the little being's
future—"I tell you her lot will be the worst of
any. I never saw a baby sleep as she sleeps
with such starts, and twitches, and turns; then
it was not for nothing she was sent into the world
on a night like this, just when her mother drew
her last breath; see how she clutches her tiny
hands, as though she were preparing for some
struggle, and Heaven knows too, she well may
be. How can it be otherwise? how can it? Oh!
no, no, she will go through life yet battling her
way, and that is the prophecy of one who was
never far wrong. I see it written across her
face—I see it there."

"What?" demanded the other.

"A copy of what is traced by no human fingers
in the book of fate," was the vague reply.

" Child," she continued, raising her yellow hand almost menacingly above the sleeping figure, " beware!"

At this moment the infant's eyes opened, and settled, with something beyond the customary vacant stare of babyhood, on the face of the hag.

" There !" she cried triumphantly, clutching her companion's shoulder with her right hand, whilst she pointed one skinny finger of the left at the helpless child—" There, did you ever see a look like that in a new-born infant's face before ?   Do you see how the lips are parted, as if there was a something within her that would answer me if it could—do you see it?—is that for nothing, is it ?"

" Let me go !" exclaimed the nurse hurriedly, shaking herself free of the speaker's grasp— " you frighten me ; and besides, I don't like to stand and listen to such things being said about an innocent baby. I don't think it is Christian. I don't see how you can know anything about her, or who ever gave you leave to speak about the future of any one, or—"

" And have I never said the truth about a future before?" interrupted the other, angrily. " I need not go out of this very room to prove

it. When that boy," turning to one of the
smaller beds, "lay in his cradle, I said he would
grow up into a miser fifty times worse than his
father; and I have seen his poor mother strive
to unclasp the hands I declared were clenched,
as only a child who was to be a miser would
clench them, till he has kicked and struggled,
infant though he was, and she has wept over
him, gentle, heart-broken soul—and now what
is he? what will he be?"

To this question came no answer; wherefore
the woman continued, walking towards the next
couch. "Suffering was revealed to me in this
one's face—and suffer she will through life—you
know, as if natural delicacy were not enough,
Mrs. Renelle let her fall one day, and made her
lame for life; and this new one will have to
battle her way painfully to the grave, if she will
not be warned in time, for I have said it."

" And I say you should never come near child
of mine," retorted the nurse; " it is a sin to
prophesy evil about a living thing; talking about
misfortune often brings it—and if it comes in
God's own time, surely He knows it is hard
enough to bear, without looking out for it years
before, as you do."

There was at once a something defiant and fearful in the nurse's manner: her love and pity for the poor little stranger ushered into the world and making its first feeble bow on the stage of life under such melancholy auspices, induced her to raise a dissenting voice to her companion's dismal croakings, even while her superstition echoed the other's sentiment.

"It could not be for good—such a storm raging, when this, the last child of a dead mother, came unwished-for into existence!" she half whispered to herself; and the old ghostly house, rendered more ghostly by the all-pervading presence of a corpse, and the howling of the tempest increased the fears of a naturally superstitious mind to such a degree, that she absolutely shrunk back, when, after her daring speech, the prophetess, laying a hand again on her shoulder, began :

"There was once another family "—

"Concerning which you foretold much which came eventually to pass, much which did not," here interrupted a voice that caused both to start and almost tremble, as Millicent Ridsdale advanced out of the gloom towards the bedside, and bending down, kissed the infant tenderly.

"But for the love of God," she continued
almost passionately; "speak no evil of this
one's future; let her work it out as best
she can, either with tears or smiles, but with
no absurd forebodings disturbing her peace. If
any effort of mine can avert misfortune from
her; if my experience can prove useful to her;
if different circumstances, a more wholesome
education, can make her lot a better one, it
shall resemble none of ours, for it was of us
you were about to speak. There are two
kinds of fate, as well you know: one which
we make for ourselves, another which is made
for us; one which we cannot control, another
which we can; one dependant on the inscrutable will of a Higher power, on the actions
of others, on the decrees of destiny, another
influenced by what we do, and choose, and by
that alone; and if ill come to this child through
the first, His will be done; if through the
last, none of the blame can fall upon me, for I
will do my best, so help me Heaven, to avert
it from her."

What answer the crone might have returned
to this speech, which was uttered, half in rebuke
half in sorrow, or whether she would have re-

turned any, it is impossible to determine, for just as Millicent concluded, the door of the room was flung noisily open, and a tall, handsome man, of about three or four and twenty strode in, followed by the bowed figure of the new-made widower, Mr. Renelle.

" Your brother-in-law was in such grief, I brought him here," said the former, addressing Miss Ridsdale. " I thought it might do him good to see the little one." And as he spoke, he drew his friend forward to the couch, and lifted the candle to enable him to see with greater distinctness the face of his child.

" I cannot bear it," half murmured the widower, turning with a look of so much anguish from the spectacle, that Millicent took him gently by the hand, and led him from the room, and stayed beside him till daylight dawned, subduing her own grief and speaking such words of comfort to him as were to be found in a place whence comfort seemed to her to have departed years previously.

For a little time after their exit from the children's chamber, however, Mr. Mazingford remained in it, scanning the features of the new comer.

"I wonder if she will be as handsome as her mother, nurse," he said. "I wish she would open her eyes, to let me see what colour they are;" and before the nurse had time to stay his hand, he rudely placed it on the infant's forehead and pulled back the lids, that, fringed with dark lashes, had lain until then, from the period of his entrance, calmly on the soft, round cheek.

With a cry, the only one save that first convulsive sob, wherewith all living greet life, which she had uttered since her entrance into existence —the child awoke; and, with the same fascinated stare the woman had previously remarked, fixed its eyes on the man who contemplated it.

"I tell you what it is, little stranger," he said; "you are about the only infant I ever saw, that had a look of anything in its face. I wonder if you can think about any mortal thing, and if you can, what you are thinking about now? Don't she look as if she were marvelling concerning me; far greater promise in her, than any of the others ever had. Here nurse, this is what I'll do. If I find her in the daylight likely to be handsome, I will stand godfather for her; what is she to be called—do you know?"

The nurse did not, only she remembered the

mother had wished her last child to be called
Judith; but Mr. Renelle insisting she should be
named after his wife and mother; Lillian Margery
was substituted for Judith. " Perhaps, however," the woman added, applying a corner of
her apron to her eyes, " now Mrs. Renelle is
gone for ever, he may remember how vexed she
was about the last christening, and call this darling by a name she would have chosen had she
been still living, which God grant she were !"
concluded the speaker.

" Judith—Judith Renelle !" repeated Mr.
Mazingford, slowly, unmindful of the last part
of the sentence, and keeping his eyes steadily
fixed on the infant, as if he were striving first to
fasten the name on her, and then to impress it
on his own brain. " Judith Renelle—a strange,
pretty, uncommon name; yes, that shall be it.
Judith Lestock—if she grow up like what she
was six years ago, she will be the handsomest
woman in the kingdom."

" If she be like her own mother, sir," interposed the nurse; " she will be the handsomest
and the best; she need go no further for a
pattern."

" Pooh !" returned Mr. Mazingford; " Lady

Lestock had more beauty than the whole of her sisters—I wonder she married Sir John ; but she got what she wanted—money ; and he got what he wanted—a young and handsome wife— a fair exchange ; and yet I think, had I been the father of four such daughters, I could have done better for them ; I am sure I could."

" As well, perhaps, as you did for yourself, Mr. Lewis Mazingford," sharply retorted the old crone, who had remained resolutely silent up to this point. " As well, perhaps, but no better ; and you could hardly have done as well either, unless you had been able to put heart and feeling out of them."

" Heart and feeling !" sneered Mr. Mazingford, bitterly. " It is something new to hear the Ridsdales were overburdened with such commodities. Heart and feeling !—Jupiter Ammon ! deliver me from a wife possessed of such as they had. The world tells strange falsehoods of the race, if they were blessed or cursed with either."

" It is false to say Mrs. Renelle was not an angel from heaven !" sobbed forth the nurse. "God pardon you, sir, for speaking ill of the dead, that never harmed you, nor yours, nor any living thing."

"Take it coolly, my good woman," said Mr. Mazingford. "Of Mrs. Renelle I have nothing evil to say; she was 'placed out' so young by her prudent father, and imprisoned here so closely by her still more prudent husband, that the world never had an opportunity of testing her qualities; but of the other sisters," he added, turning to the former speaker—"Eleanor, for instance, what have you to say?"

"That the curse of her race was on her!" replied the old Welshwoman, mournfully, and her glance fell, as she spoke, on the child who had been the unconscious origin of the discussion. "It has lain on them, men and women, for generations; but even Miss Eleanor, sir, had a heart, and a warm, and a good one."

"When she first jilted a poor man to marry a rich one, and then—"

"And did no one else ever play the same game?" hurriedly interposed the other, her cheek flushing as she spoke. "Did no one else ever leave an old love to wed for money? Have you a right to show the black spots in a family better born than ever you were? Are your own hands so clean, that the stone you would throw at another, won't stick to them and rebound on yourself? If there were tales about the Ridsdales, there are stories about the owner of Wavour Hall; if Eleanor Maskell and Judith Lestock, ay, and for that matter, Lillian Renelle, married for money, or seemed to marry for it; others have done so really before now. Can you deny it?"

"Neither generally nor particularly," he answered, with a well assumed air of indifference. "I am not finding fault with any of the ladies you mention for taking their beauty to market; all I meant to say at first was, that they, or their father for them, might have effected a better sale, and all I intended to remark at last, was, that if Mrs. Maskell's conduct be a sample of the goods that are usually woven out of the valuable commodities, heart and feeling, I think women would be better without either: however," he continued, hurriedly preventing a reply from his antagonist, for the dispute had approached too near the confines of his own affairs to be agreeable—"however there is no use in talking about the Ridsdales now, excepting that I hope this young Renelle may inherit the beauty poor Lady Lestock will soon have to yield up possession of. Good night, little

Judith," he said, by way of a finish, inflicting so rough and thoughtless a kiss on the half sleeping infant, that it instantly broke forth into one of those prolonged shrieks, which only babies can raise or sustain.

"Why, what the deuce is the matter now?" exclaimed Mr. Mazingford.

"You have hurt her, sir, with your whiskers," answered the nurse, vainly trying to pacify the screaming child ; " or perhaps your hair got into her eye and fretted her."

"No, no, she knew you were talking evil of her race, Mr. Lewis Mazingford," explained the old Welsh prophetess.

"Stuff!" retorted that gentleman, a flush of anger mounting his temples. "If I were Mr. Renelle, I would not have such a superstitious old crone hovering over my child's cradle, filling every corner in the house with ghastly phantoms, and darkening the whole of life with a supernatural veil. If I could not keep my home free of sorrow, I would at all events clear it of witches."

"And if I were Mr. Renelle," murmured the person so addressed, in an under key, "I would keep better company than the upstart son of a

low-born attorney—but good lack! money works
wonders, and Henry Renelle is proud to receive
the master of Wavour Hall when he would have
kept his father from him at arm's length.
Money—money—always money," and so the
old woman went maundering on to herself,
whilst the nurse hushed the infant again to
sleep, until at length she bethought her she
would go and watch all night by the side of the
corpse, which vigil she materially enlivened by
ruminating concerning ghosts and goblins, and
evil spirits and warnings, and other such pleasant subjects. For this wizened retainer of the
Ridsdale family, was a firm believer in everything, save apparently the love and mercy of
God. She liked to transform the earth into an
unhealthy mystical region, haunted by shapes
invisible to other eyes than hers; to make everybody with whom she came in contact miserable
and unhappy. Her food was others' poison:
and yet, with all, she had a keen appreciation of
things beautiful and good; an instinctive repug-
nance to natures sordid and mean. She was,
in brief, a strange, faithful old creature, whom
some considered mad, whom others regarded
with superstitious awe and terror, who never

was thoroughly comprehended by any one else, and who certainly had not the faintest understanding of herself.

Mr. Mazingford perfectly detested her, and did his very best to have her removed from the house; but, for some unexplained reason—perhaps, because she had tended his dead wife with untiring devotion—perhaps, because Millicent Ridsdale pleaded in her behalf—the wealthy *parvenu* was unable to accomplish his feat; but he performed another, which proved most beneficial to the children; he persuaded Mr. Renelle to issue an order that no half-crazed ravings were to be uttered in the nursery; that all her prophecies and superstitions were to be confined exclusively to the kitchen; and further, he advised Mr. Renelle to ask Millicent to remain and manage his household for him. " For, good heavens !" he said, " what can you expect your daughters to grow up into, if they have no one to look after them ?" and accordingly, when Millicent spoke of retiring to London, almost immediately after her sister's death, he entreated her not to depart.

Then Millicent Ridsdale looked with her sorrowful eyes into his, and answered,—

"Oh, Mr. Renelle, why did not a request like this come years since, when it might have made Lillian's life a happier one? Why should I stay now, when I was never asked to do so then?"

"Because," he answered, "*her* children have need of you, and you can forgive and forget the past for their sake."

It was a reply wrung from the very depths of a broken heart, wherefore Millicent yielded to its power.

"For so long as you wish then," she replied, "I will make your house my home—after I have performed one single promise; one, who is nearer to me, nearer and dearer even, than Lillian's children, has need of me, too. I must go back to her, but when——"

She did not complete the sentence, but her brother-in-law understood it to mean, that when she had closed the eyes of another sister, when Lady Lestock required her presence no longer, she would return to him.

And this arrangement being completed, she prepared for a journey back to London, her departure being greatly accelerated by an express from town bearing the following note:—

" Milly, Milly, have you forgotten your promise?   Come to me at once, or you will not be in time.   I am very, very ill.

" Your dying

" JUDITH."

Two stages from Llandyl Hall, however, her course was stopped by another messenger, who handed to her a black-edged missive, bearing a huge seal, on which was impressed the Lestock Arms.

" MADAM," it commenced,

" I regret to inform you that Lady Lestock expired this morning at half past three o'clock.

" She had been much worse for some days, and yesterday broke a blood-vessel, which was the immediate cause of dissolution.   Under these circumstances you will perceive, that your return to town on her account is needless.   I have the honour to remain, madam,

" Yours faithfully,

" JOHN LESTOCK.

" St. James's Square,

" 25th January, 18   ."

The lady dashed the epistle to the ground when she had finished reading it, and then burst into a perfect passion of uncontrollable grief.

When, after a pause she regained her self-possession, and raised her head, she was presented by the servant with the letter she had flung from her.

" Leave it there," she said, for the haughty spirit of her race was swelling even then within her —" and yet no !" she added, the next minute, taking the missive, all muddy as it was, from the hand of the man who held it ; " give it me, and tell me all you know about the death of my sister, Lady Lestock."

He knew nothing ; that was the sum total of his answer ; wherefore she bade her driver turn his horses' heads, and vainly weeping, she wended her way back to Llandyl Hall.

Mr. Renelle met her at the threshold.

" Millicent !" he exclaimed.

" I was too late," she answered. " I could not fulfil my promise to her. I was not back in time—Judith and I may never meet again "— She was right—Never in time ! oh, never, never more.

CHAPTER V.

Seven years and a half passed away after the events recorded in the last chapter, and then glad tidings came from a great city, to fill with triumphant joy the home of Evan Crepton, a man who rented a farm from Sir Watkyn Shenkin, the largest landed proprietor extant at that period in Wales, rented a farm from that knight, and worked thereon himself, living literally by the sweat of his brow, and the strength of his hand.

To his home came tidings that his youngest son, the darling of his heart and the pride of his declining days, the Benjamin on whom he had poured out a perfect flood of paternal affection, was married to a baronet's daughter in London. A creature endowed, (if her husband's

report were to be received and believed in implicitly,) with every charming attribute to be
looked for, out of heaven ; with beauty unsur-
passable, grace unutterable, all feminine accomplishments, all the cardinal virtues—youth,
beauty, birth—the daughter of a baronet, who
was possessed of money *ad libitum.* " It was
in every sense, a great and a good match." So
wrote the son, and attendant upon the letter
containing these words, joy came tripping across
the threshold of the humble homestead, filling
the same full with its presence, full unto over-
flowing.

Joy! it swept in torrents through human
hearts that lovely summer's day ;—hearts which
throbbed almost to bursting with loving pride
and expectant selfishness, and gratified ambition,
and hopeful anticipation.

" My boy—my own—my darling ;" said the
father, in broken sentences, " he is made up
for life ;" whilst daughters rapidly considered
they should now be "ladies," and brothers felt
this marriage would give them a lift in the
world.

And accordingly, for once unanimous, they
devoted the entire of that day, to conversing

about Watkyn's bride, and they talked of how
they would now resume their right position
again, and cease labour, and become gentry upon
the strength of this grand alliance, which was
to bring to them wealth, and power, and standing, and consideration.

True the wedding had taken place at Gretna
Green, and the baronet had, in the most approved fashion followed the run-away couple, and
in the strongest language, denounced both man
and wife, when he found he had come on their
track, just half-a-dozen hours too late. True,
he had cursed her and hers, renounced her, from
that time forth for ever—sworn that a Crepton
should never darken his doors. True, there
had been coarse, rough language, but what after
all, did that matter?

Nothing!—She was his only child, his pride,
his idol; and such an effusion was only to be
expected under the circumstances, but he would
relent—he must relent—they were equals in
some respects; if she were lovely, he was a
perfect specimen of manly beauty, if she were
not eighteen, he was scarcely four-and-twenty—
if she were accomplished, he was learned, if she
were a baronet's daughter, he was a relative,

(Heaven knows how many hundred degrees removed,) of Sir Watkyn Shenkin; who had tact, and talent, and sense, and who had taken orders, and who was the Rev. Watkyn Crepton, M.A.—waiting merely for a rectory, in order to become a substantial and world-renowned pillar of the church.

It was true, Watkyn had no money—that he was so short of cash, indeed, at that particular time, as to be fearfully in want of twenty pounds, in order to discharge their hotel bill, and defray their expenses to Wales, whither he purposed journeying, and for want of a better shelter, bringing his wife, too; he had barely three guineas left, but what did that signify? once again the exultant Creptons demanded. When the baronet cooled down, he would portion their sister-in-law, and buy Watkyn a living, and who knew? perhaps they might see him archbishop yet; less unlikely things had come to pass. When Sir Watkyn Shenkin first cast patronizing eyes on the lad, they never expected he would pay for his education; and when he had done that, they never dreamed he would help him through college and recommend him to Sir John Lestock, as private secretary, for it

was to his child he was married; wherefore
the same post which took Watkyn's letter to
his parents, conveyed also, one from Mr. Mazingford to his friends at Llandyl Hall, informing them that their relative had made a " pretty
business of herself;" run off, with a " parishless
parson," son to a poor Welsh farmer or labourer,
or something equally low.

And thus it came to pass, Millicent Ridsdale
was mourning concerning the *mésalliance* of her
dead sister's child, whilst the Creptons were
exulting over it, rejoicing in such unprecedented
fashion, that for once the old farmer's other
children seconded their father's proposal to
send the twenty pounds forthwith, and did not
say, according to wont, that Watkyn was
pampered, whilst they slaved. They were
anxious to get the fashionable bride amongst
them, and accordingly the sum required was
forwarded, and accordingly, the bride came,
with all her aristocratic notions and fashionable airs, and indolent, useless habits, to the
Welsh home, where she despised the " best
parlour," turned up her nose at the state bed-
room, made the Misses Crepton dress and wait
on her, ignored the possibility of any relationship

existing betwixt herself and the three shrewd, common, farmerish men who called her sister, and finally shut herself up in her own apartments, declining all intercourse with any one, even Evan Crepton himself, on the ground that he, and his sons, and his daughters were " vulgar."

"Watkyn," said the old man, with a quivering voice to his youngest-born, when this last feat of that son's well-born wife brought matters to a climax some ten days after their arrival; " Watkyn, my boy, I fear you have made a mistake."

The young husband's lip trembled, but he answered not; Heaven knew, he had thought her perfection, and was unwilling even then to admit the gem was full of flaws, fairer to look upon than valuable to possess. The enchantment was not quite dispelled, but still so little of it remained that he felt his father's words were words of mournful truth. He had made a mistake—fallen into an error for life.

"I am grieved for you, my son," resumed the parent, after a painful pause, seating himself as he spoke on the trunk of an ancient beech and motioning the young clergyman to a place

beside him; "grieved for you, and for her, and
for myself, and for ourselves. · Through the fulfilment of my hopes, I have been chastened ;
through the gratification of my pride, I have
been humbled; through the granting of the
wishes of my soul, I have heen brought to
sorrow ;" and as he uttered the last sentence in
a subdued, husky voice, Evan Crepton bent his
eyes on the ground, like one who had no spirit
left ever to look up again. As the joy had
been great, the grief was extreme; as the triumph
had been unreasonable, so the disappointment
was severe ; as the exultation had been inordinate,
so the reaction was tremendous. Watkyn felt
cut to the soul, when he beheld the mortification
he had been the means of bringing to as good
and kind a parent as ever breathed ; and as he
gazed at his grey-haired father, he found a sensation of indignation rising in his breast against
his wife ; for what had he or his done, that they
should be insulted by a heartless woman ?—Had
she not been received kindly by them ? had she
not been made a species of idol amongst them ?
had they not, according to the best of their poor
ability, provided for her wants, and studied her
whims, and bent before her will, and entertained

sher a well as they could, and greeted her as
few brides are ever greeted in any circle? Had
his brothers not urged that no money should be
spared in making her comfortable? Had his
sisters not changed themselves into slaves to do
her bidding? Had his father not told her he
knew his house was unlike what she had a right
to expect, but that still, if she could make
herself happy in it till Watkyn had a home of
his own to take her to, he would be honoured
and thankful to keep her there? What was there
about an honest heart and grey hairs and a
furrowed brow which had given his wife liberty
to insult his father?

If the old man were unduly proud and fond
of him whom she had voluntarily married, was
that any reason this girl should scorn his proffers
of love and friendship? Was her own parent,
Sir John, one half so worthy of respect as the
Welsh farmer? He knew a sort of hankering
ambition was, and had always been a trait of his
father's character, but if it were, what then?
Because of this solitary foible, had she a right to
make him curse the day, when the one great
desire of his existence was fulfilled?

Faults he knew were possessed in abundance

by his brothers and sisters, but they had never revealed their existence to her—oh! Woe for the day when he brought her home! Woe for the trust gone, and the faith destroyed, and the dreams vanished, and the idol shattered! Woe for the illusions fled for ever!—for the love so freely lavished on one who already repented her marriage vow: Woe for the faded flowers and withered buds, for the blight that had fallen on a human heart, which had placed a sham in the best niche it possessed, which had believed and been deceived—taken a wife unto itself to be a care and burden, and a torment for evermore.

Woe, for the pain and the grief and the sorrow, for the dust and the sackcloth and the ashes, for the simple mistake of a too hasty choice, for the error, the error for life!

The young husband dropped his head despairingly on his hands—for had he not changed away everything he possessed in life for one of the beautiful Dead Sea Apples,—and had he not just opened it, and found what its fabled contents really were?

"Don't think Watkyn," resumed his father, noticing his emotion, laying a hand, hardened and browned with honest honourable labour, on the bridegroom's superfine broad cloth.—" Don't think I blame you at all—or her much—or any of us. It is not a natural thing, I see, to expect a person used to splendour and luxury to be happy without them. I only say you have made a mistake, and I am grieved in my soul for it. But there is no use now fretting about the matter, for as you have put your hand to the plough, you must just make the best sort of furrow you can. The land does look stony, and unlikely, I confess, but still you must work bravely on and be a man; for this girl, your wife, Watkyn, has to be fed and clothed, and housed, and I am sure it is now as plain to you as that it is to me, that she cannot be either fed or clothed, or housed much longer here."

" If she loved me," began the young man— " My God if she only————" but his father interrupted him with—

" Hush, hush boy, and look at the thing sensibly, no doubt she loved you as————much as she could, but love is not the only thing needed after marriage, though it may be plenty before ; she loved you enough to be fond of you, and to quit her father's house and to go to Gretna with you, but not enough, to be able to put up with

our common way of living and our——Evan
paused, but immediately re-commenced.

"Don't be unjust to her Watkyn, she is your
wife now, and ought to come nearer to you than
any other human being.   Don't let me or your
brothers, or your sisters bring a bitter feeling
between you just at the start; but in Heaven's
name take her away from here, and try whether
you cannot be happier alone together, than you
are ever likely to be with us.   I am disappointed,
my son, I don't deny it—but if you and she can
agree in some home far from the old Welsh
farm, I shall be more than content, far more."

Oh ! the love of the heart that prompted this
speech ; none could estimate better than he who
listened to it—and as his parent proceeded, he
found himself putting the bitter question to his
own sense, whether any woman could ever love
him as that old man did—any woman, least of
all the beautiful being he called wife, who was
now about to separate them for ever.   With a
very pale face—he took his father's hand in his
and answered,

"Whatever you advise, that I will do—for I
have sown the storm, and I must reap the
whirlwind.   I have put enmity betwixt her

and her parent, and it is but just that the punishment of my fault should be inflicted on me, through the love I bear you. I have made a mistake, but on my head be the consequences. I am ready to labour for her, slave for her, work my fingers to the bone. Anything I will do, but permit her to insult you—only point out the path you want me to tread, and I will follow it, no matter how rough and weary it may prove."

" Your path is plain," replied the old man, " it is that of duty; do what is right, and God will smooth it; don't be unjust to her, nor harsh, nor exacting, nor forgetful of all she has given up for you, nor of all she was taught in her father's house to expect, try and avoid quarrelling, and for the rest, do the best you can."

" But what is the best?" demanded Watkyn. " That is just what I want to know."

" The best you can do at present is to take her away from here at once, " was the answer.

" But how? and where am I to take her to and what am I to do with her when I get her there? I have no money; you cannot afford to support us, Sir Watkyn Shenkin declines to see me, and her father will do nothing."

" How do you know that ? "

The young clergyman made no audible response, but pulling a letter from his pocket, presented it to his father.

Evan Crepton opened it slowly, smoothed it out flat upon his knee, and then, with some difficulty (for it was written in hieroglyphics by a lawyer) read the missive out as follows :

" Furnival's Inn, London,

20th July, 18—

" Rev. Sir,

" We are instructed by Sir John Lestock to inform you, that he declines relieving you, as Mrs. Crepton's natural protector, of any portion of the burden you voluntarily took upon yourself when you married her ; and further, as Sir John Lestock desires no future correspondence on the subject, he wishes you distinctly to understand that any letters you may do him the favour of addressing, either here or to St. James's Square, will be, after this date, returned to you unopened.

" We have the honor to remain, Rev. Sir,

" Your most obedient Servants,

" BROWN AND CARTER.

To the Rev. Watkyn Crepton,

Ewmclydllam Farm,

near Tryddmordest, Wales."

Mr. Crepton, senior, perused this polite epistle through from the first to the last word ; having finished which agreeable performance, he handed the missive back to his son, with a very hopeless " Humph."

" You see that, Sir," said Watkyn.

" I do," was the reply ; " and more than that, you must now shift for yourself, and the sooner you set about the work, the better."

"But I am completely adrift," was the sorrowful answer ; " I cannot go and be a secretary again ; I cannot buy a living, or hope Sir Watkyn will present me with one. I have not five pounds in the world, and————."

" And you must set about making money at once," interposed his father gravely—"You cannot dig, I know, nor work for your living as we work for ours, for you have been brought up to be a gentleman, but still you have education, talent, experience. Come now, think what can you, what will you do ? "

" What can I do ?" repeated Watkyn, after a long and thoughtful pause. " I can preach, and I can write poetry and essays, and I can translate tolerably well, and gain a prize for a Latin theme. I can conduct myself like a gen-

tleman in good society, and read the church
service as well as an archdeacon. These are
the things I can do; and now, as I must make
money, for your next question, of what I will do?
I will go to London at all hazards ; take lodgings
for Adelaide there; battle and fight my way as
other and better men have fought it before : try
for a curacy : obtain tuition, copying, a thousand
things—father, I thank you for making me at
least what is better than a gentleman, *a man.*
I will dream and repine here no longer: I will
make the best thing I can out of life: I will
strive to repair my error, to make her, and
myself, and consequently you, happy: I will
wait no longer for something to turn up—for I
will go, and turn up something for myself."

He had been a disappointed youth when he
sate down on that old stump, bowed to the earth
by the great trial which had come upon him,
terrified at the responsibilities he had so rashly
undertaken, relying upon others to assist him
in the dilemma, hopeless of ever being able to
effect a deliverance for himself—but something
had during the progress of the conversation,
sprung to life within him; he seemed all at
once to have changed from a dependent boy to

an energetic man, and his father looked at him with wonder when having uttered the foregoing sentence he suddenly started to his feet as though he were going to set forth there and then on his journey out into the troubles of the world.

"I have been a burden upon you too long," he exclaimed, noticing the old man's expression of countenance. "I have trusted heretofore more to your love and kindness than to my own exertions and earnings—I have received all and given back nothing—but, please God, it shall be different for the future. Something has come into my heart to-day to feel, and into my mind to think, which will alter my ideas and actions for life. Father, forgive my selfishness in the past, and speak a blessing on my purpose for the future. I will make a way for myself in the world; give you cause still to be proud of your son—for I will obtain a position yet—though not—by marriage—"

Then the farmer told him he was proud of his boy already, prouder of him than if he were a bishop—and under the clear cloudless sky of that glorious summer's day, he blessed the young pilgrim, whom he was about to send forth, from the home of his childhood so heavily burdened, to encounter the storms and the blasts of existence, to work out the troublous destiny he had made all recklessly for himself.—It was for his son's good, Evan Crepton had bade him depart—it was the love of his heart which had made him counsel the separation, it was the unselfishness of the parent making him consider Watkyn's happiness before his own, which had induced him to plead the cause of the heartless being who had brought sorrow and disappointment to his soul; but these things could not render the idea of an almost permanent parting otherwise than inexpressibly bitter; could not take the sting out of his son's marriage; nor heal the wounds the well-born bride had inflicted on his pride — and when he laid his hands on the head of his youngest son—and prayed the Divine Ruler of all Events, to guide his steps to pleasant pastures far from his father's home, the old man's long-sustained firmness fairly forsook him—and he sobbed aloud..

It was a trying moment for both—trying for the love of the father, trying for the new-born fortitude of the son, but each felt there was no help for it; new ties had snapped old ones

asunder—fresh duties had dissipated former
visions. She had come between them—she,
for whom God hath commanded that a man
shall leave father, and mother, brother, and
sister, and for the sake of that one, Evan Crepton bade farewell to his boy, and the young
clergyman relinquished his father. That was
the first step the latter took along the road of
duty, a specimen of its future weariness: But
still he did take it bravely and departed.

Not, however, before his bride bethought her
she had relatives in Wales, of whom she had
often heard in her childish days, ere her mother
died, not before she threatened to leave her
husband's low-born connexions, and seek a home
amongst her own grander friends, if he did not
immediately provide a more suitable shelter for
her—not before there had been more than " rumours of wars" in Ewmclydllan farm, and
high words exchanged between brothers and
sisters, husband and wife, father and children—
not before the glory had faded from Watkyn's
eyes—before the illusion was completely dispelled.

Almost unwillingly the man and wife—one
flesh, but two hearts; full of repentance, and dis-

satisfaction, and regret—took hands and walked forth together, disenchanted out of the paradise of love into the wilderness of life.

Wherein, if ever man struggled bravely to repair an error, to conquer adversity, to subdue fate, Watkyn Crepton did.

He worked then for duty, as he might once have done for love; and if his wife were discontented—if he failed to give her all she desired— if he were unable to provide more than a maintenance for her and their two children—the fault lay in his limited ability, not in his earnest endeavour.

Still to a certain extent he did succeed, as all must who work with a righteous purpose, early and late, from morn to even; and his father heard of his rise, slow and tedious though it was; and learning how there was hope for him in the future, blessed God that he had advised the young husband to arm himself for the strife, to take courage, to battle and to succeed.

The Reverend Watkyn Crepton, curate of St. Fulbert, came in time to be quite a public character. His rector being abroad, the whole care of the parish devolved upon him; and his untiring assiduity in discharging the duties con-

sequent upon such a position, brought him in
contact with those of London's well-born children who go about ministering unto the wants
of the poor and the lowly, the desolate and the
oppressed—who give out of their abundance to
the widow and the orphan, the sick and the
maimed—who act the part of the good Sama-
ritan unto those that lie pining in filthy lanes
and unwholesome alleys.   He delivered lectures,
and published pamphlets, and addressed meetings, and assisted to form charitable societies.
He was a known man in England's great metropolis, though only a poor, struggling, energetic
curate, who did his duty nobly, and bore his
burden all the better, because, whilst carrying it,
he strove to lighten the heavier loads of his
fellows.

What though he could not love his wife—
though he marvelled how the glare of beauty
could ever have blinded his perceptions to the
heartlessness of her nature—though he discovered she was but a graceful statue, destitute of
heart, feeling, attachment—who had wed him
in haste to repent at leisure—who had fallen in
love, as the phrase goes, at eighteen with his
handsome face and fine figure, and eloped with

and married him, to the end that she might fall
out of love again the moment she discovered
poverty to be an unromantic, uncomfortable
reality, pleasanter to read about in novels and
books of poetry than to meet face to face in
actual life and form a personal acquaintance
with.   What if he had made one mistake?
Was that a reason he should make a hundred
more?   He did his best for her.   They lived in
a comfortable rectory-house, where as well-born
ladies as she had been content before their time.
His means were small; but still she wanted no
necessary, or even luxury, that might be considered an essential to their station.   Carriages,
footmen, amusements, society, he could not give
her; but Watkyn Crepton, after the first fierce,
regretful struggle, came to the philosophic conclusion, that as repining was useless, repine he
would not.

As she had chosen to marry, she must abide
by the consequences of her step, just as he abode
by the consequences of his.   If she were a sufferer, he was a struggler; if she had few pleasures, he had many labours; if she had given
up rank and position for him, he was working
incessantly to bestow rank and position on her.

Their trials were different, yet equal. Let her perform her part or not, he would conscientiously do his; but having done that, he would resolutely shut his ears to her repinings and murmurings, earnestly strive to forget the boydream of the past, and fit himself to encounter the never-ceasing man's toil of the future.

For had he not others to labour for beside his wife; and should he permit his own bitter disappointment and her ceaseless discontent to prevent his faithfully discharging his duties to his children, his fellows, and his God? He would not look on the dark side of existence: he would not forget his many blessings, nor be unthankful for the great mercies heaven had vouchsafed unto him. Eternal employment of mind and body left him little leisure for brooding thought: he had so much to do that the demon of discontent never discovered an opportunity of whispering evil unto him. Idleness, the parent of mischief, was far from his home; and so at last, when he found he possessed enough to provide for their daily wants—when the great anxiety of absolute scarcity of money had ceased to hang like a mill-stone around his neck—he wrote down to his father that he was happy—happier

than in his old secretary days—happier than if
he had remained a comparatively idle being,
standing contemplating the battle of life, instead
of being a soldier in the ranks of the world's
best fighting army.

For when the toil of the day was over,
prattling children climbed his knees—little arms
were twined around his neck—soft, warm cheeks
were laid against his shoulder—and rosy lips
pressed his.   A son and a daughter—Evan and
Alice—nestled into his heart, and occupied
with their pure presence, the great void in
a man's nature that nothing but human affection can ever fill; for in the breast of every
living creature there yawns a gulf like unto that
which gaped in the centre of the Roman city;
and as the inhabitants thereof vainly flung treasures and offerings into the abyss, as nothing
proved availing, till a warrior voluntarily buried
himself in the rent, which then closed over and
swallowed him up—so man vainly piles up gold,
and fame, and learning, and fruitlessly strives
therewith to supply the eternal craving, which
ever keeps shrieking for something to fill up the
cavity, till a wife or a friend—a weak woman or
a little child—leaping abruptly in, closes, with

loving devotion and gentle hands, the wound that otherwise had bled on for ever.

And thus the two tiny dark-haired mortals—two romping, healthy, noisy children, dependent upon his exertions for food, raiment, shelter, happiness, supplied to the better part of the clergyman's nature all the nutriment it required; and closer and closer his heart-strings twined about them, whilst the young tendrils of their affections clung tenaciously around their father.

For Mrs. Crepton did not love them. She loved nothing but herself; and whilst they and Watkyn were playing at all sorts of childish games in the long winter's evenings, she reclined, solitary and unhappy, on a sofa in the drawing-room.

"They were so ill-behaved and noisy," she said, "they gave her a headache;" and so the boy and girl—laughing, mischievous imps at all other times—hushed their voices, when summoned to their mamma's side, and scuttled out of the apartment with most unmistakeable signs of joy and relief, when dismissed from the "presence chamber."

Five and seven—such were the number of years they had spent in existence—Evan the

latter, Alice the former—when the first great
sorrow of life came darkly upon them. Contagion—fever—death; it took but a fortnight
to accomplish the tragedy; and then, when it
was finished, the Rectory blinds were all drawn
down, and two weeping, terrified orphans sate,
hushed and mute together, beneath a table in
one corner of the nursery. It was the place
they had selected for themselves, as if they
imagined they were somehow under shelter there,
and nobody tried to lure them from it. Mrs.
Crepton being in hysterics, it required a doctor
and two servants to look after and attend to her,
so the little, frightened, quiet children were
almost forgotten, till at length they voluntarily
quitted their corner and went, still hand clasped
in hand, to find their dear papa.

Somebody, the undertaker, it was generally
believed, discovered them crying their " little
eyes out," as he phrased it, beside the corpse,
and was so moved by the spectacle, that finding
there was not a soul in the house at leisure to
speak a word of comfort to the orphans, he
lifted both up in his arms, and carried them off
bodily to the abode of an old maiden lady living
hard by, who took care of them till the funeral

was over, till earth had returned to earth, and
dust given back to that out of which it had originally been moulded.

The newspapers announced the death of the
indefatigable clergyman, " in consequence of a
fever caught in the fearless and conscientious
discharge of his duties;" and devoted valuable
space (for Parliament was then sitting), to a
brief account of his Christian virtues and philanthropic labours; and the Honourable Horace
Jones, one of his aristocratic assistants in works
of benevolence, ascertaining that no one had
written to the old father in South Wales, penned
a most feeling and touching letter to the bereaved parent, breaking the news of the event
tenderly to him, and speaking of the worth and
goodness of the deceased in language that went
home to the heart as it had flowed from it.

But no human kindness could lessen the force
of the blow, or break the shock of the intelligence; and Evan Crepton, bending under the
weight of the unexpected trial, walked through
life from thenceforth a broken-hearted man.

CHAPTER VI.

THE announcement of the Reverend Watkin Crepton's death had barely appeared in the columns of the leading papers, when Sir John Lestock found himself all at once swamped, as one may say, with a host of visitors, with a perfect shoal of letters. Philanthropists, high and low; clergymen of all shades of opinion and standing in the church, men of position, and men of money, felt themselves, as they expressed it, " called upon in duty to entreat the Baronet, to do something for the widow and children of their dead friend." But it seems as if philanthropists, and that other large class in the community, who are only rescued by their benevolence from being termed " busybodies," were rarely overburdened with any superfluity of

the valuable commodity called common sense,
and therefore, although Honorables and Millionaires hasted away, with most praiseworthy
zeal and kindness, to plead the cause of the
widowed and the orphaned, yet they all, without
one solitary exception, returned to their respective homes, feeling not merely that they had
signally failed in their endeavour, but that they
and their friend's memory had been very un-
civilly treated into the bargain.

They lauded Mr. Crepton up to the skies, and
that made Sir John hate him worse than ever;
they spoke of the state of absolute destitution in
which he had left his wife and children—and
the Baronet could have struck them, where they
sate. They lectured him on the duties of a
parent; quoted scripture, to prove they had the
gospel on their side, and even delivered impromptu sermons, on the subject of Forgiveness,
Charity, Mercy, Christianity, and so forth. But
Sir John Lestock, albeit born, and bred, and
baptised in religious England, was a heathen
who detested preaching, and could not be con-
verted. He belonged to one class in the high
world, they to another; he was of the fashionable set, they of the holy. Mr. Crepton might

have been a saint, but that fact could have no
influence on the mind of a sinner. The late
clergyman's children might be in need of a
benefactor; but he did not feel himself called
upon to prove that benefactor to them. In fine,
very much disappointed, friend after friend departed; and when, they met together on subsequent occasions and talked about poor Crepton,
they shook their heads, and referring to Sir John
Lestock, likened him to a certain deaf adder,
mentioned in the Bible.

Perhaps they were right—very probably, indeed,
they were; but if Sir John Lestock were a deaf
adder, they had not fulfilled their part towards
him properly, inasmuch as they had never even
striven to charm him wisely.

According to their natures and characters,
they had assuredly done their best; but their
light being all of another world, it could not be
expected to dispel the darkness dwelling about
the soul of a man who lived solely for this—and
so Sir John Lestock declined to assist his grand-
children, and the clique, of whom Watkyn
Crepton had formed a most efficient one, were
fairly at their wits' ends to know what to do
with them.

The worst speech the Baronet relieved himself by audibly uttering, was addressed to the worthy Rector of St. Martha's in the North:—

" If your son-in-law had lived," said that gentleman, " he would, undoubtedly, have risen to great eminence in the church; but he died a martyr's death, sir—fell a victim, as even the most ungodly and secular publications of the day confess, to a fever, caught in the zealous and faithful discharge of his duties."

" And was not that precisely what he was paid for doing?" demanded the Baronet. " I really cannot see what right a soldier's wife would have to ask a pension, simply because her husband fell in battle; and, on exactly the same principle, it puzzles me why a clergyman's family should expect relief solely because, whilst attending at his post, he contracted a malady which proved mortal. I cannot comprehend the force of your argument, unless"—and here a disagreeable smile flitted over Sir John's cold face—" unless the general opinion be correct, namely, that rectors and curates alike so universally neglect their duty, that when a clergyman happens accidentally to discharge it, he fancies he ought to be rewarded, for simply doing what he is paid to do."

This was a personal insult; so the visitor felt, as he haughtily bowed, and withdrew, and left Sir John Lestock in peace—a peace which was never afterwards disturbed by any one of his late son-in-law's friends or relatives, till a letter arrived from the clergyman's widow. It was couched in terms of the most abject repentance; contained not a sentence of regret for her husband's melancholy death; breathed no syllable which jarred on her father's proud, selfish heart; implored assistance, and declared the writer was willing to do anything he wished, providing only he saved her from the frightful alternative of the workhouse, or Mr. Crepton's low relatives in Wales. She never mentioned her children, except incidentally, when stating how small were her means, and how heavy her burdens.

The two natures were like instruments of the same pitch and compass, in tune together; wherefore, the appeal of a selfish, heartless, cold-minded woman went home, when that of noble, disinterested, amiable men had been contemptuously disregarded. According to the fashion of this world she charmed wisely. At length the adder was roused, and answered—

" If she gave up her children, if she resumed her maiden name, and forbore ever to make mention of that of Watkyn Crepton—if she sent her son and daughter back to the Welsh farmer, and chose to forget how she had disgraced both her father and herself, by becoming a wife and a mother, he would receive her back, not otherwise. They would go abroad for two years, so as totally to break off the connection; and, at the expiration of that period, she could resume the position in the world of fashion she had so justly forfeited. But he begged her to remember, it was not as a widow, but as his daughter, she was to return; that she must relinquish the guardianship of her children, and never hold any subsequent communication with them, or the Creptons. He left her at perfect liberty to choose—only ' a choice now was a choice for life.' "

With this significant hint, he finished his epistle and dispatched the same, to work out whatever effect it could.

In due course, an answer arrived from his daughter—then followed an interview, then un-

conditional submission on her part, and splendid
patronage on his.

And the children?

If Adelaide Crepton ever hesitated about
parting from them, the circumstances remained a
mystery; if a thought of their future ever disturbed her mind, no human being was so fortunate as to hear of it; if a tear fell from her
beautiful eyes, on the young faces she was sending away from her sight to a distant home,
neither Evan nor his sister was cognizant of
the fact; Mrs. Crepton may inwardly have
suffered agonies untold, on the occasion of
bidding farewell to her offspring; only as no
outward sign of pain manifested itself, some
people were so ill-natured as to hint that she
was rather glad than otherwise, to get rid of
them; and that she felt quite as thankful to "cut
the connection as her father, Sir John."

The affair was much canvassed, even in very
fashionable circles, and many comments were
made, by no means flattering either to the baronet
or Miss Lestock as she was now called.

"For anything in the shape of a woman,"
commenced a *bas bleu* one evening, years afterwards, when telling the tale to a man of the

world, who had just been speaking almost en-
thusiastically on the subject of Mrs. Crepton's
charms—" For anything in the form of a
woman—"

" My dear madam," interrupted her auditor,
" excuse me, Miss Lestock is not a woman, but
a beauty ;" and the cutting remark was just ; for
she had scarce a feminine trait about her, save
her vanity ; not a soft, tender, gentle, winning
feeling—no feeling at all, except a sort of animal
sensation concerning her own comfort, her own
good, and her own pleasure.

Well, if she were simply a beauty and not a
woman, she was truer and more faithful to her
character than women often prove to theirs, and
perhaps it was because she was so consistent as
to adhere to her original nature, that nobody
worth having ever again asked her to venture to
the altar ; for it is an undoubted fact that men
have a weakness for something beyond mere
beauty, and that an unaccountable prejudice exists
in the world against changing away a heart for
a face. Sir John attributed the want of suitors
to his daughter's one false step, and mourned
over it accordingly. He did not like the men
who proposed, as one may say, for her fortune,

reluctantly guaranteeing at the same time to take
the encumbrance along with it. Anxious as he felt
for her to form a second matrimonial alliance,
which might obliterate all memory of the first,
he was too proud and too wise to countenance
any save a really good match; wherefore as a
good match he could not bring about, Adelaide
remained on his hands. There was a prejudice
against the "lot" in the matrimonial market—
heaven be praised for it! a stain on the goods;
a flaw in the human gem; a counterbalance to
the advantages of an alliance with the rich Sir
John Lestock's beautiful daughter.

People received her very cordially in society,
and she was much admired and flattered, and
flirted with; but beyond this—ah! no one worth
thinking about or accepting, desired to have for
a wife a woman who had deserted her children.
The past could not be obliterated—mothers
spread no lures for her, but rather warned their
sons off the dangerous premises—sisters never
desired to officiate as bridesmaids' to her, no
respectable family wanted a closer alliance with
one whose filial disobedience might have been
forgotten—but whose maternal shortcomings
could never be forgiven.

So Adelaide Lestock blazed on, a solitary star in the great world of fashion—very bright and very cold, very beautiful and very heartless—appearing every evening after her return from the continent at some ball, or concert, or theatre, or dinner party; whilst her little children——

Ah! it was a mournful day for Evan Crepton, that on which he received a letter stating that the boy and girl, his dead son's tender darlings, had been left by a clerk of Messrs. Brown and Carter, at an hotel in Tryddmordest, whence he was requested at once to fetch them. It was a cruel thing for him to read a haughty epistle written by Sir John Lestock, who flung as it were, the children and a fifty-pound note at him, bidding him be thankful the while, and encroach no further on such unparalleled generosity; it was a bitter thing for a parent to think how his son's memory was treated; most sorrowful and most cruel, and most bitter of all, to consider that the mother of the little deserted ones had once been truly loved by aught of his flesh and blood; that they had built up proud hopes on the strength of the alliance—that she had been Watkyn's *wife*.

The last word seemed to bring the whole of

his misery home to the old man's heart, and also to give him a clearer idea of what had happened, and of what he had to do. Without saying a word to anybody on the subject, he first wrote on a sheet of paper, the brief sentence :—

"Returned by Evan Crepton to Sir John Lestock;" then folded the fifty pounds therein, and finally directed the letter to St. James' Square.

Having accomplished which act, he put on his great coat, and harnessed his horse, and drove off to bring his grand-children home.

"Where are you going, father?" inquired one of his daughters, as he passed forth from the house.

"To Tryddmordest," he briefly answered, and without another syllable of explanation departed.

After he had dropped the letter in the post-office, he proceeded to the hotel, when telling the landlord of what he had come in search, he was ushered into a private sanctorum, wherein he found the good woman of the house, talking to the children, and trying. but unsuccessfully, to stop their tears. Hand clasped in hand, they nestled close together on a hard, old-fashioned sofa, refusing comfort, and food, and kindness.

As if all in the world had been taken from them save each other, they stuck resolutely side by side—Evan mopping his sister's tears away, even whilst his own were flowing like a mountain torrent. They did not speak, nor move, nor ask for anything ; they did not sob, nor make any violent demonstration of grief—they just cried on quietly and incessantly, in a sort of hopeless, helpless, despairing way ; which moved unto the most intense sympathy the soul of the landlady, who poured forth a tide of lamentations in Welsh which they could not understand, and addressed words of encouragement to them in English, which they did not heed.

For a time, Evan Crepton stood unnoticed in the doorway, contemplating the pair of dark-haired, grief-stricken children ; but at length, unable to endure the sight longer, he stretched out his arms towards them with a sort of cry.

Both looked hurriedly up, and Alice catching through her tears a vision of an old, grey-haired man, weeping like herself—suddenly released her hand from her brother's—and bounding from her seat across the room, cried, " Papa's papa," and was clasped next instant to her grandfather's heart.

Very pitiful it was to behold that trio when the landlord and his wife left them alone together, the old man and the young children, mourning with one soul and one voice for the dead and the gone—very strange and very suggestive, to contrast their pretty clothes and his coarse garments; very good to see how blood linked blood together; how the boy and the girl clung with tenacious grasp around the neck of their father's father—how he, without a thought of the expense or trouble, or annoyance they might prove, took the little orphans to his bosom, and welcomed them home.

Home he conveyed them, to the amazement of his daughters, the irritation of his sons, and indignation of all parties concerned. There was a stormy scene that night at Ewmclydllan farm, where women forgot the tenderness of their sex to wonder, "who was to attend to the town-bred brats?" and men fiercely demanded if their portions were to be taken from them to fit the intruders out as ladies and gentlemen.

"Watkyn usurped everything from, and gave nothing to us," they said; "and here are his children brought home, that the same game may be played over again. We have had one

gentleman too many in the family already.
Send the pair back to their baronet grandfather,
and let him provide for them ; give them to the
proud woman who brought them into existence;
they are nearer to her than to us—why should
we be burdened with them ?"

"Because I choose it," thundered Evan
Crepton, "and the first one who speaks an
unkind word to them, leaves my house then, at
once, and for ever." With which decisive sentence, the farmer finished the discussion and
retired to bed.

But although he possessed sufficient authority
to give the children a shelter, and to preserve
them from absolute harshness, it was beyond
his power to make their Welsh home a happy
one.

True, with the fortunate adaptability of youth,
they soon became accustomed to the coarser
style of living, which was at once the fashion
and the necessity at Ewmclydllan Farm. True,
the fresh, pure, country air gave them appetites
for any food ; and all memories of, or care for
better furniture, and softer beds, soon vanished
from their minds. Mere bodily luxuries consti-
tute no portion of the joys of childhood; but

there were mental necessities denied them, which
are absolute essentials to the happiness of every
heart, and Evan Crepton writhed under the
consciousness, that the boy and girl, the offspring
of his dead son, were coldly and unkindly
treated; that they were made eternally to feel
themselves intruders; that not a tongue in the
house, save his own, ever spoke a loving word to
them; not a hand but his was ever laid gently
and caressingly on their heads.

It grieved him also to perceive how, as their
own stock of pretty clothes was either worn out,
or out-grown, the fine garments of old were
replaced with commoner ones. He could not
bear to see Watkyn's children thus palpably
" going down" in the world; and when Alice
complained that the hard leather shoes hurt her
feet, and Evan wept about having to exchange
his blue cloth tunic and little white trousers for
a skeleton suit of corduroy, the old farmer
felt as though some serious trouble had fallen
upon him, and bought a lighter pair of boots
for his grand-daughter, and comforted her brother
with a pint of nuts.

The whole system was wrong—he felt it was
ruining the children body and soul—chafing

their tempers and injuring their healths; he could not absolutely complain of the treatment they received, because there was no one individual act which could be taken hold of— yet, still he saw that in his presence they were treated with cold dislike, and knew when his back was turned, a sort of systematic harshness was pursued towards them.

He kept Evan by his own side as constantly as possible. Ploughing, sowing, reaping, stacking, mowing, the lad was always near him: a quick, intelligent child, full of talent and promise, whose misfortune it was to have been born a gentleman. There was no need to rear him above his station; for the tastes, and the feelings, and the manners, of a higher grade than that in which he was placed, had been bestowed on him by nature. From all things coarse and common, he shrank instinctively, and to personal cleanliness he was almost a martyr; washing his hands and face, free from spot or taint, a dozen times a day, in the stream which ran at the back of his grandfather's cottage. He had a dislike to rough, loud conversation, and possessed so pure an accent, that his schoolfellows, referring to that, and his erect carriage, always

sneeringly called him "the lord." He was to
be found during every leisure moment, either
close to his grandfather's side, or else sitting
with his arm round his sister's neck, reading to,
or with her—for, perhaps, the most touching
thing about the children, was to notice how,
through all chances and changes, they clung and
remained true to one another.

They seemed to Evan Crepton like beings of
a different race from his own sons and daughters; and it was this love and union existing
between the pair, which induced him to keep
them still together at the farm, long after his
common sense had told him they would be better
away from it. The old man thought it hard
to separate the young things, and harder still to
part from them himself, for they were dearer
and nearer to his heart than any others in the
wide world; and he felt it almost impossible to
give them up—even for their own good.

But it was necessary—his plain, practical,
common sense, and his never subdued, eternal,
hankering pride alike, told him that. It would
be an impossibility, he saw clearly, to bring either
brother or sister down to the level he had so
long occupied; and even had the effect been

practicable, his wishes would not have tended in that direction. The universal human desire to rise was busy within the farmer—not for himself, but for these children—besides, had they not a right to a good station ?

Was it fair to bring Alice up to tend poultry and milk cows, or well to break Evan's spirit and make him a tiller of the ground, a mere drudge on the earth ? Did the boy not carry within himself the elements of success ? and if he were properly educated, might he not make a way for himself in the world, as his father had done, and support his sister, and become a happy and a prosperous man ? Sir Watkyn Shenkin had often stopped the lad on his way to school, and spoken kindly and encouragingly to him; and the farmer entertained little doubt, but that in after-years, the knight might prove a friend to him, for Sir Watkyn, be it known, was childless, and entertained a fondness for protegès.

Altogether, Evan determined it was best to send the children to some respectable boarding school ; and accordingly, after much and anxious deliberation, he took Alice to a bleak sea-side town in Wales, where a Mrs. Crickieth, who was greatly thought of amongst parents and guardians, kept a select seminary for young ladies, and subsequently drove his grandson twenty-five miles further on, to the abode of Dr. Miles, the principal of a classical and commercial academy.

The parting between the children had been so fearful a one, that Evan's grief was perfectly exhausted when he came to say farewell to his grandfather ; he had wept so much before, that there was little occasion for his aged relative's trembling exhortation for him to be " a man" then.

The boy had done crying, and so he remained very pale, and very quiet, whilst his grandfather stood stroking down his hair and vainly essaying to bid " good bye."

" I must go now, my lad," Evan Crepton found voice to say at last—" I must go now, but don't let down your spirits, for I will come soon again to see you ; and you will keep up your heart, my boy, and try to learn a great deal, and make haste to be a man, and then you and Ally and I can live together always.—Remember, when you grow up, you are to be her protector and support. There, there, don't begin to cry again—for you shall both come home together at the summer holidays, and——."

Evan's stock, both of comfort and exhortation here appeared fairly exhausted, for he took the lad silently in his arms and held him there.

But, when he attempted to release himself, the boy detained him with a convulsive clutch.

" Let me go, child!" he exclaimed, as though in some bodily suffering; "don't hold me so tight, you hurt me—there—there"—and he gently unclasped the still twining fingers, and then left a long, lingering kiss of farewell on the broad, open forehead of his dead son's boy.

" God bless you for ever!" he said; and without a word of adieu to schoolmaster or any one else, hurried from the house, as if mistrusting his ability to leave the lad behind.

" How ill the old man looked," Doctor Miles remarked afterwards to his wife; " do you know, I think he will scarcely live to see his grandson again." And the worthy pedagogue's words proved prophetic, for ere three months passed away, Evan Crepton was dead and buried, and his sons and his daughters were talking of going to law about the stock and lease of Ewmclydllan farm, and the money their father had left behind

him in the bank.   Before the old man passed
away from earth, however, he made, as he
thought, ample provision for his grandchildren.
He paid over a certain sum both to Dr. Miles
and Mrs. Crickieth, who agreed therefor to
educate Alice and Evan, and to support them
till old enough to provide for themselves.   Alice
was to remain a governess at Mrs. Crickieth's,
till the brother had "pushed his way in the
world;" and the last act of a temporal nature the
old farmer performed on this earth, was to
address a most touching letter to his grandson,
exhorting him to become a wise and a good
man, and leaving Alice as a sacred charge upon
him.

" My mind is almost easy about the children
now," he said to his clergyman, when these arrangements had been completed.   " No one can
law them out of a good education, or deprive
them of it ; they are provided for till they grow
up; but still, sir, it would be a comfort to me
if you would see how they are getting on twice
a year or so, poor lonely, desolate, little things."

The clergyman promised, and Evan died content ; but somehow the former being shortly
after removed to a better living, forgot to per-

form, and so the children, whose mother had
forsaken, and whose aunts and uncles hated
them, were left to get through the world as best
they could, without a single friend or relative to
whom to turn in any emergency for assistance
or support.

It was as mournful a situation as can well be
conceived, but still neither sank under it; Alice
bearing every trouble and trial with that hopeless
sort of patience which seems natural to women and
girls, and Evan taking his grandfather's letter as
a text, and preaching thereupon to himself
ceaselessly. Dr. Miles said no boy before, ever
so hungered and thirsted after knowledge; and
from the time he was eleven years old, the lad
counted the very months till he should become
a man, tall enough and strong enough to work
and take Alice home. What plans and schemes,
and projects for the future the boy wrought out
in the mine of his own fertile brain!

CHAPTER VII.

MEANWHILE there had been changes in the old house among the Welsh hills—such changes as time works everywhere on every one, and a few others, such as men and women, work out for themselves, either needlessly, or because of the force of circumstances, which impel them onward along the broad stream of destiny to meet their fate.

What a beautifying hand time lays on all things, up to a certain period! How it brings forth the buds, unfolds the flowers, adds ring to ring in the giant oak; how it causes the fresh bright grass to spring, and nations to progress, and towns to improve, and the body to develop, and the mind to expand; outwardly, how it beautifies up to a certain period, and after that?

—it pulls down and destroys inanimate objects
to rebuild and re-create them in fresh shapes;
and for immortal souls?—When the picture is
reversed and the garment of youth turned, and the
bright day breaking, a half-real memory, a half-
sorrowful recollection, a dream of the morning
passed away for ever; when the evening shadows
come stealing over the prospect, and the sun that
never rises again in this world, is near its setting:
then Time, the improver and the destroyer, the
foe and the friend, hath a word to whisper in
the ears of departing ones—a soft, low, murmuring sound, concerning that timeless Eternity
whither they are bound.

But for the young, what rapid changes he
makes! With what an almost imperceptible
touch he metamorphoses infants into children;
children into men and women; with what silent,
skilful fingers, he fashions features, and moulds
figures, and darkens hair, and regulates movements, and forms manners, and changes expressions.

Time can accomplish all things with all men;
but people, forgetting that simple truism, marvelled unceasingly at the alteration a few years
wrought on Judith Renelle, who, from not

having been a particularly handsome child, expanded, as she grew up, into a something which was in those regions considered a miracle of beauty.

The old Welsh farmers touched their hats to, and turned to gaze after her as she sped over the hills; whilst their wives. relaxed their hard features and harder household cares when they talked of Miss Judith, the loveliest creature their eyes had ever rested on.

Children gave her their confidence on the shortest notice; the shyest among them coming to her as they would draw near to no one else. Even the clergyman of the parish church, who was one of that sect which seems to imagine that to admire anything in animate or inanimate nature overmuch, or, in fact, at all, is a deadly sin, and who, acting on this principle, had married one of the ugliest women mortal man ever performed the daily, hourly penance of looking at ;—even he, I repeat, puritanical, rigid, white-neck-clothed, ungraceful, unbending, unsusceptible as he was, could not avoid absolutely smiling with pleasure whenever Judith came tripping across the threshold of the gloomy rectory-house, filling their prim, sanctimonious drawing-room with some of the bright, gladsome sunshine she brought there and took away thence again with her.

All unconsciously it is true, but still the place seemed none the less light whilst she remained in it, because she never seemed to know that wherever her footsteps strayed a sort of flower of happiness sprang up around, which withered and died away when she departed from the spot.

"Beauty is a snare and device of the devil;" and "the eye maketh vain idols for itself;" and "the lost heart of man worshippeth the fleshly tabernacle wherein the spirit dwelleth, and forgetteth the immortal soul, and the God Who made it!"

These were favourite forms of expression with the gloomily righteous, though really conscientious clergyman; but somehow he always refrained from applying them to Judith Renelle, and he contrived to forget that beauty was a snare, and a lovely face a device of the Evil one to lead mortals to destruction, when he looked forth from the parsonage-window after her retreating figure, and noted how even the rough school-boys, creatures that were wont to pull faces

at, and utter rude remarks concerning every unhappy passer-by whose evil destiny led him near
the village-green at the hour when the young
imps were released from lessons, refrained from
jeer and jest as she passed, and paused in their
romping games to gaze on the lady, as though
she had been a pretty picture, a something presented for their wondering and admiring contemplation. Her walk, her carriage, her words, were
never mimicked by the unlicked herd of rising
cubs, who respected nothing on earth, and
dreaded no one save the master—the parson and
his wife, to all of whom, it is needless to add,
they applied opprobrious nick-names in private.

Judith, however, could have tamed the
boldest of them with a sentence, and always
wended her way through the group, followed by
a score of eager eyes, that fastened on her
face as they might had she been a fabulous
being exhibited in a show at so much the peep.

The clergyman used occasionally to turn away
from the casement with a perplexed sigh, for the
young beauty was far too good to style a mere
tool of the Evil one, being almost as perfect
mentally, as might have proved the case had she
been plain as his own wife, and seamed with the

small-pox into the bargain. Judith Renelle was
an exception to every unpleasant rule—she puzzled everybody, and no wonder. So liberal and
frank-hearted, albeit the daughter of Mr. Henry
Renelle; so active and healthy, and yet the sister
of a delicate cripple; so gay, although born in
that desolate, gloomy mansion, on a night when
all the storm-fiends held jubilee together; so
clever, and learned and fashionable, notwithstanding she had never crossed the mountains, nor
been at school, nor journeyed twenty miles from
home in her life; so capable of winning affection; so cheerful and light-hearted and loveable,
and still the same of whom it had been prophesied by one, whose word had never before
been uttered in vain, that her life would be a
hard and weary struggle; that with hands upraised against every one, with sorrow and grief
haunting and dogging her footsteps, she should
pass to an early grave, battling her way.

She puzzled everybody; even the old crone who
had croaked forth her note of ill omen over the
unconscious infant, that night when a fresh soul
was born into the world, when a tired and weary
soul went back to God—Judith puzzled even
her.

" It is before her yet," she would say to those
who rejoiced over the failure of the prediction;
shaking her head mysteriously, and looking away
with bleared eyes into the distance of time, as
though the future had been a sort of flat landscape, over which she could gaze and track out
the route of each individual across it. " It is
before her yet—let her beware ! She has
scarcely begun life yet, the cup has just touched
her lips, and the first sip out of it comes sweet
to most, but she will find the bitter soon—too
soon."

" What are seventeen years at the first part of
life—what are they ? no test, nor proof, nor trial
—none. The first couple spent in crying and
sleeping; the next ten in getting strength for
the body ; the next five in acquiring some sense,
book knowledge, a little experience : the first
seventeen years are like going to bed at night
to rest the frame and refresh the mind for the
coming struggle. Because there is peace then,
you dare not say the next day would be free
from trouble It is just a preparation, and the
waking must come for all that; a waking to
work, to suffer, to struggle, to battle. I saw it
in her face that night; I read it in lines you

could not perceive, in a look which 'twas given
unto me to interpret, in the first motion of the
hands, in the way she bent her brows, baby
though she was, when stranger eyes came and
stared upon her, by the shade that darkened her
countenance in her earliest sleep, as if the spirits
were whispering evil fortune to her in dreams.
I saw something in the infant's features, in the
eyes especially, which gave me leave to prophesy, for that something never came into the
world with her for nought.

"I watched for it again years after, and failing
to find it, thought it was destined perhaps to be
only a trouble for a time; and I prayed that it
might be so, that I might have been mistaken,
but now, though my sight is dim, and she so
altered, I can catch the look—the fatal look
once more—ay, and what is worse when it fades
from her face, I can see that in herself which
may be the source of grief and repentance—the
same as more than one of her race had before
her. She will battle through life yet—let her
beware!"

And the old woman repeated this caution so
often to Judith, that the girl grew weary of it.

"If it be so written," she was wont to an-

"Why should I ?" persisted the other.

"That your life may in no single respect resemble theirs," was the reply.

"What happened them ?" said Judith.

"What happened them !" repeated the old woman, pressing her skinny hands almost convulsively together; "years upon years of misery, shame, humiliation. What happened them !—oh, the stories of those women's lives, of the way their haughty spirits were bent, their strong hearts broken, might wring tears from stone. They could love, and they did so, with the whole force of their souls, and yet not one of them married for it. The eldest and the handsomest, vowed before Heaven to honour and obey a man she hated—a cold, heartless, selfish creature, who treated her like a slave, till the day of her death, which came not an hour too soon. The next first jilted a poor suitor, then married a rich one, and finally separated from him; she brought sorrow and agony to more hearts than her own — made more unhappiness in more homes than could well be believed. She is dead now, so I will talk no more about her to you, for it is a story I do not care to think of.

The third of these sisters never wedded at all—
why she knew best—and the fourth——"

The woman paused, and Judith impatiently
queried, " Well ?"

"The fourth," she pursued, " had her fate
thrust upon her by her own character, rather
than by her own actions, and yet still she made a
good deal of it for herself, and a great deal was
made for her by the other sisters. She found
her fate : some say because of home harshness ;
others, because of a love cross ; a few because
she wanted to better her condition ; let that be
as it will, one thing is certain, she married a
jealous miser, who brought her away to a lonely
house, and crushed her spirit, and broke her
heart and killed her. It was so fated for all of
them, and yet, still I repeat, they all, excepting,
perhaps, the youngest, made their fates entirely
for themselves. Take care, Miss Judith, I say
again, for the same thing which crushed their
lives is in you also. The last of the four was
your own mother—the other three your aunts.
There is a future before you, which you would
not go forth to meet if you could read it as I
can, unless you take heed in time. Don't re-

member my words when it is too late, but lay them to heart now."

And judging by the girl's face she did lay them to heart just then, but it was merely for the moment; for it seemed impossible to the gay, buoyant spirit that she should ever be stricken by care; that with upraised hands, with faces averted from her, and a home difficult to find, she should ever go battling through life; she, who had always found a welcome and a smile whithersoever she turned, and had never had a quarrel with living mortal, save perhaps her own brother, Stephen. With whom she had indeed battled and fought verbally, and by might of hand, since the day she first flew at him, when only four years of age; and twisted her fingers in his hair, and pulled it, spite of kicks and thumps, till the lad of ten absolutely yelled with pain.

Since then, up to her seventeenth winter—for it was winter, and very near her birth-night again—there had been a perpetual series of petty skirmishes betwixt the pair; for the warm, daring, generous nature of the sister, and the mean, suspicious, sneaking character of the brother, agreed about as well together as fire

and water; that is, they never came into direct
contact with one another without a terrific hiss
and splutter ensuing.

"I wish I had the strength to beat you well,
Stephen," she said, one day, after some contro-
versy, more violent than usual, when both had
arrived at what might be termed years of discretion.

"I am sure you don't want the will," he
retorted; "but I can't see what good it would
do you."

"It might not do me any good, nor you any
good," she replied, "but still I would do it, for
the mere pleasure. I am sure, if I had been a
man, I should have killed you long ago."

"It is fortunate, then, you were not," replied
Stephen, who, whilst his sister's eyes were
sparkling, and her cheeks crimsoned with anger,
could outwardly remain quite calm, with a sneer
on his lips, and without a trace of heightened
colour in his face.

"Fortunate for myself, perhaps, but not for
the world at large," said Judith, flouncing suddenly out of the room, to end a contest in which
she felt she should be certain to come off second
best.

"It is of no use quarrelling with Stephen papa," she was wont to say, "because I can't hurt him, either bodily or mentally, and he comes out so quietly with speeches that make me perfectly wild, and stays quite calm no matter what answers I make. It is of no manner of use quarrelling with him."

"Then why do you quarrel with him, my dear?"

"Because I can't help myself; if we could once have it fairly out—a real war of words or hands—if I could nip and pinch, and box him now as I did when I was a little girl, I think I should feel the better for it."

"Judith, Judith," said her father, shaking his head.

"Only once, papa—of course I don't mean for a continuance; but if I could overthrow his imperturbable composure, even for an instant—take him out of himself, and make him look like anybody else—it would satisfy me for ever after."

"If you are quite sure of that, Judith, it is a pity you do not declare war at once, in order that we may·have a speedy peace."

"And so I would this minute, only that he

is twice as strong as I am, and I should be sure to get the worst of the battle."

"In that case, then, had you not better yield at once?"

"Yield, sir!" she repeated; "yield, I would die sooner;" and then, when the old man looked sorrowfully at her, she would fling her arms about his neck, and call him her own dear, good papa, and push the grey hairs back from his forehead, and kiss his pale cheeks, and remind him Stephen was the only person she ever did quarrel with, and finish by putting his hand on her shoulder, and taking him out for a ramble over the hills.

And Mr. Renelle was satisfied, for he loved his daughter, and did not love his son—he clung to the impulsive being who so little resembled himself: and turned coldly from the lad who was his fac-simile only with the darker lines more strongly traced, with every bad and un-amiable characteristic more intensely developed, more mournfully apparent. He did not love his second self—but he idolized Judith with the whole strength of his nature; and Judith, though she saw his every fault—though she knew he could not bear to part with a shilling,

and was perfectly conscious of his failings of
temper and errors of judgment—would have laid
down her life for the " dear papa," as she always
termed him.   It was little marvel Mr. Renelle
followed her about with his eyes, and liked to
roam with her through the valleys and across
the mountains—that he only seemed to live
when she was by his side—for Judith was the
only being on earth who had ever been sincerely
devoted to him.

He had loved his wife much, but he loved
his daughter better.   He had just such good in
his nature—and no more—that he was capable
of intense affection; and this child, this girl,
filled up a void in his soul that no human being
had ever striven to close before.

And Judith understood him ; for she had
such a simple, childish manner, and such an
earnest woman's heart that she could do with
him what she chose, even to making the reserved man communicative; and so, sitting
together on the summit of one of the steepest
of the neighbouring hills, gazing away over the
landscape lying below, she got him, one lovely
summer's day, to tell her his history, to tell

her all which he had never mentioned before to mortal.

There was not much in it, not much of struggle, nor event, nor excitement, merely an unsatisfactory catalogue of misfortunes and disappointments; he had not the art of making a story out of it; he repeated facts but never attempted scenes; there was no enlargement, nor elaboration, nor striving after effect, nor demand for sympathy. The tale resembled something given to a jury by a witness on the table of a county court; he had not been accustomed to talk about himself, and the effort seemed strange to him; but still, at her request, he cast back his eyes to his boyhood, and stated every circumstance of his existence, just as it happened; and Judith with her usual quickness fitted the fragments together, and made a life out of them; and when at last, being near the end, he said how his wife had never cared for him, there was such a touch of nature about his trembling voice, that Judith, forgetting all his faults, and thinking only of his lonely, desolate, unhappy existence fairly laid her head on his shoulder and wept.

"If my mother were here now," she exclaimed, " she would love you ; but as she is not, my own papa, I will love you enough for both, enough to make up for all the long weary time when you had nobody to care for you."

Would any one have known Henry Renelle then, as he clasped the speaker to his heart, and murmured forth a broken sentence to the effect that the only portion of happiness he had ever felt, had been conferred by her, his Judith, his own dear, darling, beautiful child ?

What a power she had over him !—what sunshine she made in the desolate rooms for lonely widower, what music there seemed to him in her silvery laugh, in her clear, young happy voice, as she ran about the house, carolling songs that she had learned, nobody knew when or how.

As she advanced to the frontier lands of womanhood, she began to take an active share in domestic matters, and, like all very new and fresh, and good brooms, she swept remarkably clean.

·She carried the moth-eaten draperies away bodily from her father's rooms, she saved up

the money her aunt gave her, from time to time,
and bought white muslin and glazed calico, and
put up snowy curtains in lieu of the old, faded
damask, and made his bed-chamber really look
quite cheerful with some fresh carpeting and
clean hangings.

She would sit sewing for the length of a day,
looking so bright and happy, that you would
have imagined it the most amusing occupation in
the world; she washed the old portraits, frames
and painting, and all, and if she did nothing else,
cleared the soot, and smoke and dust effectually
off them; she put flowers in the cracked china
vases; she discovered a chest of ancient brocade
dresses, some of which she altered for herself
and Lillian, others whereof she tore up into covers
for the old tattered gilded chairs; she discarded
hosts of useless rubbish, and had rooms washed
and floors scoured, and tables polished, till
Llandyl Hall really put on an agreeable face
once more. She got her father to help her in
the garden, and together they cleared away
brambles, and trained roses, and grubbed down
among dandelions and thistles and weeds of all
sorts, and they raked, and dug, and delved, till
Judith got as brown as a berry and Mr. Renelle

became quite a practical gardener; and in the winter evenings, she darned his threadbare clothes, and manufactured all sorts of outlandish garments for him; her fingers were never idle, mending, making, patching, sewing on buttons and inspecting holes, arranging sofas, and easy chairs and footstools in comfortable positions for poor lame Lillian; trimming lamps, that she might see to read easily; singing old ballads for her, talking to her aunt, and trying to cook little dainties for all three. Judith Renelle never had a single unoccupied moment. She was as gay as a lark, and as busy as a bee.

Nobody in the house could have done without her, save, perhaps, her brother Stephen; for who could have dressed Lillian so quickly and neatly as she? who taken the dear papa such long healthy rambles? who accomplished so much with so little, and in so short a space of time, who thought so continually about every one else, and so very seldom about herself? There was not a creature like Judith in the mansion—not a creature in the world like Judith, Mr. Renelle felt satisfied.

And her aunt, as she gazed upon her, trusted that the bann of their race was lifted off the girl. She hoped, in that quiet country place, temptation would for ever be kept from her; and night and morning she prayed that sorrow might be long a stranger to the gay young heart; prayed, and hoped, and trusted—all in vain.

CHAPTER VIII.

MR. RENELLE was not the only being in existence who considered Judith "perfect." There were others in the world who had long previously arrived at the same extravagant conclusion ; and among those who admired her more than he ever previously admired any of Eve's fair daughters, and who loved her about as well as he was capable of loving any woman, which, to say truth, was very badly indeed—was Mr. Lewis Mazingford, her godfather.

During the years it had required to convert Judith from a helpless infant into a very beautiful girl, time and death had done him the good service of removing Mrs. Mazingford from earth, and leaving him once again free. When Judith was almost sixteen, he became a widower

of forty summers, left by a generous wife in
affluent circumstances—at liberty to marry a
second time for love, or beauty, or connection,
or anything he chose; to remain single, or embrace celibacy, just as best suited his inclinations. A life-interest in Wavour Hall, its rent-
rolls, woods, forests, acres; a small sum in
ready money, all the ancient furniture, and
books, and plate, and pictures. With these
things Mr. Mazingford might, in a worldly point
of view, have safely been pronounced a capital
catch, and accordingly, amongst worldly people
nets were laid for him, and traps set—nets
through which he very unceremoniously put his
foot—traps wherein no one ever caught so much
as his little finger. Mr. Mazingford was not to
be ensnared, even by manœuvring mothers;
papas vainly poured out claret for him; brothers
uselessly asked him to dinner, and told him
about their sister's virtues, portions, and accomplishments; Mr. Mazingford was too old,
and too wise a bird to be deluded by chaff, but
beauty was his weakness, wherefore he spent
a good deal of his time at Llandyl Hall, and
tried to establish a closer connexion betwixt
himself and Judith than that of godfather and

goddaughter. She was the handsomest creature he had ever seen—handsomer than her mother —handsomer than Lady Lestock—handsomer than anybody. Dressed in the height of the fashion, glittering with diamonds and jewels— there would not be such another wife in England. He fancied her sitting at the head of his table— imagined the sensation she would produce in London ;—criticized her manners, accent, carriage ; and determined she should be his wife.

But Judith determined something too, although she said nothing about it, which was, that let who else become Mrs. Mazingford the second, she never would ; perhaps, she was influenced in this decision by a secret distrust of the man—perhaps, by an indifference to the things he possessed—perhaps by a liking for the things he lacked—perhaps also, by a little love-affair she had managed for herself, and kept— so she imagined—a most profound secret ; at all events, she always treated her godfather with so resolute a misunderstanding of his intentions, with so total an ignoring of the very possibility of his entertaining any matrimonial ideas concerning her, that Miss Ridsdale was delighted.

"Thank God," she used to murmur fifty

times a month, during the course of that summer
and autumn—"Thank God, my dear child is no
flirt."

But Judith's conscience could perhaps have
told a different tale. She knew best if there
were not times when she wrung and teazed and
tortured as noble a heart as ever throbbed in a
man's breast; a " flirt," in the ordinary sense of
the word, she had not yet become, but every in-
gredient for making the character was in her.
The essences which had descended through generations in the Ridsdale family, were strong within
her, as if nature had only connected them that
minute, instead of centuries previously; there
they were, ready to be mixed together any day,
at hand to assist in working out whatever mischief the young beauty pleased. The plague-spot
was on her; imperceptible for so far to ordinary
observers, hidden from her father, brother, sister,
aunt ; but visible to some other eyes, occasionally
palpable to her own. A pin's point covered
the cancer then—she might have rooted the evil
out—she might have arrested its further progress
—she might have cast the accursed thing from
her, had she only acknowledged to herself
that it was an evil; but she nourished and petted

and watched the plant of ill-omen, till it spread and put out branches, and grew into a goodly tree, which she was impotent to cut down, or escape from the shadow of. This was the weak point in that otherwise loveable nature; the stain that blackened one portion of her character —the solitary defect, which rendered her, spite of Mr. Renelle's excusable vanity, imperfect; this had been the bane of her race, this was the curse.

But because she never flirted with Mr. Mazingford, and because she never saw her flirting with any one else, Miss Ridsdale fancied she was safe; and breathing, after years of fear and dread and anxiety, freely again, thanked God for it.

And so without a dread of the future, or a suspicion of the fact, her aunt saw winter arrive for the sixteenth time since Judith's entrance into life, and Christmas day came round once more—the Christmas day before the girl's seventeenth birthday. A cheerful party sate around the social board that evening, chatting and laughing, within convenient distance of the blazing logs—for Mr. Mazingford was spending a week with the owner of Llandyl Hall, and the parson and his wife, and his wife's cousin, Marcus

Lansing, had come through the snow to dine and pass the evening with the Renelles and their guest.

Judith faced her father. Mr. Renelle always liked her to do so—and more than one at the table thought she had never looked so beautiful before, never could look more beautiful again.

A half-high dress of thick green brocade—manufactured out of what had once been her great-grandmother's train—gave a quaint, antique air to the girl's appearance, a sort of half-coquettish, half-demure style to her costume. And then the old lace-tucker, how softly it lay against her neck—over which fell a perfect wilderness of dark brown curls; the deep ruffles, too—with what careless simplicity they were caught up, in order to shew the prettiest arm that ever was rounded; what small, clever little hands those looked, out of which Mr. Mazingford took the carving knife, in order to relieve her of the trouble! How her large eyes sparkled as she glanced across at the dear papa, and caught him looking fondly on her; what a very fine forehead she had, and how exquisitely every feature in her face was chiselled, and how gracefully she bore herself, and did the honours, she so young and

gay, and unaccustomed to general society ! There
was a sort of dignity in her manner, which indicated the carriage of the future woman, and gave
a fresh charm to the child-girl playing at hostess
—as demurely and calmly, as though she were
not thinking it all the while great fun, for
once to be acting the " old lady."

Mr. Mazingford sate next her, looking ten
years younger than he really was, and so handsome, that Marcus Lansing mentally cursed him
from behind a dish of sea-kale.   With his
light hair brushed and oiled, and combed,
and curled; with his blue eyes fastened on the
young thing at his side, in his black dress coat,
his white vest, and cambric shirt; with his
diamond studs, and glittering rings, and assured
manner, he appeared so sure of his prize, and so
certain to win it, that Marcus could have choked
him in his chair.

For he was not handsome like his rival, and
lacked moreover the advantages of dress, self-
possession, and self-assurance.   Long, dark
hair, which would not curl, and would get into
tangled masses, no matter what efforts he made
to keep it in order; deeply set, thoughtful, earnest, melancholy eyes, black whiskers, a straight

nose, a broad forehead, marked by lines of care
and anxiety, though he was but eight and twenty.
A somewhat wide mouth, cheeks pale, and thin,
and sunken, with over-study and over-work—a
tall, emaciated figure—bony hands, and somewhat
threadbare garments, made up the *tout ensemble*
of as true a man as ever breathed ; one who
loved Judith with all his heart and soul, and
power and strength.

Beside him, Lillian, a fair, delicate cripple, had
her appointed place, and nearer Mr. Renelle, his
sister-in-law, Millicent Ridsdale.   Stephen, a
low-browed, unsocial cub, who had passed three
and twenty summers in the world, apparently for
the sole purpose of clouding everybody's sunshine
in it, kept the Rector and his lady company at
the other side of the table.

They are not worth describing ; besides nobody
there had eyes for any one but Judith, beautiful
Judith Renelle.

Save her aunt, to whose mind, two things
which had hitherto been enveloped in gloom,
became fearfully apparent during the progress of
that meal ; one that the poor young lawyer from
London loved her niece; another—she grew white
and cold as a corpse when it flashed across her

mind—that the disease of her race had fallen upon the girl—that the malady was at length revealing itself—that it was not extinct, that it had only been slumbering, that it was there.

Heaven knows what spirit of evil tempted Judith on that night; whether it was the pride of her beauty, or the sudden consciousness of power, or flattered vanity, or a feminine love of teazing, or simple thoughtlessness—only one thing is certain, she did sitting there at the head of her father's table, don for the first time in public, the manners of a coquette.

Perhaps it was Mr. Lansing's gloomy brow which urged her on; the gay, childish heart, that would not appear to be bound with the trammels of his love, but flung it back to him, pettishly and defiantly; perhaps she wanted to show him she could be mistress of Wavour Hall if she listed; perhaps she wished to arouse his jealousy again, for the hundredth time; perhaps she really did feel flattered at being so much admired by one who had seen such a deal of the world as Mr. Mazingford; perhaps she had not an idea of what she either felt or meant herself; and it is useless speculating about what passed then through her giddy brain, for in spite of her aunt's

grave looks, and Marcus's imploring glances—
and the Rector's stare of startled surprise, and
his wife's ill-concealed expression of matronly
disapproval, Judith did flirt with the great man
of the company—flirt with him to her heart's
content, making him, in an hour's space of time,
do what he had never previously dreamed of,
despise the girl, even whilst he admired the
beauty.

"Yes, yes," he muttered, as he returned to
his seat after the ladies had retired; "yes, yes,
the taint of the Ridsdales is on her, the foible of
her sex is in her. It is all very well, pretty
Judith, *now* ; but when you are my wife, as be
my wife you shall, I won't stand any of those
tricks, and so you will find. It might do well
enough for the fools who married your aunts,
but not for me—little flirt, not for me."

And with a slight shade on his brow, and an
almost imperceptible sneer hovering about his
mouth, Mr. Mazingford replenished his wine-
glass, passed the decanter on to the Rector, and
then turned to contemplate Mr. Lansing.

That gentleman's gaze was fastened upon him,
and as the eyes of the two men, of the good and
the bad, the false and the true, met—each de-

tected a something in the expression of the other
which revealed a history unto him ; the exchange
of glances was but momentary, yet when the
brief scrutiny had ended, when Marcus removed
his dark orbs from his rival's face, and the owner
of Wavour Hall, was interrupted in his employment of reading thoughts by a question from his
host, the barrister thoroughly comprehended the
purpose of Mr. Mazingford's heart, and Mr.
Mazingford felt it would perhaps be prudent to
cut short further intimacy between him and
Judith ; for " hang it," he thought, " it would
be scarcely pleasant to have a second . Eleanor
Maskell for a wife—one of such in a generation
is sufficient for any family ; more than sufficient
for me."

" What about the coal mine, Renelle, eh ?"
he added aloud. " Any hopes of a black El
Dorado held out by the geologist ?"

" That there is coal in my estate is a matter
of certainty," replied the host, with a flush of
face and a flurry of manner, which told how
powerfully the subject interested him ; " but
whether it will turn out. an El Dorado for me
or not, I cannot tell.

" Pooh !—nonsense !" returned Mr. Mazingford; "we shall see you a millionaire owner of black diamonds yet; and when that day comes, our reverend friend here will insist on your build‐ ing him a new schoolhouse. What say you, Mr. Berbige? Is not that the boon you will crave when rough-visaged men come swarming over the hills, and guineas flow in so fast that Mr. Renelle will scarce be able to count them?"

With a start, Mr. Lansing turned a quick, keen glance, first on his host and then on the last speaker. The hands of the man who had hitherto been so unsuccessful in the great battle of life, were literally trembling with excitement; and as he vainly strove to cut an apple in twain, the knife fell from his useless fingers: the veins in his forehead were swollen with the sudden rush of blood which had poured in a torrent from his heart at the words of the tempter; his lips moved under the influence of strong and irre‐ pressible emotion, and his eyes, usually dull and grey, sparkled so eagerly with such a look of rest‐ less joy, that Marcus felt a chill pang shoot through his heart as the real state of the case suddenly dawned upon him.

"Devil!" he thought, and Mr. Mazingford absolutely cowered under the stern gaze the young man fixed upon him; whilst the Rector wonderingly exclaimed:

" Coal, Mr. Renelles !—is it possible ?—I never heard of it, are you certain about it ?—allow me to congratulate you with all my heart."

" Not yet—not yet !" began the host, striving, though vainly, to subdue the hope which at times he feared might never become a certainty. " Not yet."

But Mr. Mazingford cut him short with a decided

" Yes, congratulate him to your heart's content, Mr. Berbige, and if you want the school-house, present your petition—propose the motion, and I will second it ; for coal has been found on the estate of Llandyl Hall, and Mr. Renelle will make a fortune out of the barren acres yet, and we are going to get up a company first to find the mine and then work it ; and if Stephen play his cards well, he may be M.P. for our shire, and Lord Renelle, before he is ten years older ; and so, gentlemen, if you will fill your glasses, we will empty them, if you please, to the success of the Llandyl coal mines—Mr. Lansing, you prefer port, I believe ?"

But Mr. Lansing pushed the bottle some

what rudely away, rose abruptly, and left the room without a word.

"He must be ill, poor fellow," said Mr. Mazingford, somewhat disconcerted by this movement. "However, Renelle, I swallow this bumper to your speedy prosperity;" and the wine went rapidly down the speaker's throat, whilst Mr. Renelle steadied his hand sufficiently to enable him to drain his glass, after which exploit he murmured a few words of thanks and hopes:

"God grant!" he finished with — "God grant—"

"For in His hands lies the issue," added the clergyman; "and, oh! Mr. Renelle, may He in His mercy so govern your heart, that if fulfilment arrive unto you, it may not be unduly exalted; if disappointment, it may not be hopelessly cast down!" and so saying, Mr. Berbige arose to seek his relative.

"A croaking parson," sneered Mr. Mazingford, when the door closed behind him; "a sanctimonious, canting bird of ill-omen. I wonder, Renelle, you tolerate such a fellow—but let him pass. Come, Stephen, what are you thinking so intently about?"

Stephen was thinking about nothing, and as this was, according to his own statement, his usual occupation, Mr. Mazingford, by way of variety, tried to divert him from it, by making him nearly tipsy whilst he talked eagerly and confidently to Mr. Renelle about the coal mine that was to be.

That was to be—ah! when?

Meanwhile, Mr. Berbige had found his way to the drawing-room, as it was termed; which was merely, however, the nursery of old turned back again to its original purpose of a reception chamber.

To a modern drawing-room—one of those apartments filled with frail chairs, and ottomans, and lounges, littered with unmeaning odds and ends of furniture, and strewed with the wrecks of old china and foreign curiosities—the place bore about as much resemblance as did Llandyl Hall itself to a fashionable town house in a London square; still, as it was Judith's pleasure to call it such, we can scarcely do better than follow her example.

For she it was who had performed the part of renovator to it; she had routed the canopied bedstead out of the field, and ousted dressing-tables

and wardrobes, chests of drawers and toilet glasses
from their long possession of the apartment.

"It is the best room in the house," she said,
in answer to Stephen's remonstrances on the
occasion, for time had metamorphosed it into his
sleeping chamber—"It is the best room in the
house—far too good to be merely used for going
to bed in ; and besides, we absolutely require a
second apartment on the ground floor." And
accordingly the state couch was translated to the
next story ; and Judith carried Stephen's goods
and chattels defiantly past him up to his new
sanctorum, for Mr. Renelle was on his daughter's
side this time, and Stephen in consequence dare
offer no decided opposition to the move—merely
expressing a determination to Judith in private
to " pay her out" at some future time.

Little she cared whether he did or not—she
was in such glee at having at last carried her
point, and got a " drawing-room ;" what a clear-
ance she effected, of the old draperies—how she
made her father hammer and screw, and labour
at her command ; with what resolution she
insisted on a stout Welsh servant scouring away
apparently impossible stains ; how cleverly she
put up fresh curtains, and with what miraculous

expedition she collected everything which was good in the house to furnish out that apartment.

· When her work was finished, she had arranged a very strange-looking place—filled with an equally extraordinary assortment of goods— ancient chairs, covered with brocade; stools and ottomans which her father and she had manufactured between them ; tables of ebony without covers, and tables of painted deal, with cloths flung over them to conceal their real material. The centre of the floor alone was graced with a carpet—the edges being left bare, as Judith remarked, according to French fashion—but as the boards were of oak this fact did not greatly signify ; then she had a mirror over the mantle-piece, which was green and cracked and shabby, and spotted with flymarks, but still she said it did very well, particularly when there were flowers in the vases before it ; the old harpsi-chord, polished and dusted, stood in one corner, propped up against the wall, and a writing-stand of arbutus wood, which she ferreted out of a lumber-room in the top of the house, was placed in the recess of one of the windows. A heavy sofa occupied a position near the hearth, and in a convenient recess, Judith had bestowed the one great treasure she possessed — the only modern thing the apartment contained — a tolerably good pianoforte.

It was really wonderful, how, out of such materials, the girl managed to make the room look, not merely habitable, but also even stylish; and Mr. Mazingford, when introduced thereto, had passed a very warm eulogium on her taste and tact, whilst mentally considering for the hundred and fiftieth time, what a capital wife Judith Renelle would prove, and marvelling where on earth the young beauty had learned all she knew. "I believe from my soul it was born with her, like her face and her manners," he concluded; and the conclusion was right.

He had fastened his eyes for a moment on the piano, doubtingly—

"Mrs. Berbige gave it me," Judith explained, with a certain flurry of manner, which did not escape Mr. Mazingford's observation either, though he received the information with a pleasant smile, that was instantly exchanged for a hearty laugh as he beheld his god-daughter, with most feminine promptitude, deal Stephen a rapid box on the ear by way of punishment for having pulled the cover off one of the deal tables

for the amiable purpose of exhibiting the naked-
ness of the land—which, by the way, was one of
the modes he adopted of annoying his sister in
the presence of visitors.

" We shall have to fetter your hands, Judith,"
he said, taking both of them in his, and looking
intently in her face the while ; " you really are
dangerous."

Perhaps she understood what he meant, for
the blood came rushing to her face, and somehow she involuntarily glanced towards the
piano ; but instantly recovering herself, she
hastily released her fingers, and replying with
some warmth that

" Stephen would provoke a saint !" immediately left the apartment.

" Which you are not," added Stephen to her
sentence as she closed the door behind her ; " but
I say, Mr. Mazingford, don't you believe what
she tells you about that jingling old piano ; I am
sure Mrs. Berbige never gave it her at all."

" Indeed—and who pray did ?" inquired Mr.
Mazingford, with some interest ; whereupon
Stephen informed him that, " Maybe if he
looked sharp, he'd find out."

" And another thing, too," he added , " you

might have thought of buying her one long ago.
It would have been the best move you ever
made." Over which suggestion which he had only
given because it was too late to be acted on, and
which proved extremely galling to Mr. Mazingford, the heir of the Renelles chuckled audibly, till
Judith's godfather growing provoked at the
youth's merriment, went off on a stroll through
the grounds in search of his host.

It was before the instrument which Stephen
had called jingling, that Mr. Berbige found
Judith seated. She seemed playing less to
amuse herself than to torment others, for Miss
Ridsdale stood near the fire, uneasily regarding
the way in which she went rattling over the
notes—and Marcus Lansing leaned on the end
of the piano, vainly essaying to edge in a solitary
word between the chords and runs, and oc-
taves, wherein Judith was unconnectedly indulging. She looked up in the face of the
clergyman with such an amused expression, that
the stern preacher could not but feel provoked.
Well he knew the history of that instrument,
though Judith only suspected it—well he remembered how Marcus, hearing how fond the
girl, who had learned to play somehow on the

old harpsichord, was of coming over to the Rectory and practising for an hour or so in the week, had arranged with his cousin that she, who never touched the keys by any chance, should make a present of her piano to Judith, and that afterwards Marcus should pay her for it.

He, yes, even he, Mr. Berbige, had silently countenanced the deception, and this was the mode in which Judith evinced her gratitude to all parties concerned. Thoughts of lures of the evil one, and phrases about fleshly tabernacles, and snares for the soul, came into his mind as he turned abruptly from Judith's side, and crossing the apartment, put back the curtains and looked forth into the night.

"It has re-commenced snowing," he said. "I fear we are going to have a heavy fall."

And Mrs. Berbige and Miss Ridsdale followed him, in order that they also might make their observations on the weather.

As they stood by the distant window, Marcus, who had striven to attract Judith's attention hitherto without success, suddenly stopped the melody, which sounded like a hundred discords in his ears, by laying a nervous hand on the girl's fingers.

"I want to speak to you," he said; "give me half an hour, I pray."

He added the last words in a lower accent, and in a tone of pained entreaty; but he might as well have asked serious attention from a monkey as from Judith, then.

She took her white hands most demurely off the keys, and crossing them on her still whiter arms, told him very patronizingly to "proceed."

"Not here," he answered; "I cannot speak here."

"Ah, well then," she retorted, "you must defer speaking at present, for I cannot hear elsewhere."

For a moment he looked angry, but the expression changed instantly, into one of the deepest sorrow, as Judith, flinging a half-saucy, half-dignified glance upon him, rose and joined the group at the window, remaining with the trio till Miss Ridsdale proposed a return to the fire.

Then Mr. Lansing came and stood quite close to Judith, whilst he addressed a sentence to her aunt.

"Miss Ridsdale," he said, "I wish to say something of great importance to Miss Renelle; can you spare her for a few minutes ? I will not detain her long."

The lady glanced at her niece to see if she would rise; but she did not, and noticing the expression which came into the young lawyer's face, Miss Ridsdale said :—

"Of course, Mr. Lansing," and added,— "Judith, I *desire* you to grant the interview he requests at once."

Judith felt wonderfully inclined to rebel, but something in her aunt's voice, and something also in her own heart, prevented any outward sign of irritation from displaying itself, and, obedient to the word of command, she arose, and taking a candlestick from the piano, walked across the apartment without answering a word.

Mr. Lansing opened the door for her, and then passed out himself; silently he followed her footsteps up the broad staircase.

"Will you sit down and talk to me here?" she asked, with something of her usual manner, when they got to the second flight.

"No," answered her companion, gravely—and they passed on together into one of the upper rooms.

CHAPTER IX.

MR. LANSING first closed the door, and then placed a chair for Judith. He did not take one himself, but remained standing gazing abstractedly round the apartment, though very possibly he did not see a single article in it.

It was a small sitting-room appropriated to Miss Ridsdale's private use,—a light, cheerful, pleasant, summer chamber, commanding a view of the hills and the mountains, the river and the distant villages—there was scarce a nicer nook in the house, when the windows were thrown open to admit spring's breezes or summer's perfumes ; but it looked chill and miserable in the winter, with its white draperies, and empty grate, and carpetless floor, and scanty furniture.

Judith tried hard to keep from shivering, but she could not help it at last, and the action attracted Mr. Lansing's attention. What movement of her's, however trivial, but had an interest for him?

"Are you cold?" he asked.

"Very," she answered. "Please not to stand freezing all night, but tell me quickly what you have got to say, now you have me here."

He pulled a chair opposite to her at the question, and taking abrupt possession of it, remained for a moment with hands clasped, and body slightly bent forward, steadfastly regarding her.

She had to let her eyes sink under that glance, for something in it told her he was true, even whilst it reminded her that she—yes, she was true too, but——

"I am going back to London to-morrow," he at last began.

"I hope you may have a pleasant journey," she replied.

"Judith will you endeavour to listen seriously to me, if only for five minutes?" he entreated.

"I will try," she answered, "if you do not keep me long, and will call me Miss Renelle."

He started impatiently from his chair as she spoke; but then placing a strong curb on his feelings, he reseated himself, and commenced speaking after a pause, in a very low and agitated voice.

"Judith, for Heaven's sake don't teaze me now, but hear what I have to say, for it is of vital import to me, and may hereafter prove of equal importance to you. I need not tell you that I love you, for you know it as well as I do; but I must explain why I never said so before; why, when the words have been hovering on my lips, I have restrained their utterance; I wanted to be rich before I asked you to marry me—to be possessed of that which might render me acceptable in your father's eyes; I thought you were so young that a little, a very little while could make no difference. Oh! Judith, I was so sure of you, and your love, and your faith, and your truth, that I thought I might wait without fear.—Would to God, though, that I had spoken both to you and your father sooner, —would to God!"—

A sort of choking arose in Judith's throat, but she kept both that and her tears determinedly down: she was not going to cry before *him*— she had made up her mind on that point.

"But now," he continued, "I feel I must speak or die.—I am very poor, Judith, very low stills in my profession. I have nothing to offer but a heart that never loved any other than you, and a home which I will do my best to make a happy one for you. I will work night and day that I may gain riches and honor, and be able to give you all I can only hope for now. I know you might marry better in a worldly sense; that you have teazed, and tormented, and grieved me often; but still—still I do believe you love me; I am not afraid to ask you to marry me. Will you?"

"No," she answered.

He dropped his head on his hands with a sort of groan—as the monosyllable firmly uttered smote on his ear. Judith had little thought of flirting then, but she was angry for the moment, at his having made so very sure of her love, without ever asking for it, and she flung her refusal at him as a temporary sort of punishment for his presumption. She had done the thing in a very real manner, however, and Marcus was for once deceived.

"It cannot be," he said, after a short silence, "that you never loved me, I will not believe that."

" Why not ? " she asked.

" Because," he answered vehemently, " I had as soon relinquish my hopes of heaven—Oh ! Judith, for mercy's sake, say you love me still."

" I will not," she said, and she rose from her seat and drew her hand coldly away from him.

" Have you said all you intended ? " she added, making a movement as if to leave the room.

" One question more," he pleaded, " only one —do you love any other person ? "

" Perhaps I do," she replied.

" No, no—you do not, you must not," he cried in a voice that literally did pierce Judith's heart " Girl, you do not know what you are saying, you do not know what you are feeling. Love him—love Mr. Mazingford—impossible."

" Why so ?" she asked ; and the old coquettish manner, which had so frequently before driven him almost frantic, came back to her once aga'n. "Why so?—Mr. Mazingford is a very nice person, and— "

" He is the greatest scoundrel that ever breathed ! " broke in Marcus Lansing. " He is dragging your father down to ruin, he is puffing him up with hopes of a ridiculous coal-mine that will never be found."

" Yes it will," interrupted Judith ; " and when it is, I shall be an heiress—and perhaps marry a Duke."

He saw then that she had been only teazing him, but still no man likes to have his honest affection made a sport of.   No man, particularly if love be to him a thing as holy as his religion, as sacred as his belief in immortal.ty—and accordingly Marcus for the first time refused to submit to be jested at, and swung from the confines of hope to despair at the caprice of a coquttish girl.

" Judith," he said, " you must be serious now, if you would save yourself from misery hereafter —I tell you ere three years pass over, Mr. Mazingford will have totally beggared your father; that this coal-mine is an entire delusion, which he has encouraged for purposes of his own— that he wants to force you into becoming his wife—and—"

" Would not it be a good match ? " interrupted Judith, saucily.

" No it would not," replied Mr. Lansing. " Oh ! Judith, remember what this man really is, and remember that it is possible to carry a flirtation too far—you are about as competent to deal with him as a bird is to escape from its snarer; but only once give me the right to watch over you and I will do it—I will save your father if I can, and be a son to him in any case: I will be a brother to your sister, and to you—"

He stretched out his arms towards her, as if forgeful that he was pleading his cause a second time after a first refusal:—suddenly recalled to the fact by the expression of her face: he added—

" In brief, the time has come when you must finally choose between me and Mr. Mazingford."

" I don't see why I should choose either of you," she interrupted in a half pettish, half coquettish tone; " but if I must take one—"

" Well," he eagerly queried, for he was wound up to a pitch of feverish excitement.

" It would certainly be Mr. Mazingford," because—"

"Oh! Judith—false, false, Judith Renelle, may God forgive you!" he cried; and ere Judith had time to finish her sentence, or answer him even by a word, he abruptly quitted the apartment.

She stood in the same attitude of mock dignity, with the same look of raillery on her

face, with the same mischievous expression lurking in her eye, for a moment after he left the room.

Expecting his immediate return, feeling sure
he *could not* leave her so she did not throw off
the mask, but remained ready to resume the discussion the instant he came back to plead again.

" He will go to the head of the staircase and
then turn," she thought; but the hurried footsteps paused not there, she heard him descend
the flight, cross the broad hall—open the strong
oaken door.

" Good Heavens, he won't go !" she exclaimed.
There was a loud bang in answer to her thought.

Then something—Judith never could tell
exactly what came swelling up in her heart; all
the true womanly feeling of her nature, all the
real good, and genuine amiability of her character rose up in arms and denounced her former
coquetry ; a strong blast of wind shook the
casement at the moment, and in that storm she
had sent him out, miserable and despairing—on
such a night she had driven him forth.

" I do love him with all my soul !" she suddenly cried aloud; "and I will bring him back and
tell him so, and never torment him again," and

forthwith she darted out of the room, down the staircase, across the hall, out of the front door, and along the shrubbery walk she knew he would choose as the nearest route home.

It was snowing fast, and the flakes fell white and thick on Judith's uncovered head; but, unheeding the inclemency of the weather, on she sped, her long hair tossed by the wind and saturated with wet.

" Marcus ! " she cried, " Marcus ! " but the howling blast bore back the sound of her voice towards the house. Her appeal ! her soul-felt recal never reached the ear of him for whom it was intended.

At last she reached the open moor. " Marcus ! Marcus ! Marcus !" she called ; but Marcus heard her not.

" Marcus, Marcus, do come back—do—do come back !" she cried through the smothering snow.

The tempest caught the words as they fell from the girl's lips, and whirled them off through the woods on the hill side ; but even had it been otherwise, there was a tempest raging in Marcus Lansing's breast, which might have prevented his hearing that voice, on the calmest of summer

K 2

days. On he hurried through the snow, his faithful dog beside him, all unconscious of the white arms which were stretched out after him, so imploringly, in the darkness, of the half-clad, shivering little penitent, who still kept sobbing out, so short a way behind him—

"Oh! Marcus, come back—oh! do, do come back!"

She could not stand there, shrieking that out long, for the drift choked her utterance, and caused her to gasp for breath; so at last, when she was hoarse, and sick, and tired, she turned and ran back to the house.

She entered it by a side passage, and reached her own room, unperceived, just as a servant was carrying the tea equipage to the drawing-room.

Poor Judith! she stood wet and trembling before the glass, trying to fasten up her soaking hair, with numbed and aching fingers; she tried to stop crying, and wash the traces of tears from her eyes. She wiped, as well as she could, the wet off her dress, and arms and neck—and then crept like a culprit down into the drawing-room.

Her father met her on the threshold. Perhaps Miss Ridsdale had found an opportunity of exchanging a few words with him, for he looked unusually pale and thoughtful.

"Judith," he said, "what have you done with Mr. Lansing—where is he?"

She looked for a second, almost piteously, in his face, and her lips moved as if striving to speak—but then, without answering a syllable, she stole away past him to the shadow of the tea-urn, behind which no one could follow her.

An hour afterwards she ventured to come near the fire, and Mr. Mazingford immediately saw her dress beginning to smoke.

"Good gracious, child!" he said, as he laid his hand suddenly on the green brocade, "you are wet through."

"No, no," said Judith, "it is nothing to signify, I can dry the part in a minute;" and she gave her godfather so significant a glance, to draw no further attention to the matter, that he humoured her inclination, and let her sit shivering, quietly by the fire, till Mr. and Mrs. Berbige arose to depart.

But Miss Ridsdale would not permit them to do so; she said it was a dreadful night, that the way was long, and that there were plenty of spare beds in Llandyll Hall.

" You really must not think of going, Mrs. Berbige," she concluded; " you would be ill for a month after it."

" I had rather return home, thank you, Miss Ridsdale," began the lady, rather stiffly, when Judith broke in with—

" Please don't go home, Mrs. Berbige, do stay here;" and she laid so trembling a hand on the lady's arm, and raised her eyes so imploringly to her face, that the Rector's wife was appeased.

"I suppose," she said, "Marcus can do without us for once; indeed, he could scarcely expect our return; I wonder, poor fellow, how he got home"—and she fastened a reproving glance on Judith.

Judith did not stand in need of reproof then; for she was marvelling, as much as any one, how he had got home. But she was destined to receive a long lecture that night, on the subject of flirting from her aunt, who entered the girl's apartment before herself retiring to rest.

" I could not go to bed, Judith," she said,
" without coming to speak with you on the
events of this evening ;"—and Judith, prepared
by this commencement for what was to follow,
very obstinately and very guiltily crossed her
arms behind her back, and took up a commanding position between the windows of her
room, whence she thought she might conquer
her adversary : for the little Welsh beauty had,
like many another strong nature, a dislike to
being schooled and lectured; and when you could
get Judith Renelle—not to feel, but to confess
she was wrong, you might be sure you had
sounded the deepest and best depths of her heart,
and brought lasting penitence out of them.

And on the night in question, Judith, chafed
with the conflict of passion which had swept
through her breast, wearied with the reproaches
of her own conscience, and tired of grave looks
and reproving glances—chanced to be in a singu-
larly irritable mood ; wherefore, after hearkening,
with an assumed air of indifference, to her aunt's
rebukes and warnings, for a considerable time,
she at length, when some accidental word stung
her beyond endurance, vehemently exclaimed—

"And by what right, aunt, do you lecture me thus? Is it not a question in which he and I alone have any concern—we, and no other human being? What is it to you, or any one else, how I treat him? If he do not like my manners, why, he can stay away, that is all."

Without a sign of anger, Miss Ridsdale lifted her eyes to her niece's face, and kept them rivetted sadly there, till the proud glance fell, till the dark lashes veiled the drooping orbs, till the flush of impatience faded from the beautiful cheek—then, when the girl was calm again, and the fit of momentary impatience had passed away, her aunt spoke :—   .

"Judith—dear, dear, Judith," she said, in a voice which somehow caused every nerve in her listener's frame to thrill, though it was so very low, and still, and calm—"listen, and I will tell you by what right I advise and counsel you. I assume no authority over you, because I am old, and you young; because, for years, I have stood in place of a mother to you—because I have been with you from birth, through infancy and childhood, till now. It is not because you are dearer to me than anything else now left on this

side the grave, that I have told you of this one
great stain in your nature, this one fatal fault in
your character. Oh! no—but because I and
mine suffered through it also I would have
you cure it ere it be too late; I would warn you
to weave your future peace and happiness out of
this night's sorrow.

"I have never told you our story," Miss
Ridsdale added, after a pause; "it may be well
for you to hear it now—remembering all the
while, that you are of our race, and of our blood;
and that the taint which was in us, is now in
you.

"There were four of us, four girls; our father
came from the borders of Wales; and it was
from him the curse descended to us—it had been
in the family for centuries, men and women—it
had darkened their lives, and blasted their happiness. It came into the world with the Ridsdales, as much a part and parcel of themselves,
as the fingers on their hands, or the skin on
their bodies. Every male of the family was a
flirt, every female a coquette—this was the characteristic of the race. Whilst others of the
border families were noted for avarice, for genius,

K 3

for amiability, or for bad temper, we were noted
for caprice in love, for unhappy marriages, for
jiltings, and separations, and divorces, and domestic infelicity.   It seems hard that mental traits
should descend through races, as surely as gout
or insanity; but, when the good is transmitted,
why not the evil?   At all events the taint came
down to my father, whose marriage, after the
fashion of the whole family, was an unhappy one.

" He had married for money, and was disappointed; his wife wedded for a position, and was
likewise disappointed; for whilst his estates
were mortgaged past all hope, her father was
on the eve of bankruptcy.   So the old manor
house passed into the hands of strangers, and
Oswald Ridsdale had to accept a situation under
Government.

" It was a good one, but he never could grow
reconciled to work of any kind; he loathed the
confinement, little as it was; detested London;
sickened for the ancient house, and trees and
gardens of his forefathers.   His temper was
soured by misfortunes, and living in a style
which he could ill afford, he was daily worretted
by the degrading cares of genteel poverty, until

finally he grew to consider money the best thing in life—the only thing almost in life worth caring for.

"We were all born in London—and we entered life—most of us at least with an inheritance from one side the house of wayward coquettish natures, and strong, almost ungovernable wills, and from the other of personal beauty and bodily disease. Judith, my eldest sister, was the handsomest; and she might have married happily and well, but the perverse fate of our race tracked her footsteps, and even when she was engaged to a man for whom she really cared, the could not resist the temptation of flirting with a baronet, who was looking out for a wife, and had been struck by her extraordinary beauty. Like a sensible man, her lover did not bear it patiently, but remonstrated, and then Judith like a foolish woman————ah! Heaven!" exclaimed Miss Ridsdale raising her clasped hands despairingly above her head; "the girl—for she was but a girl then—flung the happiness of a life-time pettishly from her in a moment, and one short month after she married Sir John Lestock, the coldest, proudest, most heartless————but why talk about him ? she never had one happy hour from the morning of her wedding, and died of the malady she inherited from our mother's family—consumption.

"And Eleanor, my next sister"—the lady paused for an instant, and laid her hand on her heart as if some pain shot through it—" she fell in love, as the phrase goes, against my father's consent, and remained in it till that consent was obtained; when—I tell you the plain unvarnished tale, Judith, as it happened, not as it was glossed over to the world; she jilted him, and then, because he wedded another, she in pique married a man who was fifty times too good for her himself, but whose relatives made life wretched to one who had scarcely pronounced the marriage vows ere she repented them.

" Years passed away, and then she—one of the London belles—met again with her old lover, who had become a widower,—just as he was on the eve of setting out for Canada. They saw each other, I think, only at a ball, a concert or flower show ; and whether Eleanor did actually commence the coquetting of old, or whether her mother-in-law only fancied it I cannot tell, but one thing is certain, that a very angry altercation took place between the pair, even in public, which ended in my sister taking Captain Maskell's arm, and requesting him to see her to her carriage, into which she got, and, accompanied by her mother-in-law, drove home.

"So fierce a discussion then ensued, that Eleanor vowed she would not remain another night under her roof—and that she would make her husband's family repent the part they had acted towards her. It was a threat perhaps rashly uttered, but it was fatally kept; for when Captain Maskell sailed for Canada, she went with him. A divorce was afterwards obtained, and then they married; but Eleanor did not live long. He was a handsome, unprincipled spendthrift, and treated her most cruelly. It was not to be expected good could come of it, and the few years she dragged out were ages of miserable repentance.

"She brought grief to many hearts—tears to eyes that had never wept before, sorrow to those who were innocent of her crime. It fell hard on two, Lady Lestock and your mother, for it gave Sir John a pretext for bringing his wife down to the condition of a slave, and it rendered my father painfully anxious to have his youngest child placed under sure and certain guardianship; up to this point, money had been all he thought of—but then an early settlement for Lillian became the one grand object of his life, and so—it is hard to say the truth to you child, because he is so near you—she was literally sold to your father. She did worse than not love—she almost hated him, and when he in very despair, resolved to bring her here, thinking perhaps that when she was away from us she might grow to love him, she tore the wedding ring from her finger and cried she would live with him no longer, that she had been forced to marry a man she detested, and that she would not go to a distant home with him. But she had to do it, Judith—and so she broke her heart and died too. I do not know now which to pity most, your father or your mother; the love which was poured out in vain, or the love which could not be won. I used to feel indignant at your father. I feel more sorry for him now.

"I am the only one left of the four, and my

story is a kaleidoscope likeness of the rest—
the same with a difference. My godmother
adopted me, and, therefore, I was relieved from
the inexorable home influence which drove my
sisters into matrimony; but the curse lay on
me as it lay on the rest. Once, Judith, only
once, I did care well enough for any human
being to marry him—he was Sir John Lestock's
half brother, but there reigned bitter enmity between the two. He had a small fortune, and a
turn and a taste for literature; but when he
came to care for me he tried to better his position in the world, and at last obtained a lucrative
appointment in India. Now, Judith, I knew it
was for my sake he was leaving his native
country, I knew he was one of the proudest,
most sensitive creatures living—I had often
heard him say he would never ask any woman
to be his wife twice, let her be who she might—
and still withal I refused him—solely to try
my power over the man's heart.

"'Millicent,' he said, 'I once almost swore
that I would never be rejected twice—but as
the love I bear you is stronger than my pride,
as the whole of my future is bound up in you,

I pray you for the love of Heaven to reconsider your answer. I do not ask you to be my wife yet—I will not hold you to your promise, if you wish to be free on my return—I only ask you to give me hope—to say you love me now—to whisper that you think you will consent to be mine hereafter. I am not a boy to be trifled with, nor a child to be laughed at. I will not be flirted with, even by you; nor refused one day and accepted the next, by any one. If my love is worth taking, take it now—if you like me well enough, to think of me as a future husband, tell me so, for God's sake, at once.'

"But I would not—and still the love of the man's heart overpowered his pride—and I exulted in the mastery I had over him.

"'For the third time,' he said, and his voice was trembling like a nervous woman's, 'and for the last time—do you love me—will you marry me?'

"I had fancied, Judith, that I held him to me by his very heartstrings; but I drew them too tightly at last, and they snapped in my fingers."

With a sort of cry, Judith flung herself on her knees beside her aunt, and buried her face in the folds of her dress. Miss Ridsdale passed an arm around the girl's neck, and proceeded

with the self-inflicted torture she had undertaken
for that wayward being's benefit.

"So it comes to pass that I am an old maid—
so it chanced that when friends died and sisters
married, I remained alone—so it happens that
I am here preaching to you—therefore it is that
I claim a right to warn you ere it be too late."

She stooped down to kiss the averted face,
and found it wet with tears. "It is so like,"
sobbed Judith—"your story is so like to mine,
that I felt as though my heart would break
while I was listening to it." And then the poor
child told her tale in a few brief words, and
finished by declaring she would never displease
anybody again, and that she was very sorry—
very, very sorry.

This was the climax : Miss Ridsdale knew
when that confession of wrong, that promise of
amendment, was wrung from her, Judith was safe,
for the girl's was, after all, a strong noble nature ;
one with which sense and kindness could accomplish almost anything ;—and so, when it had
grown very late, or rather very early, the lady
arose to seek her chamber.

"Good night, my own dear child !" she said ;

" now I may go to bed, knowing that as you would not marry Mr. Mazingford under any circumstances, you will never flirt with him again."

Very meekly Judith kissed her aunt, and very tenderly they two parted for the night; Miss Ridsdale, who had no very serious fear but that Mr. Lansing would either return or write before he left Wales, bidding the girl, as a last injunction, " Go to sleep."

But Judith could not sleep; she walked to the window and looked out.   Nothing but snow —snow on everything—snow everywhere; and it was on such a night she had driven him forth; —that was the eternal refrain of her meditation. How busy the little flirt's conscience was that night!   What a mine of self-reproach she worked down in during those weary hours; how very humbly she went into Lillian's room, and laid her aching head on the side of her sister's bed, and began muttering sentences of regret and repentance, and good resolves, in confidence, to the darkness.   First, she was afraid she had lost him for ever, and mourned out accordingly:

" What a brother he would have made you,

Lillie, and what a home you should have had, and how proud I would have felt of him, and how happy I might have been as his wife, and what a heartless wretch I was, and what misery I have brought on myself."

At which idea she commenced to weep, for she was very young, and it seemed the most natural thing in the world for her to take to; but then after a while growing comforted, she murmured forth—

"It is impossible though that he can leave me altogether; he will surely return in a few hours, and I will tell him all then—of how sorry I am, and how I would not marry that odious wretch—no, not if he had five millions a year, and of how I ran after him through the snow, and he would not hear; and I will never teaze him again; and I will say I am fonder of him than of all the earth beside, and I will never flirt with anybody any more, and I will make him a good, faithful, honest friend, companion, wife; and I will strive to be better than I am, and I will keep this night's sorrow before me as a warning, and try never to grieve that noble heart of his again so long as I live; and I will from this time forth, turn over a wiser and a better leaf, and endeavour with all my strength to be more worthy of him; I will—I will, so help me God!"

And so the hours of darkness wore away in picturing the scene of that reconciliation and forgiveness—in thinking of all she should say to him, of all he would say to her when he returned—when Marcus came back.

Towards morning, she fell asleep—sitting on the floor with her face buried in her hands, she dropped into a troubled slumber, from which she awoke with a start when a kind of misty daylight had dawned over the white earth.

Judith was very cold; though she had wrapped a heavy shawl about her figure, and had sat huddled up together, still she was very cold and stiff and uncomfortable: her limbs were aching, and her teeth chattering: she felt shooting pains through her head, and flashes of fire seemed darting across her eyes. "I am afraid I am going to be ill," she thought, as she drew the shawl more closely around her, and walked with uncertain steps to the window. It had ceased snowing, she saw, but the hills and the trees

were covered with it—everything lay wrapped
in a white mantle—the shubbery walks and distant mountains ; it was wearisome to look out
and contemplate that waste of scenery from
which every landmark of old seemed obliterated,
every variety and relief passed away for ever.
The prospect was irksome to the mind, sadden-
ing to the heart, painful to the sight, and Judith's
eyes grew somehow so weak and dim as she
looked, that after a moment or two, she was
forced to close the lids over them, and so shut
the snowy landscape out. It appeared though
as if some fascination held her chained to the
window that commanded a view of the path by
which Marcus must come back—by which he
would come back to her. True, she could only
gaze out for a moment at a time, but still that
moment was sufficient ; poor, restless little heart
that had so tormented him when it had him
nigh, that fluttered so ceaselessly at the thought
of his return—poor little girl, who had not
known the value of the thing she was toying
with, till she had flung it beyond her reach,
when she began to cry for some one to bring it
back to her.

At last, after a longer interval than usual, for she had fallen, even whilst standing there, into a sort of doze—Judith opened her eyes and roused herself with a sudden effort; then along the broadest of the shrubbery walks she saw something coming — she did know what, at the first; there was a film over her sight, and everything dazzled her; but by degrees objects grew more distinct, and then she beheld four men coming slowly along—they bore a burden, and apparently a heavy one—for they often paused and rested; and as they emerged into a wider avenue, Judith perceived a huge dog following the party—his black tail sweeping mournfully upon the snow.

The girl did not know then, could never tell afterwards what she felt at the moment; she did not cry, or faint, or scream, but rushed from the apartment, down the staircase, out of the hall door, along the avenue.

"What have you there?" she asked of the bearers; and they said afterwards that her lip never trembled, her voice never faltered.

The men looked from one to another, and then tried to move past her without answering.

"Stop!" she said ;—"I bid you stop;" and they did it. But when she stepped forward to examine the nature of their burden, one of the men interposed :

"Don't do that, Miss Judith," he almost whispered ; "don't!"

With a strong hand Judith pushed him aside —she lifted the cloak that covered the object they carried—she stood looking, for about the time you could have counted twenty, upon it— whilst the men stood gazing pitifully on her ; and then, without a shriek or groan, she fell heavily to the ground.

"God help us all!" exclaimed the man who had previously spoken, as he lifted her gently from the earth, and carried her back to the house.

CHAPTER X.

WEEKS after, Judith Renelle awoke to consciousness. From the horrors of brain fever, and
ravings of delirium, from dreams of pain, and
terrors of imagination, she awoke to the more
frightful horror, the more awful pain of her own
actual situation. Memory did not return to her
all at once; slowly the shadows of the past came
flitting back to their old homes, the vacant chambers of her mind; one by one they took possession
of their former dominions; and when they did
so, Judith knew all. Lying there, weak, silent,
motionless, she dwelt on the one fearful sorrow
that had fallen upon her—with her eyes closed
she still looked on that spectacle which was
destined never after to leave her sight till she

had ceased to breathe for ever—when she had not strength to move a finger, she was still able to think ; and it was during this period she acquired a habit, which abode with her for months afterwards—viz. : that of brooding in silence concerning the events of that frightful night and morning, till their horror overpowered her, and she shrieked aloud.

It was the most unendurable form of grief that can be conceived. She would remain apparently in a state of apathy for half an hour or so, without moving a muscle, without shedding a tear ; but then would come that short, sharp cry, as of one in some mortal agony, when she would start wildly up, and seem meditating an escape of some kind—perhaps out of the world, poor child, away from her own thoughts. The doctors shook their heads, and said they did not like it ; Miss Ridsdale tried in vain to rouse her from her meditations ; Lillian came and talked to her, but Judith disregarding them all, would still give utterance to that horrid scream, which was sufficient to chill, with its sharp, ringing sound, the blood of every person who heard it. At stated intervals only, it echoed through the chamber,

but during the intervening periods no one could
avoid listening for it; and then when it did come,
there was a something about its peculiar tone
which caused it to ring in the ear for long, long
afterwards.

It was a nervous affection, the men of medicine affirmed, but they liked it none the better
for that—a peculiarly pernicious form of grief—
they feared the effect on Miss Renelle's intellect
—the shock had been too frightful; it had injured her altogether, bodily and mentally; unless
some change very speedily took place, they could
not answer for the consequences.

During the entire of her illness, Mr. Renelle
had watched by his daughter's couch; night and
day, morning, noon, and evening, he never left
his post beside her, till the crisis was past. But
when the first anxiety for her life was over, he
gave way; for days he was confined to his bed
by sickness; for days Judith, after her return to
consciousness, never saw him. At last he came
creeping back to his child; very pale, and wan,
and altered, with wasted hands, and haggard
face, and many grey hairs, he entered her room,
and dropped into his usual chair beside her. At

first Judith did not notice him. With her white, hollow cheek resting on the pillow, and the lids closed tightly over her aching eyes, she lay in one of her darkest moods, thinking of Marcus living, of Marcus dead, and of the awful burden she was destined to carry to the grave with her, until at length that particular nerve in her frame which always vibrated audibly, was struck, and she shrieked aloud.

According to wont, she started up in bed, and opened her eyes to their fullest extent; but as she did so, her gaze fell, for the first time since her recovery, on her father.

"Judith, Judith," he exclaimed in agony, for something about that cry froze his very soul within him—"my child, my own dear darling child!"

Heaven knows what it was in his look or his words which opened the floodgates within her, only one thing is certain, that as if suddenly recalled to a memory of others besides herself, she flung her arms about his neck, and crying out, "Papa, oh! my poor papa!" she burst into a perfect paroxysm of tears. He was so fearfully shattered by *her* illness, so totally broken down by *her* trouble, so changed, so wrecked, that the sight of him moved Judith when perhaps nothing else could have done, and saved her.

From that day forth, her escape from the arms of a more fearful foe than death was ensured; and so at length, weeping, and wailing, and shrieking by turns, she recovered, so far at least as to be able to get up and walk about the house and grounds.

But the Judith Renelle of old was as much dead as though she had been laid stiff and cold in her coffin; trouble having pressed its heavy hand on the girl's head, had changed her bodily and mentally. The gay, buoyant spirit, the happy, joyous expression; the light, bounding step— the heart so free from care—these things she had left behind her for ever: they were dead and buried, memories of the past; things which had been, but which for her might never be more. Her beauty was not gone, but its character was altered; dignified, cold, and broken-hearted, she stood on the very threshold of life, looking with world-tired eyes on the scene before her. She was a girl no longer, for sorrow had made a woman of her all too soon; she did everything mechanically; she went through existence apparently with a sort of cloud resting on her understanding; wherever she turned, whatever she was doing, whomsoever she was with, she was haunted by one fearful vision, "day and night it never left her sight," she said; sleeping or waking, it was always there.

"Ah! heaven," she once exclaimed, "for rest from it—if only for five minutes. He haunts me, aunt; he is ever with me."

And she said it so very wearily, that Miss Ridsdale rained tears over her, although Judith's eyes were dry and bright. Bright with a certain peculiar light, that had never left them since her illness; there was a fixed brilliancy about them, on which her aunt could scarcely bear to look.

Months passed away before she mentioned Marcus's name, or asked for particulars of his death; but at last, one lovely summer's evening, Miss Ridsdale told her all she knew, all any human being knew concerning the manner of his untimely end.

Early on the morning following that fearful night, a labourer crossing the hills, was met by a large, black dog, who made such signs as a dumb brute could, that his human friend was to leave the path and follow him; which accordingly the man did, for the distance of about twenty yards; when the guide coming to a stand-still and whining piteously, he was induced to examine the spot, which proved a kind of hollow, filled with a deep drift of snow, and there he found—

"Don't tell me the rest," here broke in Judith. "I know it all, he had strayed from the path, and—and I am alive to hear the tale. I, who was the cause of his death."

It was all in vain Miss Ridsdale tried to comfort her, it was to no purpose she strove to turn Judith's mind from the one all-absorbing subject; she could not give the girl a draught from Lethe; she was powerless to guide her to the waters of oblivion.

"If you could get her to take an interest in anything," suggested the family doctor.

"I cannot," replied Miss Ridsdale, "and yet I am sure there is something which would rouse her, if I could only find out what it is. Another heavy trouble, for instance—"

"Might serve as a counter-irritant, certainly," concluded the man of medicine, despondingly,

for he thought the remedy rather a severe one,
and besides he knew that troubles to be heavy,
must be real—and even supposing a fresh grief
were sure to prove successful, who was to manu-
facture it?

He saw a point indeed from whence the storm
might come—a spot where, sooner or later, it
was sure to burst; but he dreaded the consequences of that trial, and tried to keep knowledge of its approach from Judith Renelle.

"Aunt," said the girl, one autumn day, when
the purple heather was blooming over the spot
where Marcus had fallen asleep for ever, and the
fresh September wind was fanning her cheek as
she stood listlessly near the open window of Miss
Renelle's sitting-room—"Aunt, what are you
writing?"

"Stories," answered the other briefly.

"Yes, I know that," responded Judith; "but
why so eternally?"

"Because money is very scarce," explained
her aunt, pausing in her occupation, and looking
earnestly in the face of her questioner—"because
my dead sister's husband, and my dead sister's
children have need of all the little I can make."

"Have we?" asked Judith, and for once the question had a touch of human interest about it.—"How is that?"

"Shall I tell you," queried the lady, "all the truth?"

And Judith answered, "Yes."

"Well, then, my child, your father is almost beggared; that coal mine has proved a myth—nobody will help him to look for what nobody can find : his money is gone, and his credit likewise. Mr. Mazingford has a mortgage over Llandyl Hall ; and very often lately—very often, indeed, Judith, your father has been literally without a sixpence."

"Poor papa ! and he so fond of it," said the girl; and with this slight mention of his love of money, and trifling amount of sympathy for his disappointment, she apparently dismissed the subject from her consideration, and relapsed into silence.

Miss Ridsdale sat contemplating her for a few minutes, and then, with a heavy sigh, resumed her occupation.

After a long pause, however, Judith came over to the table and took up a pen.

"I wonder could I write too," she said; "is it hard?"

"Will you copy for me?" cried her aunt, eagerly catching at the idea of any employment, no matter how trivial. "I want this to go by to-morrow's post, will you copy it for me?"

"No," answered Judith, "I won't copy—I'll write. What shall it be about?"

She sat there for an hour answering the question on paper; but then she said she got tired, and tearing her work in fragments went away out. Miss Ridsdale pieced the bits together, after her departure, and read that first vague effort through. She could make nothing out of it. Perhaps the girl had talent, or perhaps she had none; the brief production did not resemble that of a boarding-school miss, or of a well informed woman of moderate ability; it was more like the disjointed labours of a lunatic—an unconnected, crude, collection of words, apparently with some meaning in them, which, however, even their author barely comprehended. There was genius in that bald, unfinished sketch, though if Miss Ridsdale could have discovered it—genius which only wanted

L 3

wakening to be resistless; which only required cultivation and clothing to be universally recognized.

Still the acorn was so very small that the lady could see no shadow of the future oak—the style, the wording, the ideas were so different from her own, that she recognized no kindred spirit in the girl. Nor was there—for Judith Renelle's genius soared as far above her aunt's intellect, as the lark does above the green fields and simple flowers of earth; and it would have been as easy for the latter to measure and limit the flight of the bird, as for Miss Ridsdale to tell to what height the girl might attain; if once she fairly took wing, as a writer.

It is strange to consider how many authors might have been, who are not; and how many there are who might never have been, had circumstances varied a little in their respective cases. How few would ever write if something stronger than nature did not make them think of or compel them to it? Association or misfortune, makes authors out of men who otherwise might have remained unstained by ink till the grave closed over them; and the curious part

of the thing is to consider how many hundreds
of men and women there are in England, now
living quietly and peaceably, who might, without
any alteration in character, or greater amount of
genius, have become, by the simplest accident,
stars, or, at all events, planets in the literary
firmament. Life's chances turn on the merest
atom of a pivot—and so, we doubt not there
are scores now earning their bread by the labours
of their pen, who would never have tried their
hand at authorship but for some strange chance
or domestic misfortune : whilst on the other
side there are numbers who, had they lived in
literary circles, or been beggared by a bank failure, an unsuccessful speculation, an unhappy law-
suit, or any other sudden accident—might have
burst out on the world as capital writers of novels, histories, poems, and so forth. We all know
cases in point which support this theory ; which
go far to prove, that although genius may and
must be born with a man, it does not develope
with his growth : circumstances form authors as
they do soldiers, statesmen, surgeons, engineers,
and lawyers ; sometimes out of good stuff—
frequently out of bad—and it is not going too

far to affirm, that had fate so ordered it, some of
our worst writers might have become first-rate
physicians, and many a medical humbug have
astonished the world with the marvels he could
perform by the aid, not of pestle and mortar,
but of pen and ink.

It is no doubt for the best, that half the
people in the word are standing in their wrong
places—that square pins are jammed in round
holes, and round pins rattle rather loosely in
places which they are not big enough to fill;
and we do not desire to quarrel with the arrangement, only it is singular, as above remarked, to
stoop down into the darkest recesses of our
fellows' histories, and see the little pivot on which
the whole machinery of their beings turns, to
note the insignificant pebble which flung them
off one line of rails and forced them to try another; the word that caused then to think of that
profession, and the sentence which drove them
into this.

And so it was that thing which men call
chance, that made an authoress out of Judith
Renelle; the train had been laid by nature years
previously, but the want of money lit the match

thereto, and once ignited, it burned steadily on, till the lamp of genius was quenched in the night of death for ever.

The girl felt the fire within her, and was as impotent to forget its existence or to extinguish its blaze, as she seemed to rule the wayward destiny that had been given unto her as an inheritance.

But for nearly a couple of months, Miss Ridsdale heard no more of Judith's literary efforts; for the energy of the girl's character, which had previously been demonstrative, was now silent and secret as the grave. Work having ceased to be a pastime or a recreation, had become an earnest labour—a thing not to be carried about and shown, but to be ceaselessly brooded over and performed.

Quietly but incessantly the steady hand pursued its labours over sheets of paper, through bottles of ink—slowly and wearily, for the knack of composition did not lie in Judith's fingers; it abode in her brain, and, for want of practice and experience, she had trouble in drawing it thence down to the tip of her pen. It was easier for her to think than say—therefore, the thoughts were but imperfectly represented by the words. She had never been much of a scribbler, even in a letter-writing sense—never been given to poetry—never had even tried a theme. She started in the race of authorship without a minute's preparation for the task; she scarcely understood what she had to do, till she was in the midst of the fray, trying to fight it out as bravely as the rest.

She pursued that as she had never pursued aught else—not for love of itself truly, but for love of what it could, of what it did bring.

For the money it might win, not for her, but for those dear to her—for the relief it gave to an aching heart, which was forced to turn from the past, when so fully occupied in the present. If authorship serve no other good, it does that of taking a man, for a period, out of himself; and but for it, many a heart had broken, many a brain reeled, ere now.

So Judith found, at all events. For the first time since her illness, she discovered something which employed mind and fingers at the same time; something which turned her thoughts out of the old beaten track, and gave her a sort of object in life, beyond brooding over a fearful tragedy—an irreparable misfortune.

True the sorrow was there always; the wound, let it heal as it might, could never be so thoroughly closed as to become painless: the agony it had caused might be judged of, by the deep, mental scar it left behind; but still, the medicine of employment, the finest tonic which has yet been discovered for all manner of morbid diseases, did its work surely on the frame of Judith Renelle, restored her to something like health, and enabled her to bear her griefs with an outward semblance of tranquillity.

The long midnight hours, which had been previously spent in conjuring up all sorts of horrible images, were now occupied in earnest, profitable toil—in labour, that bore no visible fruit for years afterwards—that seemed to the weary worker so much time, and trouble, and energy, thrown uselessly away.

For, like all who ever attain to any success worth possessing, Judith found the first part of her road rough and stony—strewed with rejections, bordered with thorny criticisms, rendered difficult with unsuspected obstacles. She, in common

with most other young authors, thought she had
nothing to do but write and be paid; but she
found out her mistake soon enough. Her first
rejection revealed the delusion to her: that refusal proceeded from the gracious pen of Mr.
Kearn, at that period editor of " The British
Lion ;" subsequently, editor and proprietor. Mr.
Kearn was one of those wolves in sheeps' clothing, who go about the world lacerating the
hearts of tender young authors, with an indescribable show of kindness, and painful adherence
to truth.

He had published two or three books himself,
and made thereby a certain reputation, which he
traded on ever after. He criticised so freely, that
people took his word for law; and Mr. Kearn
himself felt he was the highest tribunal, from
which there could be no appeal. An officious,
impertinent, literary quack, who having just sense
enough to find out the safe side of criticism,
fault-finding, scattered his " notes of censure,"
broadcast, over the kingdom ; and then called
out for the world to come to admire the work he
had accomplished. If an author succeeded, Mr.
Kearn's " hints" were, of course, the basis of his

success. If an author failed, he had either neglected Mr. Kearn's timely counsels, or else forgotten Mr. Kearn's advice, for him to abandon literature altogether; and, accordingly, in a missive, which occupied two-and-a-half sides of a sheet of letter paper, Mr. Kearns conveyed his criticism and warnings to Miss Renelle; he told her, first, still pursuing the principle on which he had won his name, what an interest he took in young authors; and then he advised her never to write another line: after which pleasant commencement, he minutely analysed the contents of her MS., and laid its faults out in the daylight, before the eyes of his lady correspondent. Finally, he told her how much he regretted being compelled to return an unfavourable answer, and remained her's, very faithfully — " Charles Clarence Kearn."

Judith read the precious missive through, from beginning to end. Standing before the fire in her aunt's sitting-room, she perused every word of Mr. Kearn's valuable advice—and then, very scornfully, flung the epistle on the top of the blazing coals, and walked out of the apartment.

It was the first sign of " temper" Miss Ridsdale had noticed for many a day; but she hailed
the ebullition thankfully, although she discovered
thereby that her dear child had commenced to
fight out the battle of life—all alone.

The change which that annoyance wrought
on Judith was surprising; Mr. Kearn seemed to
have put a sort of blister on her spirit, and to
have roused it up considerably, by the process.
In place of following his admirable counsel, she
recommenced work with greater energy than
ever, proving conclusively, to her aunt's satisfaction, that there is nothing so good for grief as a
counter-irritant—nothing so great a stimulant
to exertion, as a little wholesome opposition.
And accordingly, Judith, with a spice of her
former contrary disposition, gave herself up to
writing altogether. She neglected other duties,
to attend to that which was less a duty than a
relief. Morning, noon, and night, she might have
been found, with a pen in her hand, trying to exor-
cise the demon out of her own soul—trying to
prove Mr. Kearn wrong—trying to produce something which the publishers would buy.

All in vain; there seemed a conspiracy against

her: she got her aunt to try her connection, but it was a very small and peculiar one, and no good was to be effected there. Then she wrote to the first houses; and got no answers—then to various journals, which declined her communications, with thanks.

The worst part of the business was, that Miss Ridsdale, fearful of raising false hopes, and really not able to discover any particular talent, dared not encourage the girl. She was glad for her to write, but she dreaded disappointment: she saw Judith was again staking her all on a die, which, in no event, could bring happiness with it; she perceived trouble coming in the distance, from which her niece steadily averted her eyes. She knew it was well for Judith to write in moderation; but she also knew she was treading both a dangerous and a selfish path. Since her recovery to bodily health, Judith, once so thoughtful for others, had seemed to forget every one save herself. What she chose to do, whether weep, shriek, brood over her sorrows, or sit for hours poring over a desk, was what she did do. Great sorrow is always selfish for a time; and her time had now been a long one. Miss

Ridsdale did not like it, did not like every duty being performed on compulsion; did not like Mr. Renelle wandering about the grounds alone, looking so ill and miserable; did not like Judith's own clothes hanging about her in ribands; did not like Lilian's very existence seeming at times a thing forgotten. She made every allowance for the girl's character, considered that strong natures always go to extremes, one way or another; remembered that the best spring in her niece's character had been broken for ever—recollected that Judith fancied she was labouring from duty, working for others. She did not blame the poor sufferer, she only desired to show her that the path she had chosen, unhappily, was a wrong one. Accordingly—

"Judith," she said, one winter's day, "do you know, I think you ought to go out with your father a little more; he has grown so frail, lately, and he seems so lonely, without you."

Her auditor looked up, hastily—

"I—I can't bear to go out," she answered; "it hurts me to look on those dreadful hills; and then, besides, I have nothing to say to papa now, not a word."

"Don't you think you could find something, if you tried, Judith? You used to be able to amuse and interest him, when no other person could."

"Yes, but that was a long time ago; everything is changed now. I am not what I was once: everything is altered since then—and so am I."

"Still, you might try to make him a little happier; in fact, you ought to do it. I never saw any one so utterly broken down."

"Yes," interrupted Judith; "but when I can give him money, he will get better; it is that which is oppressing him. Whenever I am making enough to relieve his difficulties, you will see him a changed being."

"But you may never make a shilling," returned her aunt; "and, in the meantime, you are neglecting him. Besides, it is not merely money which is fretting Mr. Renelle—your illness, and the excitement and anxiety consequent thereupon, shattered his health completely; and then the sort of estrangement which has come between you and him—it must have produced a very injurious effect also."

" What estrangement?" asked Judith. " I
love him as much or more than over I did—
indeed, indeed, I do, aunt."

" Perhaps so, indeed I am sure so; but people
like a little evidence of the feeling. In days
gone past, you and he were always together;
you were his right hand, his confidante, his support, his comfort, his companion—and what are
you now?"

" I am trying to be his assistant," answered
Judith, earnestly; and the reply was true, as far
as it went.

" Very possibly," returned Miss Ridsdale;
" but why not combine all characters in one?
why neglect the great good of the present, for
the sake of a future, which may never come? I
have not forgotten your affliction, my darling,"
added the lady, noticing the look which was
coming over her niece's face, " nor do I mean to
say, but that the trouble which has fallen upon
you, will be a shade and a sorrow for life; still,
Judith, remember your grief was his grief, and
you have not been the only sufferer. Were I in
your place, I would try to combine two duties
together, pleasing and helping him. It may be

hard for you to do both, but still you might, I·
think—"

" I will go and walk with him now," said
Judith, rising, for she was one of those rare
mortals who would listen to the voice of reason,
let her tones sound as harsh as they list—one of
those women, who if once they perceive any
cause to be unkind or selfish, will immediately
abandon it; and, accordingly, she went away
down the stairs, and into the dining-room; and,
with something of her old manner, only softened
and saddened, she asked her father to come out
with her. She did not now, indeed, take his
hand, and with the petted, happy gesture of
former times, lay it on her shoulder—oh, no;
but, as if they had both known sorrow, she
drew his arm within hers, and suited her pace to
his pace, and went with him whithersoever he
chose. She tried to talk to him, to make amends
for their long alienation: with a very penitent
heart, she saw how the old man's eyes brightened, when she entered the room; how closely
he clung to her, during their ramble. She strove
to banish painful thoughts from her own mind,
painful topics from their conversation. She kept

·pacing up and down, ong after she felt quite worn
out herself; in one word, she tried to do her duty
faithfully towards the poor, shattered, broken-
down old man, who called her child.

"Papa," she said, when they got back to the
dining-room fire, and she had set him in his old
seat once more, "papa, although we have been
very unhappy of late, we don't love one another
less than ever we did—do we?"

She had crouched down on her knees as she
asked the question, and got her arms about his
neck—for the busy conscience was at work
again, reproaching her with absence of thought
for him: "Do we?" she softly repeated, as she
drew the furrowed cheek nearer, and kissed
first it, and then the tears, which came slowly
trickling from the old man's eyes—kissed the
drops away, one by one; after which, she pillowed her father's head on her shoulder, and
stroked his grey hair, with a tender, caressing
hand.

Yes, they had both been very wretched, for
the day-dream of each had vanished; and they
clung there together like two, who after having
buffeted the waves for a season separately, meet

at length on a strange, inhospitable shore, to prove a solace and a stay to one another.

And from that hour Judith Renelle turned over a different leaf in her life's story. She took counsel boldly with her own heart and her own soul, and found each had a word to say to her of reproach and warning. Happiness for herself, she discovered, was a thing never to be— that is, the happiness of old; peace and tranquillity she likewise fancied had passed away for ever; but she also saw she had sacrificed others on this shrine of her own sorrow—that she had done wrong.

Upon which discovery, the girl-woman made a solemn vow, that from that day forth she would carry her heavy burden in silence, and live to lighten others' grief, rather than indulge her own. She thought if Marcus were living, it was the path he would bid her pursue; and every pang she inflicted on her own spirit, during the course of that self-imposed path of duty, she looked on as a sort of punishment for her share in the Christmas night's tragedy: next her heart she wore the hair-cloth, with the ardour and the constancy of a devotee. Always brave and strong,

she persevered in the course she had chosen,
and thenceforth Mr. Renelle never walked alone,
nor was Lillian's comfort neglected; and Miss
Ridsdale, finding her niece so nobly battling
against the inherent selfishness of human nature, wondered if brighter days would not dawn
for the girl—if her future might still not be a
peaceful one? Alas! the future of such a past
—how could it be otherwise than stormy?

CHAPTER XI.

WHEN Judith Renelle, after so long a period of mourning, cast off the sack-cloth and ashes she had carried for such a period about, as the outward signs and tokens of her grief—when, in plainer English, she began to attend to her father again, and look after Lillian, and mend her own clothes, and take a sort of routine interest in household affairs; when, like one suddenly aroused from a useless dream, she wakened, at last, to life, and the cares and the duties thereof;—Mr. Mazingford came to the conclusion that she had indulged her sorrow for an old lover long enough, and that she ought to be about ready to take up with a new one.

M 2

" Even if they had been married," he soliloquised, " she would only have required a year, to get over the thing; but, heaven be praised! it never came to that—and yet, still, I don't know if a widow might not have been better than a girl crossed in love. I do not care for widows, though having tried one of the species already, should prefer a variety;" and as, in any case, Judith Renelle could not be made a widow of now, he determined to transform her into a wife, as speedily as might be.

For he was in love with her; and he would have done almost any mortal thing to get her to marry him, peaceably. Her beauty, though altered, was, perhaps, greater than ever; her manners were more formed; and she had lost that childish petulance, which had often provoked him in former times. Her bearing was more calm, collected, and dignified: trouble had deepened the stream of her mind, and smoothed the ripples on the surface—and last, though certainly not least, there was a certain cold repulsion, so constantly apparent towards him, that Mr. Mazingford's pique was aroused sufficiently to make him swear she should wed him, willing

or not, by some means or other.   If all these
were not reasons enough to induce him to bring
matters to a point, another might be found in
the fact, that Lewis Mazingford had set his heart
on having Judith for a wife long before; and
Lewis Mazingford was never known to set his
heart on anything for nought.   It remained to
be seen, therefore, which, Judith or he, would
get the best of the fight—for it was now almost a
pitched battle between them—she offering hatred
of Mr. Mazingford, to the manes of Marcus
Lansing — he, outwardly, all smoothness and
kindness, bringing other influences to bear upon
her, of the very existence whereof she was happily ignorant.

Money, or rather the want of it—that was
the screw Mr. Mazingford believed would ultimately prove omnipotent to bring the proud
beauty to his feet.   He longed to conquer her,
to make her feel he was conferring a favor on
her and her race, by giving her his name, a
home, and a protector.   With a sort of feverish
desire he panted for that triumph; and the
minute he saw her old love for her father re-
viving in her heart, that minute he fancied her

vulnerable point might instantly be touched, and commenced operations forthwith.

There had been a sort of coolness in Mr. Renelle's manner towards him for a long time previously; ever since, in fact, the failure of the coal-mine scheme; a coolness such as invariably ensues, after a certain period, between borrower and lender—recipient and patron. There was no absolute quarrel, it is true. Mr. Mazingford came to the house, just as freely as formerly—perhaps, indeed, a little more freely, for he looked upon it now as his own; and Mr. Renelle always received him with a show of welcome; but still, since Marcus Lansing's death, and the bursting of the coal-mine bubble, a great gulf had opened between the pair, which the owner of Wavour Hall tried in vain to span.

It was of no use, however; so, finding fair means unavailing, he bethought him of foul, and commenced pressing the screw down most unmercifully, driving the wedge tighter day by day, in between his victim's soul, and the boot of pecuniary torture he had fitted upon it.

Llandyl Hall was the one plank which stood between Mr. Renelle and absolute want; and

this plank Mr. Mazingford had the power to pull
from under his feet at any moment he pleased.

" I am too old," Mr. Renelle said one morning, " to go back into the world's strife, and
bear the heat and burden of the day ; and besides,
when I was younger, I made nothing by the experiment, — yet still I know you ought to be
repaid."

" I do not want the principal, at least at present," returned Mr. Mazingford, with amiable
consideration ; " all I desire is a fair interest
thereon ; now, can you ensure me that interest ?"

" Not unless my family starve," responded
Mr. Renelle.

There was a long pause, which was broken at
length by the owner of Wavour Hall.

" Well now, Renelle, do you know I think it
would a good thing for you just to look fairly at
your position, and really to see how you are
situated. You owe me, in round numbers,
something more than the whole of your property
would fetch, if it were brought to market to-
morrow ; you have not the remotest prospect of
repaying me that mortgage ; and, it seems, there

is no chance of interest either. Your land, for want of culture, is every day deteriorating in value—in fact, it is now almost worthless. We may give up the coal-mine as a mistake. Your acres seem to me to be producing you next to nothing; and if it were not for Miss Ridsdale, I do not believe you could meet mere household expenses. Now supposing that she were to die, or marry, which first must be some day—which last might be any day—you would be at once deprived of her annuity, which, small as it is, has been your trump card for years past. Thus, setting me out of the question altogether, you see your case is not encouraging; and putting me into it—your position becomes desperate."

Mr. Renelle inclined his head by way of assent; it was scarcely a proposition to which a man could be expected to return a verbal answer.

"Suppose, again," resumed Mr. Mazingford, "that during your lifetime I were to let that money remain on the property at merely a nominal interest—that, in brief, I were not to harass you on the subject at all, but to leave the question for future discussion—still, when after your decease, my claim is settled, and Miss Ridsdale's assistance withdrawn—what, I ask you, is to become of your children?"

" I don't know," replied the victim, hopelessly, " Stephen is not—"

" Pooh! I was not thinking of him. Stephen is a man; and no man possessed of hands, and arms, and youth and strength, need ever go begging. I meant your daughters, Renelle; what is hereafter to become of them?"

" What is the use of asking," retorted Mr. Renelle, with a sudden fierceness, which showed how tender a spot had been pressed by no gentle finger; " what is the use of asking, when you know I can return no satisfactory answer to the question? With broken health and ruined fortune — how can I ensure them dowries? I am powerless; what can I do?"

" Little, perhaps, but still a something," was the cool response. " I want to place the matter before you in a fair light, that you may understand me clearly, as I go along. Llandyl Hall, then, we may consider gone—Miss Ridsdale, doubtful. What then, I ask again, remains for your daughters?—they cannot be governesses, or

M 3

servants, or clerks, or labourers. Lillian cannot, of course, seek an asylum in matrimony; and Judith, it seems to me, is not very likely to contract, under any circumstances, a good alliance here. How, therefore, are they to be supported?"

Mr. Renelle did not even attempt a reply to this query; possibly he knew whither Mr. Mazingford was steering, and was nerving himself for the encounter: at any rate, he held his peace, and the other proceeded—

"I confess I see but one way out of the difficulty." He paused for an instant; but Mr. Renelle never inquired what that way might be.

"Which is," continued Mr. Mazingford, "for my god-daughter to become my wife."

"Judith—won't—marry," said Mr. Renelle.

"Won't marry!" echoed Mr. Mazingford; "and pray, in heaven's name, if she get the chance, why not?"

Old as he was, the girl's father felt a singular twitching in his fingers, which urged him to pitch his impertinent questioner out of the window; but he controlled his temper, and answered—

"Because, as you well know, my poor child's

heart is lying in a grave, under the elms of Llandyl Church."

"And is she, consequently, to remain a pauper for life?" demanded Mr. Mazingford; "has no woman before ever married after a love-cross?— ay, and been happy, too. I am not going to talk any sentimental nonsense; but still, I think, I am quite as fond of Judith as poor Lansing ever was; and what is more, can provide far better for her. Had he lived, ten to one you would not have consented to their marriage; for he was as poor as Job, without manner, connection, anything. But he is dead, so there is no use in talking about him—for you have now to choose not between me and him, but between me and no one."

"I do not wish to choose," interposed Mr. Renelle.

"But, sir, you *must* choose," retorted his visitor; "for between me and no one, means, in straight-forward English, between me and beggary. Listen, like a reasonable man and sensible father, to what I have to say, and then do as you like. If Judith remain for life a love-lorn maiden, she will not be one bit happier than she would

as a wife, even under the worst circumstances.
All the weeping, and wailing, and willow-wearing
in the world, won't bring Lansing to life again.
Besides, the half of a young girl's love is fancy,
which a few years' intercourse with the world
speedily dispels.   Even as matters stand at
present, therefore, she is no gainer by remaining
single.   Very well; now having made that discovery, we will take a look into the future.   She
stands there, probably, without a friend or a
shilling—unaided by a selfish brother, encum-
bered by a lame sister; unable to work, or starve,
or beg—carrying her pride, and the memory of
a foolish love-dream about with her, through
every depth of poverty, every trial, every humiliation.   But if she marry me, she is at once rescued from the phantoms of the past, and the
dangers of the future.   A new tie breaks the fetters
of the old; a tangible good takes the place of
a regretful memory.   She is not merely rescued
from penury, but placed in a position of affluence,
surrounded by every luxury, comfort, and pleasure.   If she and you will let me, I will make
her happier than she has ever been.   As a
marriage gift, I will give you back the mortgage

deed on Llandyl Hall. You can come and live
with Judith, if you like: she shall do precisely
as she list—and—"

"For heaven's sake, don't tempt me," interposed Mr. Renelle.

"I am not tempting you, I am only laying
two pictures before you, for consideration,"
returned Mr. Mazingford; "point both out to
Judith; tell her fairly and frankly how you are
situated, and what I have proposed—and then
decide as you think best."

"Judith would never," commenced Mr. Renelle—

"Possibly not, in her present frame of mind,"
hastily interrupted the other: "but a word from
you, would be sufficient to alter it. Take her out
of the sorrows of the past, by showing her the
troubles of the present. Believe me, it will be a
kindness to your daughter, in every sense; then
use your influence over her, and her happiness
and peace are ensured. May I trust to your
doing this?"

"No," answered Mr. Renelle; and the monosyllable was decided; "no, I cannot urge her
one step along the road to matrimony; I will

never force her into it. She shall do in that respect precisely as she pleases. I will use no arguments, no entreaties—she may marry you or not, just as she likes, but I will never force her to be your or any man's wife—never."

"I do not wish you to force her; I only want you to—" began Mr. Mazingford; but Mr. Renelle interrupted him with—

"Please, do not talk any more about it, Mr. Mazingford—the subject harasses and distresses me. I do not feel well, ever, now; and the least excitement, the least discussion, makes me worse."

So saying, he arose, as if to leave the room; but he had not taken three steps towards the door before he staggered, and would have fallen, but for Mr. Mazingford's timely assistance.

"What can I do?" inquired that gentleman, when he had carried him back to his chair; "what can I get you?"

"Call Judith," whispered the old man, "she knows."

Mr. Mazingford knew more, however; and after he had summoned the girl, he went off himself in search of a doctor.

" I am afraid it is all up with Mr. Renelle,"
he said, to the family physician; " the symptoms
you spoke of have appeared."

" A few weeks then," said the man of medicine, as he hurriedly put on his coat; " I fear,
that is the most we can hope; but we will see
—we will see;" and so saying, he strode out
of the house, and away up the valley, and so at
last into Llandyl Hall, where he found his patient
undressed, and in bed. Judith had administered
to her father a double dose of a draught he had
been in the habit of taking for some time past,
and the old man was better again.

His complaint was an internal one, for which
science has since discovered a sort of remedy;
but at that period, in remote districts, all or-
ganic diseases were considered incurable; and
few expedients for retarding their progress had
been introduced.

Such as his skill was conscious of, however,
the doctor had long been administering; and for
some months he thus was able to keep the
insidious enemy at bay; but the fatal symptoms
were now revealing themselves, and he whispered
to Mr. Mazingford ere he left the house—

" Mr. Renelle will not be here in a month's time. If he wish to make any disposition of his property, he ought to do it at once."

Having received which piece of information, Mr. Mazingford took a useful hint therefrom, and sedulously concealed the extent of his danger from Mr. Renelle, till he was totally incapacitated for any temporal business; and, moreover, he devoted himself with such zeal to supplying the invalid's wants, and anticipating his demands, that Judith absolutely began to feel grateful towards him.

Admirably he acted his part: simulating an anxiety he never experienced, a pity he did not feel. Very delicate and tender, too, he seemed towards Judith, during those bitter hours of trial —and in that last, bitterest one of all, when her father died, with his head resting on her breast, and her hand clasped convulsively in his. Very generously, also, he acted, in relieving the family from the care and the expense of the funeral— very wisely, in doing all he could for them, and then going away.

He knew perfectly well how matters would work now Mr. Renelle was dead and buried; he

did not feel the least hesitation about leaving his
affairs in Stephen's hands; nor need he, for
Stephen did much better for him than he could
possibly have done for himself. It is marvellous
to see how almost instantaneous a change may
be wrought by the removal of the head of a
family; it was little short of miraculous, to see
how speedy an alteration was accomplished, immediately after Mr. Renelle's death, in the interior
of Llandyl Hall.

For there, Stephen was lord and master now:
his father having died intestate, the young miser
instantly laid hands (and great, ugly, red ones
they were,) on the freehold acres, and trees, and
house, and appurtenances thereunto belonging;
proclaimed himself heir-at-law of everything and
told Judith, she would soon see "who was master
now!"

Yes, she did see, very speedily, a great deal
more than was either good or pleasant; for
Stephen, being monarch of that small territory,
made his sister "find her level," in an incredibly
short space of time. A little queen, over loving
subjects, she reigned no longer. Stephen took
the management of everything out of her hands;

ground the household expenditure down to its minimum figure; dismissed the old Welsh prophetess to an asylum amongst her own kindred, packed Judith's faithful nurse out of the house, and substituted in her place a rude, uncivilised, country girl, who had about as much idea of " domestic service," its niceties and its requirements, as an unbroken colt of the uses of saddle, bridle, currycomb and bit!

All this was done, Miss Ridsdale saw perfectly well, to mortify Judith and herself; but she never expected that Stephen would take an early opportunity of politely informing her he required her room, and should prefer it, as a whole, to her company. She had fancied her income would have proved a welcome addition to his: but in this she was mistaken; for Mr. Mazingford having hinted to Stephen, that if he could get Judith to marry him, the mortgage deed should be cancelled, the young man deemed it was best to have that little matter settled as speedily as possible; and considering Miss Ridsdale an obstacle in his path, he removed her thence, as he did all other obstacles, *sans cérémonie*. The lady dared not undertake the sup-

port of her two nieces, but she bade the younger
be of good cheer—and taking, as a forlorn hope,
a bundle of the girl's rejected manuscripts with
her, set drearily out for London.

Then, and not till then, began the great warfare of Judith's life—a ceaseless battle for herself
and sister, waged against her brother. Utterly
powerless, without a sixpence in the world, almost
without a friend—still the proud spirit never
quailed, the resolute voice was never subdued.
Before three months, Stephen and she had done
everything but come to blows: there was not a
name in the feminine vocabulary of scornful and
contemptuous epithets, which she did not call
him; not a word of anger and reproach which
she did not heap upon his head. Llandyl Hall
was a perfect battle-field, on which Judith would
not have tarried for a single night, had it not
been for the sake of her poor, suffering sister,
whom she watched and strove to protect, as a
bird does her young. But Stephen, knowing
the vulnerable point, probed Judith's spirit
through Lillian. The comforts she required
were denied to her; the rest and peace she

had always been accustomed to, were changed to strife and bitterness; she, who had always heretofore been so tenderly cared for, and thoughtfully treated, was now called a burden, and a fine lady. The fact was, Stephen wanted to get rid of both his sisters and the mortgage-deed at once; and provided the end desired were compassed, he scrupled very little at the means. Judith was no match for her brother, now her father had departed from her side: between him and Lillian, she was tortured and tormented; for, one minute, Stephen almost made her vow to leave the house for ever—and the next, Lillian detained her in it. Love for the dependant creature, who clung to her so confidingly, was the one restraining influence over Judith's heart; but, day and night, she thought what could she do to support Lilian and herself? was there no profession, no trade, no any thing?

Had she stood perfectly alone in the world, she should not have feared; but with Lillian, she dared not cast herself adrift on a strange and unknown sea. London, and authorship, had, at one period, been the hope and stay of her existence; but Miss Ridsdale wrote her word to bear anything, sooner than attempt it:—

"I cannot get a single article accepted," she said; "I fear, my child, you must give it up. Even I, who have been doing a little for so many years, can scarcely make five pounds in as many months. Perhaps things may improve at Llandyl Hall, in time; meanwhile, be patient, if you can."

But Judith could not. She formed a thousand vague schemes: to go and be governess, and hire lodgings for Lillian and get her old nurse to take care of the invalid—to set out for London, and commence a school—run off to the nearest large town, and rent a garret, for herself and sister, and try to make a living by needle-work. There was not a wild plan that she could concoct, but seemed feasible for a few minutes; and once, she absolutely put on her bonnet and shawl, and walked over to the Rectory, where, with tears in her eyes, she besought Mrs. Berbige to take her in as servant. Then the Rector insisted on her remaining with them, and went to Llandyl Hall, for the purpose of remonstrating with Stephen, who, curtly, requested the clergyman to " mind his own business;" further advising the worthy man not "to burn his fingers in other people's fires. And as to Judith," continued the hopeful heir of the Renelles—" tell her to come back here at once; or stay, I'll go myself and fetch her, for she is still under age, and I am her natural guardian; and until she is one-and-twenty, I would like to see the man dare interfere between us."

" Her unnatural guardian, I think you mean, Mr. Renelle," remarked the clergyman ; to which observation, however, Stephen only replied by a sneer.

Once Mr. Mazingford came over, and enjoyed the fray immensely, though he saw, comparatively, nothing of it. He made no proposals to Judith, however; was simply her godfather, and no more. Of the two, indeed, he paid more attention to Lillian than to her: he snubbed Stephen repeatedly, and there reigned, during his stay, almost a peace in the land. But his visit was very short; and Judith felt absolutely sarry when he departed.

Mr. Mazingford rightly described Llandyl Hall as " a hell upon earth;" but, after all, there

was little choice betwixt himself and Stephen
Renelle: they were demons of a different sort,
that was all—only, as he bore the smoother
surface to the world, and was, moreover, capi-
tally gilded, the world thought better of him
than it did of his god-daughter's brother. Stephen
was the rough diamond, Mr. Mazingford the
polished stone—but both were equally competent to cut their way through any opposing
surface, by fair means or foul. The most remarkable difference between the two was, that the
Wavour Hall monarch preferred gentle means,
whilst Stephen had a predilection for harsh proceedings. Wo! however, to the man, woman
or child, who once crossed Mr. Mazingford's
purpose: there might have been escape and
appeal from Stephen Renelle, but there was none
from the clutches of the country attorney's upstart son. He was the most dangerous animal
of the two to deal with; and, perhaps, Judith
had a suspicion of the fact.

At all events, when, during the course of the
autumn following her father's death, Mr. Mazingford invited Stephen, and Lillian, and Judith, to
come and spend a fortnight at Wavour Hall,

the younger sister most unequivocally put her veto on the matter, by stating, that " go she would not under any circumstances."

" We'll see that," retorted Stephen, and there the discussion ended; but when the girls retired to rest that night, Lilian, poor cripple, put her arms round her sister's neck, and said—

" Judith, should you think me very selfish, if I asked you to go to Wavour Hall, for my sake?"

There was silence for a few minutes, during the continuance of which, Judith was waging one of those fierce conflicts with her own spirit, that had latterly become almost of daily occurrence—there was a brief swelling in her throat, an instant's faster throbbing at her heart—but then she had gained the victory over self.

" If you wish it," she answered—" I will do whatever you wish, Lillian."

" There is a clever doctor lives near Wavour Hall; I want to see him. Mr. Jones says I had better see him;" and the invalid, who had never known the blessings of health, laid her cheek very softly and deprecatingly against her sister's, as she spoke.

Judith did not reply; perhaps she could scarcely have told herself why she took Lillian in her arms, and held her there so tightly, as if she thought to preserve her from sorrow or harm—perhaps the past had made her fear the future; perhaps she had a vague knowledge of a worse time coming, even than the dreary present. Who knows?—only long, long after her sister had fallen asleep, she still lay holding her fast, in an almost convulsive embrace—looking out with her clear, penetrating eye into the future—keeping the dear one close, close to her heart.

And of what a brave, strong heart, that was few had a conception! What a power of will the girl possessed, when she was able to conquer its eternal promptings, and—bear.

For the lesson of life which comes the easiest to the meek and the timid, which they con less from duty than because of nature—becomes a fearful task, when it is laid before a proud, high, daring, noble spirit. That which is simple repose to the one, is death to the other: to do, is difficult to the first; not to do, is a misery to the last. Work, hard, earnest, practical work, was

what Judith wanted, what Judith was fitted for;
but no other work than waiting came her
way. Waiting and bearing—the two woman's
portions; ay, and for that matter, man's portions too—that chafe the temper beyond endurance, and wear the strongest patience to a
thread.

It was a noble nature, that which had so
recently obtained another victory over self, and
which then, holding a much weaker and more
patient being in its arms, laid itself down to bear
its sorrows, without a murmur or a tear.

A noble nature cruelly used, imperfectly conscious of its own powers, forgetful that there was
virtue in the part it acted—dead to everything,
save a sense of right, and love, and duty, and
to a feeling that right, and love, and duty often
pulled different ways, and tore its heart to agony.

The season was a beautiful one; and majestic
seemed the Welsh scenery with the glory of an
autumnal sun shining down upon it. As Judith
got away, farther and farther away from home,
a sense of peace seemed to fall soft and warm
across her heart; and she thought, poor,
restless heart, as many another restless one

has thought before and since, how blessed a thing it would be thus to move on through gorge and valley, by winding rivers and waving woods—on, ever on, through life till death! Movement! it was rest and repose to her: "Oh! if it might be always thus!"—she murmured, almost in audible accents, as the carriage rolled along—and she longed, as one of old longed, " to have wings like a dove, that she might flee away, and be at rest." For the tired soul was yearning for its unknown home, even then ; and, all unconscious, that she was being brought thither through the fire of adversity, the furnace of trial, Judith, nevertheless, found herself frequently repeating passages of Scripture, that seemed to soothe and strengthen her, she knew not why nor wherefore. She could not tell either how they came to her, for she had never been much given to religious exercises and meditation. Perhaps Lillian was the prompter, for Lillian was always of a " serious" cast ; or perhaps, which is more likely, Judith's was one of those natures in which the sense of duty towards man, and of feeling of love to God, develope together.

N 2

At all events, something very good, and pure, and holy, swelled up in her breast, as she gazed at the Welsh Hills and the streaming waterfalls —as she looked through the haze of an autumn sunset, on fields where the wheat lay in rich, ripe sheaves, and pasture land, across which shadows of purple and gold were stealing. " How beautiful the world is !" she thought, and she said so to Lillian. Her sister answered, "Yes;" and as her head was averted, Judith never suspected she was weeping.

If the girl thought the world beautiful, Mr. Mazingford, however, considered she was more beautiful, when he came out to the front of Wavour Hall, and welcomed his guests thither.

The sun shone down on him, as it shone down on everything else, that lovely evening, and made him look younger, and handsomer, than ever; whilst it lit up Judith, in her plain mourning dress, as she stood there assisting Lillian—lit up her pale face, and large bright eyes, and broad, fair forehead.

She had been there before, when a child, but never since Mrs. Mazingford's death; and the widower had effected many alterations after his first wife's decease. Display was his passion; and the house was consequently a succession of exhibition rooms, kept for the admiring gaze of visitors, the reception of company, and good of the county generally.

His taste was excellent, his means ample, his will all-powerful—consequently, there was no establishment in the kingdom better conducted, none where the master reigned so supreme— none where commands were executed with such prompt obedience, such unquestioning alacrity, as that of Wavour Hall.

The carriage-horses were regularly subjected to the cambric handkerchief test; the grounds were guiltless of weeds; the gardens were full of the choicest flowers; the lawns were smooth as velvet; the drawing-rooms always kept ready for the arrival of unexpected guests. There was no noise in the house save that made by Mr. Mazing- ford himself, who had a habit of banging doors, and striding heavily across halls—otherwise, the quietude of death reigned in the mansion and around it, and accordingly Lillian said—" It was like heaven !"

Perhaps it seemed so to her; but Judith sickened of the place—she did not know why —but she felt like a prisoner in the ancient house.

The long corridors, with rooms opening off on each side, reminded her of a gaol—so did the hall, paved in white and black marble. The dark furniture, for which connoisseurs would have given any money, oppressed her; and the grinning cherubs, perched on the top of the old oak bedstead, weighed on her spirits. If she went out, she felt as if she were shut in, and could not get away. There were walls and hedges round the gardens, and walls, high and difficult, guarded the estate. The principal, and, indeed, only entrance, was defended, so to speak, by heavy iron gates, that creaked fearfully on their hinges; and two dreadful sphinxes kept watch up and down the road, from the tops of massive pillars. It was quite a long walk to this spot, from the hall, and yet still Judith went there almost daily; leaning against the iron railings she used, like the sphinxes, to look up and down the road. She longed to go

out, to that road, but somehow she never did
it, although the old porteress daily offered to
open the portal for her.

"I am thinking there must be something
wrong with the young lady at the Hall," she observed confidentially to her husband—"she
stands at the gate with such a worn, troubled
look in her face—I wonder if she is right in her
mind."

A month passed away, and then they were
going. "I am so sorry," said Lillian, as she
and Judith sate in the garden together, "there
is such peace here, I wish we could stay here
always."

Judith did not answer. She remained for a
long time pulling some flowers to pieces, and
never moved her head nor rested her fingers till
Lillian asked her what was the matter.

"Nothing," replied she shortly, flinging the
few buds she held in her hand into a marble
basin at their feet.

"And so, Lily," she added, after a pause,—
"you wish that we could stay here always?"

"Yes, if the place might be our own, don't
you?"

" No," answered Judith, " oh ! no, no !" and the restless fingers plucked some fresh flowers, and set to work destroying them. When she had bared the roses of their last leaves, she got up and looked uneasily about her.

At the moment it so chanced that a hawk was cleaving the still air in pursuit of its prey, and something about the chase attracted Judith's attention, and excited her interest.

" Look, look, Lily," she cried, " see how the poor thing strives to escape, how it sinks, and rises, and doubles and turns. There the hawk shoots past it, ah ! he is back on the track again. Look ! look now, Lily, how it flies, poor little thing—do you see it ?"

" Where ?" asked Lillian.

" Where ?" repeated her sister, impatiently; " why there right above my hand. How stupid you are, Lily !"

" Not stupid, Judith, oh ! no, not that."

In a moment bird and hawk were forgotten, and Judith was kneeling at her sister's side. There was a something in Lillian's tone which frightened her, and it was with a tear trembling

under her smile, that she asked with affected
gaiety—

"If not stupid, then what are you?"

"Going blind," was the answer.

Like one crushed by the weight of some over-
powering intelligence, Judith remained immoveable for a few minutes. She had sunk on hearing
her sister's reply from a kneeling to a half-sitting
posture, and with hands clasped together in her
lap, she stayed gazing in Lillian's face, till a touch
from the invalid's fingers brought her back to a
sort of mental life once more.

Then she heard all—heard how the bright
earth and sky, the fields, and trees, and flowers,
were growing dimmer day by day to the eyes of
the sufferer, whose one great joy had been to
gaze upon them; then Lillian told her how the
disease, though not incurable, was as bad to her
as if science and skill had discovered no remedy
for it.

"I must just submit," the patient being concluded, "and I think I can do so now, although
I felt it hard at first; Mr. Jones feared and Mr.
Mazingford's doctor says that in six months I
shall be quite blind; and that was the reason,

Judith, why I felt a little sorry to leave this place, which is so peaceful and quiet."

" But the disease can be cured," cried Judith; " did not some one say it could ?"

" Yes, if we were very rich, perhaps; but as we are not, Judith, I will consider the evil as irremediable, and indeed it won't be so bad after all. There, darling, you know the worst at last, and why I wanted to come here, and now having told you, I feel happier; it is over, and will never have to be said again; kiss me, dear; just one thing more—you will not forsake me ever, Judith ?"

" Never, so help me Heaven;" and thus the restless spirit chained itself, and the firm hand cut the last plank asunder, and the proud, high will subdued the rebellious heart for the last time, and Judith had accomplished the hardest task we poor mortals can have set us here, that of conquering self.

That night when Mr. Mazingford sate alone in his library after all his guests had, as he thought, retired to rest, Judith came gliding in.

There was a flush on her cheek, and a bright,

bright light in her eye, and Mr. Mazingford as he looked at her knew there was not another woman in England so beautiful as she.

Something, an olden phantom perhaps, had entered the apartment with her, and stood betwixt the pair; and Judith as she spoke, kept eternally stretching out her hand, as if to push the spectral shadow aside.

"I told you this morning," she began, "that I could not marry you—that my heart and soul and everything worth giving or having, were dead and buried, lying under the green sod that covers Marcus Lansing's grave. I told you my love for him was no girlish fancy, or midsummer's day dream—that it was a love for life, in death. I said I could never love you, or become your wife, but now—"

He placed her in a chair, and standing before her, asked her to go on. It was the hour he had longed for come at last; but even then he felt she had, he knew not how or wherefore, an advantage over him.

Girl as she was, with her slight figure bending and rocking, with that restless right hand pushing for ever that something so determinedly aside; with her voice trembling, and breast heaving, with her eyes dilated with emotion, in the midst of her suffering, surrounded by the wrecks and ruins of her pride, she was victor still.

Perhaps it was the utter unselfishness of the love which prompted her thus to barter away her freedom, that flung a sort of nobility around the mercenary transaction ; perhaps it was the very price she fixed upon herself which made Mr. Mazingford feel he was getting her cheap.

Other than as a buying and selling business she would not speak of it ; so plainly she stated her terms, so fairly she named her price, that she stripped the transaction of all character of meanness, of all personal degradation.

She feared not to state her motives, and accordingly she told her story so concisely and withal so mournfully, that he, not she, was the one humiliated by marrying ; he, not she, the person who ought to have blushed in recalling that scene to memory.

With an intuitive knowledge of the nature she had to deal with, the girl wanted his part of the compact fulfilled so far as might be, before their marriage: but Mr. Mazingford had many and plausible reasons to urge against such an arrangement; and at length Judith, seeing the impossibility of the thing, gave way, and agreed to become his wife—any time.

And when she said this, she got up as if in a sort of despair, and hurriedly left the apartment. Out of it after her flitted the shadow, the haunting phantom of old; and twice on the broad staircase Judith turned to face that which pursued her. She saw nothing, however, but Mr. Mazingford, who stood at the bottom of the flight following her with his eyes. When he heard the door of her room close at last behind her, he went slowly back to the library, and flung himself into his usual seat.

With a glance riveted on the smouldering fire, he sat pondering there for long. Perhaps the fulfilment had not equalled his expectations; perhaps the shadow had a word or two for his ear also, but with morning's light a different mood came on him, the mood of gratified selfishness, and unbounded triumph.

For Judith grew more lovely every hour, the rich flush deepened on her cheek, and the bright light still brighter in her eye; and she was to be his, this young, beautiful creature, to have and to hold, to form, exhibit, make a show of. The very fever which was upon her had a fascination for him; had she been a weak, reed-like, submissive being, he would have flung her contemptuously aside, but the spirit she carried about within her, he longed to grapple with and bend.

When he was lord and master over her, when she looked up to him, and acknowledged a higher monarch than herself; when her will was moulded to his will, then Mr. Mazingford felt the desire of years would be accomplished.

And he fancied the moment they were married this would be the case; wherefore the preparations were hurried on with most unusual haste; he would not hear of a return to Llandyl Hall, nor did Stephen wish it either; out of respect to Judith's feelings, and the short period which had elapsed since her father's death, the wedding was a strictly private one—and before the girl had well recovered from the first horror of being engaged, she found herself fettered hand and foot; pledged; married; a wife.

Lewis Mazingford was her husband, and that was the first intimation Miss Ridsdale received of what was going on.

"Now Heaven help the poor deluded creature," cried the lady, as she dropped her niece's heart-broken letter, "for she has made herself miserable for life."

So Judith Renelle at last became Judith Mazingford !

CHAPTER XII.

THE first six months of married life proved, considering the sort of natures thus brought into sudden contact, tolerably tranquil. The opinion of the world, that is of the high world, a bug-bear Mr. Mazingford suffered to have dominion over him, would scarcely have proved favourable to a series of festivities at Wavour Hall, six months after the death of its mistress' father; there might be reasons for the speedy marriage, but there could be none for merrymaking, and accordingly merrymaking was postponed till the orthodox period of mourning should have expired; and Wavour Hall was a very hermitage during the winter season, tenanted by a moping

bride, a poor invalid, and a dissatisfied husband.
For Mr. Mazingford found matrimony a very
" different sort of thing," as the phrase goes, to
what he had expected; and before two months
of his second married life were concluded, a kind
of uneasy conviction stole over him, that he had
" caught a tartar."   Not a virago nor a shrew;
not a cunning, manœuvring woman, nor a vindictive vixen; but a girl of something under
twenty, possessed of an indomitable will and an
unconquerable temper; possessed of no child's
fancies, few feminine weaknesses, incapable of
being ruled by anybody, or of being won by
him.

Her heart, she had said, on that well-remem-
bered night, when she offered herself to be his
wife for a price, " her heart was lying under the
green sod that covered Marcus Lansing's grave,"
and Mr. Mazingford soon discovered it were
quite as hopeful a task for him to try to move
the pyramids as to endeavour to dig it out of the
old Welsh churchyard and attain possession of it
himself.   The experiment of winning love after
marriage, which hundreds have staked their lives'
happiness on—he had tried and failed in, like

the rest; wherefore he was dissatisfied, for no man, let him be what he will, likes to have a wife who merely endures his presence. There are many who will contemptuously fling the great gift of love aside, but still they feel it a pride to be able so to dispose of the article. When the gem cannot be obtained at any price, it then acquires an artificial value in the matrimonial market. Mr. Mazingford felt piqued at Judith, because she would not—could not care for him; because she discharged the duties of a wife as though she were fulfilling her part of a business compact; because luxury made her no happier; because she never placed herself in an inferior position to himself, but always silently took an equal stand in everything. She did nothing he could find fault with, and still she irritated him every hour of the day; she asked no solitary pleasure, or comfort, or indulgence for herself, but she took all for Lillian as a matter of right. "It was for Lillian," he felt every hour of the day, "she had married; and luxuries, and delicacies, and attention for Lillian she would have."

He never repented wedding her, it is true, but

he longed with the longing of old to break the proud spirit, to bend the strong will, to make Judith Mazingford his submissive, dutiful wife.

When he recalled to mind what she was before-Marcus Lansing's death—the gay, light-hearted, impetuous creature, and then looked at her as his own wife, so grave and cold, and dig-nified, he gnashed his teeth in impotent rage, and cursed alike the dead and the living; the one who had bestowed an ocean of love on her, and she who could not give an atom of love to him.

Still for so far there was peace in the land, and in many ways the husband's unbounded pride and vanity were gratified. His wife was the handsomest woman in England, and it re-joiced his soul to see chance visitors gazing at her as though marvelling at the exceeding grace and beauty, and rarity of the gem he had managed to set, nobody knew exactly how, amongst his collection of household treasures.

Congratulations flowed in on him from every quarter. Mrs. Mazingford's beauty was talked of on all sides; the fame thereof reached even the metropolis — she was reported an eighth

wonder of the world; as to Judith herself,
people, who had previously forgotten her existence, now came forward to claim relationship
and acquaintanceship with the mistress of Wavour Hall, who had, at last, got " her promotion."
Sir John Lestock sent presents of pearls and
diamonds, and Miss Lestock added her marriage
gifts and a most affectionate letter to her dear
cousin; persons who had known Mr. Ridsdale,
others who ought to have known Mr. Renelle:
connections by wedlock, and relations a hundred
and fifty degrees removed, rapidly became
aware of their consanguinity to Mrs. Mazingford;
and Judith, accordingly, found herself, all of a
sudden, an object of at once condolence and
importance, of sympathy for having so recently
lost a parent, of still greater sympathy for
having still more recently gained a husband.
Rings and brooches, and necklaces, ear-rings,
and bracelets, valuable little nick-nacks and useless trinkets—Judith really stood aghast at the
number of people who suddenly counted kindred
and friendship with her — thanked them for
their presents with what courtesy she might,

and despised them all in the depths of her
heart.

There were but two honest expressions of
opinion concerning the marriage, which ever
reached the ear of either bride or bridegroom.
The first was uttered by Stephen in Wavour
parish church, when, with a malicious chuckle,
he wished Mr. Mazingford "joy of his bargain ;"
the other by Mrs. Berbige, who sent really a
most kind and tender letter to the girl, concluding with a heartfelt hope, that "she might be
happy ;" these two, for Miss Ridsdale said
nothing, were the only genuine remarks Judith
or her lord ever heard on the subject—few
enough, and scanty enough, Heaven knows, to
speak well for the sincerity and disinterestedness
of human nature.

But the *éclat* of the thing delighted Mr.
Mazingford ; externally all went well—internally !
ah ! there was enough to tell of the hidden volcano that would, some day or other, burst its
bounds ; but, notwithstanding this, matters did
progress for six months very tranquilly.

During this period the light had been fading
by almost imperceptible degrees from Lillian's

eyes, and when the spring blossoms came again upon the earth, all—the bright sunshine and the April showers, the drooping snowdrop and the bursting buds—was darkness unto her.

Almost impatiently Judith had waited for this consummation — impatiently, because, till total blindness came, no operation could be attempted; and with even a greater longing than the poor sufferer herself, she desired the arrival of that day, when the cure might safely be commenced. She hungered and thirsted for the gift of sight to be restored to her sister; with feverish anxiety she watched every stage of the disease, and then, when at length total blindness fell on the mild, dark eyes, she affirmed that not a day, not an hour should be lost.

But Mr. Mazingford was not exactly of her opinion; having obtained the prize beforehand, he was slow to pay the required price for it—he found Lillian's was likely to be a most tedious and expensive case; he was wearied and jealous of her, angry at the manner in which she engrossed every spare moment of Judith's time—envious of the sisterly love his wife lavished on her.

He thought her recovery in any case extremely doubtful, and felt, in brief, very reluctant to spend money on the chance. Perhaps he imagined if she were out of the way, Judith would be more easily managed; at all events, he was tired of and provoked by her—by Lillian, but for whose misfortune he had never called Judith by the name of wife. At first he staved off entreaties by an assurance that he could not leave Wales until the autumn. There was to be a contested election during the course of that summer, whereat he had been invited, and meant to stand as conservative candidate. He must stay in the country, to spend money, and bribe voters, and intimidate electors; and as to Judith—her presence would be required quite as much as his—it really was an impossibility for him to do as she wished just then, and he was, indeed, he was very sorry.

Whether Judith believed this assertion or not, never transpired, but she chafed under the delay exceedingly, and suggested that an oculist should be brought down to Wavour Hall. To this plan Mr. Mazingford opposed the ridiculous expense of such a proceeding; but not finding that argument produce much effect on his wife's understanding, he brought forward another which proved more efficacious, viz. :— that once in London it would be easier to discover the "right man" than in the country, where they would have to rest satisfied with one opinion, and that, perhaps, imperfect.

"You had better wait patiently," he finished, "till we all go up to London together—a few months can make no possible difference; it is not like a killing disease, in which every moment is precious."

And so, very unwillingly, Judith had to be patient during the entire of that summer, when the actual troubles of her married life began.

She had always been aware to a certain extent of Mr. Mazingford's love of display, of his mania for effect—but somehow, strange as it may sound, it never occurred to her proud, independent spirit that she was to become part of the show, the principal object to be set up and stared at, until she found it was even so; and then the struggling, and chafing, and enduring began—the next weary battle which

Judith waged first against herself, but finally against him.

As he might have exhibited a fine racer, or a favourite pointer, he exhibited her. Habited in purple and fine linen, with sparkling rings on her fingers, and pearls circling her slender throat, she had to sit there, and be shewn as the uncommonly fine wife Mr. Mazingford had wedded; as the handsomest woman in Wales, or in England, or anywhere. Oh! it was gall and wormwood to the haughty nature, to be hawked about from dinner to ball, from regatta to race-course : to have to show off her accomplishments, and deck out her beauty to the uttermost. " Would I had the small-pox," Lillian once heard her exclaim ; and the wish came not from the lips merely, but from the heart.

That which, as Marcus Lansing's wife, she would have prized, perhaps, inordinately for his sake—she now felt an incubus and a burden— and not the less so, because Mr. Mazingford treated her even in public as a something beneath him, which he had bought for its exceeding loveliness, and bought a bargain.

The fulsome compliments, the undisguised

stare of admiration, the scarcely suppressed
wonderment concerning her story, the prying
of ladies into the history of her past life—the
sort of sensation which succeeded her entrance
into any large assemblage : these things were
intolerable to Judith—the more intolerable, perhaps, because she felt Mr. Mazingford could
have protected her from them if he would.
But he delighted in the *éclat*—she was praised
and she was his : the more flattery, the more
incense she received, the more gratified was he.
She was his last purchase, and he was very, very
proud of her. He could not compel her to canvass
for him, but he forced her to accompany a countess who did.   He filled his house with all sorts
of well-born, indifferent company, and then had
Judith to play the stately hostess to a swarm of
the usual genteel electioneering rabble.   There
was a Duke, who condescended to flirt with
Mrs. Mazingford, and who received a cutting
sarcasm which proved his quietus from that lady
in return ; there was a young lord who dangled
after her, and a general who talked confidentially
to the owner of Wavour Hall about the sensation
his wife would produce in London ; but there

were others who marvelled at the evident coolness between Mr. Mazingford and his young bride; and this was the drop in the cup which turned all the other sweets to bitters—this was the alloy.

No one could tell precisely what was wrong, and yet every one felt there was something amiss: not merely as regarded Judith and her husband, but also as concerned Judith herself: she was so young and yet so old; so courteous and yet so frigid; so beautiful and yet so statue-like. People frequently asked if she were ill; and his most intimate friends, with that kind consideration for which friends are remarkable in all corners of the earth, were eternally enquiring of Mr. Mazingford what was the matter with his wife. They never seemed to notice that the question was an injudicious one, that they were touching with their indiscreet tongues the sorest spot in the man's nature, but with an affectation of unreal interest, went curiously blundering on.

At length the election, with its pomps and its pains, its vanities and its cares, its gratifications and its humiliations, its gains and its losses, was over, and Mr. Mazingford proved victorious.

The last independent electors were paid in full—the last voters made drunk—the last hundred was disbursed—the last ball given.   The Honourable Lodovick Standish beaten out of the field, had gone away threatening to unseat the popular member and disfranchise the borough.   The farmers (always on the conservative side everywhere but in tenant-right Ireland) had yelled themselves hoarse shouting, "Mazingford for ever!"—there had been dinners and speeches, and pledges, and chairing in abundance : but all was quiet again three days after the local newspapers announced the result of the poll in bulletins and principal columns, thus :—

Mazingford,	—	1314
Standish,	—	857
Majority for Mazingford,		457

Huzza! shouted the "incorruptibles," as the Wavour Hall greys went prancing out of the town, carrying the successful candidate along with them ; and Mr. Mazingford gratefully acknowledged the disinterested cheers, for publicity was what his soul delighted in.

Peace came to the Hall at last, when the

autumn sheaves were again lying in the golden
sunshine; when the purple heather was blooming
on the mountains; when the waterfalls and
streams were almost dry; when the richest
shadows of the year were falling on the changing leaves and beautifying them.

"I had hoped," said Judith then to Lillian,
"that by now you would have been able to look
once again over the harvest fields, at the flowers
and the rivers, and the sky—but that could not
be—this time next year, however, please God."

She did not finish the sentence, but Lillian
knew what she meant, and answered cheerfully :—

"I can wait, dear Judith, patiently."

Waiting had made her very pale during the
passing of those weary six months : that hope
deferred which maketh the heart sick, had been
her portion during the entire of that period.   To
any certain evil we can become reconciled, but
that fever of the mind, suspense—that mental
toothache, as one of our popular authors aptly
calls it—will wear out the bravest and strongest
amongst us; and so Lillian had suffered grie-

vously, though she never complained of the delay, suffered and pined in silence, and her sister knew it.

With new-born alacrity, therefore, she made all necessary preparations for their departure, when Mr. Mazingford proposed departing from Wales. A fresh life seemed infused into her, the moment he stated he must go up to London immediately after Christmas. She wanted to go before, but that might not be. January was the time he had settled, and January, accordingly, it proved.

" I really think, Judith," he said, a couple of days before that fixed for their journey, " you had best leave Lillian here, where she can be wheeled about the grounds, and have pure air, and be perfectly quiet. In London she would find herself very uncomfortable. What could we do with her there ?"

The lady of Wavour Hall listened to this speech quietly, from first to last; but then she said :—

" Mr. Mazingford, do you recollect what passed between us that night when I consented to become your wife ?"

He did—yea, verily, he had never forgotten it.

"You remember, then, precisely what I married you for?"

"Or stated you did," he retorted, with a contemptuous sneer.

"It is the same," she answered; "for with me stating and thinking are terms synonymous; and, therefore, Mr. Mazingford, my sister goes with me to London to be cured."

"We shall see about that," he said, fiercely.

"Or else," pursued Judith, "I remain here with her, and send for an oculist from town."

And on this point ensued the first pitched battle between them; but Judith sat down, as it were, before the fortress on her rights, and compelled him to surrender.

She ordered her maid to unpack her trunks. She countermanded all her previous arrangements. She did not get into a passion, or scold, or threaten, or torment; but she just held resolutely on.

"You promised me," she said to her husband, "faithfully and solemnly that, if I would become your wife, Lillian should always remain with me, always be kindly treated, always receive every attention and comfort in your house; and, further, you promised to spare no expense in having her sight restored. My part of the compact I have fulfilled; and I vow that, willing or unwilling, you shall perform yours."

"Indeed, madam!"

What a world of concentrated bitterness he managed to fling into those two words!

"You may carry me to London, if you choose," she said; "but no power on earth shall keep me there without her. I have taken my stand on that point now and for ever."

And as Mr. Mazingford had no desire to use force in the matter, he was compelled to give in, so far as Lillian's London trip was concerned; but he registered a vow, to the effect that one sixpence of his money oculist should never receive. He knew he could beat Judith there; for the strings of the purse were in his hands, and he defied her to loosen them.

Evening after evening guests came to their mansion in Mayfair in costly equipages. Mr. and Mrs. Mazingford "received" half the *beau monde* of London, and were cordially received by them in return. There was a perfect *furore* about the member's wife. The proud, cold, dignified manner; the easy courtesy, without a shadow of warmth; a certain originality of character, and power of repartee, and unfailing sarcasm, enhanced public curiosity, and made her absolutely the "fashion." She wore her beauty like a garment—as a necessary—but not a thing to be gloried in. Compliments she received with a curling lip. Admiration seemed disagreeable unto her. She was fascinating, and yet repellant. Every one felt there was something extraordinary about her; and still she beat too curious inquirers off the ground. "I stand alone," she always seemed to say, "and I am wearied of everything."

And truly so she was: of being dragged about to feed the vanity of a man she now absolutely hated; of carrying an old memory of death and sorrow into ball-rooms, through dances, to the opera box—everywhere; of the eternal whirl of fashion; of no rest, no peace, no quietness; of new faces, and coquettish women, and false men; of the tinsel and the glitter of high life; of the never-ceasing, always-commencing round of visiting; of the canker-worm, gnawing for ever at her heart; of the man she called husband, and was chained to for life.

Judith was sick—of the grand exhibition in public, of the continued strife in private, of the way Mr. Mazingford paraded her before the world, of the mode in which he quarrelled with her when alone, of the manner he adopted towards her always. Fear for Lillian made her submit to much; but Lillian was not cured yet, and that was the bitterest bone of contention between them.

At length Judith's resolution was taken.

"Mr. Mazingford," she said, "you must consult an oculist, or I shall leave the house."

"Well, leave it then," he retorted; and for once Judith was momentarily vanquished. It was but for a moment, however; for after a pause she inquired :—

"Do you, then, positively refuse to fulfil the promise you made to me before marriage?"

"I refuse to lend my countenance to any cursed folly or nonsense," he responded.

"And you will not give me money to restore my sister to sight?"

"I will not. She can't be cured, I tell you.

So there is no use tormenting about it. Besides, I am sick of the subject—so sick, that if it is ever named again, I shall send Lillian either to Miss Ridsdale, her brother, or the poor-house."

"Very well," returned Judith; and then Mr. Mazingford beheld a look in her face he had never seen previously—a look which she gave him frequent opportunity of analyzing and observing in after-times.

It had in it a sort of settled contempt, and indomitable defiance, and icy, immoveable determination. When she drew her lips into that frigid, sarcastic smile, and settled her eyes on him with that fixed stare of ridicule and disdain, he could have struck her to the earth. It was the first thing Judith discovered to have power over him. Perhaps that was the reason she afterwards treated him so freely to it; or, perhaps, which is more probable, some kind of change took place in her character, which enabled her to assume at a moment's warning that look of concentrated dislike.

Be this as it may, one thing is certain, Judith walked straight from Mr. Mazingford's presence to her sister's chamber, and told her she meant to take her that very day to Mr. Chamberton, then considered the first oculist in London.

"At last!" cried Lillian; and a flush came over her pale cheek, and the eager arms were stretched joyfully out towards her sister, and the sightless orbs were turned thankfully upwards. "At last! So Mr. Mazingford has consented, then, Judith?"

"He and I have just settled matters definitively," was the somewhat evasive reply.

"Oh! how kind! I wish I could go and thank him!" cried poor Lillian, out of the fulness of her heart.

"Better that you cannot," answered her sister, drily. "Some people do not like to be thanked;" and the fixed, contemptuous look came over Judith's face again—that dry, cold, hard expression, which it is pitiable to note on a woman's countenance—"but come, darling," she added, the next minute, "and let me help to get you ready;" and a softness stole over her eyes and lips, as she bent tenderly over the invalid, and tied her bonnet, and fastened her cloak, just as she had been wont to do in the old, old days that were gone, never to return.

Never to return—the words passed through Judith's mind, if they did not escape her lips as she buttoned her sister's gloves, and then rung for an attendant to assist the cripple to Mr. Mazingford's carriage. There had been a time when servants were scarce in the home they inhabited—when landaus and barouches were luxuries undreamed of—and now—perhaps it was fortunate that a magnificent footman here banging down the steps, interrupted Judith's musings.

" Portman Square," she said—and the unexceptionable greys were off in a moment, like the wind. All the way Lillian talked about her eyes—of how thankful she was, of how thankful she should be—she did not mind any pain, oh! no, and she could wait any length of time, if she found that eventually she should be able once again to read and sew, to see the streets and the houses, the flowers and shrubs, and scenery in the country, and the brilliant equipages, and the pretty ladies, and the endless crowds of people in the town.

"Sight is such a blessing, Judith," she finished with

"It is," assented the other; "but there is to my mind a still greater blessing which you possess."

"What is that?" enquired Lillian.

And her sister answered, "A quiet heart."

It was a very touching thing to see how instantaneously Lillian's joy was turned to sadness, to watch how she felt about for Judith's hand, and then taking possession of it, held it sorrowfully in her own; how she kept eternally fidgetting closer and closer to her sister's side.

"Don't be grieved, my darling," said Mrs. Mazingford at last. "I did not mean to vex you; do not be grieved for me, Lillian, for a perfectly quiet heart is a blessing that will some day or other be enjoyed by all of us;"—and as she concluded, the carriage stopped at Mr. Chamberton's door.

He was at home, but, like all great men, being much besieged by visitors, the ladies had to wait some time for an audience.

At last, however, they were permitted ingress to the "presence," and found the oculist a tall, emaciated man, of about fifty or fifty-five years of age; one who looked as though all the flesh had been worn off his bones by eternal driving over the London stones. It was said he changed his carriage horses four times a day during the "season;" and Judith, generally somewhat sceptical of such tales, believed the story implicitly after seeing him.

"Can she be cured?"—that was the one brief straightforward question the younger lady addressed unto him; and after a professional examination of his patient's eyes, he answered that "she could, but that the process would be tedious."

Somehow it smote on Judith's heart to see the expression of delight which lit up her sister's face on hearing this confirmation of her dearest hopes. The cure might have been effected, or at least commenced months previously; and besides, it hurt her, she scarcely knew why, to see how happy Lillian looked at the prospect of this bodily infirmity being removed.

A sudden thought then occurred to her, that if she had begged her way to London, and told some one like this oculist their story, and prayed him to have pity on her, or else got Lillian into an hospital, she might have saved herself a life of slavery and humiliation—she had strength to do anything, to dare anything then, why not before her marriage?—It was but a sudden thought, a passing feeling which she put aside and conquered instantaneously, when, raising her eyes, she found Mr. Chamberton's glance fixed curiously upon her.

"Will you favour me with five minutes' private conversation?" she asked.   And the oculist bowing assent, they passed into a smaller apartment together.

"I need not sit down," replied Judith in answer to his silent offer of a chair.   "I do not wish to detain you—but merely to receive answer to a few questions it might have been painful for my sister to hear.   Pray excuse me if I seem abrupt.   I think there is nothing like coming to the point at once."

"Nothing," echoed Mr. Chamberton with a heartiness which spoke well for the sincerity of his nature.

"First, I want to know," began Judith, "exactly what is the matter with my sister."

"Soft cataract," was the concise reply.

"And it can be cured?"

"I have no doubt but it may, with care and patience."

"Patience, for how long?" she asked with a smile.

"That depends," he replied.

"Then you will not name a time?" said Judith, after a brief pause.

"I cannot; I should be only deceiving you, if I did so."

"Exactly," murmured Judith; " and now, pardon me, if my question is unusual, but the—"

Mrs. Mazingford grew very red, as she paused, for want of a suitable expression ; and Mr. Chamberton coloured a little also, though, like a true man of the world, he took up her sentence and completed it, kindly and frankly, for his visitor.

"The cost, you mean," he said—" the usual course, you are aware, is to charge for each separate operation."

"And—" commenced the lady once again— and once again he saved her the awkwardness of completing her question.

"In most cases of soft cataract, fifty guineas."

"About how many operations would be necessary?" she enquired.

" That I cannot tell," he answered, " it depends on so many things—on the extent of the disease itself, on the state of her general health, on the care with which my directions are followed, on a thousand apparent trifles, that are totally beyond our own control. If the cataract were hard—"

" Ah! but it is not," interrupted Judith— " would it had been:" then, after a moment's silence, she added, in a calmer tone, " the operations can be performed here, I presume?"

" Impossible!" he answered: " at her own residence, that is indispensable. She must remain in a darkened room, and be kept perfectly quiet. Here! why it would probably cost her her life to attempt such a thing."

" It shall not be attempted then," said Judith, quietly, though his words flung a new difficulty in her path. " And now, Mr. Chamberton, will you tell me, frankly, if you object to receive the pecuniary debt we shall owe you not, on the occasion of each separate visit, but when your visits have terminated altogether."

It would be hard to say whether Judith were most confused, on uttering the foregoing point-blank sentence, or her auditor most surprised: at all events, there ensued a very awkward pause; during the continuance thereof, the lady stood with her eyes rivetted on the carpet, and the oculist remained gazing curiously at her:—

"My usual rule is to practise either for a fixed fee, or else gratuitously," he said at length.

"But will you break through your rule for me?" she entreated; "it would make all so much smoother for me. I am not in the condition of a person who could ask you to give time, and skill, and kindness for nothing (Oh! that I were). I can pay handsomely hereafter: but—but, there are reasons why I cannot do so now, at least not conveniently. Surely the delay of a few months will not prove an insurmountable barrier to the gratification of my wishes—you are so rich—I am certain you must be."

"And you?" demanded Mr. Chamberton, with a half smile, as he looked first at her flushed, beautiful face, and pleading eyes, and imploring gesture, and then at her handsome dress and fashionable toilette—" and you?—"

"Am rich also, if you will," she hastily replied, "in one sense, not in another—rich to have, but not to give. Do you understand the difference?"

"I think I do," he answered; and a sort of pitying look came over his countenance—"I think I do."

"And you will accede to my request, without hearing my reasons for making it? I will tell you if need be, but I had rather not."

"I will do my best to cure your sister on your own terms. You shall pay me what you can, when you can; shall we settle the matter thus?"

Judith did not reply verbally, but she held out a very small hand, and then burst into tears.

It was not a weakness she frequently indulged in; and perhaps this outbreak of pent-up grief seemed the more vehement on that account.

"Do not distress yourself," said the oculist, kindly; "I am sure we shall be able to do something for your sister. Do not grieve so about her, for the evil is remediable."

"It is not that," replied Judith, "oh! no, not that."

He did not ask her what it was, but he marvelled exceedingly; and when she and Lillian
drove away, he had absolutely the curiosity to
look after their carriage.

"Mrs. Mazingford!" he murmured, as he
glanced at the card she had left in his hand,
with an intimation that she would call again in
a week—"Mrs. Mazingford—I wonder who she
is, and what her history!"

END OF VOL. I.

J. Billing, Printer and Stereotyper, Guildford, Surrey.

In Preparation.

I.

NEW NOVEL BY LADY BULWER LYTTON.

In 3 Vols., with Illustrations,

THE WORLD AND HIS WIFE;

OR,

A PERSON OF CONSEQUENCE.

By LADY BULWER LYTTON, Author of " Cheveley,"
" Behind the Scenes," &c.

II.

REDMARSH RECTORY;

OR,

HONESTY THE BEST POLICY.

A Novel, in 3 Vols.

By NONA BELLAIRS, Author of " Going Abroad," &c.

III.

OUR VETERANS OF 1854,

IN CAMP AND BEFORE THE ENEMY.

BY A REGIMENTAL OFFICER.

1 Vol. small 8vo. 10s 6d.

C. J. SKEET, PUBLISHER,
10, KING WILLIAM STREET, CHARING CROSS.

THE

RICH HUSBAND;

A NOVEL OF REAL LIFE.

BY THE AUTHOR OF

"THE RULING PASSION."

" And she was wedded ! young and beautiful—
To one whose heart was steel'd 'gainst gen'rous deeds :
She loath'd him, as the deadly Upas tree,
That blights the flow'r which grows beneath its shade."

IN THREE VOLUMES.

VOL. II.

LONDON :
CHARLES J. SKEET, PUBLISHER,
10, KING WILLIAM STREET,
CHARING CROSS.
1858.

J. Billing, Printer and Stereotyper, Guildford, Surrey.

THE

RICH HUSBAND.

CHAPTER I.

JUDITH was very silent all the way to Great
Crowland Street, whither she had desired the
coachman to proceed.   He—great aristocrat—
had once upon a time not known the way there;
but his mistress' instructions speedily recalled
its whereabouts to his recollection, and accordingly he drove thither without stoppage or
enquiry, whilst Mrs. Mazingford, leaning back
in her handsome equipage, gave herself up to
meditation. Lillian thought her somewhat mood-

ily absorbed in this occupation ; but Judith was really forming plans for her sister's convenience and comfort. She knew the operations could not take place in Mayfair ; for even had Mr. Mazingford been neutral on the subject, they were not to remain the summer in town, and then what could Lillian do? Miss Ridsdale's lodgings were unsuitable in all respects ; clearly nothing remained for it but to take a furnished house, or a portion of one, out westwards, towards Brompton, or some of those other regions which at that period were almost country. Such a place would give Lillian a residence at once healthful, pleasant, and accessible ; convenient for Mr. Chamberton, Miss Ridsdale, and Judith herself—that was the proper step to take immediately, so Judith determined ere the carriage turned into Great Crowland Street, clattering over the pavement just as another had done one cold December's evening a long time ago.

From No. 73, Mr. Henry Bultin calmly sur-

veyed this new arrival : he had quit marvelling
concerning Miss Ridsdale or her visitors now,
for he knew her history and their histories off
by heart, and he had ceased to feel more than a
neighbourly interest in the lonely woman who,
after nearly nineteen years' absence, had returned
once again to her old quarters, to take her
unsocial breakfast and eat her solitary dinner all
alone ; who still sate by the window in the twilight, and occasionally received visits from people
who were " great," in Great Crowland Street.
Twenty winters had metamorphosed Mr. Bultin
into a plump, comfortable benedict of fifty, who
had brought his dreams of a grand marriage to
a practical and unpoetical, though exceedingly
excellent close, fifteen years previously, by wedding Mrs. Hilton's daughter, the disconsolate
widow of the green-grocer opposite, who, having
died, and left her his name, his perishable stock
in trade, and the money they had mutually made
and saved—she speedily took up—as the step
matrimonial is called in certain circles, with

Mr. Bultin, bestowing on him her hand, her guineas, her good will, and her common sense.

The first Mr. Bultin honored her by putting a new ring on, the second he accepted with less scruple, in fact without any; the third he disposed of to advantage; the fourth he made use of for their joint benefit; and the result thereof was, that whilst Hilton baker nominally ruled the shop long after that worthy woman's actual demise, Bultin attorney had his name painted on the private entrance, monopolized the first floor, and fleeced as many clients there as good fortune or bad fortune sent his way.

Thus it came to pass that he could look at Miss Ridsdale with feelings merely of a friendly character, whilst he regarded her carriage friends with only a moderate portion of interest.

Professionally he had learnt their histories, as attorneys somehow do learn everybody's, and accordingly when an acquaintance from the country, who chanced to be with him on the day in question, enquired whose equipage that might be, he was able to answer—

" Oh ! Mr. Mazingford's."

" What ! the new Welsh member, who voted on the right side last night in the House, and made a decidedly sensible speech into the bargain."

" The same," replied Mr. Bultin, " and that handsome woman just now alighting is his wife ; people say they don't live happily. Isn't she beautiful though !"

Yes, she was, there could be no two opinions on that point, whatever there might be as to the merits of her lord's speech. Miss Ridsdale thought she grew more lovely day by day, and certainly Judith did look her very best as she entered her aunt's sitting room, with a deep rich color on her cheek, and that strange brightness in her eyes, which increased but never diminished. She came, she said, to tell Miss Ridsdale the oculist's opinion, and to consult what was best to do, and so at last it was agreed that the elder lady was to go house-hunting, and that Mr. Chamberton's services should be called into re-quisition as soon as possible.

" But where, dear Judith, is the money to come from to meet all this?" enquired Miss Ridsdale.

" Oh, let me manage that," was the reply. " I can get it."

" You are positive," persisted the other. And Mrs. Mazingford answered, " Certain."

Judith had reached the head of the stair-case, on her way back to Lillian, whom she had left in the carriage during her brief interview, when a sudden thought seemed to strike her, and she turned back.

" Aunt," she said, " could you keep Lily here for a few days, and I'll get a suitable house for you? I wish you would."

Yes, Miss Ridsdale was willing to do any mortal thing Mrs. Mazingford asked her, with or without an expressed reason; and accordingly Lillian, somewhat to her own surprize, was assisted out of the carriage and up the stairs, and deposited on the sofa in her aunt's sitting-room, that very sofa whereon another aunt had once flung herself wearily for rest.

Very hurriedly Judith took leave of both, and departed, promising to come back again very soon.

"Aunt," said Lillian, "what do you think is the matter with Judith?"

"Something, that for want of a better name, we call a broken heart, Lillian," was the reply; "at least, so it seems to me."

"Do you know if Mr. Mazingford is unkind to her?"

"You ought to be better informed on that point than I," answered Miss Ridsdale.

"No," said Lillian. "She never tells me anything now—perhaps she may when I can see again; but Mr. Mazingford has been very generous to me."

"Indeed!" exclaimed Miss Ridsdale, with sudden interest; "are you quite sure of that?"

"Yes, for Judith told me he and she had settled all about the oculist; so you see he must have consented to pay the expenses."

"Perhaps," murmured Miss Ridsdale, as she turned to the window and looked vacantly, first up and then down the dreary street, to which Judith's handsome carriage had only given a momentary animation.

"God help the girl," she thought again, for the hundredth time ; " she is steering a dangerous course with that most treacherous rudder, a broken, despairing heart to guide her."

And for full five minutes the lady stood thus silently communing with her own spirit—much troubled concerning Judith's face, and Judith's position, and Judith's plans, and Judith's mode of procedure—whilst Mrs. Mazingford was rolling over the London streets—to that house, which, for want of a better name to give it, she called home.

As the coachman, however, was driving his unexceptionable bays in his own unexceptionable

and peculiarly tip-top manner, past one of the
West End Clubs, he received a sign from a
gentleman standing on the steps of that public
lounge and public nuisance, which induced him,
in consideration of the signer being his master,
to pull up short, to Judith's intense disgust.

Mr. Mazingford was about the last person
she desired, at that moment, to meet—Mr.
Mazingford's club friends were always the last
individuals to whom she desired to be exhibited;
but there was no resource for it—so she quietly
resigned herself to be stared at from head to foot
by a fast young nobleman, who afterwards condescended to remark to his intimates, that
Mazingford's wife was a deucedly fine woman;
and that if she were single, she was just the sort he
would choose to drive in double harness with,
although she had such a vicious look about the
eyes;—resigned herself to be stared at by him,
and two or three others, as she resigned herself
to other things — not meekly, but defiantly;
having gone through which ordeal, and replied

with what was called her piquant Welsh accent, to the usual string of common-places spoken on such occasions;—Mr. Mazingford, who boasted, with his usual thoughtful refinement, that he had the handsomest carriage—the handsomest horses —and the handsomest wife of any commoner in London—bade good-bye to his aristocratic friends, and took his place beside his wife, informing her at the same time, that as he wanted to see Messrs. Eives and Maycombe, in Autran Street, he thought he might as well drive round there with Judith, and then they could both go home together.

"Perrins told me you had gone out with Lillian?" he remarked, interrogatively, when the "nobs" were left fairly behind.

"He was quite correct," replied Judith in her own pet manner, which was as dry and cold as can well be conceived.

"And where have you left her?" was the next query.

"With Miss Ridsdale," answered Judith, who

never called her relative Aunt, to Mr. Mazingford.

The member uttered a low, soft whistle expressive of intense satisfaction on receipt of this
intelligence. "I wish she would stay there!"
he exclaimed.

"Your desire is likely to be gratified for a
short period," retorted Judith. "Lillian remains
for a few months with Miss Ridsdale, at my
request."

Mr. Mazingford turned and stared at his
wife, to discover, if possible, from what new
quarter the wind was blowing, for he had not
forgotten the morning's conversation, and accordingly marvelled exceedingly; but Judith returned his gaze with one of such perfect indifference that he could make nothing out of it,
and so was compelled, *bongré malgré*, to rest
satisfied, as he did not choose to ask for an explanation of Judith's change of tactics.

"Here is Autran Street," said his wife, after
a moment's pause, as they turned down a dingy

thoroughfare that, but for the name of the thing,
might as well, or better, have been called a lane.
" Here is Autran Street.   Shall I wait for you,
or go home, and send the carriage back ?"

" Wait for me, of course !" was the polite
response—uttered in a tone which implied it
was her business to wait his pleasure—as the
carriage stopped with a tremendous clatter before
the door of Messrs. Eives and Maycombe's
office.

The footman threw down the steps, and after
flinging a rather triumphant glance over his
whole turn-out, Judith's husband, or, to speak
more correctly, Judith's lord and master, descended with a braggart air from his fine equipage
and went into his lawyers', whilst Judith remained in the carriage, listlessly looking away
along the dreary vista of that London street, and
thinking about anything, Heaven knew, but the
scene she was gazing at.

Until her eye chanced to fall by mere accident
on a figure cowering in a neighbouring doorway

—a something human ; barefooted, clad solely in a ragged shirt, and, if, possible still more ragged pair of trousers.

It is by no means so unusual a circumstance even in England's wealthy metropolis, for a half-naked boy to be noted sitting hopelessly on the stones, that the spectacle need have immediately arrested a lady's attention; but poverty and misery had strange attractions for the well-clad woman's weary heart, and besides there was an indescribable depth of sorrow about the lad's attitude, which might well have arrested the steps and awakened the interest of one happier and more selfish than the rich member's wife ; wherefore, leaning forward, she bestowed one long, earnest glance on the bowed figure so near her. A habit of rapid observation caused Mrs. Mazingford to note several particulars at once ; the beauty of his rich black hair, which displayed some traces of care and arrangement, the delicate whiteness of his thin hands, the cleanliness of the only two garments he wore, and also of his feet and throat

—his face she could not see; it was covered by his bony, unchildish-looking fingers.

He never looked up to beg; he seemed as if he had sate himself down there with the intention of never stirring from that doorstep again. He did not cry, nor even moan; but a strange sort of sound, like the echo of a wail of pain and despair, escaped from the drooping figure at irregular intervals. Judith did not know what to make of him: was he hurt? or was he an impostor hoping thus to attract sympathy? or was he really in need of help? She could not pass him by, at any rate; the chance of assisting a fellow-creature came in her way so seldom she dare not let it slip; better to be twenty times imposed upon, than once negligent of an opportunity.

A trifle given to a hypocrite would never harm her; a mite bestowed on a worthy object might prove an incalculable blessing to him; so Judith reasoned rapidly, though almost unconsciously.

" Thomas," she finally said, turning to the

footman, "ask that boy what is the matter with him."

Reluctantly obedient to the mandate, the fellow got down, and stooping to inspect the boy, as he might had he been a bundle of rags, instead of an imperfectly clothed mass of flesh and blood, containing an immortal soul; he commenced operations with the encouraging sentence full of genteel irony and contempt:

"Halloa, you sir !"

The lad looked up, and as he did so, Judith gazing from her carriage, caught a glimpse of his face; oh ! such an one, so worn, so pale, so thin, so marked and pinched with poverty.

"What are you sitting there for ?" queried Thomas, "what ails you ?"

"It does not signify," said a low voice, and the tired head dropped again, and Thomas returned to his mistress.

"Well," she asked, "what is it ?"

"He says it don't signify, Ma'am," returned Thomas.

The words came home to her heart—a token of grief too deep to be spoken; of sorrow which required either gentle handling or none at all.

"Open the door," she said, "I want to see what it really is ;" and the next moment she was on the pavement close beside the boy. She did not approach him, however, as her servant had done—with easy insolence, with well-fed contempt, with under-bred airs of patronage—Ah! no—as one crushed heart draws nigh unto another; as the wayworn pilgrim stretches out his hand to assist a brother toiling through a desert—the thirst, and the barrenness, and the weariness whereof he has experienced himself; so, without a thought of difference of rank, or superiority of station, did she, that proud, grief-stricken woman, lay her hand pityingly on the young head of the beggar boy, and say in a voice soft as charity's own loving tone :—

"What is the matter, my child ? why do you sit there so hopelessly ?   I want very much to know," she added, seeing a pair of large, black eyes scanning her features curiously, "why you look so miserable?"

The white lips trembled for an instant with a more powerful emotion than any which could have been caused by mere bodily suffering, and then the words, "I am so hungry," were dropped out rather than spoken.

There was a baker's shop within a few yards of the horses' heads, and thence, at a signal from Mrs. Mazingford, the footman procured a supply of biscuits, which the lady gave into the boy's hands. Instinctively his fingers clutched at the precious morsels, and the sunken eyes glanced ravenously upon them; but the next instant a feeling of a different kind swelling up in the youth's breast, caused him to drop the biscuit he was carrying to his lips, and exclaim, not in a tone of churlish pride, but in one of earnest protest against such a supposition—

"I am not a beggar, ma'am."

"I know you are not," she returned, "and neither am I; yet still we both require to eat occasionally; finish what you have there, and then go and buy more;" and she laid a piece of glittering money in the palm which never closed upon it.

"Oh! ma'am," he cried, "don't give me money; let me work for you and earn it, but don't—don't give me money. I am not a beggar —but a gentleman."

A gentleman of fourteen summers, with bare feet and ragged shirt and trousers—there would have been a something ludicrous in the sentence, had it not been part of a real tragedy; one which is enacted every day in actual life.

Pride and poverty; starvation and independence. Judith looked down with swimming eyes on the little figure that stated itself to be a gentleman, and could refuse, in its blackest hour of need, money it had not worked for.

The half-naked child had unconsciously touched a chord that vibrated in, and thrilled through the whole frame of the stately beauty. Had she been possessed of similar strength, of equal determination, had she worked and not married, gone forth and braved absolute want, sooner than bind the yoke of slavery around her neck; what an eternity of humiliation she would have been spared!

This lad would not sell his independence and self-respect, even for a moment, to a stranger; she had sold, and bound, and tied, and bartered away herself, not for a day merely, but for always; not for a term of years—seven, or ten, or twelve, but for life—till the grave closed over him—or her.

The unintentional rebuke went home; it arose from the pavement to touch the soul of one who drove over the stones of the street in luxury; but the stones of the street have voices that shout to the rich in various accents, truths of vital import, of universal interest. Yet the rich rarely hear the things it concerns them to know; because the noise of their equipages drowns the sound and destroys the effect of London's solemn warnings, subduing all to a mere vague buzz;

the national acknowledgment they fancy it of
their vast importance.

But the arrow winged all unconsciously by a
young English Arab of the nineteenth century,
had gone home for once; and some—amongst
a crowd of idlers who had collected at the unusual spectacle of a lady and a footman ministering unto one of London's most desolate ones—
marvelled to hear her voice tremble as she
answered—

"Work for me, my boy, in your sense of the
word, you cannot; but still keep the trifle without a shadow of honest scruple disturbing you—
feeling assured it but scantily repays a lesson I
have learned this day through you. For the
future, work of a different kind you shall have
by some means. Remember, however, my last
words—in whatsoever strait or temptation you
may hereafter find yourself, always maintain your
independence; it will bring you all good; it will
preserve you from all evil;" and so saying, she
passed through the knot of idlers to her carriage,

where beckoning a respectable-looking policeman to follow, she said :—

"I am interested in that boy, but do not know how to assist him myself. Will you make enquiries about him, and if he be really worthy, procure him employment of some kind, and use this for his benefit ? It is but little, yet it may be of some service."

"And if he's a thief, my lady," intetrupted the man, who of course concluded the lad must be a thief and Judith a " my lady," "where shall I return the purse to ?"

"He is no thief," she said, almost angrily— then checking herself, added, "if it can aid him, well; if not, give the contents to some one who needs it—I do not.

"What the deuce is the row ?" enquired Mr. Mazingford, making his way up to the carriage at this juncture.

"Only a child being starved to death," said Judith.

"Curse him—let him die—better die now

than be hanged after a while," was the response.

" Much better," acquiesced his wife.

" Let them starve," once again repeated the popular legislator; " it is all they are good for—let 'em all starve."

" So be it," she answered, in her usual don't-care-about or sympathise-with-anything style. " So be it."

" Home," thundered Mr. Maxingford· to the coachman, for these cheerfully.acquiescent.replies of his wife fairly threw him *hors de combat*. He never understood, he told her occasionally, " what the devil she meant, or wanted to be at." But,. as the carriage drove off, a sudden cheer from the mob, hearty though there were so few to raise or sustain it, restored his equanimity. It was not meant, however, for the member who supported the interest of the country, and had voted two nights before on the popular side; oh ! no, but for the careless, beautiful donor of a small, green silk purse, which it was reported she had given for the rescue of one of their ragged brethren; and if the motley crew were not possessed of sufficient discernment to make joyful demonstration at the sight of an M.P., they had at least heart enough left to appreciate a kindly action, even when performed by one of their natural enemies—a fashionable lady. And so they cheered her, and her husband modestly took the compliment to himself.

"Hang it," he said, with a self-satisfied grin, "how soon the vagabonds recognise a public character. Do you hear them, Judith?"

"Distinctly," she answered, and turning her head aside, smiled bitterly.

A young exquisite riding past at the moment, catching the expression, and her eyes fixed, as he imagined, intently on his face, fancied the smile was intended for him, and pulled up to stare after the carriage.

Judith was unaware such a creature had come within her range of vision, but a sneer of contempt, a smile of scorn did curl her lip. Contempt and scorn at what?

At the man whom she had married; at herself for marrying him.

CHAPTER II.

IT is now time that we should return to Wales, to see how it has fared with the Reverend Watkyn Crepton's children, who, since the reader parted from them, several chapters back, had both learned many lessons out of life's great weary school-book, experience.

Profitable lessons, albeit sorrowful ones—lessons calculated to make them energetic, practical, long-enduring, very patient mariners across the world's stormy and troublous ocean. Theirs was, perhaps, a fit training for two who were destined to make their own fortunes for themselves, without the assistance of friends or relatives—without the adjuncts of wealth, position, or high ancestry—but it proved a weary one, for all that.

The strength of the fire was fierce, that the steel might come forth from the furnace the finer-tempered, the better fitted for all the cutting and carving that lay before it—and, as was meet, the weaker nature was subjected to the more fearful test.

As Alice required more hardening to fit her for the strife, so she received it; for, until Evan attained his thirteenth year, his troubles were comparatively light.

He was snubbed, it is true, by boys bigger, and richer, and grander, and bolder than himself: his mother's desertion of him, and his father's humble origin, were flung at him on every conceivable occasion; and it was the laudable aim of every youth in the school to make the lad as unhappy and miserable as possible.

He was the cleverest and most studious of the juvenile fry—extolled by Dr. Mills—the darling of the masters; and so, because he chanced, fortunately for himself, to be less scatter-brained than the rest of his companions, they tormented him, as schoolboys, ay, even the best among them will do, ceaselessly.

They called him "the Sage," "Diogenes," and a host of similar nicknames; sometimes asserting, that "the Judge" would yet sit on the woolsack; on other occasions, assigning him a seat in the Cabinet. They quizzed him about being so fond of his sister; and drew fancy sketches of her in his books. In brief, he ran the gauntlet of petty persecution, occasionally fighting it out with his tormentors, but more frequently receiving their jokes with the imperturbably grave face which had gained him the love of his principal, and the mockery of his schoolmates.

They said he was not a boy, and they said right. He was a man, with a man's purpose, and a man's higher feelings. He worked on, through rough and smooth, for an object, which he pursued as resolutely as though he had been fifty, instead of a mere child. The first great desire of his soul was to grow old, the next to grow learned ; he wanted to " get on" in years, wealth, rank and knowledge.

The old, refined tastes never left him : in his thick shoes and rough jacket, and often well-worn trousers, in the play-ground, and in the school-room, he was a little gentleman still. With his settled manners, and thoughtful expression of countenance, he might, but for his size, have passed for thirty—for the child-sorrows of his life had sunk into his heart, and aged him before the proper time.

Sorrow! how omnipotent a thing it must be, to have power to put a man's cares in a boy's breast ; to perform the feat of putting an old head on young shoulders—of making a lad of fourteen as grave, and full of purpose, as his father, after his marriage.

Sorrow is the great alchemist of life : for it discovers and drags to light every trait which

had otherwise lain slumbering for ever. It is
the best training-school extant for forming practical, energetic characters—it made a student
out of Evan Crepton—who, at the time he
entered his fifteenth year, knew as much as
many a one of twenty.

He was getting on admirably: Dr. Mills did
his duty by the lad, faithfully and conscientiously.

Though there was no more money coming, or
likely to come from any quarter, he never forgot
that the Welsh farmer had paid him down in
full, years previously, for his grandson's education; and now the old man was gone from
earth for ever—now there was no one else to
look to the boy, and care for him, Dr. Mills stood
his friend and counsellor. He made no difference between him and the other pupils, except, perhaps, in a little extra kindness to the
orphan child. He taught him well, and trained
him better: he gave him all the advantages of
masters, and was wont to cheer on the willing

scholar with words of hope and encouragement :—

" If you go on as well for three years more,
Evan," he said to the lad, one fine morning, the
autumn before Judith Mazingford went to town
—" if you go on as well, and continue as good a
boy, and do your best to fit yourself for the
post, I will make you one of my tutors, and
give you for a beginning a salary of thirty pounds
per annum."

" And then I can have Ally near me:" and
Evan, in his delight, forgot all his dignity, and
flung his cap (for it was on the lawn this dia-
logue took place), up in the air—flung it up so
high, that it caught in the branches of an old
elm tree, whence he had infinite difficulty to get
it down again ; and he, then and there, set to
work immediately upon a huge Greek Grammar,
and laboured on for three months as indefati-
gably as though excessive study would make the
three years' probation shorter.

" Oh, Alice ! my dear, dear sister Alice," he

would exclaim, every now and then cutting such frantic antics, and indulging in such unusual contortions of delight, that the other boys occasionally thought their grave companion must suddenly have lost his senses.

But when he told them all about it—when, almost weeping with delight, and with a face beaming with pleasure, he poured out his whole heart to the motley crowd of grinning lads—there was something so genuine about his love for his sister, about his energy, his manliness, his gratitude, and his independence, that the soft spot of good, lying so far down in the hearts of the rough schoolboys was touched, and with one accord they cried out, "Success to Diogenes! Long live old Mills!"

"We'll come to see you, Wisdom, when you are tutor, and you'll introduce us to your sister, wont't you?"

Then the biggest and richest of the little community said, "Shake hands, old fellow; I'm glad you are so happy; you deserve it all.

Come, we 'll treat you to a feast:" whereupon every one in the play-ground following the lead, volunteered (such a mode of congratulation being considered manly, and " the thing," at Dr. Mills's),—to shake hands too: and each subscribed his mite towards the expenses of a public entertainment, which it was immediately arranged should be given to " the new tutor," upon the top of a hamper, under a shed that stood in one corner of the yard.

" Three years! why, man, it will go over before you know anything about it," said the young gentleman previously referred to, who was considered a good authority on all matters of importance." Then one year more, to be second usher, and two to be first—and after that old Mills will retire, and you will marry his daughter: and Oh! crimini! won't I come down and see you then, in a drag, driving four in hand! Three years, it's nothing! Bless you, I 've been here eight, already."

" And—and—there's something else," hesitated Evan, divided betwixt a desire to be confidential, and a fear of being ridiculed—" something else, if you won't laugh."

" Laugh, indeed! Out with it, man—those that win may laugh!"

"Well, you know," said the boy, " that Dr. and Mrs. Mills are not going away to any place this winter; and they have promised to invite Ally here, to spend Christmas with me."

"Gentlemen," said the eight years' resident, "I propose we remain the holidays."

" But," pursued Evan, " we are not sure Mrs. Crickieth will let her come, for she is not a kind woman."

" An old beldame," remarked the senior: and then came no end of jesting, and joking, and laughing, and badgering; but Evan could bear it all with a better face, with a happier heart. He was a man—Dr. Mills evidently thought him so—and accordingly, he set himself to work out earnestly the happy destiny that lay before him. Alas! poor boy, the sunshine of apparent prosperity so dazzled his eyes, that he could not see the many troubles and trials he should have to encounter, before he actually became what he so confidently styled himself, a man.

It was the last morning before the commencement of the Christmas holidays, and the senior pupil was just in the act of commencing the day's proceedings by washing his face, when one of the ushers rushed into the room, exclaiming, "My God! he's dead, boys!"

"Who?"

"Doctor Mills. Mr. Unwin's off for a doctor, but it's of no use—apoplexy."

Not a soul spoke; every pupil stood rooted to the spot where he stood. In the dead chill of that dreary winter's morning they remained numbed and cold, by something drearier and colder than December's frosts and snows.

For a moment Evan Crepton stayed quiet, like the rest; for a moment he was stunned and stupified, by the suddenness of the blow; but, as by degrees the full truth broke upon his

mind, he uttered a piercing cry, and rushing out
of the open door, ran towards Dr. Mills' apartment.   Mrs. Mills was there, kneeling beside
the bed, but she never prevented the lad flinging
himself across the corpse; she never interrupted
his cries, and wailings, and passionate, ungovernable sorrow for the dead.   She never interfered
with him by word or sign, except that when
some one tore him from the body, she put
her arms, broken-hearted widow as she was,
about the boy's neck, and sobbed aloud.

"Oh! don't, ma'am—please don't—it hurts
me—don't cry;" and in his great agony, the
tears poured down Evan's cheeks, and somehow,
from the genuine love of that child for the deceased, the lonely woman took more comfort
than from any other thing or person.

What a dreadful time that was which inter-
vened between the death and the funeral, when
men in black came slipping into the house at
unusual hours — when the boys went home
quietly and sorrowfully, without any preparation

or formal leave-taking — when the good old
Doctor was laid in his coffin—when Evan moped,
solitary and miserable, about the desolate play-
ground and school-room, and corridors—

" He was the best man that ever lived," he
said, with a sort of hysterical gulp to everybody
who spoke to him—" and he was the best friend
ever I had; and if it were not for Alley, I wish
I were dead too—" and then came a perfect
paroxysm of grief, and the boy quite forgot he
was a man, and was always seeking out remote
corners, where he might sit down and cry.

During all this time he had no leisure to think
of himself.   When he was not moaning over
the Doctor's death, he was carrying messages,
and running from place to place, in a sort of
dream.   He heard, indeed, that the schoolmaster's affairs were embarrassed, that his money
was all gone—but somehow, it never occurred to
him, that the death would make any change
in his own position.   He thought school would
go on just the same as usual, only without the

Doctor; and that he would have to creep back to his books—oh! so lonely and so desolate, without him. That old house had been a home to the lad; little marvel he could not realise the idea of leaving it.

Next day after the funeral, however, he was summoned to the parlour: there sat Mrs. Mills and two men—one a stranger to him, the other his uncle. Evan paused on the threshold—a kind of faintness crept over him—he did not know what ailed him, or what he feared. Long sobbing had made him sick—perhaps that was it.

" Sit down, Sir," said his uncle, coldly, " I have a few words to say to you."

Almost involuntarily, Mrs. Mills held out her hand to him, and accordingly he went and took a seat by her. He looked at her, and saw her eyes were red, with recent weeping.

" I suppose I need not tell you, an end has come to all your fine learning and expensive education," proceeded Mr. Crepton; " you know that."

" I have told him nothing," interrupted Mrs. Mills: " Evan," she continued, in an almost choking voice, " my poor husband died a beggar. For my sake, and that of his child, he toiled and slaved through years. For our sakes he speculated; and when he lost, he died. Don't reproach him, child, because he left no provision for you—don't reproach me! God knows, if I had a shilling in the world, I would give it to you. If I could have prevented this, I would. If there had been anything for anybody, I would have taken from my own daughter, and done justice to you. Never reproach him, Evan— never, even in thought."

" Oh! he was the best friend ever I had: I don't reproach him, no matter what it is; and I wish I were a man, and I'd work for you—he was so good to me, so kind to me"—and then came a torrent of tears, which Mrs. Mills vainly tried to stop.

" Poor boy, poor child!" she said, looking despairingly at his uncle, who interposed with—

" I think, Madam, it would be better not to encourage him in such childish ways. He is not a baby now; and it is time he learned to control his feelings, and behave like a man, not like a little girl."

" And did you never see a man cry before?" demanded Evan, checking his sobs, and speaking with kindling eyes, and a flushed cheek: " I have seen my grandfather, your father, cry; and what he has done I may do, and will do."

" Come, my lad, less talk if you please, and listen to what I have to say. Money was taken from us to give to this lady's husband for your education. I don't mean to say anything against Doctor Mills, because he's dead, and all the speaking in the world won't bring a shilling of that money back again; but it appears that every halfpenny is gone, and that your superfine education is not finished. Now we have not the means to pamper you up any further; and I have therefore come this day to offer you a choice of three things, viz. to come home to the

farm with me; to be apprenticed to this gentleman; or to go the workhouse!"

It would be impossible to describe the expression of the boy's face, as the concluding portion
of his uncle's speech sounded on his ear. His
features worked convulsively—he looked in a
sort of bewilderment round the room, and then,
with a cry of " Save me!" fell prostrate at the
widow's feet.

" We had better settle this matter at Ewm-
cylldlan; don't you think so?" said Mr. Crepton,
addressing his companion: and the latter as-
senting, with a grunt—he got up, raised Evan
from the ground, and desired him at once to
put his things together, and get ready to ac-
pany him home.

" Make haste, now," added his interesting
relative, as the boy slowly turned the handle of
the door—" I'll just give you twenty minutes,
for I want to be off—so look sharp!"

Up the broad staircase, along the desolate
corridors, the boy crept, hopelessly. This was

the end of all. In one moment the cup of sweetness had been dashed from his lips, and this was the bitter potion substituted in its place.

He had not forgotten his uncles, and their previous unkindness; he had not forgotten Ewm-cylldlan Farm, and he knew, as well as if he had endured it all, what lay before him there:—

"I won't go," he said out loud, as he reached the end of the corridor. "I will never go:" and he banged right into his sleeping-room, col-lected, as he had read of other boys in similar situations, and with similar intentions, doing before him, the few trinkets and valuables he possessed—these, and a very limited stock of clothes, he tied up in a bundle, and, slipping through a back door, before the twenty minutes had elapsed, he was taking the road to London.

He did not keep along the regular highway, for he was afraid (although the short winter's day was growing dark,) of pursuit and detection; so he held on his route under cover of walls,

and plantations, and leafless hedges, until he
was thoroughly worn out, when he crept into a
ruinous barn, and slept soundly for hours.

When he awoke, the sun was again near its
setting; and, under the friendly canopy of night,
he ventured to pursue his way along the turnpike road, carefully eschewing, however, scattered villages and detached habitations—striking
out of his path for rest and provisions—consulting the mile-stones, in preference to asking
questions of any traveller, he walked on for
miles and miles, foot-sore and weary—until at
last, his limping gait attracted the attention of a
carrier, who offered him a seat in his waggon.

This was a great help; and at the place where
the man put up for the night, the landlady
washed his feet, and bound them up with linen,
steeped in oil and spirits; so that when he arose
next morning, he felt able to walk with tolerable
ease again.   But the carrier kept the lad with
him till they reached Birmingham.   Safe under
cover, in the bottom of his waggon, Evan lay

secure, in the assurance of his new-formed
friend, that he would " never peach upon him ;"
for the desolate boy had done the wisest thing
he could do—made a confidante of his companion—who applauded his spirit, and called
him " a brick," and " a fine fellow"—and said
that Doctor Mills must have been a " good
'un !"

And at Birmingham, where they were to part,
the man furnished him with a second-hand
page's suit, in which disguise both thought he
was likely to travel more safely to London,
where Evan said his mother lived.

"An unnatural baggage !" remarked the carter;
"but still go to her, my lad ; she can't help
doing a summut for you and your little sister ; so
put on these clothes till you get to town, and
keep your good ones to see her in—and go to
the place I told you about, ' The Three Stars,'
and tell the landlord I sent you."

With the native generosity of his character,
Evan, at parting, pressed upon the man a

little knitted bag, containing all his worldly
wealth, a single guinea; but the honest fellow
put it back, with his horny hand—

"Noa, noa," he said, "I have children of my
own; and I am not going to take money from
a youngster like you. Keep all you have, Master,
you will need it in Lunnun; and if you want to
do something for me when you are a great gentleman, as you will be, may be, one day—don't
forget Job Wilkins, of Mostyn-cum-Sape. Now,
God bless you, young master! good bye"—and
the child and the man wrung each other's hands,
and many a time Evan turned his head, to look
after the departing figure of his friend, who
always waved his hat, in an encouraging manner,
after the young adventurer.

And so with lifts now and then for ten miles
or even a fewer number, riding and walking,
resting and limping, the boy went on steadily,
lessening the distance between himself and London, until at length, as the shades of evening
were gathering about him on the last day of

his pilgrimage, he saw reflected in the sky before him, the lights of the great city : " London at last," he cried, and forgetting his weariness, he ran eagerly forward, as though that great Babylon had been his home.

It was with a strange throb of delight, and a still stranger sense of bewilderment, that Evan Crepton wandered through the streets and across the squares, and among the various turnings and twistings of that interminable labyrinth, London. There was no end to it. He walked on and on, staring at the shops and the houses, the thoroughfares and the passers-by, till he grew tired and frightened at the immensity of the leviathan he had come to seek. Then he bethought him for the first time of the hostel to which the carter had directed him, and accosting a man who was leaning against a lamp post, asked if he could tell him where " Melville Street was ?"

" And what may you want in Melville Street,

youngster?" demanded the person so interrogated in his turn.

" I want 'The Three Stars,'" answered Evan,
simply, upon receiving which reply, the fellow
stated he was going there too, and offered to
show the boy his way; an offer which Evan
accepted with more gratitude than was at all
needful under the circumstances.

For some time his companion led the way
through broad thoroughfares and well-lighted
streets; but at last he struck out of the more
frequented parts of the town, and commenced
taking so many turnings down questionable
lanes and courts, and alleys, that finally it became patent even to the understanding of the
inexperienced Welsh schoolboy, that they were
getting into a very bad neighbourhood.

" Are we near the Three Stars now ?" asked
Evan, at last.

" Yes, close to," replied the man making a
sudden clutch at Evan as he spoke; but the
lad was too quick for him.   In a moment he

forgot his weariness, and with fear lending wings to his heels, he sped along the lane with a rapidity which astonished his pursuer. Doubling and turning and panting, Evan pursued his flight, and it was not till he reached a broad street filled with people, that, assured of safety, he paused to take breath. Then he discovered he had lost his bundle—then he felt what it was to stand alone—a stranger and an orphan, on the stones of England's vast metropolis. Very wretched and miserable, he wandered on till he came to an inviting porch, under which he crept, and cried himself to sleep.

Morning came, and with it a "guardian of the night," who waked the slumberer roughly, and bade him be moving. So, sore and stiff and cold, Evan rose up from the stones, and shaking and shivering, went out into the world.

He had his guinea, and a couple of shillings still left; so turning into a neighbouring cook-shop, he bought some bread, which he ate at a coffee-stand close by, where a poor Irishwoman furnished him with a cup of the hot beverage.

The boy thought he had never in all his life tasted anything one half so good; for the best tonics on earth, hunger and thirst, lent him appetite and relish, whilst the warm coffee sent a glow of heat through his half-numbed body. Whilst he was eating and drinking, he consulted the Irishwoman as to the possibility of washing his face and hands, and putting himself generally to rights; and with wonderful discrimination and sense, considering the dislike of her countrypeople to soap and water, she advised him to go to the "bats," which suggestion Evan followed, when he found that "bats" in Irish meant baths in English. Oh, the unspeakable luxury of that bath—the delight of putting on his clothes, shabby as they were, over a clean skin—the pleasure of feeling, as he emerged from the baths, that if he did look poor, he did not look dirty. In his thread-worn suit, with his hair properly arranged with a little cloth cap set jauntily on the top, the undaunted boy, with courage renewed and body invigorated, started off once again on his travels, through that great, overgrown city, London. It was to St. James's Square he bent his steps this time, where he arrived just as a splendid carriage drew up at Sir John Lestock's door.

"That's my mother's," thought the boy; and a sort of throb, half of mortification, half of pride, caused his heart to bound and swell for a moment—the next he was talking to a powdered footman.

"I want to see Mrs. Crepton," he said.

"There is no lady of that name resides in the Square," retorted Jeames, whose dignity was hurt by Evan's unceremonious address; "and if you go to look for her any place else, young man, I should advise you to use more respect to your betters. Coming to gentlemen's house, wanting this and wanting that indeed!"

"Is not this where Sir John Lestock lives?" persisted Evan.

"And if it be, Mr. Impudence, what's that to you?"

"Nothing; except that I want to see his daughter."

"Oh, Lord, Simpson! do you hear this? he is talking of Miss Lestock as 'his' daughter."

"Well, I suppose she's not his mother, though she is——"

"Mine," the boy was going to have added, but he choked back the word, while a hearty peal of laughter from the coachman filled up the unspoken sentence.

"Come, come, my lad, be off; we don't want any hangers-on about our doors—at least, not of *your* sort. Do we, Simpson?" and Jeames, who had commenced with looking severe, was so delighted with this witticism at the expense of his mistress, that he ended in a chuckle.

"Will you tell Miss Lestock, as you call her, that I want to see her?" said Evan, when the merriment had subsided.

"No I won't, and I should advise you to be

off out of that, insulting gentlemen at a baronet's door."

"If you knew who I was," began the youth, vehemently—but just at the instant the hall-door was flung open, and matting was thrown hastily down the steps, and out came a lady magnificently dressed, accompanied by a gray-haired gentleman.

With a sort of cry, Evan sprang forward, but the footman pushed him back.

"I want to speak—I must speak," he exclaimed, struggling to be free—"let me go—I tell you I must speak to her."

"There, there, give the lad a sixpence, and don't hurt him," said Sir John Lestock, stepping into his carriage.

"Oh! I'm not a beggar. I don't want money;" cried Evan, rushing to the window of the vehicle. "I want to tell you about Alice and about myself. Mother, mother, listen to me—I am your son—I am Evan Crepton."

Bang went down the window, and at one blow the baronet struck his grandson to the earth.

" Take him away—let him come back at your peril," he cried out fiercely to the footman ; then flinging himself back in the carriage, he added: —" Drive on like the devil !"

Evan Crepton was not hurt, he was barely down before he was up again, and shaking his clenched hand in a paroxysm of rage after the departing vehicle.

" Hands off !" he almost yelled to the footmen. "'Hereafter I will be amply revenged—see if I don't ;" and without uttering another word, he turned his back on his mother's home—with bitterness in his heart, and indignation, and anger, and all uncharitableness boiling in his breast.

For days he wandered objectless about London —lodging in mean inns at night, and prowling through the crowded streets by day.   As his finances got lower, he sought for employment, but without success—sometimes he got a stray sixpence for holding a gentleman's horse, or carrying a parcel, but by degrees he got poorer and poorer—unable to pay for nightly accommodation, and obliged to spend night after night in waste houses—under porches and on door-steps. He sought and enquired for Melville Street and the Three Stars, but nobody knew anything of either. He parted with his cap, his neck-handkerchief, his old shoes, his jacket and waistcoat —everything but his shirt and trousers for food —and at length, utterly famished, exhausted, and weary, he sat him down perfectly heartsick in Autram Street, where Judith met him on the day and in the manner described in the preceding chapter.

He would not beg, but she would give ; she just came to rescue the boy from absolute starvation, and then disappeared, leaving him whom her husband so kindly cursed, the hero of a group of idlers, whose enthusiasm, if such it might be called, for Mrs. Mazingford, gradually subsiding into a very natural though perhaps not equally laudable desire to share the spoil—they commenced making interest with the youth in a

mode anything but pleasing to the policeman who
chanced to be his guardian for the all-important
time being.

"Now just you make yourselves scarce," began that functionary, after a brief pause devoted
to serious reflection.   "I should advise you to
take your rags out of that, if you don't want a
night's lodging in the station-house. Come
along you, what's your name," and, adding example to precept, the policeman laid a rough
hand on the boy's collar—and so, took him, as
it were, in charge.

"Let me go," exclaimed the youth vigorously,
extricating himself from the detaining grasp—
"Don't lay a finger on me, sir; wherever you
want me to go, there I will follow you quietly,
but I am not a criminal, and you have no right
to drag me along the street as if I had stolen
something."

"Which maybe you have," retorted the other,
making no attempt, however, to resume his hold
of the supposed culprit, whom he eyed with con-

siderable suspicion. "I should be very sorry to go bail that you have never had a hand in any little affair, such as picking a pocket in a quiet way, or creeping in through a back kitchen window on a pinch—"

"No—no—no," exclaimed Evan, vehemently. "I would not steal. I have not stolen to save myself from starving."

There was a something about the tone in which this denial was uttered which carried a momentary conviction with it to the mind of the public character to whom it was addressed; but rags and poverty are strong evidences of guilt, and words and manner are by no means good proofs of innocence, and accordingly he answered, still doubtingly—

"Ay, ay, that's what you all say, 'No,' and take it—like the women; there was a heavy job done over at Pimlico two or three weeks ago, and a lad in it just about your age and size, and—"

"Do you mean to say I'm *a thief*?" hurriedly

interrupted the boy, pausing short, and asking the question with flashing eyes. " Do you dare to say I'm a thief?"

" I should not like to say you were not one," was the cool response; " but thief or no thief, come along quietly with me, for at present you and this purse are a sort of charge upon me, and I want to be peaceably rid of both."

" I would rather not go with you," said Evan, choking back a few words of angry import, and swallowing at the same time his rage. " Keep the purse or give it away, that is, keep the money, I mean, and give me the purse—I don't want the lady's gold, I want—"

" To get clear off," was the response. " Yes, yes, clench your fists if you like, but it won't do. No, no, it won't, I'm too old a bird to be caught by chaff, so now don't let's have any more chat, but come along;" and he again laid a hand on the boy's collar, which polite attention was instantly repaid by a smart blow in the face.

"I told you before," said Evan, "I was willing to go with you to any place if you treated me properly. I am a gentleman, and I will not be dragged along the streets like a prisoner by any one. I have committed no crime, so you cannot take me in charge. If I had wanted to escape, I could have done so long ago. I do not wish to break any law, or to create any disturbance, but I should advise you to be careful how you annoy me, for I—"

"Am a gentleman! no doubt!" ejaculated the policeman, with a grimace, surveying the lad's clothes, or rather rags. "Well, so as you come with me peaceably, it don't much matter how we go along; and you can tell me by the way who you are and where you are from, and how so well-born a young gent as yourself came to be begging in the street."

"That's a lie," was the straightforward retort. "I was not begging—I was starving—as to who I am, that's my business; and as to where I'm from, that's no affair of yours; and as to where

I'm going—you know that better than I do."

"But you must tell me your name," said X, in a more civil tone, for something in Evan's manner was at length beginning to produce an impression on him. "I must have your name."

"Why, does it belong to you?"

This was rather an unsatisfactory reply, and on the strength of it the policeman and his protégé walked on together for a few minutes in silence. At length—"I tell you what it is, young man," he said stopping abruptly, and staring the lad straight in the face; "I expect you have run away from your friends."

"Then you are wrong," returned Evan, "for I have no friends—no home—not a relation in the world to love me but one, who perhaps— God help her—stands as much in need of aid as I do."

"And still you say you are—"

"Better than what I seem," was the answer

"but what are we going in here for? it is a Police Court, and I am not a criminal;" and the speaker's face grew very red, and he made a movement as if to depart.

"Now just be quiet, will you?" said the policeman, "and listen to reason. A lady whom I know nothing about, gives me a purse for the benefit of a——of a boy that I know nothing about either; bids me do what I can for him if he is worthy, and the rest of it, and drives off and leaves me in a pretty fix. I am an honest man, and neither want to keep the money myself, nor to throw it away on you if you don't deserve to have it; and so I think the best thing I can do in the matter is to take you before Mr. Maund, tell him the way of the case, and let him decide what is best to be done. If you are honest, you need not be afraid to come with me; and if you are not honest, why there is still the more reason that, willing or unwilling, you should."

The result of which lucid speech was that youth and guardian went into Court; the former to be questioned, the latter to talk; but as Evan resolutely refused to throw any light on his own history, the magistrate felt puzzled how to act. It was of no use to ask the stranger for any explanation of his anomalous position.

He declined to give his name; declared he had no friends, no home, no money, no place to go, no employment, no plan for the future; he said he was not a Londoner, but refused to state why he had come to the metropolis, and how long he had been in it—whence he had come, or where any one belonging to him resided.

He admitted he had relations in London, but said application to them would be useless, and that at any rate he did not wish to ask favours from any one. He stated he was willing to work, and would be thankful for employment; he did not care what he worked at, provided he could earn a living by it. He did not want to be a burden on man or woman. If the magistrate could return the money to the lady, he should be glad, only he would like to keep the purse, if he were allowed; he could not say who she was; had never seen her before; should scarcely know her if they met again, because there were so many people about, and such a confusion, but she had spoken kindly to him—her's was the only friendly voice he had heard since —"

Here Evan stopped short, and resolutely "shut up," as a bystander phrased it. No questioning could wring further information out of him, and as a *dernier resort*, Mr. Maund remanded him, so to speak, for a few days, and his guardian took him to his own home, where, by the magistrate's directions, he was provided with a decent suit of clothes, and desired to wait until further enquiries could be made concerning him. The green silk purse he had, as it was of no value to any one else, been permitted to retain, but the money, less a small sum for immediate expenses, remained in Mr. Maund's hands, until such time as something definitive should be learned about the boy.

Evan took the whole business very quietly,

shewed no sign of vexation when it was proposed
to insert an advertisement in the papers descrip-
tive of him; made not the slightest objection to
anything Mr. Maund suggested; and finally
succeeded in totally blinding the judgment of
the policeman, who gradually relaxed his vigilance
over him.

The following evening Evan expressed a desire
to write to the magistrate, and accordingly pen,
ink, and paper, were provided him for that purpose. The epistle seemed to be a voluminous
one, for it took a long time to write, and his
host, whose name be it known was Woods,
imagined it was intended to clear up all mysteries,
and thought the boy must at length be coming
to his senses.

On the strength of which supposition he
exercised so very moderate a degree of sur-
veillance over him, that next day, when Mr.
Maund wanted Evan, he was nowhere to be
found.

He had "bolted," as the brief but expressive phrase goes, taking nothing with him but the green silk purse, the clothes he "stood up in," and leaving no information behind him but that contained in Mr. Maund's note.

Little enough it proved. He enclosed a letter addressed to Miss Crepton, at Mrs. Crickeith's, Klicksturvyd, North Wales, which he requested might be forwarded to that person without being opened. He said he was going away, as he feared the advertisements would bring enemies upon him—that he thanked all who had been kind to him, and remained

E. C.

So the matter rested for a few days, but then much light was thrown on the boy's history. "He had run away," said letters from Wales, "a couple of months previously." His relatives wished him to be returned to Wales, and one of them absolutely travelled to London in order to identify his nephew and escort him home; but Evan was gone, no one knew when or how for many a long day afterwards, when it was ascertained that a lad answering printed descriptions of him had entered on board a ship at Southampton and sailed out " foreign." When he reached the Cape, however, whither the vessel was bound, he exchanged into a merchantman going on to China, and so all trace of him was lost. Years passed away—summer suns rose and set—winter came and went—the buds of spring withered, the fruits of many autumns were gathered in, but still no news of the wanderer came back to Wales, where his young sister watched and waited for tidings till her cheek grew pale, and her soul weary, because of that " hope deferred which maketh the heart sick."

CHAPTER III.

KLICKSTURVYD, where Mrs. Crickeith "held court," was one of the very coldest and dampest seaports in North Wales ; cold by reason of its exposed situation, damp by virtue of a line of hills that poured down moisture on the little town lying in the valley beneath.

This " retreat," which might perhaps have contained some two or three thousand inhabitants, boasted of course a High Street, a market-place, a church, an hotel, a doctor's shop, and the ruins of an ancient castle, built Heaven knows how long before the flood ; and besides the above-mentioned thoroughfare, public buildings, and offices—never to speak of back streets and front streets, old lanes and bye-lanes, and new lanes, it contained an aristocratic parade, place, square, or crescent (for it was called by any of the preceding names according to the taste of the speaker or fancy of the dweller) where abode the " nobs " of the neighbourhood; to wit, the clergyman, the magistrate, the four maiden Misses Breffni (lineal descendants of the Irish prince of that name who lived in the time of Henry II., and who never married, so they averred, because they had vowed in early youth not to wed any one whose genealogical tree boasted no such antique roots as their own), and Mr. Owen Davis, the unmarried attorney, to say nothing of a few minor widows and half-pay officers, who either let or took lodgings at Klicksturvyd during the bathing season.

This genteel portion of the town fronted north-west, and consequently the evening sun, when there was any, shone full upon it, revealing every broken pane, every crooked blind, every discoloured atom of cement to view; but in storm, darkness, sunshine or light, one house stood out from all the rest, distinguished from its fellows by its awful, gloomy, and of course extremely respectable appearance.

Including the basement, this house was four storeys high, and it looked as though the architect who had planned it must have flourished ere comfort, ventilation, warmth, and cleanliness were things deemed necessary to the happiness and well-being of society.

The edifice resembled a prison, or a store, or a vault; and assuredly it was a prison wherein young hearts pined and panted, and wept for liberty. A store in which were contained things precious and valuable; the treasures of childish love—the best affections of youthful bosoms—the trustful feelings of that bright spring-time of life, ere experience has touched and sullied the soul—the intellects of those who were to become, if they lived, wives, mothers, governesses, all were stored in that gloomy warehouse. They

were gathered in—the doors were shut on them,
and the treasures rotted away in the unwholesome
atmosphere; and when they came forth again,
they were all more or less tarnished, adulterated,
altered, or disfigured.   It was a vault, not for the
dead but for the living; not for cold, pulseless
corpses, but for warm throbbing hearts.   Young
frames there grew diseased; young lives there
wasted away and decayed.   It was a grave, not
for the body from which the soul had winged
its flight, not for bones and dust and clay, but
for strength and health, and hope and joy, and
childish happiness, and confidence and trust.

The house was encircled with iron railings;
there were long blinds on the lower windows,
which were kept down winter and summer, and
never raised unless the casements required clean-
ing: there were blinds, likewise, on the next
story; but the light of heaven was sometimes
permitted to enter these privileged apartments;
and then there were whole blinds, and half-
blinds, and muffing, and all sorts of inventions

on the upper story, to prevent the occupants gazing forth at the sea; or Mr. Owen Davis, or the clergyman, or even the Misses Breffni. No servant, in that dreary abode, was ever known to converse with her lover, through the kitchen windows. One had tried it, and been dismissed instanter; and from that day forth the sashes were nailed up, and the area-door shut, and locked for good, and bad, and all.

The place was a blot in creation; the sun could not make it look brighter—nor the tempest darker than it was; in daylight it frowned sullenly at the bright heavens, the dancing waves, the lonely thoroughfare; when night veiled the town in its impenetrable curtain, it seemed as though a blacker shade hung over the edifice— as though a darker shadow were thrown from it, than from any other house across the uneven pavement, along which the pedestrian groped his uncertain way.

What parents saw about the place, or the mistress thereof, to induce them to consign their

offspring to her tender care and mercies, I
cannot tell : what the inhabitants beheld in that
gloomy abode to make them observe, "it was a
capital place for a school !" they knew best; it
was called "respectable," "commodious," "healthful ;" the owner was termed " indefatigable,"
"amiable," " high-minded," " conscientious ;"
if ever any one disputed any of these proposi-
tions, he was cried down as a heathen, a savage,
a presumptuous stranger, who understood nothing—and who was ultimately forced to take
refuge in silence, whilst busy tongues sounded
Mrs. Crickieth's praise ; for learn, gentle reader,
the fact, and remember it when you have learnt
it, that the gloomy house was an Establishment
for Young Ladies, and Mrs. Crickieth the pre-
siding deity thereof.

No one ever exactly knew whence that lady
came, where she had been born, what had been
the system of the early education of one, who so
confidently undertook to train up children of her
own sex in the way they should go.   No one

was precisely aware of what had been her maiden
name—when she had changed it for the honourable cognomen of " Crickieth;" when, nor how,
nor why her lord had departed this life—nor her
reason for selecting Klicksturvyd, as the scene of
her widowed operations.   No one knew anything, accurately, about her; but it was universally circulated and believed, that the deceased
Mr. Crickieth had been not merely " not so good
as he should have been," but a great deal worse
than he might and ought to have been; that
Mrs. Crickieth was a miserable, illused and most
unfortunate woman, and a wonderful one to boot
—that her heroic endurance of evils, which had
been none of her own making, was something
miraculous, and that, in short, she ought to be
encouraged in her praiseworthy efforts, and com-
passionated because circumstances had rendered
it absolutely necessary for her to make those
efforts, in order to obtain a competence or even
a livelihood.

In the present day there are some who obstinately and stoutly deny, that, because a woman's husband has been an idiot, or a swindler, or a pauper, she is by consequence fitted to undertake the temporal and spiritual guidance of those fragile plants called girls—who prefer principles to misfortunes, knowledge to pretension, goodness to birth; there are some who like to enquire, more particularly, into the character of the woman who is to educate their daughters, than concerning her list of ancestors, or standing in the fashionable world; there are some who ask whether she can make their children good and happy as well as learned; truthful, straightforward and open-hearted, as well as graceful and elegant; religious as well as accomplished; there are some who think of these things, but would that there were thousands instead of tens, and we should see fewer pale cheeks, and sullen faces, and artful hearts, and crooked spines, and deficient intellects, and vacant minds, and frivolous souls, than may be noted any day, in those fashionable abodes where girls pass the most important years of their life—abodes of gentility and misery, and captivity, and outward adornment known to all the world by the name of Select Establishments for Young Ladies.

But still in our days there are many schools presided over by christian and well-educated ladies, where girls are tended and cared for as conscientiously as they could be anywhere, beyond the safe shelter of the paternal roof; and perhaps these homes for youth are quite as numerous as those abodes which are not homes but prisons, and are as readily to be found, if parents would only seek for them; there has been a vast improvement effected in seminaries of all kinds and for all classes, since the period when Mrs. Crickieth lived, and reigned, and flourished, for at that time you might have counted the good schools in Great Britain, on your fingers; she was the model school-mistress of a long time ago.

In person angular, erect, repelling, in face stern, not without traces of former beauty, but very severe in expression; possessed of manners

that were plausible to parents, and said as plainly
to the girls as manners could say, disobey me if
you dare. Her black dresses fitted as though
they were pasted to her figure; her widows' caps
were of miraculous whiteness, and the strings of
them never curled and got soiled like those of
other mortals; her hair never fell out of place
and blew about in a disreputable manner after
the fashion of ordinary women.

Oh! no, Mrs. Crickieth was an extraordinary
woman, and parents and guardians knelt down
and worshipped her accordingly. Then she had
a daughter, who was, so said the brother of a
refractory pupil, a "worse devil than herself;"
and altogether, what with Mrs. Crickieth and
her daughter, a cunning French governess, and
two half-starved English ones, a tremendous
garrison of rats, and a perfect guerilla force of
mice, the select seminary was a pleasant place.
Long had been Mrs. Crickieth's reign—long
and prosperous. She had made money, and
saved it; cribbed her pupils' silver forks and

spoons, and laid ambuscades for presents. She had acquired an " European and Asiatic reputation"—if England be Europe, and India Asia— she had turned out girls so accomplished, that parents getting husbands for them in no time, wrote grateful letters to the old widow of —— Crickieth deceased, and recommended other parents to offer up more victims at her shrine.

As for what the girls themselves said, that was deemed a matter of secondary importance, and, besides, rich pupils had seldom any great cause for complaint—absolute ill-usage being reserved for those whose bills were not punctually paid, or who were there at reduced rates. The élite of the school propitiated Mrs. Crickieth with services of china, knick-knacks, and netted purses, filled with nice little yellow coins; and got into the daughter's good graces by dint of silk dresses, scarfs, writing desks, and work-boxes. These young ladies had interest for their money out in quiet luncheons, more patient teaching, fewer scoldings, and a slight degree greater liberty of thought and action than was enjoyed by less favoured individuals.

Nothing more dissimilar from Dr. Mills' establishment can be conceived than Mrs. Crickieth's seminary; yet there was one point of resemblance between the two, viz., that at both the pupils received good educations, and no girl who would learn, or who could be made to learn, was ever known to leave Mrs. Crickieth's school an ignoramus.

Instruction, be it clearly understood, however, was merely given to the head. As to that great field of labor, the heart, it was left fallow, or worse than fallow, by the lady who undertook to train up children in the way they should go.

She had masters and governesses, and saw that they taught, and that the young ladies learnt. If a girl left her school a dunce, assuredly it was not Mrs. Crickieth's fault, and, accordingly, Alice Crepton, possessed of fair

abilities, and much application, gained knowledge, as her brother Evan had done, rapidly.

In the chill, ungenial atmosphere of the
schoolroom, she grew up, as orphan children do
in such places, tall and slight, and pale and melancholy. She was a thorn in Mrs. Crickieth's
side—for she would not submit, and she did
not rebel. Mother and daughter both felt that
some day that girl would get the better of them.
She never repined—she never said a word they
could take hold of—she only bore. Now, what
they wanted her to do, was to sink down submissive and broken-hearted, but in this she
would not gratify them. She was the strongest
girl in the school, and yet she looked the most
delicate; they knew her appearance did them no
good; they wanted to show her off as a sample
of their kindness to a pauper orphan, and she
was not fit to make a show or a sample of.
She obstinately and defiantly took side with the
weakest and poorest children; not in such a
manner as to give the mistresses a pretext for

interfering, but in her own provoking quiet way.
She had passed dreary years in the house and
hated it, yet was her spirit as firm as ever; firm
—yes, there was the rub—she was not fiery,
nor stubborn, nor impertinent, nor stupid—she
was only firm; they felt they could never make
use of her, and that was what they wanted.
"In a very short time," said Miss Crickieth,
"just when she might have been a saving to
us, and given me a little more leisure, she will
leave, see if she don't, an ungrateful wretch."

"She would have stayed if Bessie had lived,"
remarked Mrs. Crickieth, sententiously. "Bessie
is a bad business, Miss.Crickieth."

Whereupon that lady, who was always called
Miss Crickieth by her mother, because her
name was Sally and not genteel, looked down to
the carpet, and assented that Bessie was a bad
business.

"Not but what," continued Mrs. Crickieth,
"I think the child would have died any way.
The seeds of disease were in her; but still if

you had taken better care of her last winter, and
called in medical advice when she began to
sink so rapidly, I think the case might not have
been so hopeless."

"Bless me!" exclaimed the younger lady,
impatiently; "the brat is not dead yet, and she
may get quite well again, and at any rate will
linger a long time. Besides, that sort always
live."

"Do not speak of illegitimacy as 'a sort,'
Miss Crickieth," remonstrated her parent. "It
is immoral and unlady-like, and is a mode of
expression unbefitting your position in society.
Is the child's room in proper order for the
doctor to see her?—I hear his knock."

And Miss Crickieth replying in the affirmative,
both she and her parent smoothed their faces
into an amiable expression, and set their ruffled
plumage in order for the benefit of Dr. Duvard,
who was a young man, and a new comer—and
whom, it was an undeniable fact, that Miss
Crickieth wanted "to catch."

Had he chanced to be " physician in chief "
of Klicksturvyd one month before, it is probable
that Bessie Gay might have sooner been favoured
with medical advice—but the Christmas holidays
fell just when old Dr. Jones was negociating the
sale of his practice, and taking in his successor,
and he and Miss Crickieth not being on particularly good terms, and she and Bessie being on
worse, and Mrs. Crickieth being from home—
the child's cough was just " never mended,"—
it was let go on much as it liked, and accordingly
when Dr. Duvard at last came to see her—the
poor little thing lay in a very dreary upper room,
in a sadly precarious state.

" What a wretched life that little Gay has,"
some of the elder girls occasionally ventured to
whisper ; and what a wretched life she had,
Alice Crepton's heart indignantly echoed.
She was one of those unfortunate creatures who
seem to have no place assigned to them, in any
heart, or in any spot on this wide earth. She
was delicate—she was illegitimate—poor and

friendless. She had no mother living—she knew nothing of any relatives, of kindred of any kind—excepting of her father, who had placed her at Mrs. Crickieth's—left immediately afterwards for India—and after paying a few quarters regularly enough, had apparently forgotten her existence.

He was an officer—he may be dead, or he may be married, thought Mrs. Crickieth; and really not knowing what to do with the child thus thrown entirely on her charge, she kept her still an inmate of the select establishment for young ladies—on sufferance—and beat and half starved the little being who was patience and meekness—and all the cardinal virtues personified.

It was not in Alice Crepton's nature to see Bessie ill-treated, and refuse sympathy and affection to her.

The great, strong heart of the elder girl, which had grown brave and hard with trials, and afflictions, and anxieties of her own, which

had, through all trouble and grief, pined and
sickened for something to bestow its affections
upon, melted into tenderness, at sight of the
long-enduring child, and her troubles. " God
knows !" Alice often said, in after-life, " whatever of good is in me, I learned from Bessie
Gay ;" and where the little creature had learned
all she taught Alice, was one of those inscrutable
mysteries, which are sometimes presented for
our wondering consideration.

It was strange to see Alice, who knew so
much more than her child friend, taking lessons
from her, in that lore which is not taught by
the sage or the philosopher. Forsaken by all
earthly friends, Bessie had turned to her Great
Friend on High, and she talked to Watkyn
Crepton's daughter about the love of Jesus and
the joys of heaven, as if she *knew* both—not by
mere faith, but by something better, closer still.

A child's religion is always good : it is innocent of cant ; it knows nothing of theological
differences or polemical controversies ; it is not

an abstract idea, it is a tangible fact. If a child meet with a sceptic or an unbeliever, it does not hate the man for being unhappy, it only wonders and marvels exceedingly. It has no idea of justifying, or arguing, about its love for God and trust in Him—it would seem as strange to do so, as to begin to defend its love for its mother. Have you, dear reader, never felt all your superfine theories, all your divings into futurity, all your false bigotry and sectarianism, great profession and little faith, impatience, repining and unbelief, put to shame by the trusting Christianity of a young child? Have you never repented eating of that tree of knowledge, which sent our first parents out of Paradise—never wished you could unlearn some of that lore which leadeth to the devil, and acquire a little of the despised wisdom which bringeth to God? Oh! I have seen some proud hearts, proud in the strength of their intellects—proud of their pharisaical observance of man-created doctrines —proud of their own knowledge, and of their own subtlety of argument, turn aside abashed, at a few words spoken by a young child.

I have always thought that children, when they are religious—not saints, or casuists, or miniature bigots, or embryo missionaries—but children loving God, purely and simply after their own imaginative and innocent fashion, were better teachers of Christianity than an assembly of reverend divines. For religion is a matter of the heart, not of the head; and these little ones trouble not their brains about vexed questions and vehement discussions; they love God without pretence, in spirit and in truth—and of such, we are assured, " is the kingdom of heaven !"

And so, with her little hymns, and incidents from Scripture History, moulded into a sort of childish narrative, Bessie Gay taught Alice Crepton great lessons, that might never otherwise have found entrance in her heart; while she, in her turn, amused Bessie with more worldly stories, which she invented for her entertainment and gratification—and thus all unconsciously, in that dreary school at Klicksturvyd she was commencing the exercise of a talent, which enabled her in after-years to tell tales that the world was glad to hear.

That sort of genius for story telling, which seems to run in some families as a talent for music does in others, was already developing in her; but as yet she never dreamed of turning it to any other use than that of amusing Bessie Gay, to whose bedside she often stole in the dark (though forbidden to do so,) on winter evenings, when the child was lying in her desolate chamber, all alone.

But soon Alice felt even that companionship must come to an end. She could not get a satisfactory answer from any one about Bessie; but her own sense told her that her little playmate, the poor, little, suffering, neglected one, was going away from the clouds, and storms, and tempests, and sorrows of earth, to the green pastures, and bright flowers, and flowing waters, and ceaseless joys of heaven. She would have kept her with her though, for all that, if she could—so inconsistent and selfish is the human heart; and she grew perfectly desperate, when having crept to the sick room on the morning in question, she saw how much worse Bessie looked.

" Bessie, are you very ill?" she exclaimed. " Yes, dear, I think I am very bad indeed;" and the little thing made a desperate effort to sit up, and kissed Alice, somehow as she had never kissed her before: " Hush, there is somebody coming—run, Ally!"

But Ally was in no temper to run. She marched deliberately down the principal staircase of that rambling, ricketty, old-fashioned house, encountering on the way Mrs. and Miss Crickieth, and Dr. Duvard. The former bade her go to her lessons; but, disregarding this mandate, the moment they turned into the sick room, she sat down on the bottom step of the flight, and waited for the doctor's return from the sick chamber.

He did not remain in it very long, and Alice hearing them come forth, arose, and stood so as to face the man of medicine, as he descended the staircase.

"Miss Crepton, did I not desire you to retire to your studies?" demanded Mrs. Crickieth, in an imperious tone.

"Yes, ma'am," replied Alice; then, turning to Dr. Duvard, she said, "Please tell me about Bessie. Oh! Sir, is there any hope for her? Is she really so very ill?"

"She is dying," answered the doctor, in a subdued voice—"poor child, there is no chance for her at all!"

For an instant Alice stood pale and silent; then turning to Miss Crickieth, she exclaimed, with a violent revulsion of feeling, and sort of concentrated essence of hatred and passion—

"Well, if she dies, I say that *you* killed her."

Dr. Duvard looked from one to the other with considerable embarrassment.

" It's true," repeated Alice, before any one else could interpose a word—" Bessie Gay has been just as much murdered, as if Miss Crickieth had taken a knife and stabbed her."

" You bad, ungrateful girl," spurted out Miss Crickieth ; but Dr. Duvard interrupted any further observations she might have felt it necessary to make, by hastily bidding all parties good morning and descending the stairs with somewhat unprofessional celerity. Before he reached the hall-door, however, he heard the accents of violent altercation—then came a muffled sound as of blows—and while he was hesitating whether to return or not, a loud crash and cry decided him ; and recrossing the hall almost at a bound, he darted up a couple of flights to the landing he had just left, where he found Alice lying under a heavy flower-stand, which had, apparently, been thrown over on her—as all the pots and plants were scattered about, shivered to pieces, broken in bits.

"She pulled it over on herself," commenced Miss Crickieth, who absolutely stood appalled amidst the ruins—"she pulled it over on herself—if you don't believe me, ask mamma—"

"It matters very little, madam, how the accident occurred," said Dr. Duvard as he lifted the stand, and stooping down raised Alice from the floor—"but it is likely to prove a very serious one — shall I carry her into the drawing room?—her arm is broken, and must be seen to directly."

"Better carry her up to bed," said poor Mrs. Crickieth, who wished to have the drawing-room clear for visitors. "I will show you her apartment."

"She must be quiet, madam," said Dr. Duvard—passing on the threshold of one of the dormitories. "I will just set the arm here, and then, if you please, take her into the room with my other patient. I saw three small beds there."

Though Dr. Duvard said "if you please," he spoke with a tone of authority, and accordingly Mrs. Crickieth felt herself constrained to consent to this arrangement; but as the doctor, after depositing his burden on a couch, was leaving the house to get the necessary bandages and other medical etceteras, the lady stopped him with—

"I hope, Doctor, you will attach no importance to Miss Crepton's slanderous remark—she and poor little Miss Gay were much attached, and—'

"Excuse me, madam, but you really must not detain me now," he said. "Every moment is precious;" and he hurried past the stately school-mistress with a lack of ceremony and civility which annoyed that portly individual not a little.

"You see what your temper has brought on us, Miss Crickieth," said the elder lady; and Miss Crickieth having nothing to oppose to this excepting the statement that it was not she who upset the stand, she beat an ignominious re-

treat from the scene of action, and sulked in the
drawing room for the remainder of the day.

And having most skilfully set his patient's
arm, and seen her deposited in a bed near to
her little friend, Dr. Duvard took leave of Alice,
after giving her strict injunctions not to move;
and in answer to a question from Mrs. Crickieth
at the door, said—

"With care and good nourishment I think
you may keep the child alive some days, or even
longer—there is no immediate danger, it all
depends on the care you give her."

And on the strength of this, Mrs. Crickieth
forced Bessie to swallow some bad wine and
weak beef tea, which made her desperately sick,
and towards evening she got much worse; but
as the schoolmistress was accustomed to these
fluctuations, and had moreover the Doctor's
assurance that no immediate danger was to be
expected, she told Bessie when she came to see
her before retiring to rest—that if she made
haste and got to sleep, she would be much better

in the morning; after which fiction and a look
at Alice, who resolutely refused to speak to her—
she took away the candle and left them in darkness and coldness alone.

Yes—they were alone—the sick and the
dying each occupying the little narrow bed in
which one, or perhaps both, must soon close
their eyes, never on this side time to open them
again.

It did not suit Mrs. Crickieth's convenience
to permit a servant to sit up during the night
with the invalids; sitting up at night involves
sleeping during the day, and that, of course, was a
thing not to be thought of; besides which, the
burning of coals and candles would have been a
useless waste of both, seeing that the girls
were not likely to want anything; and " if they
do," argued Mrs Crickieth and her daughter,
with equal sense and feeling, " an hour or two
can't make much difference."

Then, as to the governesses; how could
they leave the other dormitories, and how could

they attend to their pupils the day following a
long winter night's vigil? And with respect
to Mrs and Miss Crickieth they hated to be
near sickness of any kind, and silenced their con-
sciences by murmuring that the two invalids
"would be better alone—the doctor had
said so."

Better alone, than with their delectable
society, no doubt—but was it good for one in
the commencement of a fever, with a broken
arm, to lie there with parched lips and a
burning brow, tossing as much as the pain of
her limb and head would let her, without a kind
hand to straighten her pillow, to moisten her
mouth with even a draught of water, to soothe,
by a single womanly attention, her sick bed?
and was it well for the other—speeding to that
world where no shadow of the cares which
cloud this, enters; was it well for her to gaze
forth on the frosty stars and cold still sky,
thinking of how soon she would be dead, and
not have one to tell her to be of good cheer—
to be comforted?

True, Mrs Crickieth affirmed that Alice's arm "would not signify, as she was naturally so strong," and that Bessie might rally yet—at any rate, last for a considerable time. But the former was experiencing the agonies of a fractured bone, and the latter felt her hours were numbered on the earth.

What she saw written on the winter sky, God only knew, but at last the tears coursed slowly down her cheeks. They may have been wrung from her young heart by the memory of earlier and happier days, when her mother was living, and she was loved by some one. It may have been that thoughts of that parent and of the father, who had deserted and left her to a miserable fate, harrowed her soul, and that in that last musing before death, the whole of her sad but short life, with its agonies, its humilia-tions, its bodily and mental pain, passed in mournful review before her. No human being, at any rate, ever knew what caused those tears to steal down her young pale face—whether the near prospect of death affrighted her—whether the memory of life pained her—whether the absence of friends, kindred, home, health, kindness, affection, afflicted the sensitive and overburdened heart of the dying child.

It made very little difference then, for she had almost reached that stage of mortal suffering in which sympathy avails not. It was, indeed, very nearly the same what she thought about, only no one ever knew what she felt and imagined that winter's night, when she looked with her large, liquid melancholy eyes up at th frosty stars for the last time.

When next they gleamed forth in the coronet of night she had passed to that shadowy land, which human vision cannot reach to—which is only partially visible to the keen swift glance of faith,; which may lie amongst the orbs of heaven; which may soar above them or stretch away into some immeasurable distance beyond that vast azure field in which the hosts of light keep eternal watch,

sentinels pursuing one steady round, obedient
to the mandate of their Great Maker, who set
them there and appointed unto each a necessary
task, the nature whereof man can merely
theorize upon and speculate concerning, till he ex-
changes time for Eternity, this little speck of
creation for the infinitude of space.   Down on
the frosty stars, she may, if such things be
permitted, have looked in spirit, perhaps, from
the High courts of Him who maketh of this earth
His footstool she may have surveyed the wonders
of His hands, the works of the most High but up
again—she never looked—never with eyes dimmed
by traces of earthly trouble to the bright lamps
that He hath ordained to shine on this scene of
mortal trouble, till their destined purpose, which
it is beyond our knowledge to divine, is accomplished—till it pleases the Lord and Ruler of
all, to shroud their brilliancy in the mantle of
darkness for ever.

But by degrees the quiet little being resigned
herself to what she knew was coming—the grave

was dark, very dark—and her childish heart recoiled from it—but life had been to her a very terrible scene. Heaven was bright she believed, and so, after her own simple fashion, Bessie began to prepare herself for it.

For hours her fellow-sufferer heard her repeat at intervals the little hymns and psalms she could recollect, together with such verses of scripture and prayers as seemed appropriate. It was touching to hear that meek sad voice whispering forth those holy things, and Alice's pillow was moistened by the tears the sounds wrung from her.

The moon at last arose and shone into that little dreary chamber, and in after-years the survivor never saw those cold beams lying like death-shadows across a floor or a wall without remembering Bessie Gay's last night on earth. They always in after-days made her shudder— the horror of that scene never left her heart.

The moon rose higher and higher and climbed up into the centre of the heavens, but as the Queen of Night became more full and lustrous, the child's voice grew fainter and fainter, and the verses and the hymns became more inaudible, and sometimes a sob reached Alice's ear, who could not comfort Bessie because her own grief was choking her; but still, whenever one of those mortal tremors seized the sufferer—whenever her poor fluttering heart shrunk back with horror from the idea of death and judgment and eternity—the dying child murmured, as if to comfort and reassure herself—"The wicked cease from troubling, and the weary are at rest."

Through life the sound of that young voice whispering those words rang in Alice's ears—in the silence of night they floated to her—by the quiet fireside they obtruded their sad presence—in the bright hour of morn they seemed echoed to her soul.

Something like a groan at last burst from the lips of the child, and the words "Water, Alley, water," caused the latter, regardless of her own bodily pain, to arise and bear the water-jug to the sufferer's couch; there was no cup, nor glass, nor mug, to pour the clear cold fluid into. She raised it to Bessie's lips and then took herself a long, deep, refreshing draught.

"Don't leave me, darling," said the child— "don't, for a minute or two"—and Alice sat down on the edge of the bed, and Bessie clasped her arms about her neck.

"You have been very kind to me," she murmured, "very; I forgive them all—they have starved and beaten me to death, but 1 forgive them all; I am very happy to go. I think," she added after a pause, and looking once more up at the sky—then, laying her head on Alice's shoulder, she said faintly, almost as if reasoning with herself, "Yes I am quite sure I am happy, because I am going at last to 'where the wicked cease from troubling, and the weary are at rest.'"

Alice felt the chill hand become stiff and cold —she laid her back on the pillow—poor Bessie was at rest.

She never dreamed of rousing the household

or of summoning assistance; the child was dead, no one could alter that fact, and if she could have done so, she would scarcely have wished it, for Bessie was happy now, she felt certain. So with her one uninjured arm she straightened the emaciated limbs, closed the blue-veined eyelids over the stony eyes, crossed the little hands on the cold bosom which had suffered and borne so much, and left her to her dreamless sleep.

She called no one—Mrs. Crickieth might not like to be disturbed, would probably scold her for having risen. It was time enough to tell her in the morning; no one could alter the past nor mend the present; so the survivor went back to her bed, and lay there within a yard of the dead.

She did not weep, nor sob, nor moan, but she lay there for long, still hearing the child's last words murmuring faintly; and as the moon went down and the stars grew dim, an intense horror, born partly of fever and partly of fear, came over her soul, and she shook, and quivered, and trembled to think she was alone almost in the dark with a corpse. What she dreaded she could never exactly tell, but the room seemed filled with coffins, and graves, and spirits, and bones, and skulls; the bed appeared to be whirling round, and Bessie's arms felt still to cling cold and stiff about her neck. She tried to push them away, but it was all in vain, for they still remained, and Alice quivered with terror as she endeavoured to convince herself it was all imagination.

For an instant she lay quiet, trying to calm herself—but the faintest pitty-pattying as of light feet, caused her heart to throb again, and the next moment she saw, or fancied she saw, what froze her very soul—something black, indistinct and shadowy, on the white sheet which covered the dead child's body—the hands and head alone being exposed.

She knew right well what it was.—It was no illusion—it was real, living—but still she could not move, or speak, or stir.—She was chilled to her very heart's core.

This bringing home of the mysteries and horrors of the churchyard to her very side—this premature desecration of the body—this sight of that which the flesh would fain believe unreal—kept her mute and spell-bound. She tried to rise and drive away the horrible intruder, but she seemed glued to her bed—the sheets and blankets—all scanty, though they were pressed on her like a ton weight, and kept her there with eyes rivetted on the dark creature so faintly revealed to view by the dim glimmering light of a winter's morning.

Oh! To have been able to stretch forth her arm, to fling something at it—to chase the animal away—but she felt like one in a nightmare, unable to move, or act, or stir, but compelled to feel, and see, and know all.

At length the spell was broken. A slight cracking, crunching sound, echoed through the apartment, and fell on the ear of its living tenant, and as though some band had been burst—some string snapped, shriek upon shriek, each louder and shriller, and more agonized than the last, rang through the house and brought assistance.

The person who first entered with a candle, saw something large and black spring from Bessie's body and disappear. Alice was in a raging brain fever, and could tell nothing about it for weeks after—but the mangled flesh and broken fingers of one hand told the whole story, that was hushed up as speedily as possible, the evidences of which were shortly covered from sight by the lid of a coffin.

It was never repeated excepting in whispers —those who had seen the body never cared to talk about the frightful occurrence; but no one in that house ever forgot till the latest hour of life, the night when Bessie died, and the shrieks which roused them from slumber, and brought them to the death chamber.

CHAPTER IV.

WHEN next Alice Crepton, weary, feeble, and exhausted, opened her bodily and mental vision to a consciousness of surrounding objects, she found herself lying in an unaccustomed bed in a strange room.

Nothing about her—not a solitary article in the chamber—not an object she could see reminded her of Mrs. Crickieth's establishment, and weak and astonished she shut her eyes for a few minutes and tried to remember what had happened—to recollect where she was.

All in vain—true, her memory brought her back, in due course, a faithful summary of events prior to her illness—faint at first—shadowy and unsubstantial were the forms that came flittering across the retina of her mind's eye—but, by degrees, a stronger light was flung on the page of the past, and she read it clearly up to a certain point. There she stopped and opened the doors of her outward senses—half expecting to find she had been mistaken—that previous impressions must have been parts and parcels of the delirium that had reduced her to a mere skeleton —to a creature so feeble and emaciated, that she lacked strength to raise herself in bed.

But no! let the dreams of fever be vivid as they will, there is, after all, no mistaking sober realities, joyful or sorrowful, for them ; and accordingly it was with a sigh of unspeakable relief that Alice assured herself *this* was, at all events, no illusion—no trick of the imagination, but an actual and blessed deliverance.

She was quite awake and in full possession of

all her senses, and yet she was not in any room of Mrs. Crickieth's house. Thank God for that, at any rate, she thought.

To that feeling of devout gratitude succeeded another—the former one of intense wonderment and curiosity. If not there, where could she be? and the very tired eyes—tired with even the little exercise she had given them—set out on their travels again, on a journey of discovery round the room.

It was not large—she saw that, and it was neither a very abundantly nor a very handsomely furnished one, though it had enough furniture in it, good and plain of its kind. There were two chairs—yes, she had mastered that fact, and was sure there were no more; and the dressing table, with its snowy cover and looking-glass, stood between her and the window; then she detected a wash-hand-stand up in one corner, and making a more general survey, she found the windows and bed-curtains were of white dimity, edged with green fringe—that a little table,

ornamented by a phial or two, occupied a convenient position at her elbow—there was a fire—
there were a few spring flowers grouped together
in a vase on the chimney piece—the floor was
not entirely carpeted, and that was all. Having
swallowed which stock of valuable materials,
Alice shut her eyes again, and commenced
chewing the cud, making the most out of everything she saw and remembered, and trying to
dovetail the disconnected fragments together.
It was but very sorry patchwork she made of
the pieces after all.

First she reviewed—by way of getting a sure
starting-ground for her ideas—all the events
with which the reader has already been made
acquainted. From the memory of Bessie's death,
however, and the circumstances attendant upon
it, she recoiled with horror, taking refuge from
the appalling phantoms that came up before
her in the thought—half dream-like though
it was—of a sweet kind face and a soft
gentle hand that had seemed ever near her during

that. illness, from which she was but just recovering.

Then what had that illness been, and who—
eyes there was another vague recollection worth
trying to get into tangible shape—who was the
man, the tall dark figure she dreamt lifted her
out of bed and carried her down, down to unfathomable depths where she lost herself ?

Who could he be? Was it Evan, who had
unexpectedly returned and borne her off in
triumph to a home of his own? Was he
married—would he soon come into the room?
The loving heart began to flutter, and the poor
exhausted body to tremble at the bare idea. She
strained her eyes on the door by which alone he
could enter till they ached for very weariness, until
with the sheer force of pain and feebleness she was
compelled to close them again; but the imagination, always more vivid when outward objects
are shut out from sight, would not be quiet, and
kept busying itself in picturing the joys of that
long-deferred visit in colours so radiant, in words

so cheerful, and tender, and affectionate, that tears at length began to steal down the invalid's cheeks—great big drops that slowly trickled on till they were tenderly and gently wiped away by some one.

With a slight start, Alice looked up. "Oh! I thought it was Evan," she murmured in a tone of disappointment.

"Who, dear?" and the speaker bent down low to catch her answer.

"Evan, my brother, are you not his—"

"I am Mary Duvard," interrupted the lady, anxious apparently to prevent her talking, "and now lie still and keep yourself quiet. Thank God you are better, but you must not be excited nor allowed to exhaust yourself."

"Yes, but Evan—is he here?" She had so deluded herself into the belief that he must be, it was hard to think otherwise all at once; and so when her new friend assured her he was not, Alice fretted like a child over the demolition of the air-castle she had pleased herself by building.

In vain Miss Duvard tried to soothe her—in vain she gave her wine and jelly, and various other things, to counteract the effects of what she considered a fit of nervous exhaustion.

The sufferer took all she was bidden indeed, but obstinately and determinedly cried on, swallowing port diluted with tears and beaten-up eggs flavoured with brine. She did not seem able to stop weeping, and so at last her nurse did the wisest thing she could do, under the circumstances, viz., let her sob herself to sleep, pillowed on the breast of as gentle a woman as ever walked the earth and beautified it.

When she awoke she was much better, and appeared to have come back to consciousness, with a fairly insatiable appetite. Chicken broth and beef tea, sago, arrowroot and light puddings, were devoured by her with a relish which betokened an absolute craving—a hunger and thirst for food and stimulants.

"I don't know how it is," she said some few

days after, "but I feel just starving. I want to do nothing but eat. Mutton broth seems to give me no strength—might I not have a little meat, I should like it, and some porter?"

"Ah, you little glutton!" said Dr. Duvard, who had been watching with the most intense delight every mouthful she swallowed—"I shall put you on a short allowance soon!"

"Shall you?" answered Alice, as she drained the wine glass his sister gave, and returned it to her with a gay smile. "Then I shall make interest with Miss Duvard for not less than two pounds of meat a day, and bread and wine in proportion; I think I must be eating now for all my life before. I never knew what hunger was till I got sick."

"Till you got well, you mean," said Doctor Duvard; "and now lie down again, and go to sleep."

"I don't do one single thing, but eat and drink, and sleep," remarked Alice, settling herself down on her pillow, like a person who was thoroughly comfortable; " and I find them the pleasantest occupations I ever had, and I think I am very happy, and want nothing nor nobody more but Evan."

" Well, we must try to find him, when you get better, so shut your eyes, and make haste about doing so. Good-bye for the present." And Dr. Duvard held out his hand to her.

Heaven knows what impulse seized the girl, but flinging her arms suddenly around him, she kissed him in a very unschool-girl-like manner, and exclaiming—" Oh, how kind you have been to me !" fell to sobbing on his neck.

Very gently he unclasped her hands, and laid her back on her pillow; then with a strange sensation quivering through his frame, and swelling at his heart, he went silently out of the room, and down to his own especial sanctum, where he found that during the course of that dangerous illness and tedious convalescence, he had been fool enough to fall in love with his patient.

Now lest it should be for one moment imagined at Alice Crepton was of that school of young ladies which Sheridan Knowles, I believe, first made fashionable, and who are in the habit of taking the initiative in *affaires de cœur*, I beg it to be distinctly understood, that when the little emancipated slave made such a frightful attack on Doctor Duvard's heart, as the one above recorded, she had no more idea of doing anything improper than the old musical amateur, who was so delighted with the singing of a young debutante, that he stepped on the platform and hugged her like a bear, to the extreme amazement of a hall full of spectators.

He was pleased, and Alice was happy; neither intended any harm—neither thought of *les convenances*. In the case of the girl, a torrent of happiness had been poured too suddenly upon her, and swept away in its impetuous course every feeling but gratitude and thankfulness to those who had thrown the first gleam

of sunshine, she had ever known, across her path;
the string of misery had been drawn so tight,
that when it snapped, Alice's closed-up heart
started open to a width which seemed to take in
and embrace every feeling of ecstacy that human
nature is capable of experiencing. Have you,
dear reader, never seen a man — bronzed
whiskered, travel-stained, stoop down, and in
his wild raptures at the sight of home, kiss
even the old house-dog that greets him at his
father's threshold?

It was something of the same uncontrollable
sensation as that which seems as though it would
choke the wanderer if he did not give vent, in
some way, to it, that induced the foolish weakened girl to sob out her happiness on her new
friend's shoulder; and had he taken the act as
a man with a disengaged heart would, poor Alice
need never have turned to his sister with a
piteous exclamation of—

"Oh, dear, Miss Duvard! what have I
done?"

"Done?—kissed Charles, that's all!" was the reply.

"And I should not! oh, I meant no harm, indeed I did not. I am very sorry, but I could not help it, I was so happy, and I have been so miserable; do not be angry, don't think me—"

"What?"

There could not be a doubt but that Mary Duvard was laughing; and Alice Crepton felt so mortified and vexed, that she buried her face amongst the pillows, and cried till she was tired. Poor, foolish child, she had all unconsciously stretched out her feeble hands and gathered some of the fruit of the tree of knowledge — that fruit which once tasted, leaves some of its mingled sweet and bitter on the palate for ever after. She did not know, it is true, of what she had eaten, but the effects produced were the same, for all that.

Love! how strangely and variously it comes to each man and woman, each boy and girl amongst us. What a very simple thing it seems to talk about! What a very fatal dose it often proves when swallowed.

God help us! True love forms only one chapter in the lives of any; and yet, still how it seems to influence the incidents of every future page in the lives of all. What a strong light, dark or sunshiny, as the case may be — it flings on every line, on every word, written throughout the remainder of the mortal missal. But Alice knew not the name of the fruit she had tasted. Her school-life had been too practical; her girlhood too sad for her to be learned in that lore which makes children wo-men before their time, and sets half our fem-nine population husband-hunting, almost ere they have entered their teens.

The sublime art of flirting did not come pat to her as it had done to poor Judith Renelle, in the days that were gone. The mysteries of love-making, and the signs and tokens of that inexplic-able disease, were things which had never chanced to fall under her range of observation; she had heard her companions talking about beaux, and husbands, as silly school-girls will, more's the pity, and she had mentally and audibly denounced love as "stuff," as people do who mistake the shadow for the substance, and who know, moreover, nothing about the actual nature of the substance; but on love in the abstract, as a thing which might come to herself as a sensation she should one day experience, Alice had never speculated; and accordingly, when the disease touched her so slightly, she did not know what to call it, and cried like a frightened child.

"Well, I am sure," she said at length, defiantly raising her head from the pillow, and looking round at her friend with very red and swelled eyes, "I don't see why I should not kiss him —for I am very nearly as fond of your brother as of mine."

Miss Duvard, who had a "little affair" of her own on hand at the time, did not think it necessary to explain, and her silence on points of propriety will shew you, most patient reader, what a remarkably sensible woman she was. She was discreet, and only answered Alice's implied question with another.

"Did any one ever say you should not, dear?"

"No—no—but he thought it, I know he did. I wish you would go and tell him I am very sorry, and that I will never do it again."

"What! when you do not see why you should not?" queried Miss Duvard.

"I don't—but he might, and indeed I don't suppose I ought to have done it—because you see—only, only, he was so kind—and I was so happy;" and by way of an explanatory finish to this lucid sentence Alice took to weeping again in a manner which alarmed Miss Duvard so much, that she threatened to go down and fetch her brother up if she heard another sob.

"You will bring on a fit of hysterics, Alice," she said, authoritatively, "and remember, we cannot do with that.   I do not know what you

are crying about, and neither I believe do you—
and I think you are a very silly little puss. Now
go to sleep as Charles told you. Recollect, you
must obey orders."

"Tell me one thing first, and I will," pleaded
Alice. "I do not know yet how I happen
to be here—how is it?"

Miss Duvard paused for a moment, then
answered; "Charles brought you."

"But why? how? did Mrs. Crickieth make
no objection?" persisted Alice.

"He brought you here because he thought
you would never get better there—as to the how
—he carried you across here one night wrapped
up in blankets; and with regard to your last
question, I believe Mrs. Crickieth did make ob-
jections, which, however, he overruled."

"How did he overrule them?" enquired the
girl.

"That he can tell you better himself, when
you are quite strong, meantime go to
sleep."

"And you have nursed me through it all, and watched me, and fed me."

"And dosed you and scolded you," finished Miss Duvard, "which last part of the performance I shall repeat if—"

But Alice creeping close up to her, interrupted the threat that was coming. Very lovingly were a pair of wasted arms put about the slender neck of the doctor's sister. Very trustfully did a pale, thin cheek nestle against hers. Very pleadingly and gratefully did Alice Crepton draw nearer, nearer to her still, and make Mary Duvard understand that she felt towards her a depth of affection and thankfulness that might never be spoken in words.

"You don't think your brother is angry then?" Alice whispered, just before she settled herself to sleep.

"Angry, dear child, why should he be? you have done nothing wrong."

"Are you quite sure of that?"

"Quite;" and so on the strength of this assurance, the invalid fell into a tranquil slumber.

And Charles Duvard, what during all this time was he thinking about, in the room which, for want of a more appropriate name, he called his study? he was thinking, as men have done before and since, and will do again, of conquering himself—of nipping his 'folly in the bud—of concealing the best feelings of his heart in order to leave her free; of being that impossible thing, in love, and not shewing it.

He was thinking, as all poor, true-hearted men do think, more of the girl than of himself, more of her happiness than of his own—more of her battle with poverty than of his struggle with himself. He saw it was impossible they should marry, for he was poor as a man without private means who gave advice and drugs gratis to the lower classes, and got very little money from the rich, could be.

Dr. Shaw (Charles breathed anything rather than a blessing concerning him under his breath,

as his name came into his mind) had deluded
him shamefully into purchasing a practice which
was really not worth twenty pounds a year.   He
had spent nearly all his money in buying the
confounded right to kill the Misses Breffni and
all Mrs. Crickieth's young ladies ; and now the
Misses Breffni were scandalized at his improprie-
ties (as they were pleased to term the threats he
had used to bring Mrs. Crickieth to reason, and
the fact of his having carried Alice out of the
house of her " lawful guardian"), and the school-
mistress had audibly announced her intention of
sending for the future to Llangollwernt for advice,
instead of trusting any case in the hands of *that*
Dr. Duvard.

He had already determined to leave Klicksturvyd, and with the little money still remaining, try
to push his fortunes elsewhere—as for his practice, it was not worth twopence-farthing—he
knew he could never get anything back for it
unless he swindled somebody as Shaw had
swindled him, and short of gold though he

was, he did not feel inclined to better his condition by roguery. No, his fixtures, stock, and furniture, were the only commodities he possessed out of which he could hope to make money at Klicksturvyd; as for other places, he had his brains, and knowledge, and patience; and could push his way, surely he could? others had done so before—why not he? why should he alone be fainthearted, broken-spirited, unsuccessful?

Almost despairingly, he got up, and pacing the limits of his narrow chamber, began to consider his past and his future: his great struggles and many disappointments; the numberless efforts he had made to woo the favour of that fickle jade, Fortune, and the malignity with which she had persisted in dealing him blow after blow.

Marry! Why he was an absolute pauper! should he drag Alice down with him into an abyss of poverty, care, trouble, anxiety? should he try to win her heart, or rather encourage her

to lose it, and then marry, and make her
miserable? would it not be more honourable,
nobler, better altogether to leave her free and
unfettered, and to go on his way striving to
forget her?

What were they to one another, that he
should feel his heart almost break at the idea
of relinquishing her? what did he know of her?
What was it had induced him to beard Mrs.
Crickieth in her own den, for the sake of that
girl which had compelled him to save her life;
which had made him take an interest in her,
such as he had never taken before in any human
being? Ah! it was very well a few days previously to call it pity, but Charles Duvard felt
now, that it had all along been a germ of the
plant called Love. But he would crush it! he
would stand to what he had said to Mrs.
Crickieth, that he wanted to remove her solely to
save her life; and that if the schoolmistress
persisted in refusing, and fatal consequences
supervened, he would demand a coroner's inquest,

such as ought to have been held in Bessie Gay's case, and swear he believed Miss Crepton was killed through " wilful neglect ;" he would do his duty to the girl, faithfully and fairly, spare no expense in hastening her recovery ; and then, why then they must part for ever. His sister was to be married almost immediately, then he should leave Klicksturvyd and Alice? What Alice was to do, remained a sublime mystery to him : only, he determined he would not make love to her ; that he would crush the feeling out—trample it under foot—or better still, still keep it a precious memory in his heart to make him miserable and melancholy for life ! she should be his patient, nothing more.

It was all very well for Doctor Duvard to determine these things in private ; but Charles Duvard found it very difficult to act up to his resolutions in public.

He was compelled, professionally, to see Alice frequently : and it was not long ere the marked change in his manners, and the studied coldness of his address, began to produce an injurious effect on the girl's health and spirits; she began to feel herself *de trop:* to think of the trouble she had been—of the expense she must have caused: she commenced to refuse wine and eschew porter; no persuasions could induce her to touch jellies—nothing but the very plainest viands would she eat.   She was getting so strong, she said, that she did not require cooking up; but her pale cheeks and languid step told a different tale.

"What on earth, Charles, possesses you?" demanded his sister, one day: " don't you see you are throwing Alice back?"

"I am!" he repeated; "how do you make that out?"

"Oh! with your stiff manners and grave face, and short sentences: the girl thinks we are growing tired of her, and getting impatient of the long illness; really I wonder at you, that you have not more consideration—just come and look at her;" and Mary dragged her brother to a room where his patient reclined in an easy chair, near the fire, looking so wretchedly ill and woe-begone, that the Doctor's heart smote him; what a change had come over all of them since the first days of her convalescence—what a restraint and reserve was visible now in every sentence : how very shyly Alice spoke to him— and how very much like a physician, and little like a friend he seemed when he addressed her.

The room looked cosy and cheerful by the bright firelight, as he drew a chair near the fender and sat down.

The curtains were drawn, and the tea-table was pulled up to the fire, Mary was gone to see after some domestic matters : the candles stood on it ready to be lighted, and the young man, as he glanced around, wished to Heaven he could afford to keep on even such a shelter, for then he might have asked Alice to share it with him ; he the rich Rector's pauper-son—she the poor Curate's still poorer daughter.

" You do not seem to be gaining much

ground," he said, addressing Alice, after a brief
pause given to dangerous musings, " I fear you
are not any better."

" I am afraid not," she answered, a flush
coming up into her pale cheek, " but as the
weather gets warmer I shall get stronger. It
has been such a long cold dreary winter."

Had she found it such all through? the
thought just flitted across his mind as he drew his
chair closer to hers in order to feel the feeble pulse.

" Humph !" he said as he removed his fingers
from her wrist, " you do not eat enough."

" I am never hungry," she answered.

" You must take beef tea and wine as medicine," he replied. And having issued this royal
command, in a tone from which there was no
appeal, he relapsed into silence, and then ensued
one of those dreadful pauses which usually seem
premonitory symptoms of the speedy death and
burial of conversation. In this case, however,
the symptoms proved fallacious, for having at
length mustered self-command enough to ask

Alice what she was thinking about, he was somewhat staggered by her reply.

"I was thinking of my mother, and wondering
if she be still alive."

"Still alive!" repeated Doctor Duvard in a
very bewildered manner, "why should you
suppose she was? I thought you were an
orphan: Mrs. Crickieth told me so."

"Yes, I am an orphan in one way, but not
in another," replied Alice simply. "You see
my father married much above himself, and then
when he died, she left us, and I have never seen
her since."

"Good Heavens! you don't mean to say that
she deserted you?"

He had let the words escape his lips without
reflection, but next moment he repeated his
indiscretion; for the word "desertion," although
it really meant nothing more than she herself
had stated, seemed to put the matter in a
stronger light before her—to touch some painful
chord that had hitherto remained mute—and

covering her face with her hands, Alice Crepton wept aloud.

"What a cursed fool I am!" exclaimed the young man. "Miss Crepton—Alice—do stop crying. I did not mean what I said—forgive my hurting your feelings. I do think I am the most confounded ass that ever——"

"Walked on two legs," replied Alice, laughing at his energy even through her tears. "No, no, Doctor Duvard, you were quite right. You called the thing for once by its true name, for she did desert us most cruelly and heartlessly. I will tell you all about it," she added, "and then perhaps you and your sister would think what I ought to do. You know my father was the son of a farmer, but a neighbouring gentleman educated him, made him study for the church, and got him temporarily a very good appointment as secretary to Sir John Lestock, who he hoped would be able after a time to give him a living. There he met our mother, Sir John's daughter, and they ran away together, and then the Baronet renounced her, and refused to do anything for him. He got a London curacy however, and I believe had every prospect of advancement at the time of his death, which happened when we were very little children. I remember it perfectly, though," she added in a lower tone.

"After he was gone," continued the girl, "my mother wrote to Sir John, who consented to receive her back if she gave us up altogether and resumed her maiden name, and become as though she had never been married, and so she chose to go home again, and left us. I have never seen her since. I don't think she cared about her children."

Alice paused as she uttered the last words, in a manner which seemed to imply that she was debating the point within herself. For a minute or two she looked musingly into the fire, but all at once raising her eyes, and finding her companion's glance fixed on her with a peculiar expression, she hurried on with her tale, speaking rapidly, almost confusedly.

" So we were sent back to Wales, to my dear old grandfather. I could not tell you or any one half the worth of that good grey-haired man.   His sons and daughters thought we were intruders, but still, spite of opposition, he took us to his heart and his home ; fed and clothed and cared for the desolate children thrown entirely on his love ; and then, for fear others might deal hardly with us after he was gone, he paid for our education in advance, and settled us comfortably, as he thought, in places where we could complete our education, and he rendered competent afterwards to earn our bread, if not easily, at least respectably.

" Had he lived, things might have gone better with us ; you know Doctor Mills' death left Evan without a friend, and had it not been for you, I should by this time have found a resting-place in Klicksturvyd church-yard.   You see, I am very desolate, and I want to know what it would be best for me to do—write to my mother and see if she will do anything to help me ; and then, if she fail, look out for a situation, or strive to get one by myself, without asking aid from her at all ; what ought I to do ?"

" Marry me !" thought Charles Duvard, but he had sufficient delicacy and generosity to refrain from uttering the words. It took him but a moment to survey her actual position, and to see that if her mother could be induced to receive Alice to her heart, that it would at once raise the girl to a much higher rank than he had any right to aspire to.

Then he felt it would be wrong to fetter the girl by an engagement to him ; and still more wrong to advise her not to apply to the baronet's daughter. With a fierce struggle he conquered himself, and answered—

" If I were you, I should write to your mother ; state how you are situated, and request assistance. Do you know where she lives ?"

" With her father ; some place in London ;
I don't know the exact direction. Evan told
me it once, but I forget—St.—St.—"

" James'," suggested Doctor Duvard.

" Yes ; I think St. James' Square ; is there
such a place ?"

" I believe so : but I can easily ascertain Sir
John Lestock's address. You had better write
to-night."

" There is one thing," objected Alice, " she
is always called Miss Lestock : and I should not
like to put that on my letter. It looks as if I
slighted my father and his name—and he was so
fond of us, and so good, and so kind."

For a moment the Doctor hesitated. Here
was sufficient objection to knock the whole matter on the head at once ; but he put the temptation aside, and replied—

" If you will write the letter and direct it as
you please, I will forward it in such a way as to
ensure its delivery. Now that matter is settled,
let us have tea. I have just been advising our

invalid to write to her mother, Mary," he added, as his sister entered. "Miss Crepton tells me she is still living—"

Miss Duvard looked enquiringly at her brother, and then doubtingly at Alice.—" I think," she said after the Doctor had explained the state of affairs to her, "that Alice would be happier with us, than at Sir John Lestock's; and I for one don't approve of the letter at all."

"Yes, but I cannot stay on with you," interposed Alice, with a flushed cheek and moistened eye; "I think I have been a burden and a trouble to you long enough. God knows you have been kinder to me than any stranger ever was to another before; and have made me feel happier and more at home, than I ever thought I could feel anywhere but with Evan. But I am now getting strong and well again, and must chalk out some plan for my future. Even if my brother were in England (and I don't know where he is, or whether he is living or dead), I should still like to try to do something to support myself. I know a good deal of one sort and another, and I believe I am quite as well fitted to be a governess as any Mrs. Crickieth ever had. I can teach children, indeed I have taught them, and if my mother do nothing for me, I should like to go to some quiet family, where they would not want great learning and accomplishments, but just about what I have got. If there were even no salary at first, I should not care in the least, providing I could be only happy and contented. Do you know of any one, Miss Duvard, who would have me? I think I should get well quicker, if I had some settled plan for the future. Do you know any kind lady requiring a governess?"

"Yes; there is a cousin of ours in want of just such a person as yourself; and I really think, Charles," she added, "the mild climate would be of service to her. Only, Alice, I don't like to part with you."

"And I don't like to leave you, in one way, though I do in another," cried the girl, putting out her hand to the lady : who, during all this time had kept her eyes steadily fixed on her brother's face. "But you see, Miss Duvard, I must go ; it is right ; and then, perhaps, you will send me a letter occasionally, and—and— you have been so kind to me, and I am so grateful, and though it is not likely I shall ever be able to shew you how much I feel about it ; still I will try to prove my gratitude, sometime or other."

"Should you like to prove it now ?" asked Miss Duvard, laughingly, and yet so earnestly, that her brother roused himself from a reverie, to listen to the answer.

"Yes ; more than I could tell you !"

"Come here, then, and I will show you," Miss Duvard said, drawing the girl's ear close down to her lips : "Go, and tell Charles, that you love him !" she whispered wickedly.

A burning blush came over Alice's face, and brow, and neck. She could not speak, or move, or recover her self-possession at all.

"What did Mary say to you ?" asked Doctor

Duvard, coming up close beside her, as his sister, shaking her finger at him, left the room.

"Oh! I don't know—let me go!" she exclaimed, striving to extricate herself from his detaining grasp; but he would not let her go— he had a few words to say to her. For he had found out there was a grand middle course open for him to pursue; that convenient medium between matrimony and separation, which usually entails torment, and vexation, and doubt, and anxiety: and accordingly he told her how he loved her—how he was situated—how he would leave her free, if she wished it—and free, whether she wished it or not, providing her mother consented to receive her back.

He told her he could not marry for a time; but that he should work with double zeal, looking forward to being united to her. He spoke of a year of struggle, and then a life of happiness; and said a host of things, such as men in love do say, and sate down in brief, (now he had taken the matter in hand) so determinedly before the citadel of Alice Crepton's heart, that she was forced to surrender at discretion.

And so the end of all Charles Duvard's good resolutions, was, that Alice Crepton and he exchanged promises of unalterable affection, vows of unswerving constancy; and that in place of marrying at once, like sensible Christians, and taking the best and the worst of life together, from that time forth, in each other's company; they were so very simple, or as they thought, so extremely sensible, as to agree to wait, and add another instance to the number already extant in the world, of the folly of those pre-eminently absurd and ridiculous things called—long engagements.

CHAPTER V.

MRS MAZINGFORD, for weeks, had been "not at home." Day after day, that was the standing order in Mayfair: when she was out, why then she was out; when she was in, she was "not at home!" Morning concerts and west-end drawing-rooms knew her not—she never now appeared in the ring. Her carriage was scarcely ever visible, except occasionally whirling off towards Brompton. She "received," as usual, once a week; still sat at the head of her husband's dinner-table; still came, proud and haughty, to aristocratic balls; still occasionally occupied her box at the Opera; still sneered down com-

pliments, and nipped incipient flirtations in the
bud. She had not retired altogether into private
life—she only kept her mornings sacred from public invasions.   In vain Mr. Mazingford remonstrated, argued, commanded, insisted—Judith
either replied with that look which so irritated him,
or else moderately and dutifully stated, that to one
of the Blood Royal she would not appear, unless
it suited her own special convenience to do so.

And Judith, as usual, kept her word.   In the
evenings she was his slave; in the mornings,
she was her own mistress—or rather, in the
mornings, she bowed her neck under the yoke
of two stern masters, labour and duty—and
worked at their bidding, ceaselessly.

How she did work, her pale cheeks began,
after a time, to tell; and then medical advice
was called in, which, dreaming not of the mental
exertions she was making, confessed itself virtually at sea, by ordering change of air, and
horse exercise.   The former, it was not convenient to Mr. Mazingford she should have just

then ; the latter, it did not suit Mrs. Mazingford to take ; so the lady went on getting paler, and thinner, and more interesting-looking every day, as befitted an authoress.

For Judith was writing. Although the world did not know it, and her husband suspected not, she had taken up her pen again, with as holy an object, as righteous a purpose as ever was entertained by woman. She was spinning her brains into books, to give sight to her sister. Fame she wanted not, her art she loved not—but money she required, and money she was determined to have.

So Judith, after years of idleness, took out her papers and manuscripts once more, and commenced writing, what she had never previously attempted, a novel.

There was the old style still, but it was polished—the old, strange, wild ideas crowded her teeming brain, but they came forth from it moulded and fashioned into form, by the ever-improving hands of time and experience. Her

mode of expression was still bald and abrupt;
incidents came too suddenly down upon the
page; and her book resembled a succession of
startling scenes, rather than a narrative of actual
occurrences. She still lacked the power to throw
in the softening touches that fascinate a particular class of readers. She wrote of life, as
she had found it, hard, practical, calm in its
joys, exciting in its anguish. She could tell of
the soul's strife, but she could not speak of its
rest. With firm and steady hand she stretched
the outlines of characters, that were fierce, alike
in their hates and their loves, in their gratitude
and their vengeance—violent in anger, ungovernable in sorrow—who knew no medium, whether
of grief or of pleasure, in attachment or dislike
—who were fond immeasurably, or false in-
conceivably—who were not ordinary men and
women, but devils or angels. It really seemed
as if she could not draw any character for the
original, of which she had not dived into hell, or
ascended into heaven. She had no chance to

write a really good book, there, in the middle of
London, with her mind distracted about her
sister—with her heart sick, at the pomps and
vanities of the mighty Babylon—with her whole
nature revolting against her position—with her
bodily powers sinking, with her brain in a
whirl!

A natural story could scarcely have been expected
from herself or her surroundings: and yet the
tale was a striking one, striking, from its very
disdain of established customs; from the very
ignorance the author displayed of all the rules
and regulations that fetter the literary hack, who
has ambled along the path of popular opinion,
till he has no thought, nor care, nor idea of his
own—till he has come to live, and move, and
have his being at the instigation of a liberal
publisher, and nod of an old-established review.

Judith had yet to learn one of the best tricks
of her trade, and therefore writing was a torment
and a vexation to her. It was no trouble to

sketch a scene here and there; to take a part of
the whole, and finish that off like an act in a
melo-drama—but to string those scenes together
on a good strong thread of narrative; to put in
explanatory chapters, and tell a story through
connectedly, and work out a purpose gradually
and naturally, was insufferable—Judith could
not stand it. She flung all her characters, pell-
mell, on the stage; made them effect improbable
things in an impossible manner, and then left
them all to do, what the Manchester clergymen,
who married people in scores at a time, did—
viz. " sort themselves !"

A rapid ride to Brompton, a half-hour spent
in a darkened room with the dear invalid, a few
hopeful earnest words of affection and trust of
her speedy restoration to sight, and Judith
hurried away again back to her lonely chamber,
where she wrote, as those alone have ever written,
who go on blotting foolscap against time, and
who work with their pen as labourers do with
their spades, as sempstresses do with their

VOL II. H

shattered, into port, were coming down on Judith
even then, but she could not wait their advent;
and in all pride and confidence, launching her frail
skiff upon the stream, beheld it come back to
shore again and go down amongst the breakers.

Mrs. Mazingford knew little of life—that is,
literary life—or she never would have gone in
her carriage to ask payment for a novel.

Rich authors are considered, in publishing
circles, able to afford the risks attendant on
bringing out a new work themselves. Justly or
unjustly as you, dear reader, may please to consider it, they are compelled, except in very rare
instances, to pay for their whistle.

Her shrewd sense, however, soon told her
what the eminent firm of Noxley and Mobelle
were driving at. They talked of per centages—
but Mrs. Mazingford shook her head—of subscribing a hundred and fifty copies amongst her
acquaintances. On which suggestion Judith put
a somewhat peremptory veto at once—of clearing
expenses—a plan, the lady said, was not to be

thought of; and then the polite publishers, being at their wits' end, held their tongues.

"I really do not see what we can do, madam," remarked Mr. Noxley, after a dreary pause, during the continuance of which he had waited for Judith to speak, which, however, she did not.

"Can you think of any plan, Mr. Mobelle?"

Mr. Mobelle was unable to aid his partner's imagination.

"Publishing, you see, is a very uncertain affair," remarked Mr. Noxley sententiously, "and therefore, in a general way, we do not care to take the entire risk of a new work, by an author as yet unknown to fame (Mr. Noxley bowed politely.) We like to be secured against any great amount of loss by a well-known name—that is, a name which will sell a book, or else by a certain number of copies being taken by the writer. Now, amongst your numerous connexions, Madam ——."

"Excuse me, sir," interrupted the lady haughtily, "but I do not choose to take my book begging about the world. I would rather go and ask each of my acquaintances to give me thirty shillings at once. It would, to my thinking, be a much more straightforward and independent method of effecting my object."

" It is so usual a thing," commenced Mr. Mobelle ; but Judith again interposed, with—

" I think . I might bring this matter to a satisfactory point at once, and so save you and myself much trouble, by stating first, that though you think me rich enough to waste money on publishing, I am not; second, that I don't want to publish under my own name; and third, that I wish to receive remuneration for my work. You imagine I am a fashionable lady, writing for fame. Read my manuscript, and you will find I am a woman writing for money. I do not say my work is good, but it is not a ' fashionable novel:' it is not what you think it. I do not know much about how such things are managed, or what terms authors usually propose to publishers, but I should like you, if you would not consider

me too troublesome, to read over my MS., and
then say whether you can offer me anything for
it or not. As to publishing on my own account,
it is a thing not to be thought of. If I were
rich enough to do that, I should never attempt
writing. Will you oblige me by looking at the
book?"

Messrs. Noxley and Mobelle were willing to
do anything except pay money, and accordingly,
after bowing the lady out, they placed the MS.
in the hands of their "reader"—as literary
advisers were called in those days—who laid it
aside for two months. At the expiration of
which time he condescended to listen to various
hints uncomplimentary to his punctuality, and
went through it in a couple of days.

"We regret, madam, that the result is unfavourable," remarked Mr. Noxley, with that
unvarying urbanity which is enough to drive a
rejected author out of his senses. "The reader's
report says, that although there is much merit in
the work it is scarcely complete enough as a

whole to ensure extensive popularity, and accordingly, although we should be glad to meet your
views, if possible, we fear in this instance it is
impracticable.   If you felt inclined to contri-
bute even a portion of the expenses—but, really
trade is so bad, and we require to be so very
careful, and the market is so overstocked,
that——"

"You decidedly refuse to accept my book?"
finished Judith, who felt her love for the bantling
rise as other people looked coldly on it.

"Well, on the terms you propose—Yes,"
said Mr. Noxley, with wonderful directness for a
publisher.

"So be it then," said Mrs. Mazingford, as
she haughtily rose, gathering an Indian shawl in
heavy folds about her figure.   "The time will
come, gentlemen, when you may be glad to take
a manuscript from me on any terms.   Good
morning."   And Judith beat a retreat, all colors
flying, from the publishing office, and left the
firm, thinking what a beautiful termagant she

was, and what irritable folks all the literary genus were to deal with. Ah! they did not, they could not see how—leaning back in her carriage—the tears rained down Judith's face. They beheld the waters of her soul troubled, and a momentary gleam of anger flashing across the surface, but it was not given to them to know of the deep, dark pools lying sullenly below, because of the existence of which the woman's heart was breaking.

She had staked her last throw on the result of that day's interview, and lost. They were leaving town next morning, going back to the old Welsh hills, far from Lillian, oculist, publishers, every thing and person she wanted to be near. She was looking forward to rent and taxes, and payment of bills, and all sorts of nightmare horrors. She had relied, as new beginners will, on literature as an El Dorado, and she had seen, as new beginners do, her castle crumble in the dust.

From publisher to publisher she went, finding

difficulties increase at every step, excuses multiply, her patience diminish.

The season was over—they had made arrangements for the next—they were open for tales not novels—they thought historical romances took better than domestic narratives. Mr. S. did not think there was any use in his looking at the novel, because it did not embrace theology. Mr. L. considered it fair to tell her he never paid for first productions. Mr. M. wanted a story for his magazine, but hers would be too long for that purpose. Mr. T. wondered she attempted novels—" quite gone out," he said. " Nothing will go down but biographies and travels." Mr. A. suggested bringing it out in one volume, if she would pay down fifty pounds as her share, and undertake the advertizing. Mr. D. said he published nothing but tracts, and advised her to go to Messrs. Noxley and Mobelle—the first in the novel trade in London—" but then," he added, " they never take a book unless a sum be paid down with it: their name is such an advantage to a new author. Libraries buy books that they publish, which, if sent out by any other house in the trade, would not be given shelf-room."

"In fine, Mr. Mason, I am wearied," said Judith, as she laid her manuscript down on the desk of a man, with muddy complexion and lank black hair, who was newer to the trade than most of those she had tried to talk into buying her book. "I have been to, I should say, a dozen places to day, and had 'no' for my answer at every one of them. I do not ask you to say 'yes;' but let me leave the book with you, to look over at your leisure. I really cannot take it away," she added, seeing him hesitate. "Write me what you think of it, and whether you can do anything for me—I want money—and, therefore, it is useless to propose my contributing anything to the expenses. Please send your answer to that address." And she wrote Miss Ridsdale's direction on a card, and handed it to him. "Any note or MS. left there for Mrs. Gilmore will reach me safely. And Judith looked so pale, and ill, and care-worn, that the publisher, in a state of intense bewilderment and surprise, found himself promising in a most reckless manner, to read six hundred pages of blotted manuscript through, and hoping he might be able to accept it.

"I never saw so beautiful a woman," he muttered to himself, as he beheld her drive off in that very carriage which had settled her chances with the eminent firm of Noxley and Mobelle: "it strikes me though, there is something very incongruous between herself and her statements; and then, this confounded manuscript! What a fool I was to promise to read it—I should like to see what she has to say for herself, though;"—and dimly conscious, that what the lady thought fit to write, would be worth perusing, Mr. Mason locked the parcel up in his desk, and laid it aside, till he should find time to look over it.

Meanwhile Judith and her husband went back to Wales, down to the old prison-house amongst the trees, where Mr. and Mrs. Mazingford received such shoals of visitors, that the wearied woman finding that London had been the quieter home of the two, began to pine and sicken for the comparative solitude of the great metropolis again. The old oppressed feeling came back to her heart; and under the shade of the elms, and oaks, and sycamores of Wavour Hall, she felt as though she were suffocating.

Her husband had spendthrift young noblemen, and fashionable ladies, and manœuvering mothers, and eligible daughters, and captains, and honourables innumerable, always in the house, where he expected Judith would entertain them hospitably, and she did her best; with her whole heart she tried to be courteous and kind, to hide the canker-worm, and appear content and happy—but it was all in vain. Curious eyes were always on her; curious hands were for ever baring the secret sorrows of her home; unfeeling tongues were eternally opening up old sores, causing imperfectly-concealed wounds to bleed afresh—and then last, and worst of all, her husband treated her rather like a servant than a wife—as he might have taken out a handsome horse, and compelled it to show its paces, for the gratification of his vanity, and the amusement of his guests, so he exhibited Judith to the motley throng that lodged in his house, and wandered through his gardens and pleasure-ground. He contrived to let everybody into the secret, that if Judith had been plain, he would never have conferred the distinction of Mrs. Mazingford upon her. He made every one comprehend he was first, she second; he rich, she poor; he possessed of influence, she innocent of position; he lord, she slave; he the magnificent sultan, she the English Georgian, whom he had bought for her fine points, but with whose general conduct and disposition he felt by no means satisfied. In fine, he did that which it is hardest to a high spirit to bear, he

made other people despise her—and he compelled her to despise herself. Often in the
mornings, ere any of the fashionable visitors were
stirring, the old porteress saw Judith come
down to those grim, hard gates, and press her
beautiful face against the bars, like a caged
animal.

It was not till after Christmas that she had
much leisure to think of literary matters; but
when at length Mr. Mazingford's guests departed, and a brief lull succeeded to the whirl of
carriages and hum of human voices, she began
to wonder why she had not heard from Mr.
Mason, and wrote to enquire the reason.

Days passed away and no answer arrived,
until, unable longer to endure the suspense in
idleness, she took up her pen again, and commenced scribbling short tales and magazine
articles, and all sorts of odds and ends.

The "author fever" was coming upon her
once more, as it had done in the days before her
father's death, only with tenfold virulence and

hopelessness. She was now growing impotent to resist its force—for it is one of the curses of literature, that once let the knack of composition take root in the human soil, and it spreads as inveterately through the whole system, as the parasitical convolvulus does in a neglected garden.

In the dreary winter mornings, when her husband was out — in the somewhat more cheerful evenings, when county meetings required his presence, or dinner parties, at the houses of roystering old squires who voted ladies a bore, secured his absence from home, Judith sat in her own especial sanctum writing. She had no female friends, no confidantes, no feminine attachments or amusements. There was not a solitary chord in her nature but was out of tune; not a string which, if she ventured to touch it ever so slightly, did not vibrate forth a discord. All the pulses of her heart beat one strain of misery; all the best feelings of her soul had been turned into gall and bitterness.

When in public, the powers of her mind were directed to one object, and that was to conceal— when in private, her efforts were employed to enable her to forget—writing aided her in this endeavour; nothing else did. If she read, her thoughts wandered from the page before her, to another, printed in blacker colours on a back-gone leaf of her memory. If she played, the occurrences of *that* night came up to her mind's eye—the wail of death always mingled with the song—and often, when she was thrilling forth her richest melodies at the bidding of her husband, for the amusement of his guests, and the gratification of his own inordinate vanity, she felt as though the contrast betwixt the past and the present, the honour, and depth, and truthfulness, and intensity of the love she had flung from her, and the shallow flimsiness of the thing she had taken to her, would kill her.

"I cannot sing any more," she often said, when the resistless tide of old recollections came

swelling up and mingling with the strain, " I
should be very happy to do anything you like,
but much singing pains me :" and then her husband frowned, whilst his guests noticing the
brilliant colour in Mrs. Mazingford's cheeks,
and the way in which, almost involuntarily, she
laid one hand on the white lace that covered the
front of her dress, thought amongst themselves
that the lady was not strong, and compared
notes, and pitied her when they went away.

" Take my advice, madam," said an eminent
London physician to her on one occasion, " take
my advice, and do not sing at all."

He was a man who had grown white haired
in studying the diseases of frail humanity; and
many would have asked him what he meant;
Judith did not, however.

" Mr. Mazingford wishes it," she replied, " and
I am his automaton. *I* do not sing, he does
—I am merely his instrument."

" Should you wish me to tell him I consider
it injurious to your health ?"

"No, thank you," said the lady, laughing; then seeing one, who had really meant kindly by her, turning away as if he were annoyed, she laid two fingers on his arm, and detaining him for a moment, added—

"You have wished to serve me, doctor, and I have seemed ungrateful. You misunderstand my case a little, however; for the pain I complain of is not a bodily but a mental one. I can command it less when I sing, than any other time; and when it catches me too tightly here,"—she pressed her hand upon the place— "I stop."

He looked earnestly in her face, as she paused, and gravely shook his head, but said, like a wise man, never a word.

"I know what you are thinking," she resumed, "and in one respect you are right; there is consumption in our family. Very few of its members have ever lived to be more than thirty, but you need not be afraid of its touching me; Death is very choice of his victims, and has no fancy for the unhappy."

" And are you so ?"

" Oh, fie! doctor—with all your skill and telling by the colour of my cheeks, and the look in my eyes, and the expression of my face, that the taint was in my blood—have you been so blind as not to detect the other plague-spot? Did you never hear the world, which is always liberal of kind remarks, say that the Ridsdales were born with flirting natures and diseased lungs?   Don't you know that there ˙never was a woman of our family yet who did not manage to curse her own life, and that of two or three others?   Don't you know, have not you seen, that my indifference is grief, my coldness remorse, my life a burden to me?   She spoke the last few words passionately, but immediately after added, in a quieter tone—

" If it should ever please God to give me one hour's rest, and peace, and happiness, I believe I shall then die—but till then you need not be . uneasy ; for I am strong, very strong, much more so than most people, much stronger than you imagine. So don't speak to Mr. Mazingford about the singing; it does me no harm, and it—pleases him."

Judith dropped the two last words out as if she had substituted them hurriedly for something else she had intended to say, and turning aside from the physician, went on her way just the same as heretofore—singing when she was bid, remaining silent when she could, and hating, and loathing, and detesting everything.

Fly to accomplishments, as a resource against painful memories and recent mortifications! other women might, perhaps, but not Judith Mazingford; and in her own private apartments there was no piano, no harp, no music-book, no easel, no embroidery frame. Sing! she had enough of that when there was company at the house. Draw! she had sketched Wavour Hall, at her husband's request till she knew every effect of light on the old pile, every stone, and crevice, and crack, and tree about the edifice. Study foreign languages! no; Judith would not make herself the delight of badly-shaved counts and questionable Italians. Take to the woman's resource—needlework—what was the use, when everything came ready-made to her hand?

" I will write," said the wayward heart, "for it is the only thing I have in me or on me which belongs exclusively to myself—with the joy or the sorrow of which a stranger intermeddleth not ;" and as she had spoken, so she did.

Thus the fever of old came back, never again to leave her. Thus, pen in hand, Judith Mazingford beguiled the weary hours of her sojourn at Wavour Hall. So in solitude she perfected herself in an art which some think comes more by nature than by practice—so by patient perseverance she improved herself in the cunning of her trade—so she came to feel at last the strength and the power of her genius—so she whiled away the time till the period arrived for Mr. Mazingford to resume his parliamentary duties.

And with a sort of throb of expectation she accompanied him to London, buoyed up with the hope of seeing Lillian almost well again, for good news of the patient had been forwarded by Miss Ridsdale every week, and during the whole of the dreary journey up to town she looked forward to that little gleam of sunshine at the end. "If Lillian be but restored to sight," she mentally exclaimed, "I will try to be happier and more contented than I have been, and I will take to literature as a permanent occupation, and we will enjoy the fame and the profit quietly together."

So she come to London building air castles by the way, and the first news which met her, proved that Lillian was worse!

CHAPTER VI.

LILLIAN was worse. Judith crushed the note containing the intelligence up in her hand, and then, half-passionately, half-despairingly, threw it into the fire. There was more in it than appeared, she knew that by a sort of instinct, for those who have once suffered can tell, almost intuitively, where sorrow is lurking. Out of great grief the heart learns great fear—and in those signs which prognosticate coming evil Judith was well versed. Yes, there was something in Miss Ridsdale note that implied more than it said. Mrs. Mazingford stood gazing at the paper as it blazed up the chimney, wondering what could have caused the sudden change— what could be the matter with Lillian—what she ought to do.

It did not take Judith very long to decide the latter question. The house was all in confusion, the servants had not yet fallen into their accustomed routine. Mr. Mazingford was gone to his club, and had left word he should not return for dinner, as he had to look in at the Commons. Judith paused to take no refreshment—she was in a perfect fidget of anxiety, but rapidly changing her travelling dress, she sent a servant to call a cab, and was soon *en route* to Portman Square.

"Wait," she said, briefly to the driver, as the oculist's door opened for her; and in another moment found herself in Mr. Chamberton's presence.

He was sitting alone in his study, and seemed surprised to see Mrs. Mazingford at so late an hour. He certainly had not known she was in town, and was totally unaware of the cause of her visit; but over and above this, Judith's quick eye detected a certain coldness and restraint in his manner, which she jotted down in a mental note-book of facts, and subsequently drew conclusions from—wrongly.

"I arrived in London two hours since," she said, in answer to a remark from Mr. Chamberton, to the effect that he had not expected to have the pleasure of seeing her so soon, "and found a note from Miss Ridsdale lying for me. She says my sister is worse."

"She is not so well as I could wish," acquiesced the oculist.

"When did you last see her?" pursued Judith.

"To-day; and if my advice were followed, the operations should now be suspended for a considerable period. The sight of one eye is re-stored, and if you and she can rest satisfied with that, for the present, I think it would be better."

"Why?" demanded his visitor.

"Because confinement is injuring her general health. You know it is not the restoration of one organ alone which we must consider, but the preservation of all. Now there can be no question but that your sister's state is at present far from being a satisfactory one, and, therefore—"

"What is the matter with her?" interposed Judith.

"That I am scarcely doctor enough to tell you," he replied. "In fact I never perceived the alteration in her looks until to-day. The change has been a sudden one, and was so marked that I considered it more prudent not to attempt commencing on the other eye till I had told you my opinion and consulted with you on the subject."

"Have you no idea what is wrong?" asked Judith, with that straightforward and determined pertinacity which was so strong a trait in her character. "Have you no idea—?"

"I have not," he answered; "the evil may be purely temporary, caused solely by the long confinement and the number of operations needful; for in all my experience, I never had before so difficult and tedious a case. It may be that the alteration in her appearance, and decline of her general strength, have been gradual, and that, absorbed in the question of blindness or no blindness, I have not noticed what has been going on under my eyes, day by day, and week by week. If this view of the case be the correct one, there is little or nothing to be apprehended—for perfect repose and strengthening medicines will soon bring her round again. 1 hope it may be so; but—"

"Well," exclaimed Judith, "why don't you go on? Why don't you tell me the worst at once?—Do you think I am a child, Mr. Chamberton, that you keep me in this agony of suspense? Whatever you have to say, for God's sake let me hear it at once."

She rose as she spoke, and, in the intensity of her anxiety, drew close to the oculist's chair :—

" If there be danger," she persisted, " there is

no time to lose. Speak to me as you would to a man; what do you think about Lillian?"

"I think she is in a very critical state," he replied; "I may be wrong—but I fancy the local disease she has had from childhood, is now taking some fresh and unusual turn. You know more about how that disease has always affected her than I do. Her aunt told me it has made her through life an invalid, and perfectly agreed in the propriety of calling in first-rate advice."

"Has she done so?" demanded Judith.

"She said she should prefer delaying a day or two, for the purpose of consulting you on the subject."

"What folly!" ejaculated Judith.

"But now you are in town," proceeded Mr. Chamebrton, "I should recommend that no time be lost in the matter."

"There shall not be," was the prompt reply— "whom should you advise me to consult?"

"Mr. Huron is the first in London for those

sort of cases; you cannot do better than secure him for one—but it might be well also to take the opinion of some first-rate general practitioner—say, for instance, Dr. Gresham or Dr. Staley."

"You think the case a desperate one, I see;" and, spite of all her powers of self-command, Judith turned so ghastly pale, that the oculist rose, and led her to a chair.

"You had better sit down for a moment," he said, gently, but Mrs. Mazingford would not.

There was wine on the table, and she stretched out her hand towards it: "May I take some?" she said; "my strength has all deserted me."

The look of misery which came over that woman's face, as she stood there trying to recover her self-possession, never afterwards faded from the oculist's sight. Tears he had often seen flow; expressions also of violent pain and vehement grief were no novelties to him; but this sudden breaking up of a resolute spirit, this wordless revelation of the intense anguish of a strong heart, was new to the man of sad experiences; and whilst he was considering in what form of words he might administer comfort to such a case, Judith had conquered her sudden weakness, and was speaking again—

"Where does Mr. Huron live? Please give me the addresses of all three."

"Can I not send for you?" asked Mr. Chamberton.

"No, thank you," she said—"I will go myself. If they are not at home, I can get some one else. I shall be quicker than any stranger could be—Pray do not detain me."

He wrote the place of abode of several clever doctors on a card for her, and then conducted her to the door.

"You have not your own carriage," he said; "may I accompany you?"

"No—yes—" she answered; "that is, if it would not be encroaching too much on your time."

" If you will trust it all to me," he ventured
to suggest, " and return home—you seem quite
exhausted."

" Home, without seeing Lilly !" she exclaimed;
" no, no, I must go; but I should like you also
to see the doctors, and tell them what you have
done; it might be more satisfactory—a clue and
guide, you know."

They were in the cab by the time she finished,
and driving off to Park Street. Mr. Huron was
out, and Dr. Gresham engaged; but they just
caught Dr. Staley as he was entering his own
house; and dismissing the slow vehicle they had
hitherto put up with, the physician told his
coachman to turn his horses' heads towards
Brompton, whither they all proceeded together,
talking earnestly about the patient as they
went.

" How is Lillian ?" were Judith's first words
to her aunt.

" Rather better," was the reply.

"Thank God for that," she exclaimed; and rushing past Miss Ridsdale, ran up stairs to her sister's room.

"Lilly, my darling," she cried—

"Judy, I can see you."

It was more than Judith could have said; for the whole room swam before her, and a mist of loving tears came over her eyes, as she heard the dear voice again. Someway, however, she got her arms about her sister's neck, and then falling on her knees by the side of the bed, sobbed as though her heart would break.

"Judith, dear, what is the matter?" asked Lillian, in a frightened voice.

"Nothing—only I'm so glad. God bless you, Lillian darling, you will get quite well again now I am near you. Let me see how you look;" and Mrs. Mazingford wiped her eyes, and drew Lillian's face round to the light. It was fearfully altered, and almost with a shudder she laid the dear head down on the pillow again.

" Lilly, how long have you felt ill ?" she asked.

"Two or three days.   You know I am never very strong.   I was so low this morning, I think Aunt Milly was almost frightened, but I told her it was nothing to signify, and neither it was."

" You will make haste and get well now for my sake," Judith said, hanging over the bed as if she were loth to bring in the doctor—" Tell me again that you feel better.   Your voice does not sound weak, Lilly."

" No, I am not weak," said the invalid.   You shall take me out to drive, and stay with me a few hours every day.   I think I have been moped, and that has made me fanciful."   She paused suddenly.

" Where did you feel pain then, darling?" asked her sister.

"Oh ! it's the old pain, just for a minute. You know, Judith, though I am cured of my blindness, still I can never be anything else than a cripple and a poor useless being, so don't tease about pain and illness now, but tell me what you have been doing, and how you are, and when you came up."

"I will tell you all in a little time," Judith answered, "after you have seen Doctor Staley. I was afraid you were very poorly, and brought him down with me. May he come in?"

"Yes," said Lillian resignedly; "but I don't see the good of him. I don't want any doctor, Judith, but you."

Mrs. Mazingford inwardly prayed that it might be so, as she went in search of the physician. "I do not think," she said, "I will go in with you—I am too anxious—I cannot help showing her I am afraid. You will tell me the best or the worst, Doctor, at once."

"You may rely on me, madam," he answered, and passed into the sick chamber.

The minutes seemed interminable till he returned. Judith could not rest. She walked up and down the room—she drew back the curtains and looked out into the night—she went and listened at the door—she flung herself for a moment on a sofa, and the next started to her feet.

"Well?" she said to Dr. Staley, who came slowly creaking in.

"I am happy to inform you that there is no immediate danger to be apprehended."

"No immediate danger! Do you think there is any?"

"Well, with care and proper medical treatment, I hope not; but these cases are always difficult to manage, when once they take an unfavourable turn. May I enquire if there be any hereditary tendency to decline in your family?"

"Yes; but you don't think—"

"The fact gives us a clue," he answered, "and knowledge of it will enable us to treat her case more effectually. It is her local disease which must first be seen to, and then I should advise—a change of climate. If perfectly convenient to all parties, I should like to meet Mr. Huron here to-morrow."

"And meantime?" asked Judith.

"That prescription ought to be filled up, and the dose ordered taken every three hours. It will give her strength, which is what she principally requires at present. I think you will find it do her a great deal of good. If you give her the draught as directed—part immediately, and more whenever the pain returns, she will experience considerable relief. Good night— or I beg your pardon—I had forgotten the fact of your not residing here. May I have the pleasure of giving you a seat back in my carriage?"

"No—thank you," said Judith, "I must remain with my sister, at least, until morning. You think there is no immediate danger?"

"Certainly."

"And you hold out hopes of her ultimate recovery?"

"Most decidedly."

And the doctor pocketed his fee and departed followed by Mr. Chamberton, over whose manner the same constraint Judith had formerly noticed had come again.

"He shall be paid within eight and forty hours," she mentally resolved, judging him, spite of all his kindness and consideration, harshly. Oh! woman, bending by the bed of sickness, counting the dreary hours as they drag slowly through the watches of the night, planning and devising for the future, thinking drearily over the past—soured, embittered, unsubmissive, irritable, and impatient, bless God, that from His high Throne in Heaven he judges you more leniently and righteously than you judge others. You think you know the world thoroughly, Judith Mazingford, and are able to read the hearts of the men and women in it—but, ah! me, far as you have proceeded in your study of human nature you have learned but half the lesson of life. You can guess at pretty nearly all the bad which lurks in the hearts of your fellows, but you have yet to become acquainted with the good. Yes, sit there for the present if you will, nursing all uncharitableness, but there is a time coming when light shall be let in on the dark bitterness of your heart, when the proud spirit shall be bowed to meekness, and the determined will to submission, and the restless soul be calmed to peace.

Sit still though now and muster your courage for a while, for before that period arrive you will have to weep scalding tears, and murmur earnest prayers, and suffer great trials, and make mightier efforts than any you have ever previously dreamed of; for it is through the scorching furnace of adversity, and endurance, of disappointment and endeavour, and mental and bodily anguish, that such almost unconquerable natures as yours pass to the promised rest.

.

CHAPTER VII.

LILLIAN was better! Through the long night Judith sate beside her, and when morning came that was the report she was able to give. The medicine had done its work, and all danger was past.

"You will go to bed now, Judith," said Miss Ridsdale to her niece, for whose dreary vigil there had not indeed been any necessity. "You will go to bed now, and try to get a few hours' sleep."

"No," was the reply, "I must return to

town at once. Tell me, aunt, why, when Lilly was so much exhausted yesterday, did you not send for a doctor?"

"Because I had no money to fee him, Judith," answered Miss Ridsdale. "I have not sixpence left out of your last remittance, and the landlord wants his rent, and bills are accumulating, and———"

"Give me a list of all that is owing, including Mr. Chamberton," interrupted Judith. "I know I have kept you very short, but I could not help it, for I have been short myself. We must give up this house, however, and Lilly will have to come back to me as soon as her health is sufficiently restored for her to be moved. Let me have the amount of the debts at once please, —I want to take the knowledge to town with me."

Judith laughed as she uttered the last words, but the sound did not delude her aunt.

"How are you going to pay these bills?" she asked.

"Oh! leave that to me—I shall manage," returned Judith quickly.

"But how, dear, how?" and the lady laid a loving and anxious hand on her niece's shoulder.

"With money," returned the other lightly; then added, in a different voice, "and as I have none of my own, I must get it from Mr. Mazingford someway. I told you long ago I could manage, and I shall do so. I have contrived very well hitherto, by saving and pinching, but now I must go to the fountain head. Don't detain me—let me have the bills at once."

"Judith, are you doing right?" demanded her relative, almost sternly.

"Heaven knows I have striven to do so," was the brief reply; "but do not keep me here talking, for I must see Mr. Mazingford this morning, and if I am not quick, he will have left home."

Very reluctantly Miss Ridsdale withdrew her detaining hand, and suffered Judith to depart. "I cannot make her out," she murmured, as she beheld her niece walk down the road to the nearest cab-stand. "Mr. Mazingford will never be willing to pay all those accounts at once. Oh! Judith—poor misguided, self-willed child. I wonder—and I fear."

She did not wonder or fear one-half so much as Mrs. Mazingford, however, who racked her brains, on her way back to London, for some form of words likely to move her husband to give her the sum she required. She had staked, as many a one has done before and since, her every hope on a single throw, and lost. She had built upon her books, as a means of paying every debt; and literature had proved to her a barren field, producing nothing but stinging-nettles, and thorns, and thistles. She had incurred enormous expenses, which she had no means of meeting—she wanted money to fee fresh doctors—provide comforts for her sister—preserve her life. Had it not been for the necessity of obtaining fresh funds, she would have let the old debts take care of themselves, have desired

all bills to be sent into Mr. Mazingford, and
braved the worst; but she dared not meet a crash
just then, for the danger was not over, and she
feared, as Judith Mazingford twenty-four hours
previously would not have credited herself that
she could have done.

"Gold!—oh, the accursed thing, that I sold
myself for—and cannot get now, when I most
want it.   Gold! I cannot go to ask him for it.
Drive to Mr. Mason's, —— Street," she suddenly exclaimed to the cabman; "I will try
that—and if there be no hope there, I will go to
Mr. Mazingford.   But what is the use of Mr.
Mason?—even if he bought the book and paid
me to-day: the utmost value of the thing would
not pay a tithe of these bills. You need not drive
to Mr. Mason's," she said, by way of a wind-up,
and commenced bracing up her courage for what
lay before her.   "If he refuse, there are my
jewels—his, I suppose, he calls them—they
shall go, without a moment's hesitation, but
then there may be a difficulty in selling them;

however, it must be done"—and, covering her eyes with her hand, she sat, pondering and pondering, till the vehicle she had hired drew up at the door of her husband's house.

"Mr. Mazingford has not yet gone out?" she said, inquiringly, to a servant; and being informed he was in his library, she proceeded thither without delay.

"Where have you been?" were the first words he uttered.

"With my sister," was the equally laconic rejoinder.

"Confound your sister!" rejoined Mr. Mazingford; "I tell you, madam, I won't be so treated. I will have you conduct yourself like my wife, and not be going out at all hours to all sorts of places, without my permission. I say once for all, I won't have it: driving about London in a cursed rattling cab, that has perhaps taken its last fare to the fever hospital. Don't think your movements are kept secret from me; remember you are now Mis. Mazingford, and not the only daughter of a beggarly Welshman. Remember—"

"Remember, Mr. Mazingford, to whom you are speaking, if you please," interrupted Judith; "remember that I have good blood in my veins and that you have not; remember that if you have money, I have birth; remember that I am the rarest piece of workmanship you ever purchased; and pray do not forget, that although I am your wife, you have never paid for me yet."

She looked so superbly handsome, standing within a few feet of his chair, and surveying him with a look of quiet contempt, that Mr. Mazingford felt the old sense of his inferiority come over him. He gazed up in her face, and tried, with staring steadily at it for a moment, to beat her down; but Judith was not to be beaten down—she had come there to say something, and she said it, after taking him all in, as it were, with one sweep of her scornful eyes.

"Mr. Mazingford," she began, "should you like there to be peace between us?"

"It is your own fault that there has not been," he replied.

"Because if you would," pursued Judith, "I will tell you on what terms I am ready to put my neck under your foot, to let you be my master, to sink myself into your slave. Shall I tell you?"

"As you please."

"Well then, I do please: but first I must remind you again of the fact, thát you owe me a debt, which you have never yet even proposed cancelling. Do you recollect the conversation which took place in Wavour Hall, the night I consented to marry you? Do you remember that I then said, it was for the sake of Lillian, my sister, I agreed to wed you? Do you recollect that you promised faithfully to use every effort to restore her to sight, and to make her life a happy one? Do you remember all you swore that night? I was a fool to believe you—but let that pass!"

"I have really not leisure to attend to you,"

said Mr. Mazingford, rising, as if to depart: but his wife drew him back into his chair, and proceeded—

"Nay, hear me out; I must speak now—and I will then for ever after hold my peace. Let me trace out the main facts of the story a little further. We married—and you forgot to fulfil your compact. Had I to do the same thing again, I should either not marry you at all, or else insist that you completed your part of the conditions first: but not being wise enough for that at the time, I became your wife—and tried to be a good one, until I found that you never meant to do anything for Lilly—until, in fact, you refused to do that for which I wedded you. Since that period our life has been a miserable one; if you would like to make it more endurable for the future, if you would wish to still the tittle-tattle of society about our affairs, if you would desire that there should be at least a decent semblance of peace between us, you can secure it. Let me have

Lillian always with me—treat her kindly and considerately—don't make me miserable about her—and finally, give me four hundred pounds this day. These are my requests: if you grant them, I faithfully promise never to make another to you; heaven knows I will keep my word."

Mr. Mazingford laughed: "You have gone mad this morning, Judith."

"No, I have not," she answered; "four hundred pounds is not a large sum to pay for peace. It is nothing to you—it would be everything to me. I have never asked a boon from you before," she continued, in an almost entreating tone; "grant me this one, and from this hour I will do all you tell me, no matter how contrary to my own wishes. I will make the world think we are a happy couple; I will gratify, as far as I can, every desire you have—nay, more than all this, if you will but make Lilly's life a tranquil one, I will do what I thought once I never could—try to love you."

It was pleasant to him to hear her suing for terms at his hand; pleasant for once to see her humble and suppliant before him; pleasant to feel that at last she stood below the imaginary eminence he occupied; it was pleasant for him to hear her praying, and to know he had the power of granting or refusing, as he chose. Her sister—yes, if she liked, she might have Lilly back again—he knew he had lost a hold over her, since the invalid departed; therefore he answered—

" You talk as if I had driven Lillian away; I never did.   Bring her here again if you choose; all I insist on is, that your entire time be not engrossed by her."

" But the money ?" she asked.

" Is out of the question.   Be content with what you have already got: and now that matter is settled I must be off."

" The matter is not settled," retorted Judith; " Mr. Mazingford, do stop, and listen to me—I must have that amount."

"Pooh! nonsense!" he said.

"It is not nonsense," she replied; "I am in debt, very deeply in debt. I have tried to save out of the allowance you make me for dress; I have tried to retrench in every way, but it has been useless. Besides, what is four hundred pounds to you?—you would pay that sum any day for a curious time-piece, a rare vase, a—"

"You cannot have it, I tell you," repeated her husband.

"But I tell you that I must," she persisted.

"Do not let me hear another word on the subject," he returned; "bring your sister home if you choose; let her enjoy the comforts and luxuries of this house—such luxuries as neither you nor she dreamed of in your father's life-time. You can take her out to drive, and have the use of my carriages for her, but beyond this I will not go. I know perfectly well what you want with that money; but it is useless for you to harp on that string. I gave you my final answer long ago—

and now repeat, that her blindness can never be cured—and that, if it could——"

" Finish your sentence," said Judith, bitterly, as he paused—but there was something in her face which induced Mr. Mazingford to decline to do so.

" You now know my intentions," he remarked, " and can make your arrangements accordingly."

" I want money to discharge my debts," his wife commenced; but he interrupted her, with—

" I don't believe it; you want it to fee some humbugging scoundrel."

" You don't believe me," she repeated; " well, I will compel you to do so—and having told you all, abide by the issue. Mr. Mazingford, when you refused last year to fulfil your promise, I vowed within myself that if human skill could restore my sister's eyesight, she should not remain blind, and I fulfilled that vow. I went to the first oculist in London ; I hired a house for her ; I saw she had all proper comforts; I in-

curred debt, thinking I should have been able to
defray all the expenses myself. I find my hopes
deluded me, and these bills are the result. Now
you know all; and I leave it to yourself to give
the money or not, just as you think proper. If
you do, I will never ask you for another shilling
—I will strive, so help me Heaven! to fulfil my
marriage vow to the letter—for I am weary of
strife—weary, weary of this most wretched existence. I will endeavour to forget the past, and
only remember your kindness. I will——"

" Have you nearly done?" he interrupted.

" Nearly, but not quite," she answered, in a
different tone; " as this is my first request to
you, so it shall be my last. Will you grant it?"

" No!" he vociferated.

" Well, then, I have only one thing more to
say—you had better; for if you do not, as there
is a God above us, Lewis Mazingford, I will
make you repent it."

" You threaten, do you?" he retorted; " it is
my turn now—listen to me. Your sister shall

never enter my house again so long as she lives.
I will see oculist, landlord, and all other creditors
at the devil, before I pay one shilling of any
debt incurred for or by her; and I will teach
you some lessons, madam, I should have been
wise to have commenced ere now."

He had nearly reached the door, and was just
turning the lock, when Judith, almost in despair,
sprang across the apartment after him.

" For Heaven's sake," she implored, " don't
refuse me; I am not asking you now to give
her back sight, for that she has—but life.
Without care and good advice, she will die; she
is in a very critical state. I never thought to
have prayed to you for anything; but for the
love of God, grant me this one favour—all last
night, I thought she would die. The doctors
said there was no danger, but still I got frightened. I don't exactly know what is the matter
with her, but I am sure if she is not well taken
care of she will die."

" Let her die, then," thundered Mr. Mazingford; "if you want money, write to your brother, he is rich now, or in the way of being so; write to him, if you like—but never mention her name in my presence again—I warn you never to do it."

"For the last time, Mr. Mazingford, will you give me that money?"

"For the last time, Mrs. Mazingford, I will not."

They stood there confronting each other for one brief second, then Judith opening the door, said, in a voice from which every trace of passion had vanished—

"You may go."

The tone and manner took Mr. Mazingford aback. The old look, which Judith had discarded during the course of their conversation, was once more put on, to lash him up to fury.

"What the deuce do you mean?" he demanded.

"What I say," she replied; "you may go or you may stay, it is immaterial to me—I have done with you."

"But I have not done with you," he retorted, angrily; "I will not be told by any woman living, that I may go out of a room in my own house."

"Well, stay in it then," Judith answered.

"I shall stay in it if I choose, and so shall you; I will teach you I am master here; I will show you I am your husband, a fact you latterly seem to have forgotten."

There came no verbal reply this time, only a withering laugh.

"Confound you!" exclaimed Mr. Mazingford, and almost before he was aware of his own intention, he had struck her a violent blow across the face.

It came so sharp and unexpected, that Judith was nearly stunned by it for the moment. When she recovered her self-command, she heard her husband saying to a servant, "Tell Mrs. Mazingford I shall return in time to go with her to Lady Laurent's."

" So !" muttered she—and putting her handkerchief up to her face, waited for the hall door to bang, and the message to be delivered.

" Ashley," she said, to the man who repeated it—

" Yes, madam."

" Do you think you could find me a hammer and screw-driver, or chisel, anywhere in the house? Bring them up to me here, and make haste."

No one could have told from her manner that anything unusual had occurred. An unnatural calm had succeeded to her former excitement; and as she seated herself in the chair her husband had lately occupied, to wait for the man's return, she looked as cool and collected as if every feeling within her were at peace.

" It comes all to the same in the long run," she soliloquised; " only this takes less time."

She rested her elbow on the table, and supported her head on her hand, still holding the handkerchief to screen her face, and patiently listened for the coming of the tools she needed.

" I wonder what she wants with them?" Ashley remarked to a fellow-servant; and had Judith shut the door, it is probable he would have satisfied his curiosity by a peep through the key-hole; but Judith told him to leave it open, and to order the carriage.

" She wants them to take out with her," settled the fellow, but he was wrong; she required them for a very different purpose.

" I saw him put it here," she said, half aloud, and, exerting all her strength, she forced the lock of one of her husband's private drawers, and drew forth from it a cheque-book.

" Now for it;"—and taking up a pen, she tried several times to imitate Mr. Mazingford's signature, on a piece of note paper.

Many a woman's hand would have trembled, and her cheek blanched, as she traced the letters, but Judith's did not; she seemed as perfectly indifferent and regardless, as though she were doing a right thing in a right manner.

Most people would have called what she was doing forgery, and Mrs. Mazingford knew it.

"If I were sure I should be transported for it to-morrow, I would do it to-day," she thought; and it was with a feeling of something very like pleasure, that she beheld the all-important document at length perfected before her. She had been compelled to hunt over his books for suitable copies, both for figures and letters; she tried the former at least twenty times, before she could satisfy herself, but then it was at last completed :—

"Pay self —————— or bearer four hundred pounds.

"£400.   LEWIS MAZINGFORD."

"To Lombard Street," she said to the footman; and, clutching the cheque in her hand, Judith stepped from her carriage, and entered the bank.

She stood the scrutiny of the clerk, to whom she presented the little piece of paper, without flinching; pretended not to notice first, that there was

done, I think that's Mr. Mazingford's signature, may I get an increase of salary to-morrow!"

Which last alternative capping the bounds of all probability, the cashier, who had grown grey in deciphering hieroglyphic characters, called "Customers' Signatures," directed his attention again to the cheque, observing at the same time, that " if it were not genuine, it was uncommonly well done." The more he looked, however, the more satisfied he became that Lewis Mazingford had never signed the document with · his own hand. " I beg pardon, Sir," he said, entering the manager's room, " but I cannot rest content about this four-hundred-pound affair. I am sure Mr. Mazingford never wrote that ;" and he placed his hand on the Christian name.

Mr. Bayfield pshawed, and pooh-poohed, and affirmed he knew the lady to be the member's wife; and added, " She came in Mr. Mazingford's carriage, and with his servants, who wore his livery." He said " there could be nothing wrong :" but still the cashier held to his text.

He had been " twenty-five years looking at signatures," he continued, " and never made a
mistake before. Might it not be advisable to
communicate with Mr. Mazingford?"

The manager took the cheque, held it up
between him and the light, compared it with
others that had been previously presented, and
finally observed—

" You see it would be such an awkward thing
to seem to suspect a man's wife of forgery: and
if the signature be not genuine—that, I fear, is
about the plain English of the affair—it is very
unfortunate; but, upon my word, I am coming
gradually round to your view of the matter."

The result of which violent confession of faith,
proved, first, a message to Mr. Mazingford, and
subsequently a demand if Mr. Collins had taken
the numbers of the notes. Mr. Collins had, and
so the manager considered there could not, after
all, be much harm done. But Judith, careless
as she seemed, had noticed every particular;
and her first act, after leaving the Bank, was to

get all the money changed—the large notes into
small, the small into large. Having accomplished
which feat, she drove to a shawl shop which she
occasionally patronized, and dismissing her
equipage there, immediately after took a cab
and proceeded to the residences of the various
persons she wanted to see.

Of a truth Judith was playing a dangerous
game—not with her husband—not with her
bankers, but with herself. She was just on that
broad highroad of wilful personal delusion, that
leads many a woman to perdition. Her con-
trivances and facility of invention were something marvellous, in one uninitiated in the dark
mysteries of crime.

Recklessness and cowardice—the former of
herself, her position, her good name; the latter
for Lillian—poor afflicted Lillian, were fast
converting the strong nature into a bad one;
add to all this, hatred of her husband, and contempt of what she wildly called " her own accursed
folly in marrying him," and you will see, reader,

that Judith Mazingford had set foot on, and was treading rapidly, the way that, sooner or later bringeth to the Devil. It was God's hand laid on her heart in sorrow and suffering, which turned her from it. Grievous seemed the affliction at the time; but in later life, with tears wrung from the depths of a broken spirit, she confessed that the trials she had found so hard to bear, were really angels in disguise. And thus clad in the garments of humiliation and anguish, many an angel walks the earth, of whose presence we are impatient, of whose heavenly mission we wot not, of the use of whose coming we only become aware when time, which revealeth all things, even the mystery of Eternity, unto our comprehensions, hath made darkness light.

The worst feature about Judith's mental malady was the intense calmness and the self-possession it engendered in her manner—nay, even in her mind. When guilt comes near them, those who feel innocent do not take its approach quietly.

Despair or hardness, a determination to proceed to any end, let that end prove what it may, or an utter insensibility of feeling, can alone induce this unnatural lull in the play of human emotions. The most hopeless part of the affair was, that Judith not merely seemed calm, she felt so. " She did not care ;" that one sentence sums up the state of her mind to a nicety.

She did not care !—everything in heaven or on earth was equally indifferent to her if Lillian were but secured the means of recovery, and those she felt she held in her own hand. After paying Mr. Chamberton, who, to her surprise, did not seem inclined to accept the money, and who acted most kindly and generously, even whilst retaining his previous constrained and reserved manner, she drove to Brompton, and stopping by the way to procure various deli- cacies which she thought might be acceptable to the invalid, gradually got twenty, five pound notes changed into gold.

Armed with this untraceable property, she

finally arrived at her aunt's residence, just as Mr. Huron and Dr. Staley were leaving it.

"Well, gentlemen," she inquired, "what is your opinion?"

"Our patient is much better; going on more favorably than could have been expected," said Dr. Staley, with that magnificent urbanity for which he was justly celebrated; whilst Mr. Huron, on whom Judith's anxious glance instinctively turned, stated that he saw no cause for apprehension in Miss Renelle's symptoms. "The long confinement to two darkened rooms had," he said, "been productive of bad effects, aggravating her natural delicacy, and more fully developing her disease. Had I been consulted a couple of months since," he added, "I should, certainly, have advised the operations being discontinued altogether; as it is, I wonder more serious effects have not supervened. She will require great care, and constant attention for a little time; but then I hope you will have the satisfaction of seeing her better, perhaps, than ever she was."

"She had not then laboured in vain—she had not spent her strength for nought." That was the first thought which passed through Judith's mind, as the men of medicine departed, leaving such words of hope and comfort behind them.

Yes, Lillian was continuing better, there could be no doubt about that; and the younger sister felt that any sacrifice she made, any risk she incurred was trivial, in comparison with the accomplishment of one solitary object— her recovery.

Whatsoever Judith Mazingford determined to do, that she did; and, therefore, it needed the omnipotence of an Almighty Hand to save her from the fate on which, almost unconsciously, she was rushing.

"She did not care!"—She hugged the words to her heart, and crushed out with them all dread of exposure, recrimination, personal violence. "She did not care;" Judith only found those words impossible to pronounce when she

thought that she should rarely now be able to
see her sister ; perhaps find it difficult for a time,
at least, to visit her at all."

" Aunt," she said to Miss Ridsdale, drawing
her out of Lillian's apartment—"here are a
hundred pounds—make them last as long as
you can, but still do not let Lillian want for
anything money can purchase, or skill effect. I
trust all to you, remember, because I fear I shall
scarcely ever be able to come here for the future.
Mr. Mazingford was angry at so much money
being required, and on the strength of it we
quarrelled ; in consequence of which I expect I
shall have rather an unpleasant life for a few
weeks. But I don't care for that in the least,"
she added, seeing a look of apprehension cloud
Miss Ridsdale's face. " I have got what I
wanted—money ; and as for sour glances, and
hard words, they are nothing new to me. What
I principally want to guard against is his knowing where you are, because I have crossed him
so completely to-day, that just to revenge himself,

he would, as likely as not, come down here, and grieve Lilly—perhaps throw her back altogether. He knows she is my only vulnerable point, and accordingly on that he attacks me. Now the servant who used to drive me here, before we went to Wavour Hall, has left, and fortunately I came in a cab the first night, so no one he knows is aware of your address, and for the present I wish to keep him in ignorance of it; and, therefore, when you write to me *never* put *your* direction on the paper—I will come when I can, but it must be seldom. And now good-bye—don't look so grave—for if he has vexed me, I have gained my principal point. I must just speak to Lilly and then go, for we are ' due' at Lady Laurent's to-night; and he, unlike other husbands, accompanies his wife—so I must be punctual.—Good-bye."

"One word, Judith," said Miss Ridsdale. "What is the reason of all this money being in gold ?"

"It was not in gold when I got it," answered

Judith hurriedly, for equivocation came less easily and naturally to her than forgery—concealment than absolute crime. "I had it changed for many reasons; you will find it more convenient and better altogether, I think; but if you prefer it, I can send you bank notes instead."

"It is not that, Judith," replied Miss Ridsdale gravely; "it is not a matter of convenience I am speaking of; but I want to know how you got this amount. I am not satisfied, I am anxious my dear, dear child—for the eye of affection is clear sighted, and I know all is not well with you. Tell me the truth, Judith. How did you get this money?"

"Why, I told Mr. Mazingford *I must* have it, and there is the result; it was a very painful discussion altogether, and we were both very angry; as for all being well with me, it has never been well with me for years—it never will, I believe, till my head rests in my coffin. But there is no use in talking about these things. As I have chosen my lot so I must abide by it, and strive to make the best thing out of a wretched life I can—I never said so much to you before—did I, aunty? Now let us go to Lilly."

"You are not running away from me so soon, Judith?" said the invalid, as her sister kissed her cheek. "I am sure you need not be in such a hurry—I wanted to get up."

"My darling, you had better remain in bed."

"I am tired of bed, Judith; just let me get up for ten minutes, I want to see out—I want—"

"What is not good for you, I fear," finished Judith; "but as you wish it—why, 1 suppose I must give in to you—there, wait till I wrap this cloak about you—now put your arms round my neck."

"Judith, you surely are not going to carry her?" interposed Miss Ridsdale.

"Why not? I am strong enough for any-thing," was the reply, as Mrs. Mazingford, raising her sister in her arms, carried her into the adjoining apartment.

" I am sure you ought not to attempt such a weight," said the lady.

" I have carried a more grievous one a long time," muttered Judith; and in spite of the intense anxiety she felt to get home and ward off, by her presence there, all chance of an incursion on Miss Ridsdale's temporary abode, still she sat on for another hour, by Lillian's side—stroking down the dear hair, and caressing the poor wasted hands.

" I wish you would always stay with me," said Lillian, at last.

" I wish I could," answered Judith. " But I really must go now, or I shall be regularly in the black books."

" When will you come again ?—When you do will you bring the carriage, and take me a drive in the country ?—I want to see the country—I want—"

Poor Lillian's wants were one of the worst symptoms of her disease; and Judith had some faint idea of the sort. Perhaps it was a dim feeling that these constantly increasing desires were indicative of an approaching catastrophe, which made Mrs. Mazingford so feverishly anxious to gratify them.

She would not whisper danger to herself, but she knew there was danger nevertheless. She felt her last strong tie slackening; she felt the last thing she loved, almost to idolatry, slipping out of her arms—slipping surely, though imperceptibly from life to death—from the shores of time to the fathomless ocean of Eternity.

"Aunt Milly will take you out whenever the doctors say you may venture safely," she answered, after a pause.

"Yes, but I want you," said Lillian, querulously.

"My love—I cannot come—I would if I could, but I really cannot; there—there!" she added, next moment, seeing her sister look most grievously disappointed; "don't be vexed, and I will try; I will make time—I will do something."

"Judith, you ought to go!" said Miss Ridsdale, at this juncture.

"Indeed I must," her niece replied. "Now Lilly, shall I carry you back to bed, or will you stay here a little longer?"

"No, I will go to bed—though I don't like it —I don't care where I am, when you are not here—I want to be with you, Judith—I want to go home!"

"Well, so you shall, some day—you know, dear, this has all been a probation to gain what you most desired yourself—sight; and now you have got that, all other things will soon come right."

"Yes, but they are so long coming right; and I am so tired, and I want to go out, and to be always with you. Can't you take me home to-day, Judith?"

"I am afraid Aunt Milly does not treat you well," returned Judith, as she lifted the light burden in her arms again. "Have you got any complaints to make of her?"

"No;—oh, no!" answered Lillian, listlessly, then drawing her sister's ear close to her mouth she whispered, " only I love you best!"

"And best on the wide earth I love you!" responded Judith, clasping her tighter to her heart.

"Then why do you leave me?"

"Because I cannot help it. There now, make yourself quiet and comfortable, and get well as fast as you can, and then we will keep together always," and Mrs. Mazingford put the pillows under her head, and arranged the sheets, and drew the curtains. "Good-bye, Lilly — Good-bye, my darling."

"Oh, stay with me, please stay with me!" pleaded the invalid, detaining her sister with one thin hand.

"My love, I am *afraid*," said Judith in a tone which went home to Miss Ridsdale's heart; but it produced no effect on Lillian, who apparently not heeding her reply, continued—

"I think it is very unkind of you to go, when

L 2

I want you so much to stay. You promised never to desert me, and you have done so; and I am so wearied and miserable, and you don't love me!"

"God help me!" exclaimed Judith, passionately, as the sufferer, by way of a finale to the foregoing speech, burst into tears; "What am I to do—oh, Lillian, if ever any human being loved another, I have loved you! and Heaven is my witness, I have tried to prove it!"

"Judith!" interposed Miss Ridsdale; "you had much better go—Lillian has sat up too long, and you are only exciting her; she is a little hysterical," the lady added, in a lower voice; "and does not know exactly what she is saying. Come, dear, do leave her to me, she will be better—indeed she will, when you are gone;" and Miss Ridsdale took her niece by the hand and led her towards the door. Before, however, they could pass the threshold, a faint voice cried, "Judy!" and Mrs. Mazingford, forcibly freeing herself from her aunt's grasp, sprang back to the bed-side.

"Do you think me very impatient?" asked the invalid, in a totally different manner, and with a much weaker accent—"very cross, and tiresome, and impatient?"

"No, mine own—it is I who am impatient, not you," was the reply.

"There is something the matter with me," said Lillian, laying her head lovingly on her sister's shoulder, "something different from what used to be, that makes me feel at times I don't know how. What is it, Judith, can you tell?"

"Yes, dear—it is that you have been very ill, more ill than any of us thought; and that though you are now much better, you are far from well, and feeling the effects of the illness more as you get stronger. Whenever you are well again, all that will pass away."

"Will it?—well then, good bye; you will come again soon—to-morrow?"

"If I can," answered Judith; and kissing the poor

pale cheek once more, she laid it down on the pillow, and distrusting her own resolution to go at all, if she remained much longer with her sister, hurried out of the apartment.

" Aunt," she said at the hall door, " take care of Lilly, she is very ill, dangerously ill."

" Not so ill as you think," was the reply.

" More ill than you imagine," returned Judith, gravely—" for, being with her always, you cannot see the change as I do. Let me hear every day how she is, and what the doctors say exactly; and if——" Judith paused for a moment, and then added, " if there should come any change for the worse, send for me at once; wherever I may be, tell your messenger to follow. Promise me this, and I shall be comparatively easy."

" You are needlessly alarmed," said Miss Ridsdale; " but I will promise to do what you ask. And now, Judith, the less frequently you come here the better; you really only do her harm."

" There is no fear of my coming often," answered Mrs. Mazingford, bitterly, " I shall not be able; take care of her. Remember, I give her up to you—and, for my sake, aunty, cure her if you can."

There was a quiver in Judith's voice as she spoke; and as Miss Ridsdale drew her gently towards her, all the sorrows of her life seemed to swell up in the woman's breast together.

" Oh! I wonder," she cried, almost wildly, " if there were ever anybody in the world so miserable as I am?"—and, without waiting for any answer, sped out into the darkness of night.

" Judith dear, let me send Hannah for a cab," called out Miss Ridsdale.

" I can get one close at hand for myself," was the answer echoed back through the gloomy stillness; and in five minutes more, Mrs. Mazingford was driving in company with her own thoughts—home.

CHAPTER VIII.

MR. MAZINGFORD was there, and followed his wife to her dressing-room, almost before Judith could have imagined he had heard of her arrival.

He was pale with anger, and absolutely trembling with excitement: " Dismiss your maid," he said, in a low, but peremptory tone ; and Judith, with a sign, getting rid of this unwished-for witness to a matrimonial *téte-à-téte*, flung herself into an easy chair, and prepared herself for what she knew was coming.

Whenever Mrs. Mazingford was quarrelling

with her husband, she forgot for the moment
her other causes of annoyance; and remembering nothing but the indignities he had heaped
upon her, devoted all her energies to the contest.
She was a woman who would have managed to
make a saint angry if she chose to do it; and
Mr. Mazingford being no saint, she sometin.es
drove him almost mad. He was not very calm
to start with; but her answer to the first question he put to her, the look that accompanied it,
and the way she spoke it, brought the volcano
pouring over her.

" You presented a cheque at my bankers this
morning, madam," he said.

" And got it cashed, sir," she retorted.

Perhaps if she had known what she was bringing on herself, she might have hesitated ere
uttering the foregoing sentence; for, as though
her words had set fire to a train of gunpowder,
all the pent-up ferocity and fury of the man's
nature exploded upon her.

Threats, recriminations, a torrent of fierce,

L 3

angry sentences, mingled with occasional retorts
and defiances from Mrs. Mazingford, met the
ear of the astonished abigail—who, at last, absolutely in a tremor, deserted her post at the
keyhole, and ran down for Mr. Mazingford's
French valet—betwixt whom and herself there
was a very extensive flirtation being carried on.

"For mercy's sake, Monsieur," she exclaimed,
"come up stairs, and be ready if my lady calls
for help. There is the most dreadful quarrel you
ever heard between them; and though I cannot
tell what it is all about, I am sure he struck
her."

"Ah! how the English husbands be quad-
rupeds," remarked Monsieur Chiolet, making a
very free translation of a sentence which passed
through his mind for the benefit of the lady's
maid, who, having secured so important an ally,
returned to her post in time to hear her mistress
say, in a tone that sounded strangely cold and
calm—

"I shall not give back that money, Mr. Mazingford; for if I got possession of it illegally, still, morally, it was mine. You owe me that and far more. You promised my sister sight; and if, in the regular way, she could have been attended to here, I sincerely believe her present dangerous illness might have been avoided. You promised me ease, comfort, the blessing and the boon of her society—and you know how you have kept your word. I warned you it would be better to make a friend than an enemy of me; I said I would make you repent refusing my request; and if you, Lewis Mazingford, know how to break your promises, I, Judith Mazingford, know how to keep mine. I would go to the stake, before I would tell you how I spent a shilling of the money, to whom I gave it, where I got rid of it. Try to trace the notes if you like—in the long run you must come back to me. I don't care what you say, I don't care what you do—the dread of disgrace is unknown to me. My fair name may seem a matter of importance to you; but to things of that sort I am perfectlyin'different. There is no point you can touch me on—I have not now got a vulnerable spot—all things in heaven and on earth are alike to me. What I said I should do, I have done; what I now say, that I will keep to." Having announced which determination, Judith sank back in her chair, and looked up at her husband, with a mingled smile of derision and contempt.

"Once for all, madam, will you return me that money ?"

"Not to preserve me from perdition," she retorted.

"As there is a power above, you shall !" he exclaimed.

"I should like to see the power that would make me!" was her reply.

It had barely crossed her lips, when he pulled her from the chair she occupied—shook her with all his strength, and then dashed her to the ground.

Not a cry or moan escaped her, severely as she must have been hurt. The moment her

husband left the room, she struggled to a standing position, and would accept no assistance, even
from her maid, who, without being summoned,
entered almost immediately after.

"You may go, Caroline," she said, in her
usual voice; "I shall not require you again to-
night;" and thus dismissing the woman, she
sat down by the dressing-room fire, and kept
brooding and brooding for hours.

"I think I feel ill," she murmured, at last,
getting up with a sort of shiver, and undressing
herself with what speed she might, she crept
wearily to bed.

For days she lay there unable to rise, but
resolutely refusing to see any doctor. There
were constant inquiries for Mr. Mazingford's
beautiful wife, made by members of the *beau
monde;* by stately old dowagers, and flirting
young guardsmen, who missed her face sadly
from aristocratic assemblages. At last, even her
husband came to learn what was the matter with
her; but Judith declined to see him.

"Tell Mr. Mazingford," she said to her attendant, "that any thing he wishes to say, I can hear to-morrow, as I shall then be down stairs;" and with this answer he was forced to rest satisfied.

When they met, however, the money question was never touched upon; for, during the few days of her retirement from fashionable life, he had discovered that most of the interest and attention he excited in London society, was due to his wife; and that without her he was just like other people, one unit amongst many. The world was curious about Mrs. Mazingford, as it usually is about anybody who does not care two straws for either its good or bad opinion. Her sarcasm was called wit; her coldness and indifference, eccentricity; her past life a romance; her situation as Mr. Mazingford's wife, interesting. Perhaps it was because Judith wore her beauty disdainfully, like an unnecessary encumbrance, that dowagers praised her character; perhaps, because she did not flirt, that mammas approved her conduct; perhaps, because she seemed to detest and despise admiration and flattery, that young ladies were not jealous of her.

All her antecedents were peculiar; and people never wearied of talking about her dead and living connections—Lady Lestock and Mrs. Crepton—now Miss Lestock, Mrs. Maskell, Mrs. Renelle, the flirting Ridsdales, the poor lame sister, about whom it was rumoured the member and his wife wrangled—all were brought on the tapis; and whenever the scandal-mongers of the metropolis had exhausted their other delicate morsals of lying gossip, Judith Mazing-ford was a fortress of strength for them to fall back upon. Somehow or another, after the affair of the cheque, society became informed of the fact, that the Welsh member's house in Mayfair had been the scene of a pitched do-mestic battle, and bets were made in all parts of London, in clubs, at morning visits, and after-noon strolls, as to which came off best.

" 'Pon my soul !" said Captain Lyner, of the

Guards, " I heard she forged his name to a large amount, and refused to give any account of how she spent the money.   It might not be true, you know, but I believe it, for I think she has spirit enough for anything."

Which report, flying like wildfire, brought the state of public feeling to a climax.   It was said a trial would take place ere long; that Mrs. Mazingford was not in May Fair at all; that there was to be a separation, and Heaven knows what besides; that her illness was only an excuse to cover something more serious; in fine, the world of fashion evinced such a laudable curiosity concerning his wife, and had so many vague rumours afloat concerning recent transactions, that Mr. Mazingford felt it was becoming quite necessary to produce—and, at least, appear on good terms with her; wherefore society was in due course much astonished and, perhaps, also a little disappointed to see Mr. and Mrs. Mazingford once more enter the West End drawing-rooms together.

Then some said they had never believed a word of the stories that had been told ; whilst others, more sapient, gravely shook their heads, and declared that time would show ; and so knowing nothing, and caring nothing for what was being whispered about her, Judith plunged again into the whirl of fashionable life, whilst Lillian got better.

More rapidly than could have been anticipated she was regaining her usual strength—so Miss Ridsdale wrote—so Judith, managing once to steal down to Brompton, saw for herself: and as her anxiety decreased, Mrs. Mazingford's old detestation of her " Show " existence revived in all its wonted force ; and the old loathing of her beauty, and her attractions, returned with even more than its former intensity.

" I hate these dinner parties !" she exclaimed passionately, one evening, as she swept into her drawing-room, and commenced pacing up and down it until such time as the knock of the first arrival should warn her to put on her " company manners." " I hate these dinner parties ; sitting there to be stared at and commented on by the gentlemen over their wine;" and "the handsomest woman in London" clasped her hands together over her proud, rebellious heart, and continued her dreary walk, muttering to herself, and stamping her foot every now and then on the floor, like an impatient, untamed, unsubdued, creature as she was.

She looked very lovely though through all— she always did in every dress, but an evening costume was particularly becoming to her. Her dark hair fastened up behind with a large comb, was permitted to fall loose in front in heavy curls that touched her neck, making it look by contrast, so dazzlingly white that it resembled nothing so much, in its snowy softness, as the leaf of a lilly. She was fond of pink—it suited her better, perhaps, than any other color—and with white lace, falling over the front of her dress and arms—she looked what she was—a woman who needed little extraneous aid from either milliner or jeweller to enable her to take high rank amongst the rarest and loveliest flowers in Albion's garden,

And still she was pining for a desert to bloom unseen—pining to leave the pomps and vanities and compliments, and humiliations of the great world, for a great retreat, no matter how obscure, for a peaceful home, no matter how humble.

"And when Lilly is better I will have it too," she thought. "I will not come up again to this monster Babylon! but I will have her at Wavour Hall, and live contentedly there, or if he refuse that, leave him altogether; I shall be able to make money enough for two; Mr. Mason says he will take a book from me, if I construct the plot better, and give myself more time to write it. So far well; and why should I make myself miserable by staying with a man I hate? —why indeed?"

So, like many another of her sex, before and since, Judith argued on in favor of what she wanted to do herself, until the expected guests

began to appear—when the vehement woman
became cold, and the thoroughly natural character
wrapped itself up in the mantle of forms and
ceremonies, and conventionalities; and Mrs.
Mazingford assumed the part of hostess—but
differently, oh, how differently to the mode in
which she had attempted it one Christmas night
a long time ago.

It was more a select than a large party, and
as is usual in such cases, the persons invited
made their appearance almost simultaneously—
all but one, or rather two—(unless a thin general
and his fat wife could possibly count for one, in
fashionable circles)—for whom dinner was being
kept back, when a servant entering the room,
presented Judith with a note, and added an intimation that the messenger wanted to see her.

" Excuse me," said Judith to her uncle, beside
whom she sat; and before Sir John Lestock
could, in measured accents, find time and words
to do so, she had mastered the contents of the
missive.

"Why did you not come this afternoon, when I wrote for you? For fear this should miscarry, I have desired the messenger not to leave till he sees you. Come at once—if you want to see Lilly alive.

"M. R."

She grasped it all in a minute—Lillian was dying, and her husband had kept back the note.

"I trust," she said, to her guests, "you will pardon my leaving you; Miss Lestock will kindly take my place. Don't think me rude for leaving you—my—my only sister is dying."

Not a soul present spoke a syllable. Her words and her voice touched the hearts of those assembled.

There is a something about real, genuine feeling, about the presence of a sudden and over-powering calamity, that wakes an echo for a moment, even in the most frivolous natures, and thus as Judith crossed the apartment, still holding the note open in her hand, every one rose and stood aside, making way silently for her to pass. No one spoke—not one, till she reached the door, when a young countess, recently married, followed her to the top of the stairs.

"May I go with you—can I do anything?" she asked.

"No, thank you—no—no!" returned Judith, hurriedly.

"I wish I could!" she pleaded; "but I won't detain you;" and the young girl, for she was little more, though an earl's wife, kissed Mrs. Mazingford's cheek, and told her to make haste.

Judith did not require the injunction; almost before the sentence was finished, she had reached the hall—where General Wraxmead, who at the moment arrived, began to accost her.

"Don't keep me, general!" she cried; "may I have your carriage?—Ashby, stop General Wraxmead's carriage—he will lend it me!"

"Judith, are you mad?" exclaimed Mr. Mazingford, at this juncture,

"Pretty nearly so," was her reply.

"You shall not go,". said her husband.

"No one shall hinder me," she answered.

"You have been ill, and the excitement and anxiety will throw you back again; I must really exert my authority to prevent your acting so foolishly."

"Let go my hand, Mr. Mazingford!" she almost shrieked. "No husband's commands shall keep me from going to my dying sister—if you detain me by brute force I will first kill you and then myself!"

"You are acting very foolishly, Mr. Mazingford," said General Wraxmead; "you had better let her go."

"She will injure her health!" returned the Member.

"Opposition will injure it more!" suggested the veteran. "Allow me to——"

What he was going to propose never accurately transpired, for at the moment Judith swung herself from Mr. Mazingford's grasp—bounded to the hall-door, and sprung almost off the steps into General Wraxmead's carriage.

" Drive to Brompton fast !" she cried ; " I will tell you the address by the way ;" and while the horses dashed off in the direction indicated, she stood up in the vehicle and explained to the coachman the route to take, the house to stop at. " Drive fast—drive fast !" she implored, and he did so ; but rapidly as they went, Judith felt as if they spent centuries on that short road.

" At last !" she said, when the horses, white with foam, pulled at the entrance to Miss Ridsdale's house. She ran up to the door and knocked—It was Mr. Chamberton who opened it for her.

" How is Lillian—is she living ? " Judith would have rushed past him, without waiting for an answer ; but he prevented her doing so. Gravely and mournfully he took her hand in his and led her into the sitting-room — where at length catching a full view of his face, she staggered to a chair, and covering her eyes, groaned aloud.

There was no need for him to speak a word—she knew that it was all over—that Lillian was dead!

CHAPTER IX.

IT was on the evening of a sultry August day, a considerable period after the events recorded in the last chapter, that a young man, bronzed apparently by long exposure to the rays of tropical suns, sat wearily down on a bench before one of the inns, or beershops, or half-way houses, or whatever is their legitimate name, which line, with shady verandahs, and tankards of foaming ale, that important, south-east entrance into London, called the Old Kent Road.

The wanderer's dress was of a cut and quality

frequently to be observed along the thoroughfare just mentioned, consisting of a blue jacket, pair of soiled, white trousers of the description commonly known as "Duck," a small cloth cap, striped shirt with turn-over collar, a black silk hand-kerchief, loosely knotted about his throat, strong, coarse shoes, and the inevitable stick and bundle of clothes, without which a sailor seems utterly unable to make his appearance from foreign parts. In person he was taller and slighter than men who have adopted the sea for their profession usually are; and but for a limping gait, induced apparently by some malformation, or injury of the left leg, his walk and carriage would have been pronounced good. A mass of overgrown whiskers and beard, and a profusion of tangled, dark hair, almost concealed his features from view; but when he took off his cap, and pushed back the clustering locks from his forehead, a glimpse was caught of a pair of quick, intelli-gent eyes, of a well-developed head, and rather intellectual forehead.

M 2

He seemed oppressed and wearied, either with the intense heat, or with much walking, for laying his bundle down on the seat beside him, he clasped both hands together, and bent his head forward upon them as though he were tired and sick of seeking for rest and finding none.

All these particulars were noticed by a person occupying the same bench as himself; not because there was anything interesting or remarkable in the young sailor's appearance, but simply because at that moment the observer happened to have nothing else to do—and very little else, judging from his surroundings, pleasant to think of.

For his dress was decidedly shabby—seedy, would express the style better, perhaps—only the word is so frequently employed in connection with disreputable characters, that in this case I prefer not using it.

Shabby-genteel also, would convey by far too exalted an idea of the man's costume, for it had reached a stage of extreme dilapidation, which left all attempt at gentility far behind.

You could scarcely imagine, reader, how poor
and brown his coat looked; it seemed to have
been darned, and mended, every morning he went
out, for a year previously, and to have returned
home with a fresh rent in it every night. His
hat had not a vestige of nap left on it: his
trousers were surely more poor and threadbare
than trousers ever were before; and as he had
attempted to strap them down over a pair of
boots, that but for the name of the thing he
might have left off altogether, he lived in
a state of eternal dread, lest his thin knees
should make ways for themselves through the
rotten garment.

There was nothing new or good about him
except a calico shirt, very white and clean, the
collar of which was displayed, somewhat osten-
tatiously. He had on no stockings; but the
trousers, bad as they were, concealed that want
from public observation.

The luxury of gloves was a thing not to be
thought of; and as for waistcoat—perhaps the

heat of the weather accounted for the absence of that usual article of dress. He was closely shaved, however; had his hair cut in the newest fashion; was faultless in the matter of personal cleanliness, and held himself very straight and erect. Poor old fellow—he never, in the midst of his most grievous poverty, forgot he had once been an officer and a gentleman; but who else under the sun could he imagine would ever have guessed the fact?

Heaven knew, however, it was only one of the evil chances of life, and not any fault or sin of his own, that had brought him down to the position he then occupied. For years he had been the sport of the cruel billows of fortune, which at length stranded the shattered barque on a shore like this. But he liked the shore none the better because he had not sought it himself; and accordingly, to get rid of his own sad thoughts, he first scrutinised the new comer from head to foot, and then addressed him as follows:—

" A warm day, sir."

" Warm, yes," returned the young man, starting from his reverie; " the air seems to bake one, as if in a furnace. Abroad, people talked to me of the temperate climate of England —but if this be a sample———" The speaker shrugged his shoulders by way of a finish to his uncompleted sentence.

" Are you not an Englishman, then ?" demanded the shabby individual, in a tone of some surprise—for he marvelled, if the sailor were a foreigner, that he should speak English so well— and he marvelled still more, if he were a native, at the manner and matter of his sentence.

" No—yes—that is, I suppose I may call myself one, though I have spent very little of my life in these countries—a wanderer, like myself, however," he added, in a melancholy tone, " has no land—no home—no nationality."

There was a pause for a moment after the utterance of the foregoing words, which sounded, the old man thought, less like an answer to him

make

and q

resour(

everyth

"I w

it is the

belongs (

the sorro

not ;" an(

Thus t1

to leave he:

ford beguil

Wavour H:

self in an a.

nature than

verance she i

her trade—s(

and the pow

away the tim

Mazingford t

And with ε

accompanied !

ally changed to disap-

side in ?"

ay parts," replied the

echoed—" then you

the pale, thin cheek ;

no verbal response,

n token of assent.

ive service ?" pursued

service, young man,'

ignity.

hing about the country

have headed against

ng man looked hesita-

the speaker; then,

d feeling, some strange

companion was better

M 3

than a mournful reflection uttered aloud. He felt puzzled too about the youth, whose words and manners were above his apparent station; and influenced, perhaps, as much by curiosity as anything else, he resumed the conversation by saying—" You spoke just now of India—I presume you have been there."

" There—where have I not been?" was the reply, spoken half bitterly, half thoughtfully : " China and Peru; the Cape of Good Hope, and Newfoundland—Persia and Russia—Egypt and the Slave States.   I believe I have been nearly every where; but perhaps, I know more about India than any other part of the world; for I tried to push my fortune there, and failed One always knows a country well, sir, when one chances to prove unfortunate in it. Yes, I am ' thoroughly up' in India."

" I spent thirty years of the best part of my life there," remarked the old man.

" Indeed ?" said the youth—and, facing suddenly round, he scanned his companion with a look of interest, which finally changed to disappointment.

" What part did you reside in ? "

" I was stationed in many parts," replied the other.

" Stationed !" the sailor echoed—" then you have been in the army."

A faint colour rose on the pale, thin cheek ; but the old soldier made no verbal response, he only inclined his head in token of assent.

" Were you ever in active service ?" pursued his questioner, eagerly.

" I have seen plenty of service, young man,', he answered, with some dignity.

" Then you know something about the country of the Mahrattas ? "

" Many a charge I have headed against them," was the reply.

For a moment the young man looked hesitatingly and doubtfully at the speaker ; then, moved by some unexplained feeling, some strange comprehension that his companion was better than he seemed, the sailor raised his cap from his head in a manner, and with a gesture, which proved that he, too, had at some period or another moved along a different path of life than that he was then treading.

If you are old, reader, you know how a slight token of respect from the young touches and pleases you. If you are young—you can remember the effect some small graceful tribute of reverence shown to an elder has ere now produced in your favour—and therefore no one need wonder, that after the above half-recognition of his claims and condition, the old man should feel his heart warming towards his young companion.

" Yes," he said, sadly, almost as if speaking to himself—" you would scarcely think, to look at me now, I had ever been young or brave; that I had ever served my country faithfully; that I had ever carried a sword, or worn the epaulette. You would scarcely credit these things ; and yet they are true."

"Truth is stranger than fiction," replied the other; "and the trite saying, hackneyed though it may be, rises to my lips twenty times a day. Poverty makes us acquainted with strange histories, as well as strange bedfellows; and, in my course through life, I have met beggars who had been gentlemen, and gentlemen who had been beggars. The wheel of fortune is eternally spinning round, bringing millionaires to want— and paupers to affluence. The only thing which puzzles me is, that the wheel never brings those up again which it has once set down."

"Nothing on earth tends upwards," was the answer. "The exceptions only prove the rule —for one man who rises, fifty fall—for one person that makes a gigantic fortune, twenty lose lands, estates, houses, home, all that makes a person considered by his fellows. Nothing on earth, believe me, tends upwards."

"Save the soul," replied the youth.

"And that only by the grace of God; the souls of savages do not look up; even when they can see a heaven—it is an earthly one beyond the skies. Man does what is easiest in all things temporal and eternal, unless sustained and guided by the hand of a Mightier power; and the every day experience of life proves that it is less difficult to go down a hill than up it."

"And so," said the sailor, smiling—"you consider that you and I have brought our misfortunes on ourselves, that our tendency has been downwards."

"Ah! you bring the practical application of my theory too near home to be pleasant," was the reply. "No—I don't think it is either your fault or mine that we are not what we ought to be. The tendency of our fortunes, not of our natures, has been downwards. There, will that content you?"

"You mean that we have been swimming against the tide, but that the current was too strong for us," suggested the younger man in sadder and plainer language. "Well, so be it

—what must be, must be—and though I for one cannot say I like the business, still if the stream of fortune lie before me—I had rather try to stem it and be swept away by the torrent of adversity, than sit idly down on the bank and never strive at all.   My life has been a sharp struggle for so far, Heaven knows, and so, for that matter, has that of many a better man. How many miles do you call it from here to London ? "

" To the city ? "

" Yes !—what business do you think I should have at the West?"

" I did not know.   You might have friends there."

" Friends ! I have none anywhere.   I only want to be directed to some cheap, quiet lodgings, where I can rest my body and collect my thoughts.   I can get this in the city more readily than at the West, and besides I hate the West, and the people who live there."

" I thought you knew nothing of London," remarked the old man drily.

" I know too much of it," replied his companion. "More, I dare venture to say, of its crimes and its miseries than you do. I can't bear to think of what I know about London," he added, vehemently; "if I did, I should go and do an injury to some one—but I am talking like an idiot. Which is my nearest way to the City, sir—will you take the trouble to direct me?"

" If you do not object to my company I will show you," answered the other, rising as he spoke; "and, perhaps, when we reach London, I can help you to a place such as you are in search of."

" Thank you," said the sailor; "but I must first have some porter. The heat of the day seems to have dried up my throat. Excuse me for a moment," and leaving the old man, he presently reappeared with two foaming tankards, which he set down before him. "Perhaps you will join me, I can recommend it," he began ; and when he saw the long, deep draught the old man took of the proffered beverage, he somehow grew to like him, as we always do grow to like those who stand in need of assistance, and whom we have been able to please or help, no matter how little.

"Allow me," said the elder, drawing out his purse—and, oh, what a lean purse it was—the very ghost and skeleton of a well-filled moneybag. "Allow me;" but the sailor would not. He said that was his business, and so paid the small reckoning, and led the poor shabby old man off in triumph.

They presented a curious contrast trudging along towards the metropolis side by side—the one with his stiff military strut, erect carriage, and unspeakably threadbare garments; the other with his limping gait, slightly rounded shoulders, and rough coarse clothes—they looked, indeed, the very antipodes of each other—but only to supply a fresh illustration of the fact that oppo-

sites agree. Many a one turned and asked after
the pair; but, unmindful of comment or scrutiny,
they pursued their way—talking as they went.

They conversed about India and America—
about the sea and the army—about old times
and present doings, till at length the elder of the
two suddenly demanded—

" Pray were you ever in Wales ? "

The blood mounted into the sailor's temples
at the unexpected question.

" Why did you ask ? " he replied.

" Because I wanted to know if there, or in
any of your many wanderings, you ever happened
to meet with a lad called Evan Crepton."

" And if I did, what then ? "

" Why then I would fain know how it has
fared with him since he left England."

" You never saw him," replied the youth.

" No, but I heard of him from those who
did," answered the old man; " and I and mine
have often wished to hear how he has prospered
in the world."

"If you will tell me who you are that ask, I will tell you all you want to know about the boy you named," said the other.

"Nay, nay, Mr. Crepton," answered the old gentleman, with a tone and manner that might have been called friendly and fatherly, had he happened to have had a better coat and pair of inexpressibles, but which, to any one else, perhaps, excepting the person he addressed, would have seemed familiar, and even absurd. "Nay, nay, Mr. Crepton, there need be no mysteries or disguises between you and me—for you are only Doctor Mills' favorite pupil sprung to manhood —and I am merely Mrs. Mills' uncle, Captain Darvin, grown old, and poor, and feeble."

"Good Heavens!" ejaculated Evan; and then and there, in the middle of that public thoroughfare, he wrung his new friend's hand, with a warmth and heartiness that brought tears, partly of pain and partly of pleasure, to the old man's eyes.

"I don't know," said the latter, "what it was

first made me speak to you—but could not help it; and when you talked about having no home, and no friends, and about being an Englishman and still a stranger, I felt sure it was you. So, now, you must come home with me. It is not much of a place, to be sure. There are plenty of rooms, and little furniture; many floors, and few beds; but we can make you comfortable, however, or I am much mistaken. Now, won't you come?"

"Shall I see Mrs. Mills?" hesitated Evan.

"Never again in this world, my boy. Ah! it was that broke me up. I'll tell you about it some day. I am very poor—very, very poor; but you don't mind that. Letty and I take care of an old-fashioned rambling City house, a place which was in Chancery, and that the owners want to let, on a repairing lease, but cannot do it—and although I suppose it is wrong to say so, I am very glad they cannot; for I don't know where Letty and I should go if we lost this shelter. It was a great mercy our getting it — quite a chance, but a most fortunate one."

"And so Mrs. Mills is dead," said Evan pensively, "and Letty is her daughter. Yes, I remember now. Doctor Mills was the best friend ever I had in my life, and his wife was the best woman ever breathed. May I ask you one question, sir?"

"Certainly, any—and as many as you like."

"Did she—did Mrs. Mills die poor?"

"She wanted for nothing," answered the old man—"nothing money could buy or love procure."

"Thank God for that—and her disease?"

"Was dropsy. She had been ill a long time —in fact, from the time of her husband's death she never was thoroughly well. She tried being a housekeeper—but that did not do, poor creature; and so whenever I came home from India, on half-pay, she took up her abode with me. We were very comfortable and happy while she lived; and she used so often to wonder and talk about you. She was very fond of you, and besides felt—God bless her sensitive heart —as if she and hers had, in some sort, brought misfortune down on your head. I promised her once, that if ever I met you, I would strive to push you on in the world; but that was when I was better off than I am now. It would be ridiculous for me to offer you help, when I cannot help myself—for I have grown, since her death, a poor, broken-down, unregarded ragged old creature, fit for nothing but to be carried to the graveyard, and duly allotted my six feet by three. My helping days are over—I cannot be of use to any one now, Mr. Crepton."

"You can be of use to me in many ways," answered the younger man cheerfully—"You have been of use to me already. When I met you a couple of hours, since I had not a friend in London—I did not know where to turn, nor what to do. I was weary, and dispirited, and repining; and now I have found a friend, a home, and a thankful, manly heart, again; and

I feel strong enough to commence stemming the torrent anew, with a firmer stroke and a steadier purpose. Is this your house?" And as he uttered the last few words, Evan gazed up at a huge black edifice, before the entrance to which they had stopped.

The place was, as I have said, large and gloomy. The windows were small, and the panes, in many places, cracked. It would have needed close on five hundred pounds to set the mason-work to rights, whilst a couple of thousand would scarcely have covered the expense of all the repairs needful to make the edifice "habitable." The door was of massive oak, with a large screen projecting over the top like a porch—altogether the building was an antiquity.

"It is not much to boast of," remarked Captain Darvin; "but cold and cheerless as it looks, it will give you a warmer home than an inn." And so saying, he opened the door with a latch key, and motioning Evan to enter, followed the youth into the spacious hall, which was only half-revealed to view in the ghost-like twilight of that sultry August evening.

"We live in the back rooms, finding them more private," said Evan's host. "Shall I lead the way?" and without waiting for an affirmative, the old man bustled up the oaken staircase, and turned into an apartment, situated on the first floor at the rear of the house.

"Letty, who do you think I have brought home with me?" Evan heard the old man saying, as he himself lingered behind on the landing.

"I don't know, uncle," answered a young voice. "Pussy, perhaps!"

"Better than Pussy," replied Captain Darvin.

"Oh! I am sure you could not get anything better than Pussy She caught the rats and mice so well—only we had not enough milk to give her. But what have you brought, uncle? Let us see it."

"Evan Crepton," said he.

"Evan Crepton," echoed the girl, with one

bound crossing the room and reaching the threshold where the wanderer stood.

There never was such a reception vouchsafed to a lonely, objectless man before. Without pausing to think about the wearisome forms and ceremonies of every-day life, he took the warm-hearted girl, whom he had left a child, in his arms, and kissed the pretty lips that were held so unhesitatingly up to his. It was, no doubt, very much what we have heard styled, " *Comme il fautn't* " — for a young lady to clasp a bronzed sailor round the neck, and welcome him back, after the best impulse of her guileless nature ; but Evan never thought about what was " proper " then. He was too pleased, too happy, and withal too sensible to think of finding fault with the first specimen of woman-kind who had spoken frankly and lovingly to him for years.

" Dear little Letty," he said, " I did not think you would have remembered even the sound of my name."

"Oh! you did not know how fond we were of you. But now come and sit down; I will get you something to eat, and manage to find a candle."

"Lettie!" broke in Captain Darvin.

"Yes, uncle!"—she ran to his side, and received in her hand the slender purse previously named, and in her ear an injunction how to spend it. "Now sit down," she said to Evan; "I shall be back in a minute;" and with this scrap of consolation left behind, she tripped down the stairs, and across the desolate hall, to the door.

She had not descended so quickly, however, as Evan had followed her, and, accordingly, when she stood on the threshold, he stood there likewise.

"Lettie," he began, hurriedly, "let me be your banker, will you—I see how matters stand, and don't want to be a burden, though I want to stay with you; I owe you and yours a debt I can never hope to repay, and I don't wish to repay it, for the remembrance of obligations from those I love is pleasant to me; just spend this for me as you would if I were your brother; I will try to be one to you, please God!" and he thrust a quantity of money into her hand, and was back in the sitting-room before he gave her time to utter a denial or an expostulation.

Poor Lettie! she cooked a glorious supper that night, and sat by in triumph whilst the pair of males ate it. They could not prevail on her to taste a mouthful; she said she was not hungry—that she was too warm—that she had taken her tea when her uncle was so long of returning; but Evan, scrutinizing her appearance closely, read the truth underneath all the disguises she heaped upon it—the child was half-starved, it needed no conjuror to assure him of that fact.

"·If I stay here I will set that to rights," he thought; " and if I don't I will try to mend their condition, some way!" and having made up his mind on these points, he commenced telling his story, by particular request, to Captain Darvin and his niece.

The narrative must have seemed interesting to his auditors, for they sat up till one o'clock to hear the end of it; but as it could scarcely prove equally so to the reader, in detail, I shall condense the events of many years into a few short sentences.

He had sailed almost round the globe, visited many countries, and seen some strange people—tried to get on in a mercantile house in Calcutta, but signally failed—less, perhaps, through any fault of his own, than because of his utter ignorance of business, and the impatient temper of one of the partners.

"Then," he said, "I took to sea again, not because I liked it, but because it seemed as if I could do nothing else; and probably I might have stuck at that trade for life, had it not been for a fall from the mast, which prevented my ever climbing the rigging again—as a sailor I was useless from that hour—but fortunately the captain was a kind man, and gave me a free passage to England. We threw out anchor

below Greenwich, and as I was wearied of ship-
board, I took boat ashore, and walked up to the
point where we met. And now I have only got
one thing more to tell you, which is, that during
all these years I have never heard a word of my
sister."

" Have you written ?"

" Yes, regularly as possible, under the circumstances; and also to Mrs. Crickieth, begging
her to let me know whether Alice were living or
dead. I sent some money for her, too, and its
receipt was never acknowledged. I intend going
down to Klicksturvyd, to learn some tidings of
her—but I almost fear the worst—my poor little
Alice !"

There was a pause—and then the Captain
began to administer hope. He said all that
people usually do say under such circumstances;
and the result was about what is customary on
similar occasions, viz., none at all.

"There is no use talking about it," Evan
answered, at last, " for I shall soon know the

N

best or the worst—poor child—if I dare have returned years ago, I would have done it; but till I was one-and-twenty I was afraid to face England. If she be living now—why, I am her nearest relative, and have a right to see to, and care for her stronger than that of any one else on earth: and if I have no sister—"

The young man paused abruptly, and lighting a candle, silently held out his hand to his host.

"Keep up your heart, my boy!" said the latter; "I am sure matters are not so bad as you fancy; I dare say the old schoolmistress never delivered your letters—if your sister had been dead, rely upon it you would have heard soon enough. 'Ill news travel fast,'—heaven knows that's a true proverb, at any rate. I never remember hearing of a letter miscarrying, that contained tidings of a death, or intelligence of any other misfortune—Good-night—get a sound night's sleep, and rise up more cheerful in the morning."

"Good-night!" replied Evan; "I shall sleep

all the better for having found you—I always said to myself, when far away from England, that if ever I had the means to prove my gratitude to the man who taught me all I know—I would be a son to his widow, a stay and prop to her, if I could; and now, please God, I will try to be a friend to her child, and an assistance to you, if you will let me. I shall go down to Wales in a day or two, but I want to arrange some plan for the future, first. We will talk over my prospects to-morrow—Good-night, again, sir—good-night, Lettie."

And Evan sought his chamber, and a straw palliasse, on which he slept, all unconscious that Lettie had relinquished it for his benefit, and broke her neck so grievously for his sake, over the back of a chair, during the first part of the night, that towards morning she was fain to stretch herself out at full length on the floor— where Evan, rising at day-break, and coming into the sitting-room, without any suspicion of who tenanted it—found her.

"Lettie," he said, as she started up with a color like a rose suffusing her usually pale face; "You should not have done this—it was very unkind."

"What was unkind?" she demanded.

"To treat me like a stranger—to make me feel that I have been a blind, selfish brute—that I have kept you out of bed—that—"

"No, you have not," she hastily interrupted; "I very often sit up till almost morning, and then just sleep in a chair here, till it is time to make uncle his breakfast. You don't put me out of my usual course a bit—you could not, no matter what you were to do."

"What a course yours must be then, Lettie," he said; "promise me, however, that for the future you will make no stranger of me, but treat me just like a brother—if you will do this I will forgive the past; will you?"

"Yes!" said the girl, with some reluctance.

"Well, then, as a proof that we are to be friends, that the compact is to be rigidly kept,

come and talk to me for a few minutes, before
Captain Darvin gets up—for I want to ask you
some questions that I do not like to put to him.
If I understand exactly how matters are, I think
I can make things more comfortable for all of us
—There, never mind the fire just now—sit still
and listen to me."

She obeyed him, sitting down on the chair he
placed for her, near the rusty grate, which was
filled with dust, but boasted, for so far, no blaze
of any kind.

Very demurely she crossed her hands before
her, and waited for him to speak: it seemed to
be part of her nature to do what she was told—
and the pretty submissive way she had of conquering her own feelings at the bidding of a
stronger will, touched Evan inexpressively.

"There need be no reserve between you and
me, you know, Lettie," he began; "I shall ask
nothing from impertinent curiosity; but I have
seen a good deal, and I want to understand more.

You are very fond of your uncle, are you not?"

"He is the only one I have left on earth to love," she answered, in a sorrowful voice; "I would do anything for him."

"Then you will help me to help him, won't you, dear?"

Evan put this question with the skill of a diplomatist, and Lettie replied in the affirmative.

"To enable me to be of any use to him, you must tell me how you are situated," he pursued.

"I have not got anything to tell," she said, "excepting that we are not very rich."

"Very rich!"—Evan mentally repeated the words with a smile, as he glanced round the apartment; but when his eye, after completing the inventory of its contents, fell once again on the poor little figure beside him, the smile faded away, and a look of melancholy succeeded to it.

"How does it happen that you are not so rich as you ought to be?" he asked.

She hesitated for a moment, but then said, boldly, "There is no harm in telling you: I am sure there cannot be, in showing how good, and noble, and generous that old man was. Oh! it was all for her, and she never knew—it was a sad, sad mistake—but none of us knew how it would turn out. It's pitiful to see him now—it breaks my heart—I can't bear to think of it."

And the poor child—for she was not much more in years, though so old in sorrow, began to cry.

"Did he then sell his half-pay, to meet the expenses?"—Evan hazarded, after a painful pause.

"Oh! it was worse than that," she answered; "I will tell you all about it if I can—" and she tried to check her sobs, although the effort was not altogether effectual: "Dear mamma!—we were so happy for awhile, living away down in the country, till she fell ill; but then all his half-pay went for the doctors and things that were needed, and we forestalled his next half—and by degrees we sold all the furniture, and pawned the few valuables, and dismissed our two servants, and I did all; and there was not a single article left in the house, but what was in her room; and then, when she was nearly dying, we had—don't look so hard at me, for it was no disgrace—" she interrupted, almost fiercely, " we should have starved if we had not—"

" What?" he demanded.

" Asked for out-door relief," she said.

" My God!" exclaimed Evan—" and your mother?—"

" She never knew—she died the first day we got it, I think it was. I am very glad she did, she could not have stood that. Oh! it was so hard, so hard—" and the tears came raining down the thin cheeks so fast, that Evan could have cursed himself for probing an old wound with so thoughtless and cruel a hand. The next question he put was spoken with a trembling voice:—

" I have hurt your heart, poor child," he began, " when God knows, I meant to relieve it; but I must ask just one thing more relating to the past—How did you meet the expenses of the funeral ?"

" We did not meet it," she said, "we could not, she was buried by the parish;" and Lettie hurried on—" My uncle's pay was stopped; for it appears it is a regulation of the service, that if once an officer accept relief from the poor-rates, he loses his money. The clergyman gave us a few pounds, and a letter to a lawyer in London; and my uncle has done copying for him, and he got us the care of this house—and so we have lived for nine months now."

" And what do you do, Lettie?"

" All the house-work, which is but little; and mend his clothes, and—"

" What else ?"

" Embroider, when I can get any work; but I can do nothing to signify. If I knew more, I could teach; if I could leave my uncle, I would go and be a servant; if I could do any one thing on earth to make his life easier, I would do it: I cannot bear to see him."

" And I cannot bear to see you, little one," Evan said; " but now, listen patiently, whilst you and I arrange matters. If I went to an inn, I could not live at the least under three pounds a week, and I should be very lonely and miserable besides. Now if you will manage that amount for me, I think all our means, clubbed together, would make us more comfortable. Could you make that amount do?"

" Oh! *you* would not cost a third of that," she said.

" Perhaps not—but I should have to pay it elsewhere; and if a profit is to be made out of me, it had better be made by you than a stranger. In plainer English, Lettie, for I see you are a sensible girl, and understand domestic matters, the extra sum had better go to make your uncle more comfortable, than to render a designing old landlady fat."

" But the house is in such a state, and there is not a bit of furniture in it."

" I have a hammock," he answered; "a seaman's chest, and some other odds and ends— sufficient for myself. If we need any more, we can buy them; as for the rest, from the hour I crossed this threshold, I considered myself one of the family—don't throw me back, and send me out a wanderer on the world again."

" I will tell you then what I will do," she answered. "Just what I would if you were my real brother—which I almost feel you are; for my dear mother always thought and mourned about you as though you had been her own son—and we have talked of you for years. Give me half the money you named, and let me try with that. If I cannot make matters snug on it, I will ask you for more—if less will do, you shall save whatever I tell you. I am sure we could live well for a much smaller amount, because I know how to manage better, I think, than anybody ever did."

"You have learnt economy in a hard school, I think," he said; "and now that is settled, if it please God that Alice is living, I will bring her here—and you will cater for her, too, won't you?"

"Won't I?" the pale face flushed, and the dim eyes brightened; and Lettie flung herself down in a kneeling position on the hearthstone, and commenced clearing away the ashes as if she felt she was doing something for Evan's sister on the instant.

If ever an innocent and perfectly unselfish being existed, it surely was Letitia Mills. The hardships of the world she had experienced, but of its evils she knew nothing. As God made her—art had left her—she had never been thrown with bad, or unkind, or calculating people. To love, and to deny herself every gratification, or rather to gratify herself by studying the inclinations of those she loved—

these had been the pleasures of her life. Duty was a word she had never even whispered to herself, because it came naturally to her to perform all those duties that are usually deemed the hardest without a thought of sacrifice or merit.

It seemed as much a matter of course for her to think of others and forget herself, as it was for the sparrows to chirp in London, and the sun to shine in the country.

Many heroines, so called, would have sunk under the weight of the trials she had patiently endured—and yet, still, Letitia Mills was no heroine, no self-pitying martyr, travelling drearily along the regular high road of duty. She could be styled and thought of as nothing else but a very loving little girl, who had not numbered much more than sixteen years, and who, spite of solitude and poverty, and care and trouble, managed, nevertheless, to keep herself cheerful and happy. Heaven had given her for a dowry a better gift than stores of gold, and caskets of diamonds, a bright sunshiny temper.

So her uncle said—so Evan felt sure, as he watched her take out the ashes, and brush the grate.

"Lettie," he said at last—"it won't do."

"What won't?" she asked.

"For you to work like a lodging-house servant. You must have a 'help.'"

She shook her head with a pretty gesture of dissent, and went out of the room for a few coals, which Evan took from her the moment she reappeared, saying—

"You must, indeed, get assistance, if you do not wish to have me do the entire work of the house—I cannot see you dirtying your fingers in that way."

"But you are soiling yours," she retorted; "and besides, I am used to it."

"Perhaps so, but you ought not to be used to it ; as for my great ugly hands, they have worked with pitch and all sorts of filth, till they are fit for nothing better. See how fast I have lighted the fire."

" Yes, because you have been very extravagant, and burnt four times the wood you ought,"
said Lettie, as she laid the breakfast table, and
put a kettle on the fire, and prepared things
comfortably for her uncle, who came slowly in,
after a little time, looking even poorer, and
shabbier, and thinner than he had done on the
previous day.

Evan's heart ached for him as he thought of
the great reverses the noble old soul had borne
without a murmur; and he strove, by every
effort, to raise Captain Darvin's spirit, and compel him to look forth into the future with
greater hope and confidence.

During the course of the day, they conversed
long and earnestly together over Evan's plans
and prospects. The young man had managed
to save a considerable number of Bank notes;
but all the world knows that no capital will bear
drawing upon for ever; and it was, therefore,
absolutely necessary, that before his funds were
exhausted, the son of the Welsh clergyman

should look out for, and obtain, some permanent and respectable employment.

"I have never visited any country," he said, "without striving to learn its language; and if my knowledge of foreign tongues could gain me a good situation of any kind, I think it would be well for me to see about the matter at once."

"I will speak to my employer," remarked Captain Darvin—"whenever he recovers from a serious illness which at present keeps him at home. I was down there yesterday, in the hope of seeing him about some business of my own, but I could not manage it. Whenever he gets better, however—"

"Many thanks," interrupted Evan, who had his doubts about the lawyer's liberality, and still greater doubts as to the importance which would attach to Captain Darvin's recommendation while he wore such a shocking coat. "Many thanks, but I don't think I shall wait for him, as I want to put matters in train before I go to Wales. The first thing I must do is to

get a suit of clothes fit to show myself in ;
the next, to try to hunt up a situation for myself
—or at least let it be known there is such an
individual in existence ; the third and last, to
write to my late Captain to forward my sea-traps
here. Perhaps, as time is precious, you will send
him a note for me, while I go to see about
having myself rigged perfectly out."

Which last feat he performed so effectually,
that when he returned two hours afterwards,
arrayed in black cloth from head to foot—with
a new shirt, unexceptionable pair of boots, satin
hat, hair cut, and beard properly trimmed,
Lettie scarcely knew him—and shrunk timidly
away—trying to hide her own poor garments in
the shade and gloom of the old city house.

"I have told the tradespeople," said Evan,
remarking the change in her manner, " to send
my sailor's clothes back here—and will you, like
a dear little soul, take care of them ?—for though
they are not very good, still I must continue to
wear them in the house till I am certain of a

good situation. Sometime, Lettie, we shall, I hope, be able to wear better dress all through the day—but we must be economical for a time —must we not?"

She said "yes," still shrinking back into the shadow, and looking at him as if he were a stranger; and she never seemed thoroughly at her ease again till evening, when, after a long day's round, he returned home once more for tea, and appeared, after a few minutes' absence, clad in the blue jacket and white trousers he had worn the night previous.

"I have got on very well," he said, as he sat down near the window, rubbing his hands together with much satisfaction—"I have not scrupled to demand private audiences with managing partners, nor hesitated to rate my poor abilities at their highest value. I have told any body, who seemed anxious on the subject, who I am, the occupation of my father, and the rank of my mother. I vowed long ago I would vex her if ever I could, and really have felt a pleasure in going as the grandson of Sir John Lestock, and asking for a situation of any sort, because his daughter deserted her children. To judge by the interest many seemed to take in my narrative, it must surely have been a very remarkable one. For character, and so forth, I referred all enquirers to my late captain, and astonished some of my auditors by stating I had been, for above seven years, a common sailor. I intend starting for Klicksturvyd to-morrow, and I mean to beg you, sir, to look up these gentlemen in my absence. May I intrude so far ?"

"I should do your cause harm, my boy," answered the old officer, looking down at his thread-bare unmentionables. "I believe my own dress has been one great draw-back to every effort I have made to get on in London, and it is quite enough to have lowered myself without doing you an evil turn."

"The accident of a bad coat cannot lower us, I hope, in anything but the estimation of strangers," replied Evan; "still I agree with you, that a good suit is a letter of introduction to many a man, and, therefore, as it really is of importance to me that my business should be attended to properly, I wish you would go to the fellow I got my things from, and order whatever you think necessary for the occasion. Perhaps you could do a little business for yourself at the same time; but at any rate," he said, laughingly, "if you can manage to fish up a good appointment for me, I will pay you for loss of time, in the shape of a good per centage, or, as the newspapers say, 'thanks.' It will add a little more to the debt I already owe you. And now good bye for the present," he added, "for I must be off by five o'clock in the morning, and I want to have some sleep first. Don't get up— I shall shut the front door carefully, and try to raise an appetite for breakfast on the top of the mail."

It was all very well for Evan to lay such strict injunctions on his friends, that they were not to

rise—but he might have known that Letty
would be up for all that, and have breakfast
ready for him at half-past four. Captain Darvin,
too, he had a few parting words to say to the
young man, so they walked together to the
coach office, and the old officer waited to see
the 'last' of his new-found friend, who waved
an adieu to him from the box, and was speedily
en route for the coldest and dreariest sea-port in
North Wales.

Where he could learn nothing about his sister,
excepting the fact, that if she were dead she
had not died in Klicksturvyd. Mrs. Crickieth's
information was of the very scantiest—her
manner of the very stiffest. She was not aware
of Miss Crepton's being dead : she delicately
implied that perhaps it would be as well for all
her relatives if she were so. She said she had
not received any letter from Mr. Crepton since
his sister was forcibly removed from her protection, gave a garbled account of Dr. Duvard's
interference, and so tantalized and exasperated

Evan that, had she been a man, he would assuredly have adopted summary and by no means, pleasant methods of procedure.

"Then, madam," he said at length, fairly out of patience, "am I to understand that you know nothing whatever of my sister's present place of abode?"

"I can give you no clue whatever, excepting this, that probably—if she be living—wherever Dr. Duvard resides, there is her home."

"I hope it proves a happier one than this could have been, at all events," retorted Evan; "for if I had a daughter, I would rather shut her up in Newgate than see her immured here."

"You are complimentary, sir," remarked Mrs. Crickeith.

"I should belie my conscience if I were so to you," replied Evan. "You made my sister's life wretched, I have no doubt, and now you are attempting to throw a stain on her name, and distort the motives of the only person she found to stand her friend in the hour of need. Another thing I would say to you before I go. Had you been one of my own sex, I would have thrust every word you said against Alice down your throat again. As you are a woman, however, I can do nothing but leave a warning, that if ever you speak another evil sentence, concerning her to any one, I will institute an action against you for slander, so sure as my name is Evan Crepton."

"I never wish either to mention or hear the name of Crepton again," answered the lady, with much acrimony. "Your ungrateful sister injured me sufficiently to make me loath the race for ever."

"I am very glad to hear it," he replied—"Very glad Alice had it in her power to injure you; and if ever it should fall in my way to do you the same good turn, be assured I shall not permit the opportunity to slip through my fingers. But now, madam, about the money I forwarded two years since?"

"I have not received any money," said Mrs.

Crickeith. "That is all I have got to say about the matter."

"Then all I have got to say about it is, that I do not believe you." And Evan having unburdened himself of this civil sentence, bowed stifly to the grim old schoolmistress, and walked out of the house, from which place he enquired his way to the only doctor's shop Klicksturvyd boasted.

The information, however, he gleaned from the proprietor thereof, a jovial-looking Irishman who had taken to "stimulants," profited him but little.

Dr. Macmahon knew nothing of Dr. Duvard, except that he was a very honest fellow, who sold him his fixtures, at a fair price, and told him the whole of the Klicksturvyd practice would not buy blacking for his boots. "All of which I have proved to be confoundedly true," added the unhappy apothecary; and on the strength of it he invited Evan in to take something "hot."

Mr. Crepton scrupled not to avail himself of

the hospitable invitation, and accordingly, during the course of the evening, when the doctor's heart was opened and his tongue loosened, by the genial influences of water with something in it, he heard the whole history of Bessie Gay's death, with sundry other particulars, of which the reader is still in ignorance.

"You are not the first one who has been here inquiring for Duvard," he said, with a very drunken wink; "people have come asking for Duvard, who would have made his fortune if they could only have found him—and your sister has been wanted too; but they went away and left no address, nor anything; Duvard never said where he was going, nor a sentence I could put together—I fancy he must have been intending to emigrate, for his sister married some man who went abroad, and I dare say they made a family concern of it. But it was a pity—a great pity—I wish to Heaven such a chance would come my way."

"What sort of a chance was it then?"

demanded Evan; "and why was my sister wanted—and who inquired about Doctor Duvard?"

" You see, my dear fellow, I may tell you in the strictest confidence," said the doctor, laying one finger on the young man's arm—" in the strictest confidence—all about it. It appears, one General Beaufort had a daughter at school, who when she went home for the holidays, told her pa the whole affair of the child's death, and said she would not go back to Mrs. Crickeith's unless she were dragged by force. So the General, a fine, spirited, old fellow, took the matter up hotly, and wrote to Captain Gay, calling him all sorts of names for neglecting his child, which letter brought the Captain back from India, post haste, to inquire into the matter, for it seems he had sent remittances regularly, for the girl's benefit, to some blackguard in London, who pocketed the cash; and then he heard the way she had been treated, from Miss Beaufort; and he came down here, swearing vengeance, and wishing to get the evidence of your sister and Doctor Duvard; and there were advertisements put in the paper for information of both of them, but nothing ever came of it. General Beaufort wanted to do something handsome for my predecessor, get him an appointment or something of that sort; and Captain Gay wished to provide for your sister till your return. There was a devil of a row altogether!" concluded Doctor MacMahon, with great glee and exultation at the very recollection of the excitement; "and though there was no open trial, the affair split up the old woman's school, and trumped all her best cards. She don't clear fifty pounds a year by all her teaching, at this minute; and if she had not a pupil, it would be all the better for society at large."

"Where does General Beaufort, live?" demanded Evan.

"In Cumberland, to be sure—where else?" responded the apothecary; " I can give you his address, if you want it—he left it with me in case Doctor Duvard should ever turn up—here it is—now listen:

'GENERAL BEAUFORT,

'BEAUFORT HALL,

'HAWKSHEAD,

'CUMBERLAND.'

Bear that carefully in your head, my boy, and it may be the making of you yet."

With which injunction the Irishman dismissed his visitor, who proceeded from Klicksturvyd to Beaufort Hall, where, however, he found no tidings of his sister awaiting him. The General proved a capital old veteran; he had not forgotten Bessie Gay's death; he remembered the name of Crepton; he knew Sir John Lestock, and said he was a cold-hearted worldling; and, finally, took a fancy to Evan, told him if ever he came across Doctor Duvard, to write him word, and he would try to push him on in the world; and by way of doing something for the connection gave the youth a quantity of introductory letters to people in London, who, he said, might be of use to him.

"If ever I hear of your sister," he added, "I will be sure to let you know; and if you have time to spare, I shall be glad to hear how you are getting on in the world. Ah! the time will come, never fear, when Sir John Lestock will be glad enough to acknowledge you."

And General Beaufort, who had in years gone by, plucked a few private crows with the Baronet, bade the young man a hearty good-bye, and told him when he travelled that way again, not to forget to stop at Beaufort Hall.

So Evan, in somewhat better spirits, returned to London, where he speedily obtained a good situation, and still searching about, and inquiring for Alice, and hoping in course of time to meet her once more, took up his abode with his new found friends—the elder of whom he adopted for a father, whilst Lettie, with her pretty ways, and loving, artless nature; installed herself in the innermost recesses of his heart, and was unto him as a sister.

END OF VOL. II.

J Billing, Printer and Stereotyper, Guildford, Surrey.

THE

RICH HUSBAND;

A NOVEL OF REAL LIFE.

BY THE AUTHOR OF

"THE RULING PASSION."

"And she was wedded! young and beautiful—
To one whose heart was steel'd 'gainst gen'rous deeds :
She loath'd him, as the deadly Upas tree,
That blights the flow'r which grows beneath its shade."

IN THREE VOLUMES.

VOL. III.

LONDON:

CHARLES J. SKEET, PUBLISHER,

10, KING WILLIAM STREET,

CHARING CROSS.

1858.

J. Billing, Printer and Stereotyper, Guildford, Surrey.

THE

RICH HUSBAND.

CHAPTER I.

TIME, which hath a way of improving the fortunes of some people, and of making matters
worse with others, had been kind enough to perform the latter operation for Judith Mazingford,
during the course of the two years succeeding her
sister's death.

Looking at affairs from one point of view, any
person might have concluded, that as time wore
on, Judith would become more reconciled to her

position; that years would, very likely, smooth
away the sharp edges of her chain, and habit
accustom her to the weight of the yoke she had
voluntarily chosen to wear; and with some
women, under some circumstances, such ideas
would undoubtedly have proved correct; for
general humanity, particularly the female portion
of it, certainly has a knack of accommodating
itself to any evil—if only once convinced that
the said evil is irremediable.

But as Judith was an exception to many rules,
so she proved an exception to this. She never
got used to her burden; the longer she wore her
chain, the more she tugged and tore at it, like a
furious animal; the longer she was married, with
greater intensity she hated her husband; the
more futile her efforts for independence appeared,
the more frantically she asserted her rights; the
oftener she and Mr. Mazingford waged an un-
equal war, the more eager she seemed to commence the strife *de nouveau.*

From the hour Lillian died, she flung over-
board every consideration of prudence, duty,
expediency. What she liked to say, she said—
when she wanted to be quiet, nobody could get

a word out of her; she gave Mr. Mazingford a
few specimens of what a determined woman,
crossed in any purpose, injured in any particular,
can be ;—to sum up all into four old-fashioned
lines—her husband speedily found

> "That man's a fool who strives, by force or skill,
>   To stem the torrent of a woman's will;
>   For what she will, she will, you may depend
>   on't—
>   And what she won't, she won't, and there's an
>   end on't."

He knew perfectly well what she was driving
at, understood as thoroughly as Judith herself,
that she was sick of the uncongenial tie, and
longed to sever it; saw that she was trying by
every art and stratagem to compel him to a
separation—knew, and understood, and saw all;
and swore that he would bend, and break, and
bring her under still.

It was the work he had set himself before
their marriage; it was the work he determined
sooner or later to accomplish.

But he might as well have striven to bend

and break an oak of the forest, as try to "get the better," as the phrase goes, of his indomitable wife.

His taunts touched her not; his violence never seemed to affright her: his fiercest fits of rage, only moved her to scornful laughter—she met him with the armour of despair; she dared him to warfare with one of the haughtiest and most unconquerable women that ever lived. "I defy you, Lewis Mazingford!" she said to him, once, after one of their stormiest altercations; "I defy you to break a broken heart!"

There lay her strength—he had done his worst in former times—and rising, after long prostration from the mental stupor succeeding the struggle, without any care or feeling left—she turned her proud, beautiful face on him and all the world beside, and dared the whole universe to inflict another pang upon her. It was a mournful sentence, to be spoken in the fierce anguish of her heart, by a wife to her husband.

"I defy you to break a broken heart." Yes—there lay her strength, and yet there were dreadful hours of darkness, when the giant spirit, which refused to be vanquished by the

weight of any present sorrow or humiliation—
sank under the horror of the misery and desolation of the past—the dreariness and hopelessness
of the future. There were hours when, with
nerves unstrung, and pulses quivering, she could
not put on a brave defiant face, and meet all
trouble half way—when Mr. Mazingford thought
he was gaining the mastery—when Judith herself
could have almost fancied herself that her mind
was wandering. And how far she was actually
"sane," in the correct interpretation of the word,
I, reader, cannot pretend to say, believing that
all violent passions, all tremendous griefs, shake
the understanding for a time; and that there
are times and seasons in the lives of every one
amongst us—when, if a commission of lunacy
were held, we should find it wondrously difficult
to prove ourselves reasonable beings.

No doubt Judith still retained her full compliment of senses; and was as far from being a
maniac as any human being can be—but still
the world began to whisper that Mrs. Mazingford
was "odd," "eccentric," peculiar—"more than
ordinary my dear"—and it is not for me to
declare positively that the world was wrong.

Still, if the lady were crazed, there was method in her madness—method in the way she tormented her husband—method in the manner she tortured herself. The sort of abject apathy with which she submitted to a continental tour for the benefit of her health, would have been enough to have made any other man under heaven desire to get rid of her. From town to town—from mountain to ravine, and from ravine to volcano, Judith permitted herself to be led—like a sheep to the slaughter. Her husband brought visitors to their hotel, and she would not talk to them. She did not know their language," she said, " and it was wearisome for foreigners to talk English." When she left Rome, people asked her what she thought of St. Peter's; and she declared that she had not noticed it sufficiently to be able to answer the question. She tired everybody out, but the person she wanted to tire. It proved a pitched battle between them, and they fought it out.

When, after a year of dismal travel, however, she returned to England, with her body invigo. rated, and mind restored to most of its former powers, Judith put out her canvass on another tack. Reducting herself to the condition of a dead-alive piece of the creation, had done her no good—and so she fell back upon her old style of weapon, and used it with tremendous effect. The old sneers—the old sarcasms, the old fixed look of scorn—she brought these back into her service, and tried their powers to the uttermost.

It seemed as impossible for the two to agree, as for a cat and dog to meet without a spar—and, to say truth, she usually got the best of it; for if physical strength and worldly advantages were on his side—moral courage and mental superiority were on her's.

"I don't care what you say," she once exclaimed; "I don't care what you do—you might as well talk of hurting a corpse as of touching me. You destroyed my vulnerable point, Mr. Mazingford—find another if you can."

And he did try, but he could not—he had lost the only hold over her he ever possessed; and she laughed his threats, and anger, to scorn.

"I will never do anything again that you wish, if it be possible for me to avoid it," she declared—"never, so help me Heaven." And she did not; she would not sing, she would not

play, she would not draw, she would not dance,
she would not talk—she would go out to show
society that she would not do what he requested
her.   She made him writhe, at times, under her
look of fixed contempt in public—she had
ceased striving to conceal the fact that life was
an agony to her; she flung aside the veil which
had previously partially concealed their domestic
misery from view—and, without uttering a word,
or pointing a finger to the scene, still permitted,
in her imperious way, all who would, to look at
the ghastliness of the skeleton she and Mr.
Mazingford bore between them.

The world, which had ever been good enough
to take a lively interest in all that concerned the
member and his wife, at length began to make
such candid and audible remarks on the subject
of their matrimonial unhappiness, that Judith's
husband, wearied of the useless struggle, finally
determined to change the battle-ground, and see
whether an alteration in place might not also
produce an alteration in results.

Acting upon this idea, he gave up his house in
town, and shifted his head quarters to Wales,
a home which seemed to Judith a degree more

unendurable than London; for, in the metropolis, there was something to distract her mind
from the subject of her own misfortunes, but at
Wavour Hall, the great spirit sunk under the
weight of its utter loneliness—her heart preyed
on itself—she thought till she was weary, and
she cried till she was sick.

And, besides, once arrived in Wales, her husband managed to provide a new source of irritation for her—a sight of her brother Stephen,
with whom there had been no intercourse for
years previously, in consequence of Mr. Mazingford's having forgotten to fulfil his promise and
remove the mortgage deed off the firs and weeds
—and brambles and ruins, of Llandyl Hall.

Stephen never forgave the member; but he
proved a deeper file than Mr. Mazingford had
ever given him credit for—and as thoroughly
baulked his brother-in-law of the property he
wanted to secure, as though he likewise had been
born and bred a pettifogging attorney.

He borrowed money to pay Mr. Mazingford,
from a capitalist, who shared the young man's
belief, that if the member had not thought there
was coal on the estate, he never would have ad-

vanced money on it to Mr. Renelle—employed
a lawyer to take both principal and interest to
the estimable proprietor of Wavour Hall—got
thoroughly practical men down from London,
abandoned the shafts his father had sunk at
another's prompting—bored in more promising
and likely situations, and finally, to his infinite
triumph, came on the black diamonds, and commenced coining them into gold.

Then Mr. Mazingford made overtures of
friendship to him, which Stephen accepted, to
the end that he might vex his brother-in-law,
by talking of the mines, and the wealth likely
to accrue from them ; and Judith, whom the
conversation between the two made heart-sick,
turned, with perfect loathing, from the memories
and the miseries her brother's presence conjured
up before her.

" Stephen, I hate you," she said at last, " and
I wish you would go."

" Well, I'm sure," he replied, I never asked
you to love me; and I won't go till it suits my
convenience:" and accordingly he remained, until
he and Mr. Mazingford quarrelled again, when
he went away back to his mines, leaving matters

at Wavour Hall a degree worse than he had found them.

" You know I wished you joy of your bargain," were his farewell words to his brother-in-law; and, with a " Good bye, Judith—I am glad you are so happily married!" he departed, laughing like a fiend over his sister's misfortunes.

Then came the dreary November days, with the rain streaming down, and the sky dark, and the earth damp, and the prospect gloomy—then came the most intense loneliness, the most perfect isolation and retirement—and, almost in despair, Judith flew to her pen again, and worked, for weeks and weeks together, at a novel, which, in the very agony of her soul, she entitled " The History of a Broken Heart:" and out of the fulness of sorrow came the ripeness of genius—and at length, the hand felt its power, and the imagination its intensity, and the labour of composition ceased to be a toil, and the words flowed easily from the pen.

Shrewd, sarcastic, brusque, writing of the world, and the men and women in it as she had found them, she produced, what all amongst us would be glad to do if we could, a book worth reading ;

and the craving desire for fame, for wealth earned by her own endeavours, for freedom from the yoke she had bound round her neck, for perfect untrammelled leisure, to perform the only work left her in life—came to save Judith Mazingford's soul from perdition—to rescue her from that numbness of sensation, which is death to the mind as it is death to the body.

Travellers tell us of a disease, common in Liberia, called the sleepy sickness. It is caused by want of exercise, a particular diet, and the influences of climate; and so affects the sufferer, that he sleeps on continually, being scarcely able to rouse up sufficiently even to take nourishment. When this stupor has continued for some months, the patient falls into a deeper slumber still, and never wakens on this side eternity again.

It was just such a numbness as this which was gathering over Judith's soul, when authorship roused her from it. The want of an object in life—the utter carelessness concerning both herself and everybody else—the great fountains of love turned to ice in her heart—the miseries and humiliations of her present existence, and a sort of failure in her general health, mental and bodily—these things were fast reducing her mind to a state of unnatural stupor, when she fled to her old occupation again. With her pen she cleared away the mists from before her eyes; out of the inkstand she drew medicine more potent than any ever prepared by the hand of chemist or apothecary. Of inanimate paper she made a living confidante, talking on foolscap eagerly, earnestly, well—as she had never talked before for years, in reality.

One personage in the book was Judith Mazingford, and another an ideal character, such as Marcus Lansing's might have proved; and to this imaginary friend she poured out the story of her sorrows—confessed her faults and follies—put questions and gave answers—arguing with herself and her own proud, ungovernable spirit, before the personages of her drama—wrestling and striving, and sinking and rising, as she had done in reality—fearing, repenting, hoping, praying, weeping, and working. God knows, it was no wonder the book, when finished, seemed life-like; for it was, after all, a daguerreotype of human feelings, wrongs and griefs.

The pain she described she had experienced;
the struggles she recounted had been made by
herself; the wrongs had been inflicted on her;
the faults she was conscious of, in her own
ill-regulated nature.   No marvel, that the colour-
ing was like flesh and blood—that the interest
was absorbing—the story too much resembling
reality ever to be taken for fiction.

"Out of the fulness of the heart the mouth
speaketh;" and accordingly, Mrs. Mazingford's
tale might justly have been considered—

"The History of a Broken Heart, written by
one Broken-hearted."

So she whiled away the dreary winter days—
so, when her husband was from home, she employed her leisure time—so when he was in the
room, and she with books and papers laid aside,
sitting opposite to him, she kept her thoughts
from brooding by conceiving fresh incidents for
her novel, by thinking that she still possessed
one thing, at least, with which he could never
intermeddle.

Silently she triumphed in the fact; she
thought she had at length pitched her tent on
safe ground—thought so, but was mistaken.

Christmas came—and with it guests in abundance—guests to admire the dark oak furniture, and the curiously carved chairs, and fantastic tables; to fill every apartment in the house, and to occupy in especial one drawing-room, filled with rare and curious knick-knacks, part and parcel of the valuable personal property the late Mrs. Mazingford had bequeathed unto her lord. Fires were never let out in this room, for the master of Wavour Hall delighted to receive antiquarians in it, and show them old relics, and hideous chairs, and formal settees, and oaken cabinets, and inlaid screens; Judith hated the chamber, because whenever company came to the Hall, she had to go down there, and receive them and become a figure in the pageant —the only thing requisite to complete the picture, perfect her husband's triumph, and give life and animation to the scene.

She had no time given her now to jot down her imaginings; from morning till night her existence was a perpetual torment to her. Company and show !—she, one of the puppets set to play for the amusement of a host of fashionables, idlers, *savans*, and bores of all sorts. Judith got

wearied, as well she might, more especially as old
guests only departed to make way for new;
Christmas revellers for electioneering politicians;
foolish women, for strong-minded ones; silly
flirts, for indefatigable canvassers; females who
knew little for females who knew everything;
for ministers had turned out, and there was
another contested election.   Then recommenced
the bitter wrangling between man and wife, which
had suffered a brief cessation during the preceding
months; then, when lulled into a state of delusive
security by Judith's recent comparative quiescence,
he tried once again to show her off—to humble
her and exalt himself; the spirit of old burst
forth with tenfold violence, and scenes of recrimination and passionate reproach were of daily
occurrence.

"Am I never to have peace?" she once
demanded.

"Never, till you learn to conduct yourself
properly!" he answered; and she could not but
acknowledge that in this instance he kept his
word.

Still the canvassing went bravely on, and
electors were bribed, and fed, and entertained;

still young politicians lounged about the house, with an affectation of fashionable indifference; still handsome women drove through the country in carriages with outriders, flattering, praying, beseeching, and urging for votes; still all was fuss and hurry and confusion at the Hall ;—and at length the anniversary of Lillian's death came round.

It was a day Judith always kept sacred, a day when she could not bear to hear the sound of a strange voice; when the intrusion of visitors seemed a profanation; when she shut herself up all alone with God and her own thoughts, and looked over the relics she still possessed of the dead; turned out the contents of a secret drawer which she never opened at any other time, and wiped the damp off the long, fair tress, and kissed the leaves of the rose she had lifted off her sister's breast, when she lay shrouded in her coffin—opened the old bible and read all the passages marked in pencil—held the much-worn prayer-book in her hand, and rained bitter tears over all.

Lillian herself was never absent from her thoughts; but she did not dare trust herself

often with a sight of the tangible mementoes of
the dead.

" They would unfit me for the ordinary duties
of life," she said, mentally ; and she was right.

And accordingly, it was only when the day
came round once a year that she turned the key
in the lock, and let the light of heaven stream
on the memorials of one not lost, but gone
before ; but, unfortunately, it chanced that the
election was not over when the anniversary
arrived.

In the morning Judith sent down a message
to her guests that she should be unable to leave
her own apartment during the course of the day
—and in the bustle of canvassing, driving,
riding, laughing and talking, her absence was
very little noticed, until dinner-time, when her
vacant chair at the head of the table attracted
Mr. Mazingford's attention, and turning to a
servant he demanded where his mistress was.

" Mrs. Mazingford has not been down stairs
to-day, I believe, sir," was the reply.

" Is she ill ?"

" I do not know, sir," answered the man.

All at once it flashed upon the ex-member's

memory, that this was a day his wife loved to set
apart as a sacred and peculiar season, and indignant that she should dare to permit her own
private feelings to interfere with his public in-
terests, as he called her appearance on all possible
occasions, in all possible places, he muttered a
hasty apology to his friends, and leaving the
dinner table, to ascertain, so he said, if Mrs.
Mazingford was ill, he hurried to her own especial sitting-room, where, finding the door locked,
he demanded admittance.

"What do you want?" asked Judith,
opening it for him.

"You!" he answered; "come down to dinner at once."

"Not to-day," she pleaded; "you can do
very well without me; and I like to be alone
with *her* memory."

"Alone with the devil!" responded her husband. "Put by this trash," pointing to the
relics previously referred to; "or, better still,
put the whole lot in the fire, and dress as fast
as you can. Don't hesitate, for I tell you I am
not going to stand any more of your cursed
sentimental nonsense. I am out of patience

both with you and with it. I don't intend to have you sitting here for days as you have done reading and scribbling, cramming your head with poetry and a parcel of such damned folly. I swear by——"

"Lewis, I wish you would not swear so here," interposed Judith nervously. "It makes me feel —feel —" She looked hurriedly around the room, and, by way of a finish, burst into tears.

"Come, no more of this infernal nonsense," he exclaimed. "I think no man ever was so .tormented as I am. Go and dress yourself, Mrs. Mazingford," he added, angrily, "and come down as quickly as possible. It is of importance to me that my constituents should be suitably entertained—that my wife should sit at the head of my table, that—"

"She should sit there so be stared at, and forget her own feelings that she may gratify your wishes," finished Judith bitterly. "Well, be it so—any other day in the year but this."

"You had better not refuse," he said, "or I will make you repent it."

"You could not," she answered.

The words had barely passed her lips before

every one of the relics were tossed relentlessly into the fire. With a shriek Judith sprang forward to rescue some one article—some single memento—and plunging her hand absolutely through the flame, she plucked out a volume, and, quick as thought, extinguished the blaze, by wrapping it in the skirt of her thick black dress.

"Give me that," he cried.

"I will not." And as the smell of the burnt lock of hair, and faint perfume of the rose, and bright glare of the fire told her all else had perished, she grasped the book with a tighter hold, and strove to save it from him.

In vain,—he wrenched it from her with his strong hand, and flung it once again into the flame, holding her back at the same time forcibly from rescuing it.

After the first struggle she remained quietly, till she saw it was all consumed. Then she hissed out, from between her teeth, the words:

"You have burnt a Bible, and I am glad, for I will inform against you—I will, so sure as I am Judith Mazingford."

"For which very reason, pretty one, your

testimony would be perfectly valueless. A wife cannot be a witness, false or true, against her husband. So much for that !" he finished with a sneer. "And now dress and come down to dinner, for I won't stand any more airs or nonsense—you had better. I should advise you not to cross me again."

"Very well," she answered sullenly. "Only rid me of your presence, and I will do as you desire ;" and she walked, as she spoke, towards her dressing-room, and, ringing for her maid, went through the duties of her toilette as though nothing had happened.

He had raised a devil in her again—a devil none the less dangerous because it was a silent one, and having made up her mind to a certain course ultimately, she could afford to be quiet and obey him in the interim.

Almost before Mr. Mazingford could have imagined it possible for her to change her dress, she entered the dining-room, arrayed in a deep mourning robe, with her hair simply arranged, and only a few jet ornaments relieving her sombre costume.

He looked angrily at the style of toilette, but

she sneered him down. With her pale face and commanding presence, and wonderful beauty, she had the advantage over him then, and strong in herself and her determination, she took her seat with a feeling almost of joy throbbing at her heart — at last she had made up her mind—and she was free.

A gentleman, on her right, ventured to hope that she was better.

"Thank you," she said, in a clear though quiet tone, "but I have never been ill. The reason I absented myself from your circle was, that this being the anniversary of the death of my only sister, who expired under peculiarly melancholy circumstances, I thought my presence might be dispensed with, but Mr. Mazingford judging otherwise, I, of course, deferred to his decision in the matter."

She uttered the foregoing sentence in a perfectly audible voice, and, at its conclusion, glanced towards her husband. For one instant his eye rested on her with a menacing expression, the next he was asking some one to take wine, and striving to banish the disagreeable feeling of restraint and discomfort Judith's explanation had produced on his guests. She took no notice either of him or the sensation she had managed to create. She went on her way quietly and politely, conversed, perhaps, a little more than usual, played the part of hostess with greater politeness than had latterly been her wont, tried assiduously to render the ladies of the party comfortable and happy during the course of the tedious half-hour after dinner, and finally, of her own accord, set young girls to the piano, drew out prints and folios of landscapes for the gentlemen, sang, without being ordered to do so by her husband, and, in brief, rendered all need of intervention on his part superfluous. She was a model wife, and a model hostess that night until all the outside visitors had driven off, and all the inside ones retired to rest, then closing the door of the drawing-room, containing the quaint chairs and dark tables, she said to Mr. Mazingford :

"I want to speak to you."

"And I have a good deal to say to you, madam," he retorted—"but I am too angry to say it to-night; you had better go away, and not commence talking to me now."

"I had not better go away—and I will talk to you," she replied. "I can put what I want to say into a single sentence. We are wretched together, we shall never agree. In Heaven's name, then, let us separate."

"You have been driving at this for two years; but you may just as well quit it, for I will never give in to any arrangement of the kind. Make up your mind to that."

"But is not the life we are leading a sort of hell upon earth?" she asked, putting a force of constraint upon her utterance, which gave it a sort of thrilling intensity. "Are we not more wretched than man and woman ever were before—would not anything be better than this—no change could be for the worse."

"If you like to make your own life wretched it is nothing to me," he answered. "Do what I desire, in a proper manner, and we shall get on well enough. If you just would remember, once for all, that I am master, and will be obeyed, you would make yourself, and every one else, a vast deal more comfortable than is the case at present. Put the idea of separation out of your mind altogether; recollect I have said it shall

never be—and, above all, never dare to cross me
again as you have crossed me this day ; for if
you do, I will bring you to your senses by
rougher means than any I have hitherto employed."

"Fool!" said Mrs. Mazingford, and she
dropped the word out from between her lips
with an accent of such ineffable contempt, that
Mr. Mazingford's blood boiled within him.
" You think I am afraid of violence—that I am
afraid of you—that I am afraid of anything on
earth. I showed you once before," she continued, more vehemently; "what I could do
when I would. I warned you then not to
refuse me the money, and I warn you now not
to refuse me a separation; I want no annual
allowance—I want no annuity, no sum in hand,
no any thing—I only want leave to go in peace.
Will you grant it."

" If you ever ask for it again ?" he began—

"Well," she demanded.

" I will make you wish you had never been
born," he said fiercely.

"That would be nothing new," she retorted; then fixing a withering glance of concen-

trated hatred upon him, she added, as if debating the question with herself. "I wonder, Lewis Mazingford, I have never killed you."

"And I wonder I have never killed you," he returned, growing absolutely pale at the idea that possibly at some future time she might take it into her head to finish matters quietly by such a process.

"I daresay you would long ago," was her reply—"had you not been afraid of being hung —for you are a coward as well as a bully. Don't strike me," she exclaimed, as he raised his hand threateningly. "Don't do it—for I will arouse the household with my shrieks—and nform society that Mr. Mazingford, of Wavour Hall, is in the habit of beating his wife."

With a coarse oath he sprung towards hei ; and with one hand covering her mouth, he wound the other through her luxuriant hair, and shook her by it till he was perfectly exhausted. When, at last, he flung her from him, his hand was full of dark hair, torn literally out by the roots—and, thoroughly unnerved by the intense pain he had inflicted, Judith sank on a sofa, conquered, for once in her life, by bodily suffering.

"There," he said, as he rolled the trophy of his manly conquest up, and flung it on the fire—" never anger me again, for I will not be browbeaten by any woman under Heaven, much less by one whom I raised from a station little better than that of a beggar. Name separation again to me if you dare."

" I dare do anything ; but I will never name it again," she answered, in a low husky voice. "Still, remember, Mr. Mazingford—and these are my last words on the subject to you—that any evil consequences which may ensue from your refusal will rest on yourself." And, without waiting for a reply, she picked up her comb, which had fallen on the floor, and walked out of the room, away to her own desolate chamber. That night her head never rested on a pillow.

It did not take her an hour to pull the flounces off a black dress, to put a bit of ribbon plainly across an old garden bonnet—to collect all the jewels which had been given to her by her various friends, on the occasion of her most ill-assorted marriage; to envelope herself in a coarse travelling shawl, to tie up her most important manuscripts, and burn the rest. With a wild impatience she hurried on the preparations for departure—unburdened by anything save one convenient bundle, with curls brushed out, and hair plainly braided ; she cautiously descended the back staircase, opened a glass door leading out into the garden, and unmindful of wind and rain, sallied forth in the darkness, and ran on till she was fairly out of breath.

She felt no fear of night—she did not care for the pitiless pelting of the storm that wet her through and through ; she was leaving all she hated and dreaded on earth behind her, and in the wild delirious joy of escape, forgot every danger, every risk. Crossing the drive she entered the plantations, and pursuing a narrow path, with the windings of which she was well acquainted, she at last reached a stile that conducted her into the churchyard of Wavour.

There among the long wet grass, and the mouldering head stones, she stopped for an instant to think, and, as she did so, the rumbling of distant wheels indistinctly heard during the pauses of the tempest, reached her ear.

"That's the night mail," she muttered, " I will go in it," and groping her way over the graves and mounds to the churchyard gate, she took her stand by the roadside, and as the lights came blinking up close to the spot she occupied, called out for the coachman to stop.

" Where do you want to go to?" he demanded, pulling up.

" London ;" was the brief response.

" All right," said the guard; " Now ma'am !"

" Hang it !" exclaimed the coachman, " don't bring a woman outside a night like this."

" I can't afford an inside seat," said Judith, disguising her voice as much as possible.

" Oh! it's all right, my girl," he answered; " you can get up if the inside fills; but it's not likely till the election's over we shall have many passengers. Now, look sharp!"—and suiting the action to his companion's words, the guard shoved Judith, somewhat unceremoniously, into the vehicle, banged the door after her, demanded if she had nothing but the bundle, and receiving an answer in the negative, clambered up into his place, and gathered his great coats and horse-cloths about him, as the coach whirled off towards the next stage.

" Thank God! thank God!" said Judith, " I am free at last:" and assuredly, she had chosen

her time for flight well. Had she planned her
escape for months previously, she could not have
found a better opportunity.

Long ere her departure was ever dreamed of,
she found herself eighty miles from Wavour;
and she amused herself with picturing what an
excitement and confusion would follow the first
knowledge of her departure. Mentally she beheld her husband rushing about the house; she
fancied the amazement of the servants, the con-
jectures of the guests—she knew it would be
impossible for Mr. Mazingford to follow on her
track immediately, as this was the day the election was to be decided.

"Ten thousand furies!" muttered the member
between his teeth; " she has laid her plans well.
Where the devil can she be gone?—she has
taken no clothes, no jewellery, no anything. She
cannot be gone to her brother. I have it—she
is sure to be found at Miss Ridsdale's. Colonel,"
he added, to one of his friends—"will you post
up to town for me? Employ detectives, anybody
you choose. Spare no expense to find her; and
above all, watch that house. She is sure, sooner
or later, to go to Great Crowland Street. Dog

Miss Ridsdale's movements, and you will soon
be on her track.   Don't lose a minute : inquire
along the road if any one have seen her.   She
cannot be far ahead, for it was raining so furiously until it was almost morning, that even
she would have scarcely ventured out in the
storm.   I shall be up after you to-night—thank
you—I am sure I could not leave it in better
hands:" and so saying, Mr. Mazingford flung himself on his horse, and galloped off to the county
town—where the free and independent electors,
having been tremendously bribed by the Opposition candidate, forgot to return their former
member, who lost the day by twenty-three votes.

" I shall petition against your return," were
the first words Mr. Mazingford uttered to the
Honourable Mr. Standish, when this result was
made known. " Post-chaise and pair!" he cried
to the landlord of the " Feathers;" and ten
minutes after, was driving off towards the metropolis, thinking to find his refractory wife,
and bring her back, without any extraordinary
amount of trouble.

One would have imagined he might have
known enough of Judith's character, to feel sure

she had sense enough not to dream of going to any place where he was likely to look for her. The first thing she did when she went to London was to buy a widow's cap, mourning bonnet, and mantle, trimmed with crape. Arrayed in these sable habiliments, she proceeded to Mr. Mason's, left her manuscript with him, and then wended her way to one of those convenient lodging-houses situated close to the Strand, where, as visitors to London are constantly dropping in, there is no tiresome difficulty made on the score of references. For the sake of appearances she bought a trunk, and armed with this credential, and her own quiet, lady-like appearance, she experienced no difficulty in obtaining apartments, wherein she abode for a week, daily searching those columns of the " Times " relating to the important subject of furnished lodgings ; for although the first floor in a street off the Strand did very well for a few days, it was far too expensive and noisy to suit Judith for a permanency.

" I will try this," she said at last, coming on a paragraph which stated that apartments might be had furnished, in the house of a quiet family

residing in " a favourite part of Walworth, for
Twelve Shillings a week; no other Lodgers or
Children:" and accordingly she did " try," but
found the situation so wretched, and the house
so dirty, that she unceremoniously backed off
the premises, and determined to search further, perfectly satisfied that go where she chose
she could fare no worse.

Very wearily she wandered along the dreary
Walworth Road, which resembles, like every
other road leading into London, a thing described
in an allegory—so long, so straight, so chilling
and so ugly.

She glanced at the lines of houses on each
side, with shops jutting out before them, which
look, as I once heard a Cockney say, as though
somebody had been to a chest of drawers, and
forgotten to shut the bottom one—and speedily
that lost, miserable sensation came over her,
which usually oppresses every one who wanders
about London, without having the privilege and
blessing of a settled home. She got to Camber-
well Gate; then, nearly at random, crossed Cam-
berwell Green; walked, almost without an object,
along Church Street, hoping probably, as we

all have hoped, at some time or other when
house or lodging-hunting, ultimately to come to
" some place;" and finally, sickening of endless
high-roads, she turned aside down one of those
old-fashioned streets abounding in that suburb
of London, where the houses were built of red
brick, and the windows were painted white—
and little gardens, carefully kept, relieved the
tedium of town architecture with natural effects
in *petto*.

There were lodgings to let in that Grove, as
it was called; and Judith went in to look at
many of them, but she could find nothing to
suit, and so pursued her pilgrimage, still keeping
out of the regular track, and making inquiries at
humble two-storey houses, tenanted principally
by milliners and dress-makers, people who " had
been better off," and people who wished to be;
but still, desirable as most of these individuals
considered their own especial apartments, Judith
could not make up her mind to " come to terms"
with any of the lot. Truth was, poor desolate
soul, she was searching for a home, not a lodging-house—and there was something about all
these vulgar little suburban rooms, with their

line and plummet arrangement of furniture, their tables covered with gaudy oil-cloth, their stiff chairs with horse-hair seats, their mantel-piece crockery, and black-framed prints, that disgusted her.

" I could not write here," she thought ; " the Strand, after all, would be better than this."

And thus almost determined to remain there she walked on, getting further and further from the regular high road, till at length having all unconsciously shaped her course still further away from London, she found herself, just as a few drops of rain (the forerunner of a heavy shower), began to fall, in a lane called Ashby Row, which took her fancy more than any place she had seen since she left home. The cottages on each side were tenanted she saw by a poor, low class, who earned their bread by the labour of their hands and the sweat of their brow ; but the windows were festooned with ivy, and curious chimneys, and queer old gables, abounded in all directions. A few trees grew too by the wayside ; and peeping through a paling to her right, she saw a Nursery Garden within. " Well, this is all very romantic and pretty," she thought ;

"but pretty as it is, I must take shelter from the shower—" and hurrying on to the top of the lane, she stopped by a low green gate, and asked a decent-looking woman standing on the door step, if " she would allow her to wait till the rain was over ?"

" Certainly," answered the proprietress ; and leaving her post on the threshold, she asked Judith if she would not walk up stairs?

"No, thank you," was the reply; " I will just wait in the passage for a moment till it cease."

But the moments passed away so rapidly, and the sky grew so much darker, that Mrs. Mazingford yielded at length to the old woman's entreaties, and groping her way up a dark staircase, finally emerged on a still darker landing place, from which she passed (following her hostess), into a large low room occupying the entire breadth of the house, and lighted by two windows, which must have been glazed, judging by the bull's-eyes in the panes, and dirty green of the glass, about a century and a half previously.

What between the state of the sky and the style of the glazing, Judith could scarcely distinguish objects through the gloom at first—

but as by degrees her vision got accustomed to
the peculiar shade of light, she saw the apartment was a very old-fashioned one, very strangely
furnished.   Over the chimney-piece there hung
a print of some gentleman's mansion; and scru-
tinising it a little more closely, she found written
underneath — " Mayfield, Bucks, the seat of
Thomas Alfred Hardmore, Esquire."

Between this and the mantel-piece was sus
pended a small mother-of-pearl crucifix, very
elaborately carved, the ends being tipped with
gold, while on the chimney itself, some China
vases, of a better description than any usually
seen out of nice houses—a tortoise-shell box, a
faded water-colour portrait, and a couple of
feather fans, were arranged with more taste than
could have been expected in such a region of
the habitable globe.

Pursuing her investigations still further, she
perceived that two ricketty mahogany tables,
propped up against the walls, were covered with
shells, ivory boxes, Russian punch-bowls, some
Chinese paintings on rice paper, a grass fan, a
foreign bird or two, and a little miniature canoe.
These articles told their own tale intelligibly

enough; but the print, and the crucifix, and the portrait, and the tortoise-shell box — Judith brought back her gaze to the chimney-piece, and confessed herself puzzled.

"You are looking at the picture, ma'am," said the woman at last, noticing how her visitor's eye rested on it; "it is faded and stained now—but it was the picture of as good and handsome a woman as God ever sent on the earth."

"May I take it down?" asked Judith; and stretching forth her hand, she brought the miniature nearer to her. It was that of a very lovely girl of two or three and twenty, with long fair curls, and laughing eyes, and rich colour, and small pouting mouth.

"She was different from that when last I saw her," added the woman, in a low tone—"with lines across her forehead, and wrinkles about her eyes, and the beautiful hair grey and grizzled! Aye, her life was not an overly happy one—but God has taken her to himself. They may say what they like about this religion and that not getting to Heaven, but I am just as sure that she is with her Saviour at this minute, as if I saw her among the angels :" and the woman took the picture from Judith, and wiped and replaced it on the mantel-piece, by way of a finish to her rather extraordinary speech.

When she chose to exert herself, no one had a greater power of winning love and confidence than Judith Mazingford; and accordingly, in less than fifteen minutes, she succeeded in extracting the whole of Mrs. Hardmore's history from the old woman, who had, it appeared, lived with her as lady's maid for a period of fifteen years.

" My master and she were of different religions. Ma'am," she said, " and that was the whole cause of unhappiness, for I don't think a nicer gentleman ever breathed, or a kinder lady, and they could have done well enough only the relations interfered. And he would not let the children go to chapel, and she was loth to see them go to church, and so the end of it was, they grew up nothing much, and went to their place of worship more for the name of the thing than any anything else,—and they made fun of their mother's faith—and sided with their father's sisters against her, and the end of it all was, ma'am," continued the old woman, "that her heart was broken among them, and she died. I had left her service long before that to marry a mate of a foreign vessel; but when she was so ill, I went back at her own request to nurse her, for I was about her when she was a girl, and her heart turned to those who had loved her then. She gave me a crucifix, and all the rest of the little things you see, and I have kept them ever since for her sake."

Further, Judith, by dint of judicious cross questioning, elicited the information that the mate previously referred to had been drowned, after bringing home the curiosities distributed about the room, and that his widow managed to make "off a living" by washing and doing up "fine things." From this point to the state of her finances was an easy transition for so skilful a diplomatist as Judith Mazingford, and ascertaining that the woman found it hard to make all ends meet, and having assured herself that there were no children, or lodgers, or other inmates in the house, she boldly suggested to the widow, the propriety of letting her a bed and sitting-room, on moderate terms.

" You say," she continued, " you have often
thought of taking lodgers, only you were afraid of
having ' to do' for rough people. Now I want
quietness, and so do you, and if you like to give
me this room for my books and papers, and
another to sleep in, I will conclude with you now
on the best terms I can offer, namely, fifteen
shillings per week, including attendance and
washing."

And so, as the nursery maids say, to "cut a
long story short," Judith and the laundress
finally struck a bargain, and next day, Mrs. Gilmore, as the ex-member's wife called herself,
took up her abode in the room with the foreign
birds, and beasts, and shells ;—took up her
abode there, and felt wonderfully elated as she
did so, for a sense of peace came to her heart in
the old apartment, such as for years previously
had never visited it.

" DEAR AUNT,"—she wrote to Miss Ridsdale,
posting the letter in London, " Do not be uneasy
about me, for I am safe and *happy*. I could
bear it no longer, and I believe I have done right
after all. I would come to you, or let you *come*

to me, only I am afraid. Don't be miserable about me, for I am free.

"Your own Judith."

In due time also, Mr. Mason accepted her novel, paying twenty pounds for the MS., and agreeing to halve the profits, should any accrue from the work.

"I will have it printed immediately," he said to Judith, "and you might venture, I think, to be getting another ready—another, if possible, for the autumn season;" on the strength of which suggestion she set desperately to work on a new MS., which she entitled "Canonbie," and wrote about a volume, so rapidly, that from sheer bodily exhaustion she was forced at last to lay by her pen.

"I think I will go into London," she declared, when this climax arrived. "I suppose I have been sitting too close, and want change. I have such a dreadful head-ache." And acting on this idea, she sallied forth, and not having crossed the threshold before for weeks, excepting to go to church, found herself so tired by the time she reached the Elephant and Castle, that she was fain to call a coach, and drive to Mr. Mason's.

He was in great glee; the book was out,—a success—a decided hit. He placed a pile of favourable reviews before her, and affirmed there would be a good margin of profit left for both of them. "But I beg your pardon, what is the matter," he said, stopping abruptly in the midst of his congratulations, "are you ill?"

Judith was sobbing like a child; her head bowed over the reviews,—her hands clasped almost convulsively together :—

"Yes, I believe I am ill," she said. "I must go. I was foolish to come out. Thank you, you can get me nothing. Good morning. I will call soon again," and hurrying out of the publisher's office, she flung herself into the vehicle she had bade wait, and drove back home.

"I feel very ill," were her first words to the laundress. "I believe I had better go to bed, and I wish you would make me a cup of warm tea, I am so wretchedly cold. I think I must have got a chill some way or other. You might light me a fire too; I am shivering from head to foot."

"Had I not better go for a doctor, ma'am?"

demanded the woman, as Judith, taking off her bonnet and widow's cap, which last article of dress she never wore excepting out of doors, commenced binding up her hair with trembling hands. "Had I not better go for a doctor? There's a clever young man just newly come to the neighbourhood, shall I run round for him?"

"No, oh no. I only want something warm to drink, and to get into bed. It is only a cold, and won't signify, only it makes one feel so wretchedly ill and low for the time that it lasts. Just get me a couple more blankets, there's a good soul." And having swallowed some boiling tea, and covered herself over with blankets, and shawls, and cloaks, she bade the washerwoman go quietly to bed, and never mind her.

"I feel much better now," she said, "and shall be quite well in the morning. Please to draw the window curtains close. Good night."

And the wayward head was laid quietly down on the hard pillow, and an hour afterwards, when the laundress softly opened the door to see if she wanted anything, Judith was asleep.

During the earlier part of the night she slumbered tranquilly enough, but after twelve o'clock her rest grew broken and uneasy. She moaned and tossed, and turned, and finally woke up with a sudden start, feeling so ill that, nervous and solitary as she was, with the expiring fire casting strange flickering shadows about the small apartment, and the horrors of fever fast coming upon, and all the ghosts of past events rising before her—she thought in all si cerit , that she was dying.

CHAPTER II.

WHAT a wild yearning for life came over her, as she lay on that most lowly bed, in that most humble room! what a passionate craving for a prolongation of existence! what a frantic, despairing wish for two or three years more to work, to suffer, to battle, to succeed!

A few short months previously, and she would have thankfully flung the gift of being from her, and left the wealth, and luxury, and misery of her husband's house for the perpetual quiet of the grave. A few brief months previously, and *to die* seemed to her the summit of her earthly wishes; and now to live was all she asked. To obtain permission to carry her burden a little

longer, she would make any effort, any sacrifice
—incur any danger, or trouble, or peril—do
anything save always return to him.

Fever had already laid its hot hands on her
body, quickened her pulses, scorched her frame,
parched her mouth, dried up her blood; but
there was a stronger, fiercer fever raging in her
mind.

To die thus!—to be carried to some pauper
grave, and be left to moulder to dust, without a
headstone to mark the place where so much of
beauty and talent lay!—to depart with every
design of her existence unrealized, every project
of her youth unfulfilled!—to go with the
thoughts of her soul unspoken, her genius
unrecognized, her mission undreamed of! She
beat her forehead with her clenched hands, and
groaned aloud, as she reflected that such a doom
might be in store for her; and a determination
sprang up within her, born partly of fever, but
greatly of her indomitable character, and she
felt strong to resist even the mandate of the
great angel. She could not go at his bidding
then: it was impossible for her to cease to be
on this earth ere she had fulfilled her mission

in the world. She had never yet begun that mission. It was before her, in the shadowy future, all still to do—to be commenced, persevered in, finished, whilst she, whose destiny it seemed to be to accomplish it, lay there dying.

But she would not die. She had still strength left to battle with her disease. Had it not been predicted years and years previously, as she, an unconscious infant, lay slumbering one night, when the storm spirits chaunted her lullaby, that she should pass through life " battling her way" —with her hand raised against every one, and the blessings of peace, and the smiles of fortune, and the haven of a happy home shedding a sunshine on every path save the one she trod.

And should she not fulfil her destiny? should she not battle for existence with the king of terrors, and use her hand to clear a stage for herself in the world's vast arena? should she not stay to suffer and to win—not a home, not a fortune, not even peace—but fame, success: to make one dream of her youth a reality— to tell her wild stories to the ears of thousands —to enjoy in retirement and solitude the applause of her fellow beings? If she had strength

to write, if she had time to publish, she would
succeed.

It was so written, she felt, and the vehement
desire for life grew stronger with that conviction,
and she wrestled with the power, and pain, and
suddenness of her malady; but it beat her down
with its invisible hands, and as she strove to
rise, it pinioned her to her couch; and Judith
gnashed her teeth, half in delirium, half with a
consciousness of her own impotence; and at
last the tardy daylight came and brought with
it the thought of other help besides her own
unavailing will; and the instant her humble
hostess appeared, she almost shrieked forth the
words:—

"A doctor—go for one—the best there is,
be quick."

How tardily the minutes passed—how eagerly
her ears were strained to catch the first sound
of coming footfalls—ye who have waited for the
return of a messenger with anxious soul and
throbbing heart only can imagine; and when,
at length, she heard two persons cross the
threshold, when the woman opened the door
of her room to admit a stranger, she stretched

forth both hands and welcomed him with a cry
which, though born of intense joy, sounded to
the new-comer like the suppressed shriek of a
maniac; and as she fell back again on her
pillow, he paused for an instant to gaze on one
who offered such a contrast to the mean house
and the poor neighbourhood, to the vulgarity
and coarseness of the *locale* and its inhabitants
—who had surely been accustomed to a different
home from this—whose beauty, rare at all times
and in all places, had now, with the flush of
fever on her cheek, together with the circumstances under which it was seen, acquired a
brilliancy absolutely superhuman.

One like this, lying without a friend, in such a
place; it was one of the anomalies of life, and
so the doctor felt. It was that idea which
chained his footsteps for the instant, and kept
him silent till he recovered from the surprise the
first appearance of Judith Mazingford awakened
in him.

The long slender fingers, glittering with rings,
the delicate smoothness of her hands, the haughty
chiselling of her features, the beauty of her
complexion, the rich tresses of her dark hair, a

something of indescribable grace about her attitude ; all these things told the physician of a once
different home, of trials, cares, of sins perhaps,
of wrongs possibly, of need of kindness, sympathy, succour certainly, and as she once again half
raised herself on her elbow, and opened her
cracked lips, as if to address him, he broke the
silence, and said, in a low respectful tone,—

"You wished to see me, madam, and I am here ;
what can I do for you, what do you require of
me ? "

" Life ! " she almost screamed ; " life at nearly
any cost—at any sacrifice—a cripple, a defor-
mity, I care not; only preserve my senses, and
the use of my hands.   Give me a few years, or,
if that may not be, a few months to do that
which I have found to do, and I ask no more.
Life and reason !   Surely, I am not exorbitant.
You promise me these boons—will you not ? "

He took her wrist, and pressing his fingers on
the pulse, found it flying at a rate, which, if it
continued, bade fair to bring the human machine
rapidly to a stand still.

" You must keep yourself quiet," he said.

" And you must promise me that—life you

know—life," she returned in a tone which induced him to believe she was already hopelessly delirious, but when he answered her—

"All depends on yourself—far more on you than on me. You must keep quiet ;" he discovered his mistake, for she obeyed him as quietly as a child, she saw the reasonableness of his remark—anything—anything to gain that point. Life—what could she want with life? She read theunspoken question in his face, and answered it in a hushed subdued voice.

"You marvel why I am here—and why being here, I long so to preserve that, which, until now, I never deemed a boon. To the first, I reply I am the keeper of my own bitter story, and cannot betray the trust ; to the second, that I want to triumph for once over a wayward destiny, that I desire, ere passing from earth for ever, to grasp one of the phantoms I determined years since to secure—the rest I have left far behind me, and may never dream of seeing, even in the distance, again—but that may—must still be mine. I have no relatives you can write to for me," she added, anticipating the question he was about to ask ; " there is no one I wish to see—I have no atonement to make to living man—there are but two things you can do for me—one, restore me to health; the other—can you break this?" she abruptly demanded.

He took the ring she pulled off her finger, and presented to him, and examined it attentively, whilst again an idea of her temporary or confirmed insanity occurred to him. It was a hoop of diamonds, most valuable he saw, an antique affair—probably a family heirloom—the relic of happier and more prosperous days. To talk of breaking it! He put it gently on her finger again, and remarked—

"Your case is one requiring immediate attention. I will send you over some medicine, directly, and come back again in the course of an hour or two."

"Don't go yet," she said clutching his hand. "You think me mad. I am not so—I am ill, but not delirious. Can you break that ring—(I am serious)—and take the stones out and get them sold for me? I have no money to meet the expenses of a long illness; in a few hours I shall not, perhaps, be able to make this request.

I intended to try to separate the diamonds myself, but something prevented me."

Once again the ring was in the doctor's palm.

"It seems singular," he began reluctantly.

"It does," she interrupted; "and I am singular, and everything about me is so too—but you will only be doing me a kindness if you comply with my request. You will be wronging no one —the trinket is my own—it was given me amongst other baubles on my marriage; it could be sold as it is—only the peculiar setting might give a clue to my present home. Home!" she repeated with a withering smile, "it is not much to implore to be left in undisputed possession of such a shelter. I who might—"

She broke off abruptly, and laid her head down in the middle of her sentence. Something like a comprehension of the actual state of affairs seemed glimmering on the doctor's brain. He saw her malady was making rapid progress; that it was absolutely necessary for prompt steps to be taken, yet he stood hesitating for a minute, with the jewel in his hand.

"And you wish—" he began.

"Money," she answered; "which you

can spend for me.   I shall be grateful," and she
changed her position, and moaned audibly. "I
am in such horrible pain," she murmured—"but
I don't mind it—I can bear that, and I will be
quiet—life, remember, you have promised me it
—just for a little while."   There came another
expression of bodily suffering—another rapid
change of posture—an almost convulsive repeti-
tion of the one word—Life.

It was the last syllable she uttered for days
with the slightest consciousness of its meaning,
for the spell of the fever was cast over her, and she
lay there, raving of the scenes of her childhood,
of the events and sorrows, and misfortunes of
later days; and, though the old laundress could
not understand what she said, the doctor
gathered such fragments as he heard together,
and pieced her story out of them.

A fallen house—the curse of poverty—an
old cross in love—a dead sister—a hated union
—an unfeeling husband—the knowledge of genius— these were the materials !

He understood all about her, save her character, now.   There was not sin lying heavy on
her conscience; there was only a load of sorrow

in her heart. There could be no crime in assisting one so young and so unfortunate.

Home!—where had it been—where was it now—that home, so unlike this—so unhappy, that she preferred the mean London hovel where he had found her, to the abode of proud magnificence, whence she had come?.

Home!—he heard her raving of wild waterfalls and snow-capped mountains, and of a prophecy concerning her own destiny—of a human body wrapt in a white mantle, which they carried over the hills to her.

Over and over again the sentence " I claim a separation !" was muttered by the sufferer; and then the refrain of all, " Life, life !"—came echoing forth. It was a strange sick room, and an anxious one too. Never before had the doctor beheld so fierce a battle waged between the two mighty powers Life and Death, as in that chamber. The two great foes wrestled over the body—and almost tore it asunder, in their efforts for victory. Never but once before had he met a case which interested him so much, to which he devoted so much time, skill, and energy—and Heaven knew there was need of all to save her !

"It's just a toss-up," remarked Doctor Crosby, with professional *sang froid*, as he raised himself from a scrutiny of the patient— "just a toss-up. If she be not better in an hour, the case is hopeless."

"And if there be no amendment at the end of that time," said Judith's friend, who had faith in Dr. Crosby, because he was at the head of his profession, and particularly noted for his skill in fevers, small-pox and cholera—for which reason he had posted off for him in despair—"and if there be no amendment at the end of that time, what should you recommend me to do?"

"What you like," responded the man who was learned in physics and diseases: "anything or nothing—the result can prove but the same. Perhaps the best thing, however, you could do, would be to speak to an undertaker as the body can't remain above ground twenty-four hours. Should not wonder if decomposition have set in already; very heavy smell in the room."

"It's these infernal windows, that won't open," said the younger man, impatiently. He would gladly have cursed Dr. Crosby where he stood; but failing him, he took comfort in swearing a little at the windows. "How the deuce the poor live in these dens, without ventilation, air, light——"

"There, there, my friend, don't waste your time talking about the poor—knock a few panes of glass out, or remove the sash altogether—that is better. Bless my soul! what a relief it is—you have taken down the curtains, I see. Yes, yes, very good—you have done all that any one could, but I fear it is hopeless."

"I know you do not approve of stimulants," said the other, hesitating.

"Good Heavens, no!" exclaimed Dr. Crosby, indignantly; "but," he added an instant after, "try what you like in an hour, nothing can then make any difference—for the worse, I mean; and, a word of advice, my young friend —if you want to succeed, don't be so nervously anxious about your patients; it will unfit you for your profession. Let me know the result, will you? Good evening:" and the little man of large practice bustled away, and left Judith almost in the last agonies—with one solitary friend near her, at liberty, given him by the "highest authority," to do as he chose.

He did not wait the full period named by Dr. Crosby—for the mortal throes came quicker

than either had anticipated. Almost in the
death struggle, he poured a bottle of wine down
her throat:—" There," he said, flinging aside
the empty vessel, " I have followed old customs
long enough—we shall see what that will do!"

It may seem to you, reader, that he tried a
simple and natural experiment; but it was
a new idea at the time, and an anxious trial,
and he stood beside the bed absolutely trembling
with excitement, to see what effect his expedient
might produce.

It turned the scale in Judith's favour—just
when the spark of life was leaping up for the
last time in the socket; the new oil caught the
flame, and trimmed the lamp afresh. " Thank
God, she is saved," he said at length—and he
drew a long breath of intense relief, as he felt
heat coming back into the limbs, a more natural
pulse beating in the emaciated wrist. Then she
fell asleep, and slumbered for hours—during
which interval, the young doctor, who had not
many patients, never stirred from the cottage,
scarcely moved from his chair.

" Well, Sir, what do you think of her now?"
whispered the old laundress, warned by his upraised finger that she was not to make a noise.

"Don't let a footfall be heard in the house—don't speak a word above your breath—tell your neighbours to be quiet, and she is safe."

And he bent down his head to catch the sound of her breathing, for it was so faint, that at times, any other but a professional man, might have thought she slept, indeed—but that sleep which knows no waking.

He was better instructed, however; he knew that sleep was life to her, and so he stayed quiet and content till she wakened.

Then brandy, wine, and every stimulant he dare venture on, were given to the sufferer. He poured out a quantity of silver on to the table, and saying to the laundress,

"Now let Mrs. Gilmore want for nothing; and make her swallow some nourishing food every hour," left the cottage.

Before he lay down to take a few hours' sleep, he wrote to Dr. Crosby.

"DEAR DOCTOR—The patient is saved. I gave her a bottle of wine; and, if necessary, should have doubled the dose. Yours, faithfully,

"CHARLES DUVARD."

To which, Dr. Crosby politely responded.

" MY DEAR DUVARD,—I congratulate you on the result of the treatment. You know I said you could not go *wrong*. I would persevere in a rich diet; my ideas on that point are well known. Faithfully yours,

" JOHN CROSBY."

And John Crosby, Esq., M.D., next time he came across an apparently hopeless case of fever, tried brandy, and the result proving successful—and the experiment enabling his patient to turn a very ugly corner safely, he established a fresh reputation on the solitary cure, and stood two inches higher on the strength of the idea he had stolen. And so many a good estate is held by no better title—whilst the rightful owner goes begging to his grave. So the world jogs on, and accordingly, while little Doctor Crosby drove through London in a carriage and pair, and strutted into the drawing-rooms of the " nobility, gentry, and others," (whoever they may be!) Charles Duvard remained in an obscure suburb of the vast metropolis, dispensing pills to bilious old women, and curing their children of croups and measles, and scarlatina, and various other diseases, innumerable. But he had made one great conquest; he was more proud of having brought Judith back to life, than if he had been consulted about the finger-aches of half the countesses in England.

He had waged as fierce a battle, with the gr... king of terrors, as any physician ever did; and if you, dear reader, have at any period of your earthly career waged such a battle and LOST, you may have learned out of the fierce agony and despair of your defeat, what it would be to have fought such a fight and *won*. What a tedious recovery it was! How the scales were always vibrating; now, towards death, and now towards life; how incessantly the old laundress came running to him for directions. How often he had to rise from his meals, to note the unfavourable changes which had taken place in his patient. It was indeed a tedious convalescence, with perpetual alternations of hope and fear; but at length Judith was pronounced fairly out of danger, and permitted to walk across her chamber, then into her little sitting-room, and, finally, down stairs. As she got better, she had a species of primitive arm chair carried out into the garden, where she came slowly back to health, inhaling all the strong perfumes of our commoner flowers—musk, sweet-william, pinks, and roses. "Blessed be God for flowers," the wayworn woman used to say, when leaning back in her seat, with her feet resting on the smooth green sward, she surveyed the small enclosure, and drank in the fragrance and beauty of the simple plants and herbs. Peace came to her heart there; peace, such as for years had never visited it; peace, which arose from some lessons she had learned during her illness—from a new purpose and object she had found in life—Thankfulness and submission.

How much of the tone of former days had been restored to her through much suffering, may be gathered from the fact that Judith Mazingford, after years of dissatisfaction, and repining, of finding no good in anything, of carrying a canker worm about with her, of longing for death, of weary gazing over hill and dale, and loathing the sight of earth's fairest landscapes, at length "thanked God for flowers."

Yes; in that little haven, lying so close to

life's stormy ocean—in that brief calm lying
between the billows of the past, and the billows
of the future, Judith gathered faith enough to
enable her to go forth to meet the latter ; resig-
nation and religion enough to give her fortitude
to endure the former.   Strength and weakness !
the one to battle, the other to submit, she had
learned at last ; and, with these, peace came
unto her ; peace, such as the world could never
have given—peace, such as the world could never
take away.

There she sat, the same, and yet how altered ;
at feud no longer with the whole human race,
finding good in all things ; in life with its purposes, in death, with its hopes ; in the long
struggle ; in the longer rest she ceased striving to
banish thought, but used to lean her head back
on the pillows, and dream of others beside herself, reflect about better things than her own
mournful story.   For the future she would
wander beyond—oh ! yes, far beyond herself,
away into the great human distance which she
had never previously thought of surveying,
and see the world, and the men in it, not
as weary inventions of the enemy, but as

God had made both, instruments wherewith He means to work out His mighty end.

Sitting there, she found out many new things, and jotted down her discoveries on paper, writing with a deeper meaning, and a higher, holier purpose, than had ever previously been the case. When she grew tired of the mere bodily labour, she rested herself by talking to the healthy little children, who, spite of the old laundress' attempts to preserve her lodger from their encroachments, obstinately forced their way through hedge and paling, and secret ways of their own divining, to the "great lady," who had so nearly died among them. And when Judith took the chubby urchins in her arms, the future men and women, and strength and hope of the nation, when she listened to their lisping prattle, and looked into their clear bright eyes, and contemplated their healthy innocent faces, she did more than thank God for the flowers of the garden, she blessed His name for the little human flowers He has spared from His garden in Heaven, to bloom beside and gladden man's pathway on the earth.

"Blessed be God for children," she used to

exclaim, as in the absence of all other companionship, her heart attached itself to the rosy
creatures, who daily brought fresh playfellows to
seek her, until the little grass-plat resembled a
reception room, and the washerwoman had to
abandon the bleaching of muslins, and drying
of collars thereon, as hopeless. " Blessed be
God for children ; " and well she might say so
—for they opened the fountains of old within her
they laid their tiny hands on her closed-up heart,
and tore it open to human feelings and sympa-
thies again ; they came to her fearlessly, unmindful of the differences of rank and conven-
tionalisms of society, laid their soft cheeks
against her's, and forced her after years of desolate bitterness, to love something once more.

They used to marvel at her short curly hair—
make audible comments concerning her beauty,
take the rings off her fingers, and watch the
diamonds and opals change and sparkle in the
sunbeam, till their eyes danced with delight.

As she got better, too, she told them stories,
wonderful stories, about fairies and giants, and
good children and bad children. Little Red-
Ridinghood she repeated to them till they knew

all about her and her grandmother, and the bear, off by heart; and Jack and the Bean Stalk, Whittington and his Cat, Goody Two-shoes, Puss in Boots, and other such veracious legends, she rang the changes on day after day, till she had exhausted her stock, when she took to inventing legends of her own, which, however, truth to tell, never became quite so popular as Cinderella, and Robin Redbreast, and the rest of the quaint old tales that once were, and ought to be still, familiar as household words in every nursery throughout the kingdom.

With a silky-haired little girl in her lap, and a circle of open-mouthed healthy children sitting at her feet, Judith would recount all sorts of stories for their gratification; and, perhaps, the happiest portion of all her later life, was that she spent in the widow's garden, ministering unto the amusement of very young children, writing scraps in her new book, gathering strength for future struggles, and finding the long summer days too short by half.

The only alloy to her content, was an occasional slap or scolding which the parents of her little friends were in the habit of readily admin-

istering when the children either had actually
been bold, or when their natural guardians
fancied it; but even then the tiny creatures
used to come and nestle so trustfully beside her,
and sob out their sorrows so very naturally, with
faces buried all the while in the skirt of her
dress, that there was balm to be extracted out
of the frequent rebukes they received for making
"too free" with the lady, who was looked upon,
by the way, as a sort of queen by the population
of Ashford Row.

And there, too, Judith first learned the use
and object and purpose and mission of street
music. There she first came fully to understand
the power it exercises in purifying, gladdening,
and humanizing the hearts of the dwellers in
London's most polluted portions; she had never
previously thought nor comprehended how much
cheerfulness, even the most cracked and discor-
dant instrument is capable of carrying into the
darkest places.

Out of time; out of tune: hoarse, asthmatic,
jangling, and deplorably used up were the
organs, and pipes, and cornopeans, and flutes,
and violins that ventured into Ashford Row—

yet still, Judith with her refined taste and cultivated ear, who had heard the best singers and performers in the world — whose own musical knowledge was wonderful for an amateur, could sit and listen with a species of swelling pleasure to the commonest old air hopelessly murdered by the worst among the lot, for the pleasure came home to her heart through many others.

The joy of a score was hers—the joy of laughing girls and whistling boys, of lisping beings who clapped their little hands for gladness: of care-worn matrons who danced their infants to the tune, and looked happy whilst its rattling melody lasted. Judith always felt better on a day when a "grinder" passed their road. She was wont to give the children pennies for the olive-faced Italian, and when he departed she would tell them stories about the sunny land he had wandered so far away from ; and on one happy occasion when a darker mood than usual had fallen upon the lonely woman, she bade them bring him into the garden—on to the grass-plat—where he played for ever so long, and let the smallest of his auditors try whether they could turn the handle too: and Judith gave him a shilling, and a troop of urchins, half wild with glee, followed him to the extreme end of the Row, where he ground out three airs for them for nothing, and then departed, to tell others of his countrymen about the fair signora. The consequence of which proved that the widow's cottage was besieged for days afterwards, and the children existed in an atmosphere of perpetual music: and Judith was so perfectly deafened with "Highland Laddie," "Annie Laurie," "Aileen Aroon," "All's Lost," "Sailor's Hornpipe," "British Grenadiers," and "Hear me, Norma," that from thenceforth, she carefully limited her benefactions to a penny, and never had another organ to play on the grass-plat.

When the summer was near its close, Judith Mazingford, much weaker in body, but healthier in mind, than she had been for years previously, was able once again to walk forth, and chalk out, as she did so, plans for the future, which she knew she must go on to meet — all alone.

CHAPTER III.

THE knack of authorship is a pleasant property (once after you have squeezed yourself through the thorn hedge surrounding the domain, and recovered from the numerous scratches received during the process), if you have not a large family to feed upon it—if you have self-respect enough to live quietly like any other Christian, and refuse to be lionized—if you are not very thin-skinned and do not writhe under the lash of criticism—and above all, if your habits are not very expensive, and that you can make yourself happy and content with what Heaven and the publishers send you.

Suppose all these "ifs" realities, then tolerably successful authorship is a pleasant possession. It is an easy, idle, dreamy, self-contained way of earning bread with a little butter on it—as creditable and agreeable a mode of employing time and paying the baker, as I know of—so Judith Mazingford found at all events.

Living amongst the very poor as she did; amongst those whom sickness, death, and sudden accident, or apparently trivial loss, brings, not merely to the verge of poverty, but to absolute starvation, almost in an hour—Judith's means, small as they really were, went a long way towards alleviating the distresses of those with whom she came in contact.

She had abundant charity, a generous heart, and above all, discrimination and good sense; so that, having once permitted her thoughts to wander out beyond the circle of her own individual recollections and griefs, she found she could effect much, even out of little. In trouble, danger, difficulty, she was sought with eagerness, and consulted with respect. By the bed of

death she stood pale and beautiful, like a
ministering angel; she feared no contagion; she
dreaded the sight of no disease. In houses in
which fever and pestilence were raging, she
carried—frequently health—always kind words,
consolation, and pecuniary assistance.

"My income is not a large one," she said
one day, shortly after her recovery, to Dr.
Duvard, "but still, I have enough to help a few
of my fellow-creatures along the road of life;
and whenever you meet with a case of real
distress, I should feel obliged by your informing
me of it. You must see much misery that
never reaches my eyes: tell me how to relieve
it, and I shall be truly thankful to you."

And so, whenever a brood of young children
were left orphans, or a woman made suddenly a
widow; or a man disabled, or an old couple
deprived of food by the death of some stalwart
son—their bread-winner—the doctor went to
Judith, and got help for each and all from her.
It was no wonder that, young and beautiful as
she was: good and unostentatious as he knew
her to be: wronged and miserable as he fancied
she had been—he should become deeply inte-

rested in the woman thrown so strangely across
his path—that he should seek her dwelling on
the slightest pretext, and feel something rising
within his heart for her, which almost amounted
to reverence.

Not that he ever once wavered in his alle-
giance to Alice—she to whom he had plighted
his faith—she who was to be his wife.

The time was gone past for ever when Judith
thought flirting an amusing occupation. She
was too grave, too serious, too reserved, too
matter-of-fact, to inspire any feelings but those
of friendship and respect in the breast of an
"engaged" individual; and what, perhaps, saved
Dr. Duvard from a very disagreeable *denouement*,
preserved his fidelity to Alice unshaken, and
prevented his ever dreaming of "getting into
the mire" by falling in love with the stranger,
was the fact, that Judith kept him at arm's
length. How she managed to be friendly, and
still formal, was a riddle she might have solved,
but which nobody else could. Her manners, if
kind, were certainly somewhat frigid to everybody,
except her little garden acquaintances; no one
ever dreamt of asking her a question, of en-

croaching one step beyond the line she marked out for herself.

No—she was a person to admire, respect, look up to, consult, go to as a friend, a comforter—to marvel concerning—consider a rare compound of pride and humility, genius and goodness. But love!—Doctor Duvard would as soon have thought of getting up an affection for a glacier, as of committing that folly. Alice was to be his wife; and meantime he thought he had never seen so beautiful, and accomplished, and amiable a woman as Mrs. Gilmore, concerning whom he wrote, truth to tell, a good deal more to his affianced bride, than altogether satisfied that somewhat exacting young lady. It was in the purity, and confidence, and integrity of his heart that the man poured out his admiration as he did. But Alice did not like it; she grew wonderfully suspicious of the beautiful unknown—restless, unhappy; and, shall I write it?—jealous too.

Jealousy is a necessity of the tender passion; so those learned in the moods and tenses of the verb " to love," fearlessly declare; and it is not for me to contradict the assertion, more especially as I believe that the "perfect love which casteth out fear," is unknown on this side heaven.

Be this as it may, Alice Crepton became jealous, and angry, and dissatisfied; and she thought it was an extraordinarily strange and evil chance, which had sent the widow, for so she deemed her, into that identical suburb in which poor Charles Duvard was trying to keep soul and body together; and she felt angry with her for going there, and getting ill, and sending for Doctor Duvard, as though there were no other doctor on earth she could have got to physic her, but him. And she was vexed with her being so beautiful, and good, and clever—for woman is as unreasoning in her dislikes as in her loves—and Alice being very fond of her *fiancé*, was tenacious of his affection accordingly; and besides all this, the flame of her discontent was fanned by calculating tongues and disagreeable circumstances—and doubt was fostered by separation—and at length Alice grew perfectly satisfied that Dr. Duvard was "cooling" towards her, and becoming far too much impressed by the lovely face of his new neighbour.

In brief, dear reader, the curse of a long engagement was on the girl, and producing effects which will hereafter be described; but while she continued torturing herself with all sorts of unjust suspicions and conclusions, Dr. Duvard was not falling in love with Judith—he was only asking her to assist his patients, and enjoying, as all men, whether married or single, will enjoy, half-an-hour's chat occasionally with a well-educated woman; while she, in her turn, grew to esteem the young physician, who she saw was buffeting bravely with the billows of fortune; and she would have aided him if she could. But it was beyond her ability to procure him a good practice; and so utterly unconscious of all the harm she was doing, totally unaware of the close relationship which would some day exist between them, she quietly pursued her way —writing a good deal, reading a little, sewing occasionally, walking but seldom, and doing good always.

For twenty-one tranquil months she had been an inmate of the laundress' humble abode; and still the world, usually tolerably well informed in all matters of the sort, was unacquainted with the real name of an authoress, whose works were beginning (to use a technical phrase,) to be " inquired for."

Her second book had gone through two editions ; and Judith was completing a third, the first portion of which was already in type. Much curiosity was expressed in literary circles concerning the antecedents of the lady who produced such life-like fictions—who could not be " got at" by any means—who was one of their family, and yet seemed to hold herself aloof from it—of whose real name and place of abode even her own publisher was reported to be ignorant. Miss Ridsdale was the only one who guessed the truth at that period—and she, perhaps, only surmised it, because of a certain character vaguely shadowed forth in the first book, and of a remittance her niece sent her, which, Judith said, in the note accompanying it, " had been honestly earned by the united efforts of her hand and head."

Reading, the lady marvelled to find out what a genius the little Welsh girl had turned out. Closing the volumes, she wondered how it chanced she had never believed in Judith's talent, until it was acknowledged by everybody else—and then she began to doubt whether, after all, the books were written by the same slow, unfluent pen, that had jotted down so many bald ideas on paper at Llandyl Hall—doubted, till she re-read some passages, which no other mortal upon earth but Mrs. Mazingford could have constructed—for, as no two human faces are alike, so no two human experiences are identical; and in the concentrated agony and intense despair of a few sentences, Miss Ridsdale read the life's story of her niece.

Then turning alike from the book and their success, from newspaper commendations and favourable reviews, and bitter criticism, and trade puffs, the lonely woman bent her head on her hands and wept. Wept for the existence wasted —and the genius shrouded, and the useless wealth, and the valueless fame—wept for the wrecked happiness, and the dream which had been fulfilled too late—wept, as she thought of the " home that might have been," of the proud husband and happy wife — never mated — of Marcus and Judith—of the past and the present — of the greyhaired father who had gone down to his grave broken hearted—of the youth who was borne dead across the hills, back to the house she had driven him out from; of the light-hearted girl who became a wretched woman, in the one night of anguish—who had sold herself to a man she hated, for love of her sister—who had borne and toiled and suffered—and was even then sitting by her desolate hearth, listening to the distant echoes of that which a woman never values for her own sake; which can never give balm to a wounded spirit, or heal a broken heart; which is, after all, only a foam-bell on the waters of life—Fame. And yet, though the bubble had burst, and Judith discovered the thing she once panted for was not worth possessing—though she found the real pleasure and excellence of literature consisted little in what the world thought of her works, but much in the employment it gave her; the good she was enabled by its instrumentality to perform—though the fever was over—the intense desire gratified—the flower withered, and the fountain dry—still Judith Mazingford was happy, comparatively speaking. Had she been fortunate enough to have had one loving female friend near at hand, with whom to exchange an occasional word, and not been condemned to live always " alone," with an unconfessed, but still most intense horror of discovery haunting her constantly, she would have been perfectly so.

As it was; the more reconciled she grew to her solitude—the more she grew to appreciate and quietly enjoy her freedom, the greater became her dread of detection; and, during the writing of her new work, and conveyance of it piece-meal to Mr. Mason's, she lived in a sort of agony. Perhaps it might have been the state of her bodily health, which was far from satisfactory, that induced this morbid kind of horror; perhaps she wrote too much, and thought too much; perhaps, as she got further away from the evil, its magnitude seemed to her greater; perhaps, certain rumours which had reached her anxious ear, even in that remote region, of her husband's affairs being embarrassed, had brought back painful memories, and aroused fresh apprehensions; at all events, one thing is certain, strange as it may sound, that Judith frequently found the contemplation of possible detection so terrible, that she rushed into absolute danger to get

rid of her apprehensions. She found relief in
movement, in restless walks to the great Babylon,
in rapid exercise, as if she then felt she were
fleeing from, and escaping some great danger.

She said, afterwards, it was her fate urged her
on; but if it were indeed so, the fate she found,
seemed to ordinary observers, one of her own
seeking, for under the protection of her well
prepared disguise, she traversed most of the
back streets and odd lanes of London—trying to
dispose of old manuscript tales to editors and
publishers—asking for interviews with all sorts
of people, as if she were striving for variety,
in rebuffs, refusals, cold civility, and constrained
politeness. She, the successful author, apparently liked the amusement of taking her first
born literary offspring a-begging. She never said
to anybody, "I am the writer of these books,
about which reviewers are making such a rout;"
she defiantly presented her earlier efforts to people
who would not accept them, and used to come
forth from many an office inwardly laughing at
the comments which accompanied the rejections.

"Genius is not then a plant so easily discerni-
ble," she thought; "let people talk as they like,

it is a long time of bearing fruit fit for public eating, and, therefore, it strikes me nobody can say, with any confidence, to a young writer— " Lay aside your pen, for the gift is not in you. Look at the " Shadows of the past," for instance. Not a soul in London can detect anything remarkable about it—and yet I wrote it. I felt all along the talent of authorship had been vouchsafed ; and I don't blame others for not seeing it too. I only blame people for dogmatically advising me to give up the attempt as useless. Oh ! if some of these Job's comforters had been less confident in their own judgment, and helped me ever so little in the days that are gone—what a different fate mine might have been." And as she finished, she turned into the Strand, intending to proceed from thence straight home ; but, passing by one of the cross streets with the manuscript in her hand, it suddenly occurred to Judith that she would leave it with her old correspondent, Mr. Kearn, who " held court " in that region, and see what he had to say to her now. Accordingly she went a few steps out of her way, and entering the British Lion office, asked for the editor thereof. He was out, so she consigned her parcel to the care of a clerk, and said she would call again the next time she came into town.

Very graciously Mr. Kearn received her when she did so, seated in his dark sanctum, where gas was burnt all the day long, and visitors contemplated the august personage of the editor-proprietor, across a table covered with papers, and through an atmosphere thick with dust. Heaven knows when the room had been swept or cleaned ; perhaps, about the middle of the last century. It was an unwholesome place, out of which one longed to pitch the musty old documents that littered it, for no conceivable purpose, and into which it would have done your heart good to have let the air, and light, even of a London winter, together with a painter, plasterer, and paperer.

Mr. Kearn, however, would not have had a finger laid on it for the world ; it was a part of his creed that authors should live surrounded by dust and dirt, and in a species of artificial night ; and, to do him justice, he acted up to his creed —which is more than can be said of many a man. Judith could not see him very distinctly for a minute or two, but at last she made him out, and rapidly sketched off a mental picture of her first rejector.

Between sixty and seventy ; of middle height ; neither fat nor lean ; with iron grey hair, muddy complexion, no whiskers, small sharp irritable nose, and grey eyes, that gave the lie direct to a species of benevolent smile, which he manufactured on his thin lips. The expression on his face was one of a self-sufficient, I-can-never-be-wrong " species," varied by a look of important patronage, and kind interest in the affairs of his fellows. He seemed, in brief, a grand seigneur of the literary class, who had elected himself censor-in-chief of English authors, and who would have put down Shakespeare at once, and nipped Byron in the bud—a man full to over-flowing of theoretical sympathy and benevolence, and of practical uncharitableness, intolerance, and impertinence. Judith felt her old dislike had been well founded, as she took the proffered chair, and proceeded to business.

" I left a manuscript here about a fortnight since," she said, " entitled ' Shadows of the Past :' may I enquire if you have come to any decision concerning it ?"

" Yes," answered Mr. Kearn, diving down as he spoke into a perfect chaos of papers, from out of which he finally fished up the tale in question. " I am sorry, very sorry to have to return it—more particularly as I cannot praise it in any solitary respect. I feel it a kindness to you—I feel it in fact my duty, to advise your abandoning literature as a professional pursuit in toto." And as Mr. Kearn delivered himself of this encouraging speech, he laid the offending manuscript out flat on his desk, as if it were a corpse, and he a clergyman about to read a funeral oration over it.

" It is a matter to be regretted," said Judith, a faint smile just flickering about her mouth, " that I cannot follow your counsel: the power of choice having long since been taken from me. I, sir, write for money, and if you can show me any other means of earning it as easily and respectably, I shall abandon the ranks of the literary sisterhood for ever and a day."

" I am afraid—" commenced Mr. Kearn, drumming on the desk in a perplexed and abstracted manner; " I am afraid you will not make much by your writings: I can see no sign of promise in them, excepting the total absence of fluency, which I consider to be the vice and bane of the age. That is one grand point, certainly; but one negative virtue will never make a great author—never."

"I am quite content to remain a very little one," replied Judith.

" Or a little one, or any kind," persisted Mr. Kearn, still ambling along the path of duty; "but if you must write, why I suppose there is no help for it; and what I should suggest under those circumstances, would be for you to abandon the fictitious and imaginative line altogether, and to try biographies, or translations, or—"

"In fact, anything but what I have hitherto attempted, namely, novels, tales, and essays," finished off Judith, in her cold, measured tones, which never varied, even for a moment, and deluded Mr. Kearn into a belief that she was laying his counsels to heart.

"Precisely," he answered. "I have a great sympathy for young authors; it is a crotchet of mine to give them a lift whenever I can. I like to see men mounting fortune's ladder, and think I pointed its steps out to them. Now, in biography, the industry you possess might be turned to good account; but novels and tales require a vein of original humour, pathos, and imagination, which are quite out of your beat— we have all our particular gift, and your's is not novel writing; then, essays must have depth, smartness, concentration, and piquancy: their style must be at once brilliant, and terse, and the reasoning new, close, and vigorous."

"Like the specimens lately published in the 'British Lion,' probably;" suggested Judith.

For a moment it struck Mr. Kearn as a thing within the bounds of possibility, that his visitor might be laughing at him, and, accordingly, he bent his keen eyes—for keen they were, though generally half shut—upon her; but Judith met his glance with one out of which he could make nothing, and accordingly forgetting to answer her last remark, he pursued—

"Ladies seldom develope into good essayists, their style is too slipshod; their reasoning too superficial; their ideas too contracted; their sphere of observation too limited. And then, again, their fatal facility of stringing unmeaning sentences together: their dangerous fluency of composition—"

"I thought you paid me the compliment of remarking I was not fluent," here interposed Judith.

"In that respect you differ from the rest of your sex," retorted Mr. Kearn, snappishly, for, somehow, he felt that Judith was beating him, even whilst he was rebuking her. "In that respect, and in one other—I think I never met with an unimaginative lady author before. That is women's forte in fact, and—"

"I am destitute of the gift," finished Judith, rising. "Well, it is a pity—as out of novels I must earn a living. I cannot alter my trade at the eleventh hour, and turn biographer all at once, after having served an apprenticeship to tale-telling. I fear I cannot follow your suggestion, sir—I am too old now to learn."

The majestic editor looked for a moment across at the speaker; but if there were bitterness in her words, there lay a sort of sadness in them too: wherefore he refrained from further argument, feeling a very uncomfortable conviction that, although Judith was a woman, he might possibly get the worst of it. She stood waiting there for her manuscript, which he handed to her with a polite remark, that if his lengthened experience could prove of any service, he should be most happy to furnish a few hints and suggestions on the subject of writing in general, and of her writing in particular.

"Thank you," responded the object of his proposed benevolent intentions, "but as you decline my tale, I fear there is nothing further you can do for me. I do not think ' hints,' or 'suggestions,' would be of much use in my case now."

"Yet authors—young authors—often stand greatly in need of advice," urged Mr. Kearns.

"Pray, do you often find them follow it ?" enquired Judith.

" Yes, generally," he responded.

" And you never discover your advice to have been ill-judged," she pursued.

"No," he said, but he said it somewhat hesitatingly : "No, I cannot remember an instance."

"Well," answered Judith, and leaning over the top of an ancient arm chair, upon which one arm rested, she fixed her eyes intently on Mr. Kearn's much irritated face ; " Well, I will

supply you with one: years ago, a young girl
wrote to know if you would read one of her
manuscripts, and by return of post, for you
do possess the one rare virtue of answering
letters promptly, there came a reply, stating how
happy you should feel to give your best attention, and so forth; and accordingly she sent her
tale.   In due time it was returned to her, declined: accompanied by a note full of regrets
and counsels, the principal burden of the epistle
being that you advised her not to write at all,
she having no genius for a literary career.

"Advice to that girl was of no use—money was
all she needed, assistance all she asked—money
then would have saved her a life-time of misery;
had you stretched out a helping hand in those
days, she would have gone down on her knees
and blessed you for it."

Judith's voice quivered as she spoke.

"But to the letter—instead of studying its
contents; and laying them to heart, she put it
in the fire—and now that same individual can
obtain a couple of hundred pounds for any novel
she writes—she made her reputation quickly, and
is at this moment a "popular author."

" And may I enquire ?" began Mr. Kearns.

" Yes, you may," interrupted Judith ; "you have heard, no doubt, of a book called, ' The History of a Broken Heart.' That was her first published work—she has brought out one since."

" And the authoress——" suggested Mr. Kearn.

" Has now supplied an instance, Mr. Kearn, of what she considers the absurdity of either giving or following advice—for I was that girl— I am that woman, and this manuscript which you have just rejected was one of my earlier efforts—that I wanted to turn into money. I came to you, because I wished, now I was successful, to hear your opinion pronounced on a later work than the one previously submitted to you. I wished to hear now my genius is acknowledged, whether you could find in that old manuscript any trace of latent talent ; and you know the result."

" But you are so young to have written two popular books," remarked Mr. Kearn after a pause.

" Young in years—old in sorrow—ah !

Heaven, yes !" she answered with a sort of shudder.

And the authoress died out, and the woman usurped her place, as with a rush of old memories softening her voice, she added :—

"Good bye, Mr. Kearn, what I have said may, perhaps, prove of use to some orphan girl or struggling woman ; for their sakes I hope I have not related my experiences in vain," and she held out a very small hand to the editor in token of amity, which he took and shook in an offended and dignified manner, and afterwards returned with, perhaps, unnecessary expedition to its owner.

So Judith passed forth satisfied that she had said her say—and had it out with the officious Proprietor of the British Lion, and Mr. Kearn— why he did not believe one solitary syllable of her story, and speedily recovering his equanimity, which had been somewhat ruffled by his visitor's rather uncivil comments—he put on his hat, and walked out of his office, intending to proceed on "business of importance," to a publisher of his acquaintance.

When he got into the Strand he saw Judith

waiting to cross the crowded thoroughfare. The
street was wet and dirty—a drizzling rain had
commenced to fall, which, hanging like dew on
the thick crape veil she always wore in public, to
conceal her features from observation—blinded
her so completely that almost involuntarily she
flung it back in order to effect the pilgrimage
over in safety.

At the moment she did so, Mr. Kearn noticed a man regarding her with a fixed and
puzzled stare, with an expression of such intense
surprise and eagerness, that it at once arrested
the Editor proprietor's attention, and induced
him to pause for a moment, to see what would
come of it.

He saw Judith reach the other side, followed
by the stranger :—whenever she set foot on the
opposite curb, down went the deep crape veil
again, and just as she was gathering it in close
folds over her face, the person who had excited
Mr. Kearn's curiosity, drew close up to her
side, and touching her shoulder, whispered apparently a single word in her ear. With a sudden
start she turned round, and then without a single
cry fell senseless on the pavement. The whole

affair scarcely occupied two seconds, and before
the Editor had well recovered from his amazement, the principal figures were concealed from
his view by a crowd of delighted spectators, who
pressed eagerly forward to " see the sight," and
surrounded the spot in an incredibly short space
of time.

" What is the matter ?" asked Mr. Kearn, of
a gentleman who turned away from the circle
after a glance into the centre, with a peculiarly
significant smile, " What is the matter ?"

" Only a gentleman who has found his wife,"
replied the person addressed, who chanced to be
a Member of Parliament.

" And who may the lady be ?" demanded the
other, feeling satisfied the gentleman knew all
about the parties concerned.

" Oh ! the beautiful Mrs. Mazingford, whose
disappearance nearly two years since, created
such a sensation in fashionable circles."

" Whew," exclaimed Mr. Kearn, and the
magnificent Editor absolutely emitted something
esembling a whistle from between his closed
teeth,—after which impromptu performance,
which wonderfully amused his informant, he

bowed to the gentleman who had given him such early and valuable intelligence, and posting off Eastwards, told the "news" to every publisher he came in contact with. Whereupon, long before Mr. Mason was himself aware of the fact,—all the trade knew that the two successful books he had recently brought out were written by Mrs. Mazingford, the lady who had run off—and a tremendous demand followed forthwith, as a natural consequence, somewhat to the astonishment of the publisher who, as usual, was the last person to hear that which concerned him most.

CHAPTER IV.

At length Judith Mazingford awoke from that
long, death-like swoon, and opened her large,
mournfully-beautiful eyes to the consciousness,
that through the dusk of a winter's afternoon,
she was driving in a post chaise along a dreary
country road, with the rain beating against the
windows of the vehicle; the mud splashing all
around as the wheels passed through puddles on
the high-way, and the postilions cracking their
whips, and urging their horses forward with
increased speed to the nearest place of shelter,—
their next stage.

She understood and remembered everything
in a moment. She was travelling home
with her husband, the consummation so long

dreaded had come at last. Let the future bring
what it liked unto her, of weal or woe, it could
bring nothing worse than it had now brought;
and with this desperate consolation whispered to
herself, she retreated into that last refuge of the
wretched, hopeless recklessness, and closed her
eyes once more.

Not in a swoon, however, this time. The
dreadful blow, so long dreaded, so cautiously
guarded against, so fearfully averted, had descended on her head at last. The weary, fruitless struggle, the skulking and hiding, the
determined war against circumstances, the resolute braving of poverty and difficulties, the
horror of detection, the ceaseless circumspection,
the disguise, the timid flight, the horror of discovery, which had dogged her steps by day, and
haunted her dreams by night,—they were all
over now; fear was changed into certainty;
the phantoms that had tracked her path into a
flesh and blood reality; the long dread and horror, into the sickening anguish of fulfilment;
the dark silky lashes rested again on the pallid
cheek, but from that time forth her senses never
deserted her. The pursuer, whose clutch she

had evaded for two struggling years had come
up with her at length; and the frightful shock
of that meeting,—of that voice in her ear—of
that strong, rude hand on her arm, could never
terrify her more. The worst! after fleeing from
it long, it had overtaken her in the end, she
must face it now.   For its visible embodiment
after its shadow crossing hers in the street fifty
times, had seized her there at last, carried her off
captive, was sitting beside her even now.

.   But what a worst that was.   How tremendous the shock had been, was proved by the
mere fact of such a woman as Judith Mazingford swooning at all.   If it had been any timid,
fanciful, nervous, susceptible creature, to whom
fainting came as naturally as eau de cologne and
vinaigrettes; if it had been a person who was
in the habit of letting her weak body and
weaker mind, fall into a state of lady-like insensibility, half a dozen times in the course of a
day; if it had been an individual not habituated
almost from childhood, certainly from girlhood
to exciting scenes, to sudden revulsions of feeling, to earnest self-conflict, to eternal self-
restraint, had it in brief been any one else under

the sun, any other specimen of the fragile
portion of creation, any one of the feminine sex,
xcepting Judith herself, the occurrence would
have seemed as little extraordinary as a shower
in April. But great indeed must have been the
force of the blow, well nigh incalculable the
power and horror of the shock which had struck
her down to the earth, deprived her in one instant of speech, perception, consciousness, left
her at his cruel mercy, unable to move finger to
save herself, to make even a vain effort to escape,
to utter a cry for assistance, which had hurled her
to the pavement as suddenly as though the great
king of terrors flitting through the crowded
streets, intent on his pauseless errand, had touched
her with his mysterious wand in passing, and
bidding the weary soul be free, released it from
its prison house for ever, and left but a lifeless
corpse behind, in lieu of that which had thought,
felt, suffered, and striven.

The long, death-like swoon told its own story,
without the need for another syllable to be added
to the narrative. But the shock was over now;
she had passed from a fugitive to a captive;
awakened from unconsciousness to a knowledge

of the reality, and accordingly, with lids firmly closed, and teeth tightly clenched, she sate there looking not with her outward eyes indeed, but with her inward vision at the position in which she was placed:—away, away, into the dreary future, lying beyond.

The evening merged into night, night expanded into morning's twilight, morning's twilight into day. Again day began to subside into darkness, to give place unto her gloomier sister; but ere the last streak of light disappeared from the western sky, Judith beheld the gables and chimneys of Wavour Hall, rising to view in the distance.

She thanked heaven when the shades of evening, when the clouds of night shut out the sigh of that place from other than mental observation What she had suffered in it, none, save He and she might ever know. None, save He, the Omnipotent maker of the earth, and she, one of earth's erring, suffering, heart-broken children none, save they two,—He, in the heaven which is His throne; she on that which is his footstool: none, save they two—not one.

Twenty-four hours of life—a day and a night

of weary travel : a great city, and its millions of
inhabitants ; a couple of hundred miles or more
of turnpike road they had already left behind
them, and yet still though they had spent those
hours, and travelled those miles, and come forth
out of that city in company together, not a sentence of conversation had passed betwixt the
husband and the wife ; not a syllable had been
exchanged between them. From the chaise
to the several inn doors, from the inn doors to
their comfortless sitting rooms, and from thence
back to chaise after chaise, he had conducted her
in silence. Across dusty mahogany tables, he
had pushed, without a word, refreshments over to
her, but she never tasted them ; she seemed indeed not to notice the act, to be as insensible to
his presence, to his most decided movement, as
if he had been a spider on the wall,—a creature
of whose very existence she could not be supposed conscious. She had permitted him to
lead her unresistingly, whithersoever he would,
to draw her arm through his, and escort her
thus through groups of shock-headed country
waiters and ostlers, and gaping chambermaids,
who discussing them after their departure, spoke

of how tenderly he watched her, and of what a
proud, statue-like lady she was, so cold, so
beautiful, so white, so stately, and came to the
conclusion it had been a love match on his side,
but that she hated him, though he was so fine a
gentleman that she might well have given him
her heart when she took his name. For twenty-
four hours, food she tasted not, words she spake
not, sign she made not. Drawn back into her
corner, to be as far from him as possible, looking over the heads of gossiping maids, and
obsequious landlords, and curtseying landladies
—straight forward at the great misery which
ever stayed with her, which ever walked before
her, which met her gaze, in the past, the present,
the future—self;—occupying the remotest sofa,
or the most distant chair, in the dreary hotel
rooms, keeping her aching orbs shut continually,
save when at long intervals she opened them to
glance for an instant at the external prospect;
so wore away that day and that night, like an
eternity of suffering, and once again night came,
and brought with it as the throbbings of Judith's
heart told her, Wavour Hall.

Yes—she needed no prophet to tell her that,

no light to proclaim the fact, no announcement from her companion that their journey was well nigh completed; she knew the short sharp hill, the postilions alighted, and led the horses down within a stone's-throw of its massive gates; the cringing and cracking of those same gates, as they swung back to permit the vehicle to pass, sent the old shudder through her frame as in the days of yore; the crunching of the gravel underneath the wheels—the sudden noise caused by the long branches of the trees sweeping the roof of the chaise; the twistings and windings of the interminable avenue—the soft places in the drive, over which the conveyance rolled as noiselessly as though those parts had been strewed with rushes; the distant baying of the dogs, the strange echo in front of the house— all these things were familiar unto her, as long acquaintanceship could render them; she counted every step of the way—yet another, and they should be at home. They were so.

For in a second after the postilion banged down the steps, the hall door was flung open. Mr. Mazingford assisted her to alight—drew her

arm once again within his, and led her into his
house—their home.   Judith inclined her head
to the various domestics, most of whose faces
she recognised as she passed along.   Still pulling
her onward, her husband gave a few general
directions, and hurried through the hall—up the
broad staircase, into the old, handsomely furnished
drawing-room ; the sight of every chair, and
table, and couch and mirror wherein, she detested from her innermost soul—into the scene
of so many a bitter humiliation, on to the battle
ground of yore, where they had wrangled out so
many an hour of their wretched married life—
where she had demanded a separation from him
as a right, whence she had fled in darkness, tempest, and solitude, whither she was now brought
back by him.   There, apparently, ended their
journey, and the blessed silence which had
reigned between them, for the moment Mr. Mazingford entered that apartment, and closed the
door, so shutting himself and his wife in, and
the world and its hundred-eared listeners out, he
pointed authoritatively to a chair, and said—

" Sit down, Madam."

She walked forward to the hearth, whereon,

as was the whim of the ostentatious owner of
the mansion, a fire blazed cheerfully, whether he
were at home or not, ready to welcome any grand
visitor, to whom he might desire at unexpected
and unforeseen periods to exhibit the carved
chairs, and the antique cabinets, and the inlaid
tables, and the paintings, and the gilding, wherein his soul delighted. How well she recollected
that old passion of his for display, and how it
had galled and chafed her proud spirit in the
days when she was called down and considered
part of the show. There was a frightful tempest
gathering within her, as the past swelled up in
her heart; when waves from that not remote
shore came rolling fast after one another, beating
furiously against her swelling bosom, adding an
hundredfold to the tumult and roar caused
already by the sounding waters of the present;
but, somehow, Judith restrained them within
bounds, prevented their overleaping every obstacle, obliterating every landmark of prudence,
rendering her an absolute slave to the wild passions of her soul—she shut the tempest up within
her breast, and closed her teeth determinedly
on it, walking as she did so to the fireplace,

seemingly unconscious of her husband's mandate.

"Sit down," he repeated, following her movements, and this time pointing to one of the antiquarian lounges, the envy of connoisseurs, and admiration of every one. "Sit down, I have something to say to you."

"I can hear you in any position," she opened her parched lips to respond—"and I prefer standing."

Time had been when he would have pushed her into a seat by force; but all powerless as she stood, there was a something about her silent defiance which restrained him, and waiving that point, he said—

"It has cost me much trouble to find you. Now that I have done so, however, I am determined you shall remain here."

The proud lip curled with scorn, and then assumed a peculiar smile; the precise meaning, and cause whereof, Mr. Mazingford cared not too curiously to enquire concerning. He waited for a moment or two, to afford her an opportunity of replying to his observation, but she remained mute. Leaning against the mantle-

piece, with one arm resting carelessly upon it—
she fastened her large eyes on his face, with that
fixed, passionless, and yet still ironical stare
wherewith she had been wont, in days of yore,
to lash him up to madness.　The bitterest
words, the severest reproaches, the most violent
outburst of feminine fury could never have
produced such an effect as that peculiar look,
which seemed to contain, within itself, the
concentrated essences of contempt, ridicule, re-
pugnance, mental superiority — indifference,
defiance, and carelessness.　There was no describing that stare, it was a thing to be felt, not
talked about; a sneering injury capable of stirring the very deepest sloughs of a man's temper,
whilst leaving him without a decent pretext for
anger—without a cause which might be explained
unto mortal, for the ungovernable anger and
resentment it awakened.　Even as his eye
quailed under her's on the occasion in question,
Mr. Mazingford felt that rising within him which
prompted him to strike her to the floor; but,
restraining his passion for about the first time
in his life, he proceeded:

" Now, there are two ways by which to accomplish my object—one advantageous to both, the other advantageous to neither; one, whereby you may return, if you will, to the position you formerly held here as my wife, and the mistress of Wavour Hall—another, which irksome and unpleasant as it will be for me, cannot fail to prove twenty times more so to you. The choice, however, lies entirely with yourself—as you desire, so I will act. Whichever plan you select, I shall adopt—but it is a point I desire to have settled immediately. I will give you ten minutes for reflection before requiring a definitive answer."

She never once removed her eyes from his face during the delivery of the foregoing sentence; and, consequently, when he raised his head at its conclusion, he met the old fixed look, which seemed, when once it settled on his wife's countenance, to be as immovable and unchangeable as if it had been carved in marble, instead of merely traced on features of flesh and blood. A burning flush came over his cheeks, and an angry light gleamed in his deep-set orbs; but the feeling that she was in his power, that he was at length master, she slave, endued him with power to subdue a hasty demonstration of rage, and turning with a malignant smile of triumph to the table, he coolly deposited his watch thereupon, with the air of a man who, conscious that he had the best of the dispute, could afford to be calm on the matter.

" Will you have the kindness to point out the different modes by which you propose arriving at your end ?" Judith slowly requested. " A little explanation would be desirable."

" Can you not guess them ?" he retorted.

" I may have an idea," she returned ; " but I always prefer deciding upon matter of fact. Tell me what you propose—without a moment's hesitation I shall then tell you what I prefer."

He knew as well she only said this to ruffle and annoy him as he knew he was standing within a couple of feet or so of the handsomest woman he had ever beheld, who loathed, hated, despised him; but remembering that her struggles were now but as those of the bird fluttering in the net of the snarer, he replied quietly enough:—

" The two modes are fair means, gentle lady and foul: in peace or in war I shall hold you here—if you prefer a truce or reconciliation, you shall have that—if you choose a perpetual

battle, you shall have that.   We can live without quarrelling, should you desire it: we can
remain at daggers drawn, if that suit your
temper better—one way or other, I will, however, carry my point.   If you choose harmony,
I shall prefer it—if you compel me to force, I
will employ it."

Having concluded which kind and considerate
sentence, Mr. Mazingford plunged his hands into
his coat pockets, and felt fortified to give Judith
a broadside of determined looks in return for her
unchangeable glance of indomitable scorn—but
she beat him down: even in defeat her unconquerable spirit claimed its supremacy over him:
the mind over the body : the intellect over mere
brute power and force.

  " You have spoken of our married life, our
present position, as if of a battle ground, and I
cannot say otherwise than that I admire the
truth and aptitude of your simile.—To answer
you in your own style—to pursue the imaginative and poetical a little further : still, to cling to
a metaphor which seems less like a metaphor than
a solemn truth, for Heaven knows life has been
like a battle ground to me, and a weary conflict

I have had upon it—to speak as though we were the representatives of hostile nations, and not husband and wife—man and woman—what are the terms upon which you propose an amnesty betwixt us ? What must I do to secure peace ?— what will you do, suppose I reject your proposi- tions ?"

" If you like to give me your word, that you will never separate yourself from me again, except with my consent—you shall return to your for- mer position here : I will forgive the past and never allude to it further : if you decline to make such a promise, I must use a certain degree of restraint to prevent your leaving the house of your only lawful protector, until such time as you have repented of your obstinacy, and desire a reconciliation. Considering the past—taking into account the vexation, and scandal, and malicious reports, caused by your indiscreet conduct—I feel I am now acting in a most for- bearing manner in offering you a choice in the matter—after the scandalous mode in which you have treated me."

" Do you ?" retorted Judith ; " well, under the circumstances, that may be regarded as a

blessing—considering the past, too !" she added
—" Merciful Providence—considering the past !"

She stood for a moment gazing with her
outward eye into the blazing fire; with her mental
vision into the dreary past; and as she did so,
the old fixed look departed from her face, and
she commenced gnawing her under lip, and
striking the fender impatiently with her little
foot all unwittingly.   He thought these external
signs of emotion betokened a struggle going on
within her betwixt fear and pride; betwixt
prudence and temper, obstinacy and helplessness:
he thought this, but he was mistaken—it was
the past she was considering, not the present—
what a past it had been! she recoiled from the
remembrance of it with a sudden start.

" Then, if I understand you rightly," she said
abruptly, turning towards her husband—" If
I understand you rightly, in the one case I
shall be subjected once again to the old humiliations; the old taunts; the old bondage:
guests will be requested to stare once again at
the beauty of the woman you bought ostensibly
with a price, but never yet have paid for. I
shall have to converse to show how clever l am:

to sing to prove what a magnificent voice Mrs. Mazingford has : to play, that connoisseurs may pronounce her the finest private performer they ever heard : to sketch, that the crooked old chimneys and piled gables of Wavour Hall may be carried to other lands and spoken about there ; to do all this, not because I love you and you are my husband, but because you are proud of me, and are my master.: I must either obey you without murmur, or we must quarrel ceaselessly : and even obedience cannot preserve me from insult, contempt, reproaches. What few women can forgive, I have experienced at your hands—what most consider the overflowing drop in the cup of injury you have poured out upon me; but I think little of mere personal violence. I differ from the rest of my sex in that respect, and care less for simple bodily pain than for anything else. I am not so weak or delicate but that I can bear a blow ; and you know, in days gone by, I let you do your worst, and never uttered a cry for help—never raised a hand to defend myself.

"I only speak of these things to prove how vast must have been the mental suffering I endured, when beside the remembrance of it all corporeal pain sinks into insignificance. The body !—Oh! they cannot have felt what I have felt of soul's anguish who grieve about it. The body ! if you had stabbed me to the heart—if you had poured out my life's blood like water— if you had trampled me under foot, and done your worst on it, I could have gone down on my knees and blessed you for your clemency, Lewis Mazingford !"

He had the advantage over her now; the old advantage which he always gained, when feeling and passion found vent with her in words.

"If you have quite concluded your eloquent harangue, madam," he retorted, "will you have the kindness to give me a definite answer?—the ten minutes have expired."

"Have they?" she said more calmly; "it would be to subject myself again to indignity, sorrow, humiliation, to avail myself of your most generous offer; it would be to doom myself to perpetual intercourse with you; to the eternal sight of a man I detest and despise—you need not speak," she added hastily. "I know what you would say, what you would promise, vow, swear; but I know what your oaths, vows, promises are worth—who better?

"No, sir: your harshest treatment would be to me preferable to ever again submitting myself to your will: to ever again passing my head under the yoke; free in solitude and confinement, I shall be—but as the mistress of 'Wavour Hall' I was a mere slave—ten minutes—or ten years, my answer would be the same at the expiration of either period. Take it now, once and for ever. I will give no promise. I will never be reconciled. I will have no truce. Do your worst, and I defy you; you may touch my body now, but my spirit never, never more. Yes, Lewis Mazingford—my master—my oppressor—my husband—my curse; I thank Heaven that at last, standing at your very hearth, I can say, in all sincerity—I am free and I defy you."

"You throw down the gauntlet bravely, Madam," he said, absolutely quivering with passion, for her determination was not precisely what he had anticipated; "you throw down the gauntlet bravely, and I take it up readily. That point is then settled for the present—you have taken your choice—so be it."

From that hour Judith was never left alone for a moment; three rooms on the upper story were allotted to her use, and from them she never descended for months to take even a stroll in the gardens. Sleeping or waking, wet or fine, by day or by night, keen eyes always kept vigilant watch upon her—her husband, or some of his satellites—there was not a chance of escape she saw, and her soul sickened and wearied at the long confinement, but still she remained unsubdued. She would not promise. Mr. Mazingford grew desperate, and she—she would have died but for the relief of pen, ink, and paper; but for the novel she felt herself bound to finish—a portion of which she knew was in type.

Bit by bit the manuscript was forwarded to Mr. Mason—one by one, letters of acknowledgment came from him, which were duly read by Mr. Mazingford ere they reached his wife. She was perfectly cognisant of this—saw precisely what the result would be—understood the reason why she was permitted to write at all—grieved exceedingly because a promise made under different circumstances compelled her to reveal her secret, and gratify, even in one solitary instance, her husband's vanity and cupidity—but without a syllable of comment—without a single observation or attempt at concealment, she worked resolutely on, till the last sheet was finished— the last proof corrected—the book published, and the money paid for it.

"No despicable amount this," thought her husband, as a cheque for a considerable sum dropped out of the publisher's letter. "She might readily add a thousand a year to my income—help to pay some of the expenses I have already incurred for her"—and he handed the communication, (without its enclosure, however) to Judith, who sent, by return of post, her acknowledgment of the liberal sum. Then, she laid aside her pens, and ink, and paper, and took to gazing out over the landscape.

She sat at the window of her sitting-room always : doing nothing, saying nothing ; watching the course of the sun from the time he rose in the east till he set in the west—looking away and away at the river, and the trees, and the hills, and the mountains, and the flowers.

But never writing—that pursuit she seemed

to have relinquished as completely as though the great gift had not been in her. Silently she may, indeed, have thought about her art, and chalked out plots, and plans, and schemes for future works of fiction, but she never committed any of her imaginings to paper. She was not going to write to minister to his pride—to make herself conspicuous as "the beautiful Mrs. Mazingford,—*Such* a genius, too!" to bring more notoriety upon herself than that she knew had already been wrought out.

For that fashionable world, for whose amusement she had so long catered, was now in full possession of the "dear, romantic story" of that enchanting book—"The History of a Broken Heart," and the novel was read with tenfold interest, and pronounced to be fifty times more piquant, because, so said society—"all the characters in it were drawn from life, and so easily identified." There stood Judith, herself, the centre figure in the tableau; with the various people she had encountered in her pilgrimage through life grouped about her as accessories. Delightful peeps were those the world got of her domestic relations through the medium of that

most clever book. It was currently believed
that every scene in it had been sketched, or
rather coloured from life; and, indeed, what
with Miss Lestock and her aunts, and Lillian
and her brother—and the vague story of a dead
lover—and various rumours afloat concerning
the occurrences both of her earlier and later life,
there was enough romance to be got out of her
own story to justify people in their idea that she,
who had suffered so much, had no need to draw
on imagination, either for incidents or characters.
Judith's eccentric flight—the fictitious anecdotes
abroad with regard to her doings after she left
Wavour Hall—the strange characters she was
said to have met, and the really remarkable
things she was stated to have done—furnished
such a nice budget of gossip for fashionable and
literary London to gorge itself upon, that once
again, the ci-devant member and his wife became
the fashion. Dear Mr. and dearer Mrs. Mazingford were besieged with letters from ladies who
were fond of lions, and old gentlemen who were
fond of gossip. In some of the cheaper publications of the day, a sort of biography was got
up of the new authoress, most of which com-

menced in a solemn and impressive manner
with these words—

"In an old ruinous hall in Wales there was
born at the commencement of the year 18— a
child of remarkable beauty, &c., &c., &c.;" and
then a fancy sketch was given of the old father,
and of the Welsh family circle, and a truly remarkable woodcut of Llandyl Hall and a portrait of Mrs. Mazingford graced the pages of
many a cheap periodical; and anecdotes were
invented, showing how, from her cradle, the
" child" was an authoress, and specimens of
poetry were given, said to have been written by
the infant at the tender age of six years, but
really composed by a clever gentleman who
resided in the neighbourhood of Great Queen
Street, and made a good deal of money by
burning children for the newspapers, inventing
horrible tragedies, and doing any other work of
a light and agreeable nature which Heaven sent
his way.

Publicity is an end more easily to be compassed in London than most people imagine.
Anybody who likes to run the gauntlet of
popular opinion, and either make an idiot or a

martyr of himself, may become famous *pro. tem.*; only, if he want to continue to be famous, he must keep up the steam. The greatest author, statesman, or philanthropist, scarcely creates so vast a sensation by his mightiest efforts as a "good murder," and both are forgotten equally soon; the one goes to Westminster, and the other to the gallows; the one is sometimes cited in the pages of a magazine, the other is embalmed in Causes Célèbres. Verily, oh! reader, if you want to become a great, and famous man in the sight of your fellows, the best way to compass your end is to stab your friend, poison your wife, commit some gigantic fraud, or else go through miseries enough to turn your brain, and let them be made public. The surest mode of obtaining notoriety is to do something you desire to keep secret. Believe me, if you once attempt concealment of any sort, you will soon have as much publicity as any rational being could desire.

So Judith found: people who had been striving all their days, by routs and balls, and lions, and works of art, and works of benevolence, and works of the arch fiend, to become famous—

and the fashion—had failed; whilst an ordinary Welsh Member's wife, *née* a wild, unbroken, Welsh beauty, furnished topics of conversation for half the west-end of London. Because she had innocently caused the death of her lover— because she and her husband lived like cat and dog—because she would love her sister, and chanced to be cousin to a woman who had deserted her children—because, in very weariness of spirit, she fled from her only lawful protector, and omitted to put her own name on the title-page of her books—Mrs. Mazingford obtained publicity.

It was really astonishing, when it became known that Mrs. Mazingford and the authoress of these clever books were one and the same person, how her productions were sought after! Her publisher grew anxious for another manuscript. His brethren began to speculate on the desirability of bringing out a new novel by her. Librarians eagerly demanded when she was going to write more? and insinuated to Mr. Mason, that they had a few vacant places on their shelves, they would be glad to fill with a new work with a taking title, by the so-called " Mrs. Gilmore."

In fact, there was a perfect *furore* on the matter; and at last, Messrs. Noxley and Mobelle offered terms for a fresh novel, which actually startled Mrs. Mazingford.

" Judith," he said, " these gentlemen wish a work from your pen."

" No doubt—"

" And double Mr. Mason's proposals."

" They are very liberal."

" And are desirous of having the completed manuscript placed in their hands before Christmas."

" Indeed !"

" Will you therefore write, and say that you agree to their terms—and will commence the book forthwith ?"

" No."

" And for what reason do you decline ?"

" Because I have given up scribbling. A bird cannot sing in a cage—Judith Mazingford cannot write in prison."

" Then, for Heaven's sake, let there be a truce between us, and come down stairs !"

She turned from him with a bitter, scornful laugh . " Lewis Mazingford," she said, " you do not know me yet—but I know you. I will never voluntarily cross the threshold of these rooms, unless I go forth free—or am carried out in my coffin."

"Why should there not be peace between us? Why should we not live happily?"—he demanded.

"That you well know," she replied; "but to refresh your memory, which seems to have become wonderfully defective, I answer, that we can never be happy together, because oil and water won't mix—because I cannot alter your nature, or change my own—because you have cursed my life, and darkened my existence—because, one by one, you have taken from me kindred, home, self-respect, bodily strength— the desire for fame —the hope even of comparative tranquillity. We cannot be happy together, because I have been false to myself, and you have lied to me—because in marrying you, I lost all sense of independence, all consideration, either for my own or the world's good opinion—because you cheated and juggled me out of myself—because you killed my father and my sister—and because I hate you!"

She spoke the last three words with such startling vehemence, that Mr. Mazingford was awed, for the instant, by the force of her passion; but recovering himself immediately, he answered—

"Will you, or will you not, write as I desire to Messrs. Noxley and Mobelle?"

"No—that is, I will, on two conditions."

"What may they be?"

"I will write for you, Mr. Mazingford, if this night you permit me to leave Wavour Hall—make no search for me, and leave me the privilege of seeking my own home, without intrusion from you. I will give you three-fourths of all the money I make—you shall have my fame, my earnings, everything save myself. The world need know nothing of our separation. The state of my health is far from good; let that be the ostensible reason for my retirement: only let me go—and I will do what you wish as you wish."

He hesitated for a minute, as if considering her proposition; then, however, laying a sheet of paper before her, he said, "Well, be it so; I agree to the proposition—now write."

" Before you have fulfilled your part of the contract? No, thank you, Mr. Mazingford; I did that folly once, and thereby cursed my whole after-existence. What I promise, you know I will fulfil; but your promises I know you will break. When I am free, it will be time enough to enter into fresh contracts." And Judith, pushing pen, ink, and paper from her, turned aside from her husband, with a movement of utter contempt and detestation.

There was a great struggle in Mr. Mazingford's breast for a minute, betwixt prudence and obstinacy, anger and expediency; but at last he said—

" What pleasure do you think it can be to me, to have you cooped up here? If you will not be friends with me, if you will not return to your old position as mistress of Wavour Hall, if you will insist on regarding me as a cruel task-master, in place of your husband—why then, for Heaven's sake, go. I give you liberty to leave Wales to-night; to make what arrangements you choose with these gentlemen; to follow the bent of your own inclination entirely. I believe yours is one of those tempers that grows only more determined with opposition or argument; therefore, take your own way, follow your own path, uninfluenced, uncontrolled by me."

" How sweet is liberty!"— ejaculated Judith.

" Well, take it then," retorted Mr. Mazingford, pointing to the door—"I am not now preventing your departure. If you want to be free as the birds of the air, as the winds of heaven—go!"

" You are very kind," she said, " but I don't think I shall avail myself of your most disinterested offer. You are too ready to let me go, to make me feel very wishful to depart. I suppose," she continued, after a momentary pause, " you think I am so blind as not to see every thought as it passes through your mind. You know you want to let me leave Wales and proceed to London, and enter into an engagement with these people, and start once fairly to my writing, and then bring me back. You want me to be free as a tethered horse is free. You want me to have such liberty as suits your own purpose—but it won't do. I have got accustomed to my prison, and I would rather not

G 3

leave it at all, than leave it to be dogged by you."

" Has it ever occurred to you," he demanded, " that it is a rash thing to urge a man to extremities ? "

" No," she replied.

" Has it ever crossed your mind, that some-day I might find means to avenge myself for years of disobedience, insult, caprice, crime ? Yes, madam, crime ; for a forger, let her be wife, or what else she will, is as great a criminal as ever left the dock for the Hulks. Has it ever entered your mind that I am not a person to be trifled with and defied with impunity always ? "

" No ; " Judith struck to the monosyllable, with resolute pertinacity.

" Have you never once thought, that having sworn to conquer you, I will yet do it ? "

" No—you might try to do it, and have tried, but you could not—I dare you to do your worst."

For one moment Judith absolutely quailed at the look which came over his face.

" It is the state of my health," she thought. " How weak I am getting ; " and, before she had completed her mental sentence, he was speaking again.

"Once, for all, Mrs. Mazingford, will you relinquish your present absurd line of conduct —will you consider yourself as my wife—give your word not to attempt to leave my house again without my permission, and conduct yourself in all respects as befits your rank and position in society?"

"I will not."

"On your own head be it then," he said sullenly, and left the apartment.

. For several days she did not see him again; but at last, one evening, he entered her apartment, and requested to know if she had altered her determination.

"No," she answered.

"Judith," he said, "you had better reflect. There are ways and means of bringing refractory wives to reason, from which, perhaps, even your spirit would recoil appalled."

"You are brewing mischief, I see," was the cool reply; "but even when you bend your brows to meeting—when you look at me with that cruel, stoney vindictive glance—when you draw the lines close around your eyes, and speak through compressed lips—when I know that you have invented some fresh misery for me—I am not afraid, I can defy you."

She said this while finishing a cup of coffee a servant had brought up a few minutes previously. Scarcely, however, were the final words uttered, when she suddenly exclaimed.

" Have you poisoned me ?   Gracious Heaven, what is this ! "

She attempted to rise, and walk across the room ; but a cloud seemed to come over her eyes—all strength left her limbs—a sort of heavy dizziness oppressed her head ; and stagger-ing forward she would have fallen, had not her husband caught her in his arms.

" Let me go—don't touch me," she muttered, and in another minute lay like one dead before him.

CHAPTER V.

THE place to which Alice Crepton proceeded, after her departure from Klicksturvyd, was situate in a lonely part of Dorsetshire, ten miles from any large town, three miles from the nearest village, a good half-hour's walk from any coach road, a dreary, desolate abode, tenanted by a Mr. Merdun, his discontented wife and a brood of healthy, romping, unmanageable children. Truth, to say, Mary Duvard had never visited her relatives, or she would not have sent Alice amongst them. But in any case, where else could the girl have gone? that was the great question Alice propounded to herself during the first week after her arrival, and for many a weary month subsequent to that. Where could she go—she who had no friends, no home, no anything, on earth, but a poor lover and a strong constitution?

For Miss Lestock had returned her daughter's note to Dr. Duvard, in a blank envelope—and Sir John having requested his secretary to inform the "meddling quack," who ventured to interfere with his concerns, that the baronet never had, and never would, recognise the Crepton children—that they were no relatives of his, and had no claim upon him—favoured Charles with no further correspondence on the subject. Then Mary was leaving the country, and her brother was too poor to marry; and so Alice had no alternative but to seek an asylum in the bosom of Mr. Merdun's family.

And anything but a soft pillow for a weary head to rest upon it assuredly proved; so rough, indeed, that had Alice thought fit to complain, I question whether Dr. Duvard would not, at all hazards, have rushed into matrimony at once; but Alice was proud—and somewhat reserved —and so, accordingly, as all such characters do—took her sorrows home to her heart, and nursed them into well-grown hardships at her leisure. One of the curses of thinking

alone is, that after a time it compels a person to
feel alone.   Where sympathy is not sought, sympathy will not be given ; and though many most
excellent but reserved people think the contrary, I
trust they will pardon my saying that it is utterly
impossible for anybody to understand their troubles unless they will occasionally be good enough
to explain them.   The world cannot know by
intuition where pity should be given—and, to
enable it exactly to understand where the feeling,
said to be next akin to love, might be judi-
ciously bestowed, it is absolutely necessary for
sufferers to open their lips and hearts, and tell
the hows and the wherefores, and the whys of
what is the matter with them.

But, to do Alice justice, it was not the stoical
reserve which obstinately persists in making a
martyr of itself, that kept her silent.   It was a
delicacy of sentiment—a sort of shrinking timi-
dity—a dread of seeming to force herself on
Charles Duvard—a painful memory, that innocently though it happened, still after all, it was
she, not he, who had made the first advance
into the vague region called " being engaged "—
which prevented complaint, or even desirable
explanation to the young doctor.

She was miserable at Combe Ridgis, and yet she put on a mask of contentment to deceive his understanding; she detested the home selected for her, and yet fifty causes interfered to deter her from writing the plain unvarnished state of the case to him who had, assuredly, the best right to know all about, and the nearest interest in it.

She could not even seem to ask him to marry her. She could not add to his weight of anxiety —nor appear dissatisfied with the home he had provided for her—nor speak against his relatives; she could not complain of any shelter after the den from which he had rescued her; she did not like to say she was unhappy—lonely—wretched, and yet she felt all three.

For it was a miserable house, where the master, a gentleman farmer, was eternally trying fresh experiments—keeping himself and his family in perpetual hot-water, for the sake of some new crotchet or absurd whim; where the wife, a woman of fretful temper, for ever maintained a lamentation concerning the state of her health—her husband's bad management—her children's disobedience—and her own blighted existence. She

was far too much engrossed in the contemplation
of her misfortunes, ever to dream of attempting
to lighten any of them, and thus it necessarily
came to pass that whilst she lay grumbling on the
softest sofa, the junior members of the family
scampered wild among the servants, who, in
their turn, discharged no single duty properly,
and were far more proprietors of the house and
farm than the legitimate owners.

When Alice first arrived amongst the Merdun fry—a lot of unkempt, black-eyed, brown-
faced, untidy, romping boys and girls came
rushing to meet her; and from the moment of
her appearance, evidently regarding her rather
as a new playmate than as a governess, they
harassed her life out with all sorts of elfish tricks
and hoydenish jokes, until sometimes the young
instructress, in very despair, boxed them all
round, when they rushed howling to their
mother, who thereupon desired Miss Crepton, or
Alice, as they all called her, not to be so severe
with the children; and upon the strength of this
maternal admonition, they set their teacher's
injunctions at defiance, and laughed her commands and entreaties to scorn.

Music, drawing, and a little French, she
managed to impart to the girls, whilst she
compelled the two youngest boys to learn the
rudiments of English grammar—spelling and
writing—and with great address contrived
to nip in the bud an incipient flirtation which
Mr. Merdun's nephew, an unlicked cub of
nineteen, wanted to establish with her. When
this youth, tired of experimental farming, and
went to London to study for a surgeon, Alice
devoutly thanked Heaven for his change of
mind, and residence; but the untidiness, the
irregularity, the extravagance, the democracy of
that house, baffled description. When visitors
came, as they did every Christmas, in the persons
of the young student above mentioned—his
sister—a *bas bleu*—who had the reputation, at
Combe Ridgis, of being an uncommon genius,
and Charles Duvard, who stole down twice a
year to see his inamorata, and delude her
and himself into a false hope of his prospects
speedily brightening—a better face was put on
everything, and the farm and its inmates rubbed
themselves up for the festive occasion. The
young ladies had new frocks made that almost

fitted them; the brothers having gone through the ordeal of being " measured " by the village tailor, turned out on Christmas morning in tight jackets and loose trowsers; their hair was oiled and their faces were washed, and they were bribed with fallacious promises to sit tolerably still, and behave themselves with tolerable decorum. Mr. Merdun brought forth an old suit of superfine black, and arrayed his gaunt person in it, whilst Mrs. M. took out her curl papers, and appeared languishing and beautiful in a clean lace cap, and company satin dress, with a new baby who was for ever cutting fresh teeth, and A-ba-ing, and slobbering its pinafore in her arms.

" How many children have you, Mr. Merdun ?" hazarded an inexperienced young curate, on one occasion.

" God knows," was the impressive reply; and it was a fact that he did not, and that he invariably called them all Mrs. Merdun's boys and girls, and would not have recognized one of them, had he happened to meet him or her five miles from home.

He was a careless, good natured, well-educated idiot, who had mounted farming as a hobby, and was riding himself, and not his pet, to death.

Immediately after Alice's arrival, he commenced levelling all the ditches on his property; but then finding that he required divisions of some kind between the different fields, he spent as much money in erecting new fences as it had cost him to pull down the old hedges. When once the fencings were completed, he took up the notion of spade labour, and set all the vagabonds in the country at work, to dig his land thoroughly, which, judging by results, meant turning over the ground about two inches from the surface. When the spade labour crotchet was done with, he thought fit to sow all his arable land with flax seed, which, for want of sufficient moisture, did not yield him half a crop, and storing the small portion remaining, without " rippling," the entire rotted, and could be made available only as manure. He drained his land too dry, and had the stones picked so clean off his fields, that the ground closed up, and would grow nothing. He lost half his butter by veering about from one new style of churn to another, and killed his fowls with food that was intended to make them lay two eggs a-day. His horses were lamed by experimental shoeing: the people he employed were continually being set to one job, and compelled to leave another; whilst Mr. Merdun himself, in an old thread-bare coat, and battered straw hat, roamed about the fields, thinking within himself what improvements he could next effect. He tried to reclaim a barren common, by dropping little pieces of slate over the ground; and when Alice, whose curiosity really was piqued at the process, asked him what good they were meant to accomplish, he explained to her his idea that where the slate lay, it warmed the ground, and that accordingly round each bit he dropped, a tuft of clover would spring.

"So that you see," he finished, "I shall have a fine crop of clover for the value of these pieces of broken slate."

But the clover never came any more than money, or increased stock, or greater comfort; and after she had endured the misery, and the unsettledness of that untidy house for nearly three years, Alice began to think that as Doctor Duvard seemed as far off being able to marry

as ever, she would try to better her condition,
if he could not better his.

How far vague ideas of authorship, fame, and
wealth, conspired to turn this idea into an absolute project, it is hard to say; for very soon
after her entrance into Mr. Merdun's family, the
girl found that the gift of the mother's race had
descended to her; that she had a capability of
writing easily, if not well;—that authorship
seemed to come naturally to her, and that it was
not, after all, so very hard a thing to " write a
book."

First of all, she tested her powers on the
children, reading them her own tales as if
they had been composed by somebody else:
then Miss Merdun, the *bas-bleu* previously
referred to, insisted on being taken into her confidence, and seriously recommended her em-
bracing literature as a profession; and finally,
Mr. Merdun went perfectly insane on the
subject. " She was a D'Arblay,—pooh—Miss
Burney never wrote as she could. She was an
Austen, a Ferrier, and heaven knows what
beside. In brief, he took up her books as he
had taken up experimental farming, and pro-

phesied as much success would result from her
pen as from spade labour, artificial manures, and
broken slates.

Had Alice's indeed not been a rather stronger
head than usually belongs to the members of the
fourth estate, her brain would have been completely turned with the praises Miss Merdun and
her uncle lavished on her productions.   The
former took one of the shorter tales to London,
and, though unable to dispose of it, reported how
some most "talented" friends of hers had asked
her who the delightful creature was that wrote
it, and declared that she must be an astonishing
genius, destined to take rank amongst the first
of living female writers; and even whilst doubt-
ing, Alice listened, and forgot to remember that
Mr. Merdun was an idiot and an enthusiast, and
omitted to remark that Miss Merdun herself
did not seem to have found literature a very
productive field of labour, and that it was no
less true than strange, that she was wanting to
exchange her brilliant prospects in London for
a governess' situation with thirty pounds a
year at her uncle's, or a situation as wife and
housekeeper to Dr. Duvard.

Very artfully the lady covered over both these designs, either of which would have been a move for the better, and the latter a change greatly to her liking; for she wanted to be married, and she wished Doctor Duvard for a husband, and therefore her advice to Alice to embrace a literary course was not altogether so disinterested as the girl imagined. Alice might have seen a little more clearly perhaps, had she not been looking on objects very close at hand through somewhat vain spectacles; for if she did not rate her own abilities at an inordinate height, still she was new fangled with the idea of being an authoress; and though perhaps every crow does not call its black brood white, yet there cannot be a doubt but that most scribblers consider their first ugly bantling a very respectable sort of bird.

Dr. Duvard indeed was the only individual who threw cold water on the heated schemes of his wife, that was to be. He discouraged the idea of her leaving Dorsetshire, and spoke of the desirability of her retaining her present home until she exchanged it for one of his providing; dwelt somewhat mournfully on the difficulty of getting on in the world, and finally assured her that he had an insuperable dislike to lady authors, and should be very sorry to see her pretty fingers soiled with ink.

Now all this might have done very well, and been carefully taken to heart, had not it chanced to come upon the top of a load of petty irritations, and very sufficient jealousies, caused partly by Mrs. Merdun, greatly by Dr. Duvard's admiration for Mrs. Gilmore, and most of all by Miss Merdun, who had been secretly fanning the flame of discontent in Alice's breast by a number of friendly comments on her lover's conduct and her own peculiarly disagreeable position.

She pointed out to Miss Crepton the fact that, if her *fiancé* ever intended to marry, he might just as well commit the folly soon as syne. "As for his waiting for better means, my dear, it is absurd; because he could support a wife quite as easily as himself—for his whole expenses as a married man, would be infinitely less than living as he does, in lodgings. If you had a home of your own, it would alter the case: for he then might be afraid of making you less comfortable. As it is, however, everybody knows a governess's life is not so pleasant a one—and, to wind all up, if I were in *your* place, I should not feel at all satisfied. However, every person knows his or her own business best—and I make it a rule never to inter to interfere with any one. Only *I* think Mrs. Gilmore's handsome face is at the bottom of the business."

And this final clause, containing, like the postscript to a lady's letter, the gist of the whole argument, Alice, poor deluded child, took it into her uncommonly wise head to think she was very hardly used. She had no mother to talk to and be comforted—no sister to take counsel with—no sensible friend to advise and re-assure her—so she communed with her own wounded heart, and found there such cause for sorrow, as caused her to feel herself a very miserable, desolate individual, with a long list of grievances, who had a right to cry herself to sleep—which latter portion of the performance she successfully achieved when day was dawning, on the morning following the night on which Miss Merdun had thought fit to state "her opinion."

Sleep, however, did her no good, for she awoke with a very uncomfortable sensation about her heart, as if some great calamity had happened to her the night before; and she set about completing her catalogue of miseries, as speedily as might be, by renewing the literary question with Doctor Duvard, and growing very pettish and cross when he persevered in his advice for her to relinquish the idea of " pen-work" for ever.

He urged her to consider the difficulties every literary man and woman, from the days of the Heptarchy down, had met with in the path she so rashly proposed for herself. He spoke of the folly of relinquishing a certainty for an uncertainty; said she could try literature if she chose, when they were married and settled close to the publisher's head-quarters; offered, if she liked, to take up a manuscript with him, and see whether he could get it accepted; pointed out to her the fact that she could not remain as a guest for ever at Miss Merdun's house, even if she accepted her invitation, and were to pay her a visit in London; hinted that his opinion of that lady was not of the most favourable character; and imbly, tried to " talk her round" to his views, as a sensible man, under such circumstances, would he likely to talk to a tolerably sensible girl.

But he did not understand the true position of affairs, and therefore all his arguments proved utterly unavailing: he could not comprehend Alice's pertinacity to her new scheme, until having said, in a very blind sort of way—

" You see, dear Alice, I feel almost as if you were at home here, as if I left you with a father and a mother till I can come to claim you for my very own ; and I should be miserable if you were in any other house than this, excepting as my wife ; for I know you could not be half so happy anywhere as here ;"—she somewhat vehemently answered :

" I could not be half so unhappy anywhere else you mean, for I am and have been perfectly wretched in this place." Then the truth so long and carefully concealed, suddenly burst upon him, and taking the poor tired, weary girl to his heart, he muttered, " Good Heavens ! what a fool I have been, a blind, unfeeling idiot. Look up, Alice—don't cry so bitterly—I thought you were happy here, and free from care, and that I would not drag you down to poverty with me; but if you think you could be content as my wife, we will be married immediately, and I will do my best to make life easy for you."

"I—I don't want to be married," sobbed out the proud little spirit. "I won't marry just yet. I only wish to leave Combe Ridgis, and see if I cannot push my own fortune in London."

"Yes, but you can push it as my wife—silly one," he replied.

"No, I could not. I want to be free."

"Free!" replied Dr. Duvard, and he relaxed his grasp, and looked earnestly into her eyes, which, however, sought the ground and refused to be interrogated; "Free! what do you mean by that?"

"I mean," she answered, "that I wish for a time to be free and independent, and—and able to do as I like; and I won't marry just yet."

"Will you tell me why?" he pleaded, and the true love of the man's heart came swelling up within him, as it suddenly swept across his mind that she wanted to be released from her engagement. "Will you tell me why?"

"No—I cannot—that is I—"

"Are you afraid of poverty?" he asked.
"Are you tired of my want of success? Have
you grown to despise a man who cannot win the
smiles of fortune? Have you found out at last
that I am not your equal in any one respect—
that you desire a husband every way superior to
myself—that I am only a struggling doctor,
without friends, wealth, or connexion, to give me
a lift? Are you tired of me Alice? Oh! for
mercy's sake, don't take back your love from
me. But, if that is gone, I won't hold you to
any rashly-spoken engagement; you were a
child then, and I was a fool to think I could
ever hope to be loved, as I do love still—still—"

"A letter for you, Doctor," here interposed
Miss Merdan, opening the door at the moment,
and cutting right across his sentence; and as
she did not leave the room after delivering the
missive, he was reluctantly compelled to let
Alice glide away from his side out of the apartment, whilst he remained with his relative, and
broke the seal of the missive she had presented
to him.

He looked at the epistle at first carelessly,

but as he read, an expression of curious excitement and anxiety came over his face.

" What time does the coach pass the cross roads for London?" he demanded.

" Half past two," was the reply.

" I shall just, then, be in time to catch it," he said, looking at his watch. " Tell Alice I am obliged to go. I should like to speak to her. I shall be back in a minute;" and hastily quitting the room, he went off in search of Mr. Merdun, who, as usual, was not to be found; and failing him, said good bye, in a very hurried manner, to Mrs. Merdun.

" Come, Alice, do be quick—I must be off," he cried, from the bottom of the staircase ; and his words brought the girl down, followed by Miss Merdun, who seemed determined not to lose sight of her.

" I shall only be a day or two away," he said. " I will tell you all when I come back. I want to talk to you—you—you don't want to be free, Alice ?"

He spoke the last few words in a very low tone, and was answered only by a look.

" There is nothing wrong, is there?" she asked, anxiously.

"No—not much—nothing wrong with me; it's poor Mrs. Gilmore. Now, good bye, mine own, take care of yourself, we will have a long talk over matters when I come back."

And even whilst Alice held out her hand to him for another " good bye," he was gone.

Half disappointed and a little hurt, she turned away from the hall door, and encountered Miss Merdun's black eyes fastened upon her with a strange expression.

" I wonder," said Alice, " if Mrs. Gilmore is ill again."

" No, my poor child, she is not ill," said Miss Merdun, with an air of mysterious pity.

" What is she then ?" demanded the girl.

" *Non est*," answered her friend.

" Surely not dead !" exclaimed Alice, the recollection of many an angry thought and evil feeling coming across her conscience, and troubling it. " Surely she is not dead."

" No, she is not dead," responded Miss Merdun.

" Well—what is she then?" persisted her victim.

" Why, she has disappeared, and Doctor

Duvard is in despair, and must needs leave you to hunt after her," said the lady. "There, don't look so pale and frightened; it must have shewn itself some time or another—better before your marriage than after—an artful, designing woman. Poor Charles! he is greatly to be pitied. If he never see her again, it will be a happy thing for both of you."

Alice did not answer; she staggered somehow to the bottom step of the staircase, and sat down, burying her face in her hands.

"And he loved her, and would have married me out of pity—charity—" she muttered, after a pause. "No, it shall never be. Miss Merdun, if you will take me, I will go back with you to-morrow to London. I will try literature, and if that fail, must take another situation—but I can't stay here, I—I am—"

Miss Merdun never pushed her for particulars of what she was; from that hour she kept pouring jealous poisons down her throat, and finally, so worked upon the girl, that without revealing her intention to any one else, she wrote a proud, indignant letter to Doctor Duvard, releasing him from his engagement, leaving him

free to marry Mrs. Gilmore or any one else he
chose, telling him she was leaving Combe
Ridges for ever, but giving no address at which
information of her could be obtained.

When that ridiculous epistle reached Charles
Duvard, he was ill in bed. Having walked so
hurriedly across the country as to induce a
profuse perspiration, he mounted, on a cold
winter day, to the top of the coach, where he
cooled at his leisure; getting, finally, so chilled,
in fact, that by the time he arrived in London,
he found he was unable to stand, and had barely
voice left to tell a cabman where to drive him to.
A violent rheumatic fever was the result; and
when at length, with the help of a stick, he was
able to get so far as Miss Merdun's house, he
found Alice had left her abode, and that all trace
of the girl's whereabouts was lost.

"Do you mean to tell me," he said to his
relative, "that Alice came here with you: that
she has left your house: that she gave you no
address likely to find her; that you have no
knowledge whatever of her movements?—for
mercy's sake, give me some clue to her. Don't
you know we were to have been married almost

immediately. What can have possessed the girl? I am wretched about her. I don't know what to do, or where to turn, or what to think."

Miss Merdun did not know either, but she consoled him by remarking that she believed he had brought it all on himself, by his attentions to Mrs. Gilmore.

"Attentions to Mrs. Gilmore!" The doctor raved and stormed, nay, he did worse, he swore, at the insinuation. He told Miss Merdun unpleasant truths about herself, and her wretched mischief-making propensities; he said she had acted an unchristian part towards a young and unprotected girl, and wound up by declaring that she either must have made Alice's visit wretched to her, or else was perfectly cognisant of her address, and, in refusing to enlighten him, was playing a double and most unwomanly game.

"Now, my dear Charles," she remonstrated; " do be reasonable; what possible object could I have in preventing you seeing the girl?"

"That you know best yourself," was the reply.

"I am sure," persisted the lady, " all that I have ever wanted was to promote your and her happiness; that has been my one sole aim."

"May I be hanged if I don't think your sole aim on earth is to be married yourself," vociferated Charles, with considerably more candour than politeness; "but, once for all, will you tell me where Alice is? I look upon her as my wife, and I have a right to enquire about her as if she were actually such."

"I thought she had declined ever to become the wife to a man who could leave her to run after a handsome face," sneered Miss Merdun.

"That letter was written under influence," retorted the doctor; "in plain English, yout put ideas into her mind, that never would have come there of themselves. You have done a great deal of harm, which you can only undo by telling me where she is. Do give me her address, and I will forgive all the falsehoods you have implied about me to her, and all the misery you have given me? Will you."

"Upon my word, I no more know where Alice Crepton has gone to, than you do," said Miss Merdun, earnestly. "I consider that she treated me very badly—particularly at a time when I was trying to make her as happy and comfortable as possible. She took offence on

very slight provocation, and left the house, notwithstanding all I could say to dissuade her from
such a step. I really do not think she is
thoroughly sane," finished the lady, by way of
completing her sentence in a manner gratifying
to her auditor's feelings.

"She has a good deal more sense than you, at
any rate," murmured Dr. Duvard; and after two
or three more ineffectual attempts to get anything
further out of his interesting relative, he left the
house, determining to write to Mr. Merdun concerning Alice

Very wearily, and very hopelessly, he paced
along the London streets—little dreaming that
within ten minutes' drive from Miss Merdun's
door, Alice Crepton was sitting up in a mean
little third-floor room, crying, as the popular
phrase goes, "her eyes out"—because it had, at
last, occurred to her she might have been premature in giving Charles his dismissal, and because
she was such a little simpleton as to feel ashamed
of taking any steps to ascertain whether she had
or not.

She found out, when it was "too late," that
she had only jumped out of the frying-pan into

the fire—that her change for the better, had
turned out a change for the worse; that Miss
Merdun was by no means an amiable hostess,
that her influence and abilities stood higher in
general estimation at Combe Ridgis than in
London.

It was the old story over again—of a patron
pretending to more power than she actually
possessed, of a protegée growing impatient, and
of both losing their tempers, and telling each
other truths plainer than pleasant.

Then Miss Merdun reproached her friend with
ingratitude and want of genuine talent—whilst
Alice accused her of a lack of straightforward-
ness, of having raised hopes she knew never could
be gratified, stated as facts things which turned
out to be fictions, and, altogether, done everything, saving and except that which she ought.

The end of which state of warfare was, that
Alice feeling herself *de trop*, took leave of Miss
Merdun one morning in a huff—and without so
much as informing that lady of her destination,
conveyed herself and her worldly effects to cheap
lodgings at the top of a very large house,
situated in a quiet street near Portman

Square, where she managed to pass her time,
as hath been previously recorded, very miserably.

The real state of the case was, that she had
rashly started on an untried path, without thinking whither it might conduct her—and, accordingly, following the route she had, all unconsciously, chalked out for herself, she arrived, at
last, in the third floor back room above-mentioned,
where she gathered her papers about her, and
tried to rest contented.

For so far she was not short of money, having
saved fifty pounds during her three years sojourn at
Combe Ridgis ; and, therefore, all tedious as
publishing delays are, she fancied she could
afford to wait patiently for a result ; but days
and months passed drearily away—and still,
though her pen was never idle, no gold, or fame,
or happiness (save that she always found in
writing) accrued from her labours.

Tired and sorrowful she rambled from office
to office, getting her tales read by some, skimmed
by others, and refused by all ; at last, somebody
wanting to get rid of her, and never having the
remotest intention of ever printing anything
she submitted for approval, advised, or rather

" suggested," as the phrase goes, the propriety of her trying a three-volume novel.

The idea revived Alice's spirits, when they were almost below freezing point; she clutched at the proposal as if it had been a bonâ fide offer of purchase, there made and there accepted—thanked her adviser eagerly, and gratefully declared, in a tone which, to do him justice, caused him to wince a little as he thought of how lightly he had uttered the words—that she was *very* much obliged to him, turned into a neighbouring stationer's shop, purchased a ream of paper, a pint of ink, a quarter of a hundred of quills, and hurried away home to commence, without the delay of a single hour, the " great work " which it had been recommended unto her to attempt. So she launched herself into the foaming tide of a literary life, into that stormy, troublous sea, in which so many a goodly craft has gone down, leaving no track behind it in the memories of man, no trace on the deceitful waters of popular opinion, that are ebbing and flowing, flowing and ebbing, for ever.

It seems a sad fate, that of sinking in the briny wave, and leaving no memory of good or

bad behind. God help those swimmers who
never reach the opposite shore; and yet, to my
thinking, it is a harder and a sadder fate to live
to stem the current, and buffet the billows, and
then find the wreath they have struggled for, has
been steeped in the bitter waters of the ocean
they have just passed over.

Better, to my mind, when the first cold plunge
is taken, to go down, and leave no sign behind,
than to find, on reaching the barren strand,
success—that its verdure is a mirage, its flowers
are withered, its fruits a delusion, its happiness
hollow, its plaudits vain; that the peace and the
hopes, and the dreams and the visions of youth
are all lying far behind on a lovelier shore—that
money and reputation have come, but that those
for whose sake we desired such baubles, have
departed.

Better never to taste the cup at all, than drain
the bitter drop lurking at the bottom—better
never to drink at all, than quaff till the liquor palls
on the palate; better never to touch a quill, than
ever come to write for the sake of so many
guineas a sheet.

So, at all events, thought Judith Mazingford,

who had arrived at a state of mind and body of which Alice, all lonely and miserable though she might be, had no conception. So thought one who had worked out her destiny, and done that which her hand found to do—who could ·have told any young aspirant all about the pains and the pleasures of literature, who was sick and weary of herself, and life, and the things of this troublous world—and who knew all the ins and outs, and straight paths, and bye paths of book-making by rote. Who better?

CHAPTER VI.

THE letter which summoned Dr. Duvard away from Combe Ridgis with such remarkable speed, was one announcing, in crabbed characters, and with an unwonted amount of bad spelling, the fact that Judith's landlady was most uneasy concerning her lodger, who had, at time of writing, been absent for three days. The woman expressed her apprehensions lest some serious accident had befallen the lady; "for she told me," added the laundress, "that she would be certain to be back for dinner at five, and to have all ready for her." .

Visions of all sorts of horrors immediately took possession of Dr. Duvard's mind, after perusing the epistle* just referred to. There is a nameless dread in the minds of most about being "lost" in London. It is not a desert, on whose barren sands any object may be clearly discerned—it is not a lowly Highland moor, where the disappearance of a stranger would lead to instant and successful search; but it is a great human ocean, where one wave swallows up another—where a man sinking down is no more missed than a rain-drop in the Atlantic —where, the moment that any one falls, the densely-packed ranks close around the spot, and shut out further view of him for ever. Men commit suicide, fracture their limbs, are carried to the station-house or the hospital, and, unless there be an address in their pockets, nobody ever learns who they were, or what they are, or whence they came. If you do not possess the questionable advantage of being known to the police, and drop down dead in the street, most probably your wife, living in one of the suburbs, will keep wondering for years what can have become of .you, and not dare to marry again till the orthodox seven have rendered you legally defunct. Looked at from a "possibility-of-losing-yourself" point of view, London is an awful place; and, accordingly, not having an idea of what shocking event might have happened to his mysterious patient, with a memory of all her sorrows, and goodness, and loneliness, and beauty rising before him, Dr. Duvard hurried off, as we have seen, to the metropolis, with the intention of finding her, living or dead; but the illness previously mentioned kept him chained to his couch for weeeks, almost for months afterwards, and when, feeble and emaciated, he crawled to Mr. Mason's office, he learned that search for the lady was superfluous, as no one can interfere between man and wife, and she had been only reclaimed by her husband.

Then he understood all—the long, dark story, with its tracery of intense passion and anguished endurance—then he fitted the key he had so often longed to possess, into the events of which he was already master, and read the weary, weary history of that wasted life from beginning to end. Now he comprehended the meaning of the cyphers he had previously looked at without

an idea of their actual import: now, even more
than formerly, he pitied, and respected, and felt
for her.

Love and hate—the two strong emotions of
her soul—he had heard her raving of both—he
had seen her trembling like a frightened bird—
he had listened to her unconscious outbursts of
indignant pride—he had beheld her cower back
from that white figure in the snow—he had
watched her work out again, on the stage of her
active mind, the fulfilment of that old prophecy,
which declared that she should pass to the grave
" battling her way."

And, then, had he not known her strive and
labour—labour to make one dream of her youth
a reality; and this was the end of all, to be
carried back a captive to her husband's house—
for he was convinced she never returned there
willingly—a slave to that home which she had
shuddered even in frenzy to name.

Engrossed as the man was with his own
troubles and anxieties—with his vain search
after Alice, with pecuniary difficulties, and fresh
anxieties—he had still time to spare a few

thoughts to the being he had met under such strange and painful circumstances.

Her clothes and trinkets he took into his own possession, feeling a vague conviction that some day or another she would come and claim all from him—some day when, perhaps, she might stand in need of such moneys as the valuables were likely to bring. He remembered the circumstance of the diamonds, and he thought such a chance might occur any time again. For months he expected a letter from her, but none arrived; and at last, even with her worldly goods safely stowed away under lock and key in a cupboard at his elbow, he grew to forget to look for tidings of her—grew to think that, perhaps, she and her husband were reconciled—that she had again plunged into the vortex of fashionable society, and permitted the old garden, and the children, and the doctor, and the locale of Ashford Row to escape her memory.

Since her departure, he had become almost old. His illness, for want of needful luxuries during his recovery, had left dregs in his constitution that were exhausting his system, under-

...ing his ... He was weary of the useless struggle, weary of solitude, weary of his lonely, cheerless home, weary of his vain search after ..., weary of his patients, his situation, his ... himself, everything. If he had not still clung to the hope of some day meeting the ... girl who had caused him such unhappiness again, he would have left England and joined his sister; but it was impossible to tear up hope by the roots, to cut off the last link of communication between himself and Alice—to give up, after having gone on so long.

He would wait—even if his hair grew grey, and his face furrowed in the process—he would wait, and trust, and see.

Musing and resolving somewhat after the above fashion, he was sitting one night over the fire in his little, mean parlour, when the post, a rather rare visitor at his door, brought a missive to him, directed in a woman's hand.

He recognised it instantly; he had seen her writing scores of times, and, unlike that of most of her sex, it was characteristic and peculiar. Very eagerly he tore the cover open, and read the few lines traced on the inside—traced, apparently, with an unsteady hand:

" For pity's sake, come to me: now, if you can. Come to 63, Upper Emery Street, and ask for Miss Leake. Remember, I am Miss Leake.
" Yours,
" JUDITH MAZINGFORD."

" Poor soul! a fugitive again," he muttered, as he put the note in the fire; and taking his hat, sallied forth to comply with her request.

" No rest, no peace, no assurance of either, till I am laid in my coffin—Oh! would that I were there."

The broken sentences he had heard her murmur in her delirium, strung themselves together in his mind, as he hurried away towards Emery Street: " No rest, no peace!"—the words she so often used, floated back to his memory; and then remembering the petition she had so urged upon him, her earnest and continuous prayer for life, he marvelled if the boon had been granted to her only as a punishment for her importunity. He had never felt so strong an interest for any one as for Judith Mazingford;

there was a something of romance, of energy, of
eccentricity about her which piqued his curiosity,
and kept his feelings always up to fever pitch
when in her presence.

She was more like a man in many ways than
a woman; it seemed almost as though the weaknesses and foibles of her sex had been burned
out of her, in the scorching fire of trouble she
had passed through. Even when he was mounted
on his pet hobby—a dislike of "literary women"
—the type of whom was, to his mind, Miss
Catharine Merdun, he totally forgot, mentally,
to single Judith out from amongst the lot.   He
never thought of her as a *bas blue;* he saw her
work perseveringly and unostentatiously, like a
brave-hearted man; and he would as soon have
dreamed of finding fault with her for mending a
stocking, as for writing a book.   Truth was,
though he did not know it himself—he hated
the sham, not the substance—and as Judith was
all substance, ready fashioned to his hand, he
imagined, pretty nearly, that she could do no
wrong, and was quite ready to do her a service,
in season or out of season.   It was a strange
power, strangely given, that which she possessed

of fascinating every one who approached her; a blessing turned into a curse—a power given to enable her to darken her life, and blast her existence.

From the time he turned into Upper Emery Street, until he reached the door of No. 63, he kept repeating her new name softly, over and over to himself, lest by making any mistake, he should endanger her chances of safety; and when he fairly got the sentence, "Is Miss Leake at home?" out, without a slip of any kind, he felt as if he had performed a truly remarkable exploit.

"Yes, sir," she said, "you were to be shown up stairs," was the reply of a civil servant; and following the steps of the speaker, he found himself in another minute at the drawing-room.

"The gentleman, ma'am," announced the servant, ushering in Judith's visitor—and, advancing into the room, he was seized by two trembling hands, which belonged to her who had been beautiful Judith Mazingford. Had been!—he thought he had never gazed on such a wreck in his life—pale, emaciated, frightened-looking—with a restless turn in her eyes, and quick, eager, unsettled gestures. Could it be

the same he had known in other days?   He
gazed in her face, doubtfully.

"You would not have known me?" she said,
and the very tone of her voice was altered.

"I should not," he answered.

"Thank Heaven for that," she cried, and fell
back into a chair, sobbing hysterically—"Oh!
I'm so glad," she continued; "sit down, and I
will tell you all.   No, I cannot tell you; but be
quiet, and listen while I think."

He did not answer her by words; he only
lifted a candle from the table, and looked earnestly at her for a moment—then he laid his
fingers on her pulse, and, finally, rang the bell.

"You—you won't betray me?" she exclaimed,
springing up and seizing hold of his hand; "oh,
surely I can trust you—I thought I might rely
on you."

"So you may, implicitly—" he replied, putting
her gently back into her seat; and drawing an
inket and portfolio to him, he wrote for a minute
or two:—

"Now," he said to the servant, who stood at
the door, in answer to his summons, "take that
to the nearest chemist, and tell him I want the

prescription, filled up at once—And, stop a moment—have you any brandy in the house?"

" No, sir, I am afraid not, unless Mr. Gartmore—" the woman stopped.

" Who is he?"

" Oh! it is a gentleman who occupies the ground floor," interposed Judith, " don't go to him, don't—I'm quite well. I want nothing."

" Present my—Dr. Duvard's compliments to Mr. Gartmore, and tell him I should be much obliged by his letting me have a small quantity, for a patient who is seriously indisposed;" and, putting Judith's wishes thus quietly in the background, and substituting his own commands in their place, he led her back to her chair, and told her not to excite herself.

" But you do not know who this Mr. Gartmore is—" she remonstrated.

" I do not care if he were the arch fiend," replied Doctor Duvard.

" He is a heartless old misanthrope—a perfect oyster."

" More likely to get what we want out of him, then!" returned the man of medicine.

" When once you force the shell open, oysters

are good eating—now, I want to know how long
you have been ill ?"

" Ill—I am not ill; I am only—"

" In a bad state of health," suggested Dr.
Duvard. " Precisely so; and I wish to hear for
what length of time you have been, not so well as
when I last saw you ?"

" I have been growing weak and strange for
some months—oh, I think for nearly a year. I
was not well latterly at Ashford Row—only,
only if I confess, I am ill—you must not say I
am mad."

" Say you are what ?"

" You must not think that—that—that—"
Here the old sobbing fit re-commenced so
violently, that Doctor Duvard was compelled to
say, " Now, Mrs. Mazingford—"

" No, no, not that—" she interrupted.

" Well, Miss Leake, you must not give way
in this manner, it is very injurious in every respect: if you will but help me to cure you, I
think I can do it; but you must strive to do
your part likewise."

" Mr. Gartmore's compliments," said the servant, entering at this moment, " and anything

he has, is at your and Miss Leake's service. Should you like a little port, sir? He has some which has been in bottle fifteen years."

" My master says, sir," added a middle-aged valet, following close at the maid's heels, " that if the case is a pressing one, I can go for any medicine or further advice, that may be required; also, that if he can be of any service—"

" Got the knife in," remarked Dr. Duvard; *sotto voce*,—though not so softly but that the words reached the domestics—who concluded, however, that the observation applied to some surgical operation. " Best thanks to Mr. Gartmore, and the brandy is all I require; unless, indeed, you will be good enough to have this prescription filled up for me immediately. Now," he added to Judith, when they were left once more alone, " did I not say the oyster was good eating?"

" Yes, but he is half-brother to Sir John Lestock."

" To whom?"

" Sir John Lestock—why do you know anything of him?"

" I should think I did," answered Doctor

Duvard; "but never mind who he is at present —we have got the brandy:" and he set about the work of curing Judith as zealously as if he had not another care or object in life.

"What have you eaten to-day?" he demanded, after a pause.

"Nothing," was the reply: I cannot eat—I have no appetite—I—"

"There, lie down and don't exert yourself," he interrupted "you must keep quiet, or you will have a very serious illness."

"But I cannot keep quiet," she persisted; "I am so wretched—there is a dreadful woman coming here to-night, and I have no money for her—have you any?"

He had not, and he looked enquiringly in her face.

"Oh! don't look at me that way," she cried, "if they come and say I am mad, won't you defend me, and tell them I am not? What became of the things I left in Ashford Row—they are safe, are they not?"

"Yes, you can have them turned into money at any time."

"Then will you see this creature to-night, and tell her you have valuables of mine, and promise

her what she wants?—and I'll go to bed. I
am afraid of her. Do stay here till she comes;
she will be here directly. And I may trust you,
may I not?"

" As yourself," he answered; " but I must
ask one other question—what claim has this person on you? What has given you such a horror
of insanity? What is the matter with you?"

" You could not guess;" and she came quite
close up to him, trembling from head to foot;
" if I tell you, you must not think——"

" I shall think nothing but what you would
wish me," he answered, kindly.

" Well then, don't ask me any particulars;
only when I defied him, he said he would break
my spirit, and so he lodged me in a Lunatic
Asylum—and I was not mad, Doctor—I was
sane, as sane as ever I was—as sane as you are."

" And he knew that?"

" Perfectly."

" The infernal scoundrel!" ejaculated Doctor
Duvard, heartily, reader, just as you or any other
honest man would have spoken the words.

" And—and Doctor—what I saw there nearly
made me as bad as the rest; I cannot tell you

about it—my blood curdles as I think of that place—another month, and I should have been as crazy as the maddest amongst them. But this woman—this keeper, or matron, or whatever she was, helped me to escape; and now she keeps wanting money; always, always, more money, when I have none to give her—and I am afraid—for ever afraid."

"Oh! I will satisfy her," remarked Doctor Duvard, "but now tell me, could you not manage to return to your old quarters?"

"No, — I am safer here — safer in this large lodging house, than I should be in that quiet suburb. He would never think of looking for me here—besides he knows my old name of Gilmore, and if I change it, the people down at Ashford Row would think there was a mystery hanging about me; and then, the place is damp. I cannot do with damp, latterly; there is something, Doctor, catches me here, every few minutes —what is it?"

"You must keep quiet," he returned; but there was a grave anxious look about his eyes, when he followed the movement of her hand to her chest—which Judith caught at.

"There is consumption in our family," she remarked, in a quieter tone.

"You are nervous and fanciful," said her friend, "but we will soon set you to rights again —if you could, I should now like you to go to bed; and after I have seen this woman, I will go home, and call early again to-morrow morning. Rest assured you shall never again remain a prisoner in any asylum in the kingdom— whatever occurs I will procure your release; good night!" and he shook hands with her, and then sat down, after she left him, to muse, before the fire, until the arrival of his visitor.

It was late before he was able to leave the house; for the interview with the raw-boned individual, who had Mrs Mazingford, as she phrased it, "under her thumb" lasted a considerable period. From her he learnt many particulars he was desirous of knowing; although he would have scrupled to ask Judith concerning them; and when at length the woman departed, she left him in possession of the horrors his patient had passed through; of the name of the asylum — of the actual state of

Mrs. Mazingford's health, and many other things, too numerous and trivial to enumerate.

" I have arranged matters with her," were the brief words Doctor Duvard traced on a sheet of note paper, and sent in to Judith by the hands of a servant; and having heard that she was much more tranquil, and inclined to sleep, he walked more gently than is the wont of doctors, down stairs, and had his foot on the hall door-step, when a hand was laid on his arm—

" Doctor Duvard, I believe !"

The person so addressed raised his hat in acknowledgment of the justice of the supposition.

" Would you be kind enough to favour me with a few minutes conversation ?" pursued the stranger ; and Doctor Duvard acquiescing, he led him into a dining room more handsomely furnished than apartments in lodging houses usually are.

" Pray be seated," said he, and his visitor having done so, had leisure to scrutinize the appearance of his new acquaintance.

" Under sixty, and odd," was the mental summary he made—whilst the misanthrope, as

Judith called him, opened proceedings, by asking how the lady was.

" Very ill !" answered Doctor Duvard.

" Dangerously ?"

" Not at present," was the reply.

" Pray Sir, do you know who she is ?" demanded Mr. Gartmore, with a directness which might have thrown another man off his guard —but Doctor Duvard answered without a charge of countenance.

" Yes; Miss Leake."

" Is she a friend of yours ?"

" A very intimate one ; I have known her a long time."

" Leake," mused the other, " Leake, it is strange—I know no one of that name—and yet I am sure her face is familiar to me; I met her one day on the staircase, and felt as if I ought to speak to her. It is a curious thing, her living alone in this manner, Doctor."

" Many people are left orphans and friendless, Mr. Gartmore," returned his visitor. " She has very few relatives now remaining, and besides she always seemed to like solitude. The nervous affection, under which she labours, may be both cause and effect of the excessive exclusiveness, that keeps her prisoner within free walls of a London house. It is not good for any body to live too much alone."

" Did you mean that for me, sir ?" demanded Mr. Gartmore, facing suddenly on the speaker.

" No ; I was thinking of Miss Leake and myself; for she shuts herself up in a shell from choice, and I from necessity. If you live to yourself for yourself, likewise, I say we are all three then to be equally pitied. Can I afford you any further information respecting my patient ?"

" No, not at present," answered his host.

" Then I shall wish you good night," said Charles, rising; " for I have far to go—I think it must be late ; good night !"

" Good night !" returned Mr. Gartmore, roughly; but as his visitor turned the lock of the door, he held out a hand to him, and said in a straightforward point-blank sort of way—

" Upon my soul, I believe you are an honest fellow."

" You do not know what I might be, if I were tried," retorted Doctor Duvard, who saw that if he fenced the old man it must be with his own weapons.

"Sharply put!" replied Mr. Gartmore, laughing. "Did Miss Leake say anything to you of me?"

"Yes, she remarked that you were a perfect oyster."

"And what did you reply?"

"That when you could get through the shell oysters were good eating; and, therefore, I sent for the brandy, and, therefore, I got it."

"Good—when you want anything else come to me."

"I do not think I shall—but if I do, I will, as you seem to desire it, knock first at your door!" and Charles bowed himself somewhat stiffly out, for he did not like to be condescended to —and he did not approve of being cross questioned. Besides, was Mr. Gartmore not Sir John Lestock's brother, and did he not hate Sir John Lestock, as he might have hated a fiend.

When Judith greeted him next morning, he saw with even more distinctness than the night before, the ravages a few brief months had made. Her eyes were sunken and her cheeks thin, there was a look about her mouth, which he did not like at all; but in better spirits she laughed her ailments aside, and telling him she was almost well again, commenced speaking eagerly of her books.

" Books, indeed!   Do you want to kill yourself?" demanded Doctor Duvard; "I forbid your holding a pen for months to come—write, it would be as much as your life is worth."

"My life is not worth much in one way, though it may be in another," she answered. "I am not happy enough yet to die—my whole existence has been an out-of-joint, contradictory, contrary sort of drama; and I have firm faith that I shall never be claimed by the shadow of death, until I learn to care for and enjoy that stern reality, life; you will call this superstition, doctor, and I suppose it is so—but presentiments you know often make their own fulfilment; and as for not writing, I must write to provide myself with every-day necessaries.   But what I wanted, principally to say to you was, that I have a completed manuscript if I could get it sold—that woman supplied me with the materials secretly, and we are to share the profits, that was our agreement—would you try to dispose of it for me to advantage?—you must not take it to Mr. Mason, and you might have it published under the name of any friend of yours —I should like it to be fairly copied out in a different hand than mine, and then presented to Mr. Larocca; he pays the best, I think, of any person in the trade, when once you can get a book accepted. It must be presented as a first, you understand—might I tax your friendship and kindness so far ?"

There was hardly anything she could have asked him to do for her he would not, and, accordingly, by dint of persevering attentions to the publisher, Charles managed to get the work into print, paid for and reviewed within the miraculously short space of three months from date of delivery, and during the lapse of those thirteen weeks, Judith's health rallied so much that Doctor Duvard began to hope great things for her. The prospect of more money kept her tormentor quiet, judicious treatment and perfect quietness stilled and soothed her nerves into a state of tolerable tranquillity. A shadow of her former loveliness came stealing back into her face,

With trouble once again behind her—relieved
from the incubus of its immediate presence, she
grew calm and collected, sometimes even cheerful, more able to contemplate her actual position
fairly, to act, and think and judge for herself.

Still, however, she was far from well. Doctor
Duvard never felt so thoroughly satisfied of that
fact, as when he beheld the effect the adverse
reviews, those very reviews, in fact, which, by
their intense bitterness, ensured the success of
her book, produced upon her. She tried to
laugh them off, but it would not do, there seemed
a sort of poison to her in the critic's sting which
had never abode there before, and, at last, Doctor
Duvard seriously recommended her to write no
more.

"Or if it be necessary as a means of sub-
sistence," he said, "let it be for the Magazines,
you can easily obtain enough to supply every
want from that source, without over-exerting
yourself, or running the gauntlet in a chase after
fame."

"Well, Doctor," she returned, "if you will
only consent to my writing one more book, I
am ready to follow your advice—one more, just

as a sort of farewell to my profession, and I will sink into private life, in the pages of a second-rate journal. I shall take the matter very easily, writing essays and other things,—which do not excite the imagination so much as fiction,—between. Now do be a good-natured creature, and give me leave. I shall die just at once, if you do not!"

And she looked so pleadingly at him, with those large eyes of hers, that he could not resist her petition, even whilst he felt she ought to have greater rest than ever. But then hers was a spirit which knew no repose.

" It is not that I like work," she said, on one occasion, when he remonstrated with her on the subject, " only there is a little piece of machinery in me which forces me on—often against my inclination. It has never been still for a moment, oh, not for years past—and I suppose it will never let me be quiet until I am lying in my grave—I think I must have lived as much in three or four years, as many an one in sixty—I have hurried on, always so fast."

Hurrying on—hastening forward to death as she had rushed through life.—Her friend could not disguise that fact from himself—it was impossible for medical eyes not to discern the fact, for though the beauty of old was restored to her, though her eyes were brighter than ever—though the colour had deepened in her cheek to an almost feverish glow—still—still—he perceived it was but the deceitful light of a sun near its setting, that was streaming across her face—a little while longer, and a deeper darkness than ever would succeed thereto.

And every line she wrote, drained away a life-drop from her. He saw it, and told her so ; but the proud spirit that had remained unbroken by sorrow, remorse, hardship, and cruelty, would not yield itself captive to pain. She laughed when he told her she ought to go to Madeira, and asked if he thought she could delay the fiat one hour—a sort of fatalism seemed settling down upon her. To all remonstrances she returned one invariable answer :

" It is so written—when it is appointed for me to go, I shall ; but not one moment before."

On one point alone was she vulnerable, and that the horror of detection—every sovereign she made was shared with the wretch who held her

liberty in her hands, and whose demands grew
larger day by day. It was in vain Doctor Duvard suggested flight—she seemed to have a
nervous horror of the woman, a dread of offending her, a terror of doing anything which might
cause antagonism between them, a fear of having
two pursuing her instead of one.

The incubus was weighing her down to the
earth, and at length having made such inquiries
as satisfied him that Mr. Gartmore was not one
of the same heartless species as Sir John Lestock, Charles determined to lay the state of the
case boldly before him, and demand at once
advice and assistance. An old love-cross, it was
rumoured, had sent Mr. Gartmore a wanderer
from his native land, caused him to draw an icy
mantle over his heart—made him remain an un-
loved, and unregarded, desolate man in the clime
e had chosen, and finally driven him back to
England, where he was surrounded by a set of
toadies, who courted him for the sake of the wealth
he was reported to have amassed in India. Doctor
Duvard heard he suspected everybody of sinister
motives in approaching him; that he detested
his niece, Miss Lestock, who was continually

paying him visits—that he had no faith, no trust, no love in or for any one—that he was, in brief, a misanthropical old man, to whom money had proved a curse, and life a valueless, unimproved, profitless gift.

And yet he had his redeeming points. When he could make sure that he was not flattered or sought for his money, he was kind and liberal, though, perhaps, a little roughly so. The upper surface was only a crust, a very hard and tough one certainly, but still, after all, only a crust, covering many a good, and tender, and generous emotion. He was more sick of the world than worldly, more suspicious than cold-hearted, more sinned against, perhaps, than sinning. Besides, had he not desired Charles to come to him, when Judith needed aught at his hands; and was it not at any rate a scheme worth trying, to free the delicate woman from persecution and the presence of a perpetual dread?

Dr. Duvard had just made up his mind to this course of action one afternoon, when he was summoned to attend a pressing case in his own neighbourhood.

" Mrs. Bling, sir, has been taken with cholera.

Could you go over at once to her? and here is a letter just come for you."

"Say I will be with her in five minutes," he replied, tearing open the envelope, which enclosed a note for Judith. It was forwarded by her publisher, and directed to her under her *nom de plume;* but Dr. Duvard started, when he looked at the superscription, as if a pistol had been discharged at his ear.

Never in his life had he felt so tempted to look into another person's secret affairs. His fingers positively itched to break the seal; and he had to lay the missive down before he could persuade his own conscience he had no right to look into Judith's private correspondence.

Then he thought he would go to her; but afterwards, remembering about his patient, duty got the best of the struggle with inclination, and tracing the words—"If you can help me to find the writer of the enclosed, for Heaven's sake do," he folded the missive up out of sight, and dispatched it by a special messenger to the hands of Judith Mazingford.

"What on earth can the man mean?" she

soliloquized, when she read his brief petition.
" Is he looking for an absent wife, too? or is he
in love? or what?" and even as she wondered,
she opened the note, and looked to the name at
the end.

" Alice Crepton" was the signature.

" Why, good gracious! that's my cousin!"
said Judith absolutely out loud in her amazement, "and it is dated from where? 63, Upper
Emery Street;" and when she arrived so far on
her way, her astonishment grew too great for
words, and she betook herself in very bewilderment to a perusal of the epistle, which contained,
first, many apologies for the liberty taken in
writing; secondly, an explanation of the position, views, and wishes of the writer; thirdly,
a detail of how Mr. Larocca had promised
to speak in her behalf, and of how he had
not done it; and, fourth and last, a very
earnest petition, very modestly put, that if the
authoress she addressed would not thereby sustain any loss or inconvenience, and if she approved of Alice's novel, she would lend her name
to the book, and consent to be editor for it.

Very much in Judith's own style was the letter wound up :—

" I am afraid you will think me presumptuous for addressing you at all; but I have tried so long, and been so often disappointed, that I do not seem as if I much cared what I did. I am quite tired out. Had I seen a glimpse of hope in any other quarter, I should never have thought of requesting a favour from a total stranger. Indeed the idea of an editor would never have crossed my mind, had Mr. Larocca not suggested it to me.

" ALICE CREPTON.

" 63, Upper Emery Street."

Judith repeated the name and address over again, ere she betook herself to a second perusal of an epistle which would, probably, never have received an answer from any other individual. After she had finished the last reading, and drawn her own conclusions from it, she rang the bell, and asked the servant who appeared in answer—

" Pray, Mary, how many lodgers have you in the house ?"

"Why, ma'am, besides yourself, I think we have seven. I will just count them over. There is old Mrs. Morrison has a bed-room and boards with the mistress; then Mr. and Mrs. Bute have the second floor to themselves—that's three; and the nurse and the two children, six; and Mr. Gartmore has the two parlours and a bed-room on this floor; and you have the two drawing-rooms. Yes—just seven."

"Only seven! Are you sure there is nobody else? no younger lady than any you have mentioned, either staying with some of your lodgers or else living alone?"

"Oh! yes, to be sure, ma'am, you are right—the young lady in the third floor. I always forget her, because she gives so little trouble and is out all day. Miss Crepton, ma'am, you mean, I dare say?"

"Precisely. How long has she been here?"

"I cannot say exactly. We never think about her some way, she is so quiet. It is Jane that does the little she requires; but I do not think she is ever at home. I heard her talking once, a long time ago, to my mistress about music pupils—so I suppose she teaches."

"While her mother drives up to the door three times a-week in her barouche and pair," thought Judith bitterly—then added out loud—

"Do you know if Miss Crepton is within at present?"

"Oh! she is never out so late as this, ma'am," returned Mary, who had an intense respect for Judith, and whose opinion of Alice went up a hundred per cent. from hearing her inquired about by a lady of Miss Leake's appearance.

"Should you wish to see her? Can I take any message up to her?"

"No, thank you," said Judith, coldly. "Wait a moment, though. I want to write a note to Mr. Gartmore."

CHAPTER VII.

" Miss Leake would feel obliged by Mr. Gartmore favouring her with five minutes' conversation."

So Judith, after a few moments' reflection,
wrote, not on a sheet of note paper but on a
slip torn off a piece of foolscap, which, dispensing with the usual formalities of envelope and
seal, she simply twisted up and dispatched by
the hands of Mary to the misanthrope.

Then she stirred the fire, and drew down the
blinds, so as to shut out the coming night, and
pulled forward another chair to it, and having
thus reduced the appearance of things in general

to that state which favours the prospects of a confidential conversation, she seated herself in her accustomed place ready to receive the old man, who turned the handle of the door almost instantaneously.

She did not rise to greet him as he advanced, a courtesy to which his grey hairs and position as visitor at her summons, might well, indeed, have seemed to entitle him, but merely inclining her head in her own graceful, queenly style, in return for his elaborate old-fashioned bow, she said :

" I thank you very much for acceding to my request."

" Requests from you, madam ? " he answered in his formal drawing-room manner, with which, however, there was also mingled, in the present instance, a dash of the interest wherewith Judith inspired every one who approached her. " Requests from you, madam, come so seldom that, even were it not a pleasure to comply with the slightest of them, there would be no excuse for refusing to do so."

Judith smiled — that half-mournful smile, which was the only one save a bitter sarcastic sneer that had ever hovered on her lips for years previously. It was her sole reply, and but a brief one after all, for it departed even as it came.

"Will you not be seated?" she asked. "Pray do—for I have a few words of moment to say to you, otherwise I had not intruded on your time or broken through the rule of my own seclusion."

"An unhappy rule, whether self-imposed or imposed by others," responded Mr. Gartmore, taking possession of the chair, indicated by a gesture of her hand—"a strange rule to be adopted by one so young and —"

He paused—a delicate fear of offending—a feeling that the word he was about to add, though strictly true, could scarcely fail to give her pain, stopped his further utterance. She was so altogether uncommon a creature, mentally and bodily—her habits were so peculiar, her position so anomalous, that ordinary curiosity died away in her presence, and ordinary phrases of wonderment, pity, or admiration were abandoned ere their conclusion.

Mr. Gartmore now inwardly muttered the same

sentence as many an one before him had done.

"Unless she choose to tell me I shall never know more about her—I cannot ask."

Judith gathered his thoughts from the puzzled wistful expression of his face; and after waiting a sufficient time for him to finish his sentence, if he preferred doing so, she concluded it as he had intended.

"A strange rule to be adopted by one so young and beautiful, you were about to say," she remarked. "Yet it is a long time since I was really the former, almost as long since I forfeited old claims to the perishable latter. As for my rule—it is one I would not abandon if I could, and could not if I would. Some people," she added, with that careless indifference of manner wherewith she concealed her deeper feelings—"some people might not like such total isolation, but it suits me admirably. We have all our hobby, and philosophers tell us it is well to ride the thing to death. Seclusion, in the very heart of busy, bustling, panting, suffocating London, is my whim."

"Only your whim ? " he said enquiringly,

fixing his keen grey eyes on her face so steadily
that even Judith was compelled to turn aside
from the scrutiny.

"Only your whim?" but she never answered.

"I sent for you to-night, Mr. Gartmore,"
she abruptly re-commenced, after an awkward
silence, "to do you a favour."

The announcement really seemed to produce a
startling effect upon the visitor. He was unaccustomed to having favours proffered to him
in such an unhesitating manner, and his countenance expressed the fact even though his
tongue did not.

"That is," pursued Judith, "if you are of
my opinion that it is a privilege to be able to
assist our fellow-creatures, and that considering
the little good we are enabled to do the person
who throws a chance of the kind across our
path, is doing us a favour."

"Putting the boot on the other leg with a
vengeance," thought Mr. Gartmore, but he
refrained from giving utterance to the elegant
expression, whilst with an amount of politeness
and dissimulation, which (to do him justice) he
rarely practised, he said aloud:

"Quite true, madam, and anything which I can do to serve you —"

"Stay," she interposed, "you are mistaken in imagining I want anything for myself. Man cannot help me, Mr. Gartmore, nor woman neither, but there are others in the world who stand in need of assistance. Before, however, entering into the particulars of the case, I must ask a few questions. You are acquainted, I believe, with Miss Lestock, as she is called?"

"Miss Lestock, as she is called," answered Mr. Gartmore, "is my niece."

"And being such, you are, of course, aware of all the particulars of her marriage?"

"I have heard all the particulars of that most disgraceful transaction," he acquiesced.

"Nay," exclaimed Judith, "not disgraceful, for though her husband might be of meaner birth, he was her superior in every other respect. If you think your niece's marriage with the Reverend Watkyn Crepton a disgraceful transaction, I need proceed no further with my petition, for you and I can have no solitary idea or opinion in common."

"You criticise my relations freely," he replied

K 2

with a smile, "yet am I not offended—for my conviction of the matter has always been that Adelaide Crepton is a being without heart, head, or conscience—that the Welsh curate threw himself away on her; and that having had children given her by Heaven, she had no right to fling the Divine blessing of motherhood from her. I despise and hate the woman, madam. There, is that confession of faith satisfactory to you?"

"Perfectly," she answered. "And now do you know anything of her children?"

"The Welsh grandfather adopted them, did he not?"

"Yes, but grandfathers will not live for ever," Judith replied. "Did you not read the grand *exposé* there was in the papers long ago, about a lad found starving in the streets of London—a grandson of Sir John Lestock.— do you not remember it? But no," she added next moment, "you cannot—you were out of England."

"How do you know where I was?" he demanded curiously.

"I know many things you might scarcely

give me credit for," was the reply, accompanied with a smile—" however, my ignorance or knowledge is nothing at present. The facts were so, that Evan Crepton was found starving in the streets of London—that he fled from his relations, that he went, nobody knew whither, that he may now be living or dead, for any information I have on the subject—but his sister Alice is at this moment lodging two floors above our heads, and you can aid her if you choose to do so."

" How ?" Mr. Gartmore did not pronounce the monosyllable encouragingly.

" By assisting her endeavours to make an honest livelihood. She has embarked, Heaven help her, on the stormy sea of literary adventure, and is sinking for want of a strong hand to bring her to shore.—In one word, sir, she is an authoress, and——"

"I hate authoresses, madam," interrupted Mr. Gartmore vehemently, "a confounded set of pretentious blue stockings : better the girl was a dairy-maid, than an affected, conceited, half-educated, sentimental scribbler. I can't bear literary women, madam ;" and the speaker wheeled round in his chair, and looked defiantly at Judith as he uttered the last clause.

"That is unfortunate," she coolly remarked, "for I am one of the unhappy genius, and I suppose I may therefore take your observation as an especial compliment to myself."

"You an authoress!" he repeated. "Well, there are exceptions to all rules."

"It strikes me very forcibly, Mr. Gartmore,' resumed Judith, "that there was a time when there existed a charm in the name for you—when you would have done battle for a blue-stocking, and vowed that a woman could be intellectual without vanity, learned without pretension, clever without forwardness, imaginative without mawkish sentiment. In the days when you would have married one who has since blotted her manuscripts with tears, you entertained different ideas. But so it proves always—from love to hate—a solitary step."

During the delivery of this sentence, Mr. Gartmore's face had worked painfully, and at its conclusion he rose from his seat and approaching close to Judith, demanded with an agitated voice :—

" Who, in Heaven's name, are you, that thus lay bare the secrets of my life, whom I have never spoken to before this hour, and whose voice and face are yet as familiar to me as my own—who can raise the ghosts of the past before me, and play with the hidden feelings of my heart, as if you delighted to pain and torture me ? You are closely connected with me in some way—your name is not Leake—you are either a falsehood or the Evil One, for you have spoken of things this night which no person ever knew but myself and one long since dead and forgotten."

" You have been misinformed," said Judith. " Millicent Ridsdale is not dead."

" Not dead !" he cried ; " assure me of that fact and—but it is false—she died years—long years since."

" To fashionable society, yes," was the reply ; " but though I have not seen her for years I know she is still living—a solitary, broken-hearted woman, on whom the curse of her race descended. She was more fortunate than some of the Ridsdales, though, and she may bless Heaven for it."

" And who are you that talk of the Ridsdales,

as if you were one of them, and of me, as if
you had known me always.—Since first I saw
you I felt your face was not altogether a new
one, and yet, until now, I never knew it was
Lady Lestock you resembled.   You must be—"

"Judith Mazingford," she finished ; and when
she had spoken the words, he sat down again,
and stared at her as though she had been a
"remarkable criminal."

"You have heard of me," she ventured, when
the scrutiny was becoming painful.

"Often."

"And hated and despised me, because the
taint that had cursed your life was in my blood
as well as in her's—because I made for myself a
phantom that has pursued me through life—
because you thought I was false to his memory
—you have heard my story from worldly lips,
that gloated gossipping over the miseries of my
most wretched existence.—Hear it from mine—
let me tell it for the first and last time connectedly through, and then form your own conclusions for yourself.   Should you like to hear
the secret history of Judith Mazingford, as
known only to God and herself?   I can talk or

remain silent at your bidding. Which shall it be?"

"Talk," he said briefly, but there was a softer tone in his voice, and a different look in his eye—and he bent unconsciously forward to catch her words.

"You remember Lillian Ridsdale," she began; "perhaps you knew her husband, too, Mr. Renelle, she was my mother and he my father. I was the youngest of three—the one who drew my life from her death-sigh—a little helpless infant, ushered into the world when the winter winds were howling about the house, when the great king of terrors was bearing away a soul—when my father's heart was breaking—when every sign and token predicted sorrow and misery for me. And as I lay in the first sleep of childhood, with the tempest roaring outside, and the sobs of a bereaved husband sounding within, an old Welsh woman, to whom it was given to utter ominous warnings, prophesied that my life would be a wretched one—that with faces averted from me, and with hand upraised against every one, I should pass to the grave 'battling my way.'

" But I did not seem born to battle.   I seemed
born to be loved and to love, to be cared for,
petted, and caressed—to give to my father what
he had sickened for through life, a pure and
undivided affection—to be a comfort and a pride
to   my aunt—a nurse and a solace to my
sister Lillian, a creature to be surrounded by
friends, a being to be sought, and won and wed
—to become an honoured wife and a happy mother—Oh ! my life was rich in friends and
promise then—look back with me and imagine
if you can the peace and the joy of those cloudless days—look at the bright young face, and the
tearless eyes, and the unmarked brow, and the
active step : look at that dear old home which
my hands beautified, at the girl who was all in
all to every one—assistant, councillor, friend; who
was never repelled by a frown—who was more
loved than daughter ever was before—who enjoyed life as the birds and the butterflies enjoy
it, and who looked out on existence as she
might on a long, bright .summer's day.—Look
back at all this—then glance round this lonely,
desolate chamber and pity me."

Almost involuntarily he did as she bade him,

and gazed round the room, in which, as he well knew, she had passed many a month of her wretched life. When his eyes came back again to Judith, he saw she had hidden her face in her hands, and was weeping convulsively.

He could say nothing to comfort her—he sat silent until, with that strong determined will of her's, she hushed the sound of her grief, and locked that picture once more up in the cabinet of her heart. Looking into the firelight with her dark eyes still wet with tears, she resumed.

"Then I was loved by one who was no popinjay of fashion—no oiled and perfumed, curled and heartless simperer—but by *a man*, who never had a weakness, except that of loving me; and I was worthy of his affection, I know now I was—but for the plague-spot. I never varied really in my troth, but I took a senseless pleasure in tormenting him. Thus, when he asked me to be his wife, I trifled with his patience—and, you have heard no doubt, I murdered him. It is true."

She was calm again—cold, and immovable as the ice on some polar sea, that covers briny waters of fathomless depths; and Mr. Gartmore, to whom such sudden changes seemed inexplicable, regarded her in amazement.

"I could tell," she continued, after a pause; "of how fruitlessly I followed him in his flight to death—of how amid the storm and snow of that fearful night, I cried aloud for him to return—and of how the hurricane, sweeping by me, choked the sound of my voice, and bore my entreaties back among the woods.   I could tell of hours of weeping and watching, of praying and sickening for his return, of a waking to grief, of an awful shock, and a long blank—of a restoration to life, that seemed like a descent into the valley of the shadow of death, of repentance that was unavailing, of tears which fell in vain, of years clouded by remorse, of a love that lay down in the grave beside him; of a darkness that was never lightened, of a sorrow which has never been dispelled—of a broken heart which has never since that night known a solitary gleam of joy.   I could tell much if it would undo the past, or take the weight of my soul. As it is—" she paused for a moment, and then hurried on.

"Misfortune came thickly after that, and then

it was Millicent Ridsdale who bought bread for her sister's children, and roused me from utter uselessness by her noble example, and unselfish exertions. Then I learned to write, and tasted the bitterness of rejection; then I vowed I would show the world what was in me; then my impatient spirit, chafed and disappointed, commenced its battle with the world.

"Death came once more into our home, and this time we were beggars—Lillian and I—but still I remained true to my faith, until I found that her sight was going, and that I, and I alone, could give back the blessing to her.

"For her I married—not for luxury, not for ease, not for peace did I wed a man I hated, but for her. It was the most unselfish action of my life; wrong, I admit, but I never deceived him. It was a regular bargain between us. I gave myself to him, and he was to give her sight and comfort. There was nothing she wanted he was not to let her have, and I, poor deluded dupe, believed and married him. If you know Lewis Mazingford, you may conjecture how he fulfilled his part of the contract. How he thwarted my love, forgot his promises, humbled

my pride in the dust, and made me, in the bitterness of my soul, curse the day, when, instead of
working, I married to save her.

" So it was useless. He would do nothing for
her after all, and I,—when mad with his falsehood
and invectives, I took the matter into my own
hands, they were powerless for good—strong for
evil. Did you ever hear I forged a cheque? It was
true. There is nothing I have not done to gratify
her, and vex, and mortify, and revenge myself upon
him.   Oh, if you knew what a life mine has
been—if you could only imagine for a moment
of what a chafing, and gnawing, and tearing at
the chain he made it—you would not blame me.
Pity I do not want.   Yet even in another way, I
am ready to vindicate all I did," she continued in
a calmer tone. " Thus, when I forged his name, it
was after I had prayed and supplicated, as Judith
Mazingford never prayed before to mortal, that
he would give me the means to save her life,
for Lillian was dying then—the last I had to love
like myself was dying.   I would have stolen for
her; and the money I got was mine—mine by
right, if not by law.   Heaven knows," she added
more vehemently, " it was no crime.   My

own conscience acquits me. I would do it again."

"I am glad you did," said Mr. Gartmore, " go on"—

"To her death," replied Júdith, "to how, when a note came summoning me to her side, he kept it back; to how, when a second messenger arrived, he would have prevented my departure by brute force; to how, I flew down to Brompton, and rushed in at the door, but was stayed on the threshold, and numbed by the words ' too late ;' to how, ill, and wretched, and loathing, I was hurried from place to place, led still through the world with a string round my neck by him. Oh, how I have hated the world," she exclaimed, passionately, " how I have spurned my own beauty, and mourned over my accomplishments—how I have sickened because God made me handsome, and graceful, instead of ugly and deformed—how I have longed to ' flee away and be at rest,'—at rest in my narrow grave.

"From country to country he dragged me, and at last we came home, to a sterner tyranny on his part, to a more irritating defiance on mine. You have talked of hating authoresses, Mr. Gartmore; had I not been one, I should have died then, but my pen was my voice, and my paper my confidante. Shut out from all other sympathy, I made friends out of these and talked to them, when, if I had not talked, my heart would have broken.

"It was then I finished a work which has since made some noise in the world, and it was with that, and a few trinkets, I fled from home one dreary winter night, and took my way to London."

"What made you leave him at last?" demanded Mr. Gartmore.

"Because every thing I valued—every relic I possessed of hers—her Bible—a lock of her hair—all the dear mementoes I had hidden and cherished—he flung into the fire, because into the chamber where I had been weeping and praying, he brought angry words, and ungovernable passions; because, on a day which I always set apart to her, he dragged me down before his guests, and made a show of me; because, when I asked for freedom—for a separation—for permission to leave him, and starve alone—he answered me in the language of old—with oaths, and threats, and savage violence. Do you see this?" she asked, taking up a mass of her luxuriant hair, " he retained a handful of it as a trophy when I fled from his hearth, and his house, lonely and desolate."

" And what did you do without friends or money, or——"

" I made all," she answered, " money, friends, and home. I came to London, and fell sick. I was watched through my illness by Dr. Duvard. I made friends with barefooted children, and care-worn women, and struggling men. I wrote, and was successful. I achieved fame and valued it not ; obtained wealth, and tried to make a good use of it. I found that the good one can do unto others does good to oneself. I found it possible to be content, if not happy, even on this earth, and had just made the discovery, when one day he laid a hand on my arm, and dispelled the vision."

" He, Mr. Mazingford ?"

" My husband," she acquiesced. " Then home. I went to the old prison house again ;——home to a man who after the slights, and taunts, and wrongs of years, would have cried truce, and patched up

a peace with me because I was famous,—the
fashionable to gratify his vanity—able to re-
plenish his purse.   Had I loved him, I would
have poured out my heart's blood for his sake, but
hating him as I did, can you wonder I refused to
write for his pleasure ?—that I laid down my pen ?
—that I would listen to no terms—believe no
promises—consent to no arrangement ? that I
believed any pain would be light in comparison
to the mental humiliation, and moral degradation
of obeying his commands—that prisoner and captive as he kept me, I still had strength enough
left to enable me to defy him ?"

" And then," suggested Mr. Gartmore, as she
paused and turned pale, " what did he — what
did you do then ?"

" When I defied him to do his worst — I
thought there could be no worse than that which
I had already experienced—he told me there were
ways and means of bringing refractory wives to
their senses ; what was the way he adopted do
you think, Sir ?"

" I cannot tell ; some infernal device, probably—"

" He drugged me, one night ; and when I

came back to a consciousness of where I was, I found myself in a private asylum."

"The cursed villain!" ejaculated Mr. Gartmore, passionately; "well—"

"Oh! it was not well—it was ill," she returned. "How shall I tell you what I endured in that vile place? how shall I speak of that which is not past, which will never be altogether past, until private asylums are blotted off the face of the earth?——

"True, bodily, I felt nothing—for I suppose as both husband and doctor knew, I was sane, they deemed it best to treat me as such. But the things I saw—the shrieks I heard—will never fade from my eyes—will never cease to ring in my ears, till I am laid in my coffin.——

"I tell you, Mr. Gartmore," she added, with quivering lips, "that the power possessed by the Autocrat of all the Russias, is limited in comparison to that held by the owner of a private madhouse; and the man who ruled over the destinies of these wretched lunatics, was less a man than a fiend! less a human being than a demon."

"Where was this place?" demanded Mr.

Gartmore; " At Craftcn," she answered. " Oh, if I had not shrunk, like a coward, from the idea of detection, and dread of his vengeance—what an exposure I would have made long ago, of that den—but I can think of no one but myself —my life is now one eternal horror of detection. I believe if I were to see my husband, I should die. With health broken, and nerves weakened, and strength failing I sit here inactive,—I dare not take a solitary step, likely to reveal my whereabouts to him; I can do nothing but ask others, when I am gone, to be more courageous —and remain, myself, listening, patiently, for the tardy rustling of the wings of the angel called Death."

When she had finished, her visitor turned to the fire and looked at the flame through a sort of film, that caused it to grow dim and lustreless before him. Then, after a long pause, he raised his head, and said sharply, and as if indignant that any one had found the means to touch his heart,

" You have told me all this, to rouse my feelings—to make me feel interested in you and yours—to soften me in order that you might mould me more easily to your wishes. You would not have spoken so freely, had you not had an object in view."

He uttered the words in a querulous, irritable tone—perhaps he felt provoked to have been so moved by a tale, repeated, save in one instance, without a tear or sigh—perhaps it was against his principles to be moved by any one, least of all by a Ridsdale—perhaps it was a burst of genuine suspicion, or perhaps a mere affectation of the feeling assumed, to see how she would "take it," but whatever the cause may have been, the result produced was certain. Judith took it as a real expression of his opinion ; and accordingly, after favouring him for a moment with a glance of mingled contempt and pity, she answered :

"And what, oh, most wretched, miserable man do you consider my object could have been ? Do you think your hoards of useless gold can heal a broken heart—do you imagine any efforts or care, or help of yours, could soothe a broken spirit like mine ? Oh, Mr. Gartmore, you are worse than foolish to let suspicions and doubt lock up and stifle every good avenue to your heart. In refusing to help your fellows—worthy or unworthy, as the case may be—you shut

L 2

yourself out from one of the highest pleasures God gives us—but what are you to me that I should give myself the trouble of talking thus ?" she said, abruptly checking herself—" Why should I speak so to a stranger, who thinks it a tax to benefit others—who imagines that society has entered into a conspiracy to deprive him of the money that will be squandered in some way after his death — who persists in storing up useless hoards, that moth and rust may corrupt them, and thieves break in and steal—who has no faith, no trust, no hope, no love—in or for any one save himself, and who above all," she added with a slight curl of the lip—" to follow out your own theory to the utmost, Mr. Gartmore, can be of no service to me? —I can help the girl I spoke to you about, myself—you, perhaps, could have done more, but I can do enough to make her happy. I am sorry so have intruded on your time, and to have wearied you with the details of a story, which could not possibly interest you—farewell, Sir; and when Judith Mazingford lies in her grave, remember that you met with one woman in your passage through life—who pitied you in the midst of your wealth and prosperity, more than she pitied herself, when surrounded by jibbering idiots and screaming maniacs."

She held out her hand to him, as with heightened colour and sparkling eyes, she concluded the foregoing peroration, and her visitor took it, though not in token of departure.

"Tell me what to do," he said briefly, "and I will do it—you have spoken hastily and plainly, but I like you the better for doing so. The path you bid me take I will follow in this matter. Miss Crepton is, I presume, the girl I have seen so often crossing the hall with a parcel in her hand."

"I suppose so, but have never seen her," answered Judith; "this is the note I have received from her, and it was enclosed in one from Dr. Duvard, who appears to take an interest in her, whether for his own happiness or not I cannot say."

Mr. Gartmore read the letter, and then said :—

"Now, what can I do in this business—how can I help her in these literary efforts?"

"By influence, if you have it—by money, if

you have not," Judith briefly answered. " It
would be better for her not to start with an editor,
because her book would be then depending,
not on its own merits, but on the standing of its
sponsor.   It is, in fact, a sort of patronage which
I detest, and therefore, although I have no objection to put my name on the title page, I know,
for her sake, it would be better not.   If she
have the talent, let her climb in public estimation
alone—if she have not, the sooner she make
discovery of the fact the better."

" And what is your opinion of her talent ?"

" Why, never having seen a line of her writing
except this note, I cannot judge, only I feel
pretty certain had there not been 'something,'
as the phrase goes, in her book, Mr. Larocca
would never have promised to publish it."

" Even with your name."

" Even with my name," acquiesced Judith;
" but if you give the girl a 'start' she must
then depend altogether on her own merits, and
on no extraneous circumstances.   Subscriptions
—editors—private circulation—partial one-sided
reviewers—all these things are of no earthly
use to an author beyond the first book—

they only serve to depreciate his character, not to benefit him professionally. It is merely the first getting into print that requires help—to pass through the publishing office is in literature *le premier pas*—once out, however, a work must stand or fall alone—for the reputation that is blown up like a bubble, will burst like one also."

"True," acquiesced Mr. Gartmore, "and Doctor Duvard?"

"I will communicate with him."

"And if I take up this business you must permit me to go thoroughly through with it alone?"

"Unless you require my assistance, I shall never interfere by word or deed."

"Good—as for yourself, I suppose you don't wish Miss Crepton informed of who you are?"

"You need never mention my name in any way—you go to help her from yourself not from me. I have now done with the business, and there is no necessity for me ever to appear in it again."

"And may I come to see you occasionally?" he enquired.

"I think you had better not," said Judith,

sadly. "I am safer knowing no one—seeing no one—talking to no one. The state of my health requires Dr. Duvard to visit me, besides I can trust him implicitly."

"And can you not trust me?" he asked.

"You are more in the world I was one of," she replied, "but he knows nothing of the people who once knew me—at least he knows none of them intimately. I could trust you thoroughly, but you live amongst a set that are certain of no secrecy of thought, no liberty of action. Servant and friend would be curious concerning your acquaintance—all things considered, I am better alone."

"As you wish," answered Mr. Gartmore; "but is there nothing I can do for you before I go—if you would like to sue for a separation—for a re——"

"Too late," she cried in a tone of agony— "too late. Did I not tell you man could not help me, nor woman neither—but God will.— Not very far before me in the distance I see a separation, such as you could never procure for me—wide as Eternity—vast as infinitude. It is coming slowly but surely.—Let me but have peace and quiet until then."

Mr. Gartmore uttered no reply in words, but he held out his hand to the lonely being who spoke, and looked in her face with silent sympathy.

A long pitying glance, and an earnest friendly pressure, and he left the room quietly and sorrowfully.

For a few minutes he stood as if irresolute on the landing-place, and then having apparently made up his mind to some course of action, he commenced ascending the staircase, while Judith after a pause, devoted to painful reflection, flung back the spectre " self " once again into the shade—and taking up her pen wrote two short notes ere she retired for the night.

The first was to Doctor Duvard, and ran as follows :—

" Come to me to-morrow, and I will give you Miss Crepton's address. On my own account also, I want to see you. First, about disposing of the new work—second, concerning my health.

I have finished my last work to-day, and lay down the quill for ever. I believe Miss Crepton is quite well; but if you have an interest in her you can soon learn all particulars for yourself.

" Your's,

"J. M."

And the other was to Alice.

" DEAR MADAM,

"In reply to your letter of —st inst. which only reached my hands this day, I shall be very happy to forward your views, if in my power. At the same time if you can do without an Editor I would rather not stand sponsor to your work, as it will hereafter prove more advantageous to you to have introduced yourself to the public than to have been introduced by any one else. Should you, however, fail in all other means of getting into print, you are at perfect liberty to make whatever use of my name you choose, and if such a step prove necessary you can show this note to Mr. Larocca as your authority for calling me the Editor of your book.

" You are entering upon a toilsome profession, but wishing you every success in your endeavours, and satisfaction in their results,

" Believe me,

" Your's truly,

" J. Spierson."

Folding both notes up in a parcel, Judith sent them down to the misanthrope, who posted the missives for her first thing next morning, when he sallied forth much pleased with the results of his interview with Alice on the preceding night, of which interview it may be as well to speak in the course of another chapter.

CHAPTER VIII.

The fire was low on the hearth, and the solitary
candle only dimly illuminated the dismal apartment Alice Crepton called hers. The clock had
just chimed one quarter to eleven, but still the
young aspirant for literary honours was sitting
writing; she never dreamt of weariness. Night
was the time when phantoms born half of reality
and half of ideality in that mysterious world
lying dimly in the brain of poets, authors,
musicians, and painters, came out from their
hiding places—walked across the narrow apartment, talked, looked, moved, and felt as they
might have done had they been actual persons,
and not the mere dream-like memories of experience, the spectres of fancy, or the ghastly forms

of that awful shadowy train, lengthening at every step, which we all bear after us—the innumerable but never-forgotten departed.

Dull and dreary, by the cold, sober light of day, ten feet by twelve, poor, shabby, and mean; the moment a sort of lull fell on the heart of London; the moment the curtains were closed and the paper spread, and the pale face bent eagerly over the sheet, the scene seemed changed as if by the wand of an enchanter.

Beyond the small circle within which the candle dispelled the gloom; away in the darkness beyond—Alice, in a dream-land of her own, saw the lamps of festival burning brightly; the forms of the young, the beautiful, and the gay, came, and went, and flitted joyously before her. Then the heart-broken drew near the hearth and told their tales unto the ear of the listener. She heard the voices of passion and the sobs of sorrow, the tones of tenderness, reproof, entreaty.

Men with their purposes, women with their griefs, children and their joys or troubles; the old, the young, the good and the bad, the lovely and the plain, the resolute and the weak,

walked forth from the shadowy corners, clothed
with form, individuality, face, character, and
stood before the eyes of the watcher, who never
felt lonely whilst the company thus summoned
from the " silent land" remained with her.

For to some the portraits sketched in pen and
ink by the rapid hand of the artist of imagination, seem taken from life. Every face —
every word — every thought — every sentence,
stamped by the magic of ideality with the firm,
touch of actuality. To the true author, no
character is a fictitious one. He knew his
hero. Though he never clasped his hand, nor
met him in the public haunts of men, yet he
greeted him in the dim twilight, and heard his
history in those hours when the genius of
inspiration created an artificial atmosphere
around the solitary literateur.

Some write for fame, and some for vanity,
and some—how many it were difficult to count
—for gold; and some—how few most of us
could give a guess, for pure love of the art.

Alice, however, was one of the latter. Had a
guinea never been likely to result therefrom;
had she known that not one of her works was

ever destined to see the light of Heaven shining
upon it in a bookseller's window, she would still
have sate in her little room, conjuring up all
sorts of strange forms, for pure love of their
society. She was as true an artist as ever lived.
Her heart—her soul—her purpose, centred in
her books, and those who feel this are those
alone who have the patent right direct from the
hand of Nature, to go forth and tell what their
mouth findeth, to speak unto the remainder of
their more practical fellows.

But how few there are that do feel the
"sacred flame," they who write know best.
Out of the six hundred and odd confessed
authors of this our native isle, there are, possibly, not a dozen, if, indeed, even so many, who
have wedded their art voluntarily for love of
herself, and not for love of the dower she promised to bring with her unto them, in the shape
of wealth, renown, position, or consideration.

Few are the suitors who woo the innocent,
simple-looking, yet all-powerful pen, with disinterested purpose; fewer still, those who cleave to
it afterwards without disgust, or weariness, or
dissatisfaction clogging its progress, and sullying

its endeavours; rarest of all are the one or two who, if they might choose again, would choose the apparently lovely bride, with her delusive smile, and fictitious fortune, and tardy reward wrung by exertion, wrought out by toil.

Alice, seated by the mouldering fire, was one, at all events, who worshipped the true flame, not its stolen counterfeit, and still she saw and wrote, and thought, until a tap at the door of her apartment induced her to cease for a moment and bid the new comer enter. She had fancied it might be a servant, or her landlady, but when, after her brief "come in," an old man with a keen, shrewd; expression of face, whom she recognised as Mr. Gartmore, turned the handle, and stood before her, she started up, surprised at the unusual visit, and the time selected for it. He closed the door very delibe-rately, and walked round the table without uttering a word, but when he had reached a point just opposite the girl, he said—

"You did not expect to see me here."

" I did not expect to have that pleasure," was the brief reply, somewhat formally spoken.

" Well—unexpected pleasures are always the

greatest," he said in his usual bitter, sneering tone. "I have come to talk to you."

Alice cared very little if he had come to preach to her. She was resigned to anything, and although not independent of every one, was independent, at least so she imagined, of Mr. Gartmore, who, with one hand resting on the table in the very middle of her scattered papers, remained looking intently at her, and by way of showing him the only civility she had it then in her power to evince, she pulled an old easy chair out of the corner, wherein it had been peacefully reposing, and asked him with, what civility she might, to "sit down."

"Ha!" said the old man, glancing suspiciously at her—"you offer me that chair because you have heard I am worth a couple of hundred thousand pounds."

"I offer you it, not because I know you have two hundred thousand pounds, but because I think you might, perhaps, like it better than the rest—however, if there be any other chair in the room you prefer—"

"I may take it, eh?" finished Mr. Gartmore.

"I should be sorry if you made yourself un-

comfortable out of politeness to me," answered
Alice, an amused smile flickering round her lips,
and lighting up her eye—whilst an answering
look in the old man's face assured her he understood that she comprehended him, and as he
dropped quietly into the proffered seat, he laughed
in a low, harsh key, and then commenced gazing
into the fire, and rubbing his hands and muttering odd sentences to himself.

Meanwhile, Alice waited with what patience
she might, for some further remark ; she resisted
a strong impulse which impelled her to take up
her pen and pull the feathers off it.   She refrained from collecting her papers together ; she
did not even stir the fire, but remained like a statue
immoveable, until, at length, she happily bethought her that as the candle required snuffing,
she might move without laying herself open to
any charge of feminine fidgetting from the lips
of the testy old man.

The action, however, failed to arouse him, and
for two or three interminable seconds more Alice
was doomed to sit watching her strange visitor
as he hung forward over the embers, and knit
his brows, and twisted his lips.   At last, sud-

denly starting from his musings, whatever they might be, he abruptly demanded—

"What do you mean?"

"What do I mean?" repeated Alice, taken quite by surprise. "I said nothing, sir."

"No, you said nothing, I know, but you do something. What are you doing?"

"What am I doing!" she again repeated, looking in blank astonishment in her questioner's face—"What am I doing?"

"Don't echo my words!" exclaimed her choleric visitor, "particularly when you understand me perfectly well. You need not deny it, for these speak for themselves;" and he laid an impatient hand on the blotted sheets. "You need not deny it."

"If you mean the fact of my writing, I do not wish to deny it," she replied.

"Yes—yes—I see you have started as an authoress, and are proud of it — and want it known, and—"

"No," interrupted Alice, hurriedly. "I have started as an authoress, as you say ; yet whilst I do not attempt to conceal it, neither am I proud of it. I am not ashamed to confess to the title but I have no desire to blazon to the comprehension of everybody, that such an insignificant person as myself exists."

There was something mournful in the tone of her voice, that took the sting off her visitor's tongue, and as he asked his next question, he looked almost pityingly in her face—

" Do you know what you are doing, child ?—Have you thought about it ?—Has any one ever told you what you are beginning ?"

" No one has ever explicitly told me," she answered ; " but I know.   I am beginning a profession which may gain me a livelihood and which may not ; which is full of struggle and disappointment !"

" In plain words, you write for money—for the sake of the lucre, against which all authors rail, but which all authors love in their hearts. You imagine passions, and pen scenes, and dream dreams, and rave of beauty, and anathematize vice—all for money—all."

There was a bitter scorn in the speaker's voice —it seemed as though he were talking of bartering away the heart's affections for gold— so vehement was the gesture that accompanied his words, but Alice's conscience felt clear of the implied offence, and therefore she began—

"We cannot live without money—"

"True!" interrupted Mr. Gartmore, vehemently; "but are we then to live *for* money. Is there nothing else under heaven precious to have—lovely to see—good to admire—worthy to long for, but the accursed metal—gold? How can we look for disinterested attachment when men and women consider the child of their own brain, the only heavenly thing that came out of Eden with Adam, now left to us, to be valuable only as pieces of merchandize are valuable for the price it will fetch—the number of pounds it can be made to wring out of the reluctant pockets of publishers."

Mr. Gartmore had got into such a passion during the progress of this speech, that he arose from his chair and commenced walking up and down the room, whilst Alice, after a moment's pause, answered—

"Authors must live—and to live, people must have money. If you do not like the idea of authors selling their thoughts, why not look upon it, that they are paid for the actual manual, bodily labour of writing and correcting; will not that do?"

"No, it will not," said Mr. Gartmore, "I do not object to pay,—Heaven knows, the recompense of genius in all branches is frequently a pittance, but I would not have talent always grubbing downwards. I would have genius paid —not traded with—let it have money if it can get it honestly, but let it not fret, and toil, and labour, and put forth all its best energies for money alone."

"And did ever the meanest drudge in the cause of literature labour merely for his daily bread?" demanded Alice. "Oh, surely not. I don't think that there ever was a writer yet, who would not have written on, even though money, and fame, and reputation were never destined to come to him after all."

"Do you feel thus?" demanded Mr. Gartmore, stopping abruptly in his walk, and looking with his keen, shrewd, worldly eyes into the young girl's face.

"I do," she answered, the warm blood coming up into her usually pale cheek, "for years writing has been my delight, my pleasure, my hope; long before I thought of making money, before a desire for a sort of fame was born, since that desire died, it was the one thing I cared for—why should I not care for it still?"

"I have known authors," said Mr. Gartmore, "who detested their vocation, who worked like galley slaves at their desks, loathing the toil, who catered for the 'popular taste' as it is termed, and had to hunt like dogs along the old tracks, never daring once to lift their noses from the ground, and follow their own fancies, for fear of losing the legitimate scent, and by consequence, the liberal reward which was to follow running the game, called the public, successfully to cover, and yet still these very people are the first to commence a rant about the superiority of literature to trade—about the disinterestedness of authors, and the grovelling character, and debasing influences of a life devoted to some far more independent business than their own. Bah! I am sick of the world,—sick and weary of the men and women of the world."

"Perhaps you know too much of it," ventured Alice.

"Too much—far, far too much," he said bitterly. "But now, little girl, what can I do for you? How are you succeeding in your literary endeavours—what has your experience of life taught you? I will help you if I can."

There was such a change in his voice, that Alice absolutely started; scarcely a word of kindness had greeted her ear for months previously, and her very soul had sickened for it.

Now, when with softened tone and gentler manner, her strange visitor turned out a friend in disguise, the surprise was too great, and the tears came unbidden into her eyes, as she answered—

"Thank you, sir, a thousand times, but I don't think you can help me. I am as grateful to you as if you could; but I believe there is only one person in the world who could assist me, and I am afraid I cannot expect a stranger as she is, ever to think of me."

"Humph! And who may this friend or enemy be?"

Oh, she is a lady Mr. Larocca mentioned. He said if she could be got to edit a book for me, he should not be afraid to publish it; and promised to write to her; but he was so long about doing so, and seemed to care so little about the matter, that I sent a note to him to forward to her; but I suppose she does not intend to notice it, as I have received no answer."

" And did you expect her to notice it?"

" When I sent my note? Yes."

" On what grounds?"

" Because she says in her book that it is our duty to help one another; that the mere fact of requiring aasistance is sufficient introduction without the usual formalities of society.".

" Heaven help all authors, if they were bound to act up to the exact meaning of such pretty theoretical sentences. Don't you know you have asked this woman to do almost an impossibility for you? In fact, were I an author, I had rather give you a hundred pounds than stand sponsor to any other person's literary child. You have made a most improper request, in so strange a manner, that I do not wonder at the lady's silence."

"I am very sorry," began Alice—and she looked it — and grieved, and mortified, and angry, into the bargain.

"There then, don't look so humiliated," he interposed; "forget all about her, and never do such a thing again. Where is this manuscript of yours? In the hands of Mr. Larocca."

"No," answered Alice. "I have it here; but he knows the book, and with a good editor has no objection to publish it."

"And give you how much?"

"Me! Nothing, He would have to pay the editor. Then he gives the money, and I the book, and we both would expect to make our profits out of a second——"

"Out of the devil!" almost shrieked Mr. Gartmore, as he heard this exposition of a very common literary procedure. "Give me your manuscript, child, and I will get you better terms than that. Pay an editor, and make—humbug! I will squeeze something for you out of them, or my name is not Thomas Gartmore."

"But you, sir, are as much a stranger to me as Mrs. Spierson, and I do not see why I should put you to so much trouble and annoyance,—and——"

"Because I choose to do it," responded Mr. Gartmore, shortly. "Now make over the copy-

right of that book to me—write as I dictate—
so—sign your name and date to the document. You are of course aware," he added, as
he pocketed the transfer, "that I can now sell
that work, and keep the proceeds—that you have
made it over, not in trust, but in fact, to me."

"If you get anything for the book, I am
not afraid of losing it," answered Alice with a
smile.

"More fool you," he retorted. "But then,
indeed, women are the greatest fools in creation,
—except men."

Having delivered himself of which complimentary speech, Mr. Gartmore nodded to Miss
Crepton, and left the room, with the manuscript
under his arm, and a very grim sort of smile
hovering upon his lips.

"I think he is the strangest being I ever
met," soliloquized Alice as he departed. "I
wonder whether any good will come of it?"

Perhaps it was because Mr. Gartmore had
experienced in his own person a good deal of
that hope deferred, "which maketh the heart
sick," or, more probably, because he was of a
very impatient disposition, that he hurried on

matters with the publishing office of Mr. Larocca with such impetuosity as resulted in his quarrelling with that gentleman, in the course of one brief interview, and finished matters off by telling that friend of authors that, if he went down on his knees, and prayed for the manuscript, he should not get it—a threat, be it remarked, which affected the publisher's peace of mind not in the least.

Finally, after he had rated half the novel publishers in London in a manner which was, to say the least of it, extremely unreasonable—after arguing, and storming, and, may I add it, swearing, he came to the conclusion that, if he waited for any of the " caterers of public taste " to pay for the book, he would have to wait a long time.

They hummed, and hawed, and talked about sharing the profits, which meant *nil*—and of taking half the risk, which meant relieving Mr. Gartmore of a few superfluous hundreds—and of subscribing a hundred copies amongst his friends, which meant giving them a hundred and fifty pounds clear—and of getting an editor to

advance the author's standing, which meant an
extra profit for themselves. Or they would take
the book on chance, and pay nothing. If it
were a failure, run the risk; if it were a profit,
pocket the gains. Or they very rationally wanted
to read the manuscript before saying any thing
about it; and the cool men of business threw
so many obstacles in Mr. Gartmore's path that
at last, fairly losing his temper, or, rather, gaining an accession of it, he threw an unoffending,
middle-aged, decorous-looking individual off his
balance, by muttering a withering denunciation
against all authors, publishers, printers, editors,
and all the rest of the "confounded rubbish,"
and rushing out of the last office on his list in a
state bordering on lunacy.

"My dear Mr. Maxwell," he exclaimed, entering his solicitor's office with an unwonted
excitement of manner, "do you think you could
find me out in London such a thing as an honest
publisher?"

"Well, I don't know," replied the lawyer.
"They, like ourselves, all think themselves
honest."

"Because," continued Mr. Gartmore, unheeding this interruption, "I have been running about all day, and cannot find even a sensible one amongst the lot—so—you see that manuscript," and he thumped the offending parcel down on the table with a tremendous bang. "Now listen to my instructions. It *must* be on the library shelves by this day six weeks—it *must* succeed—it must be brought out by a good house—it must not have an editor—it must have every fair chance given it—and I must not, in any case, lose more than a couple of hundred pounds by the transaction. It must not be published by any of these people," jotting down a list of those he had not been able, as he styled it, "to make listen to reason." "Now do you understand my wishes? and can you arrange the matter for me?"

"Without difficulty—only, if the book have not talent in it, no money will ever make it a success."

"·I tell you, sir, the book has talent, and it shall be a success," retorted Mr. Gartmore, having relieved himself of which decided expression of opinion, he walked off to his banker's, and returned thence to Upper Emery Street with a new fifty-pound Bank-of-England note in his pocket.

"Take my compliments to Miss Leake. I particularly wish to see her," he said to a servant, who returned next minute to request him to walk up stairs.

"I want to speak to little Crepton" was the manner and fashion of his salutation to Judith. "Will you let me see her here?"

"Little Crepton is at this minute engaged in a very interesting conversation with Dr. Duvard," answered Judith, with a smile. "I imagine they are making up a lover's quarrel, and will get through the performance a great deal better without our assistance;" and as she concluded, the old man and the young woman, to both of whom such things seemed as sad, dreamy memories of a lovelier and brighter shore, looked into each other's faces, and smiled mournfully.

"Sit down," said Judith, after a pause. "Dr. Duvard will call in with me as he comes down, and we can then send him back for her. I dare say he will not object to execute the commission."

"So he is smitten there?" remarked Mr. Gartmore, taking a chair. "Poor fellow!"

"Yes, he has caught the infection," said Judith. "It is one few escape; and though the hearts of some can be healed after the ordeal, they are, to my thinking, never worth the having; there is a deal said against first love, Mr. Gartmore, but I believe in none other."

"Do you believe in love at all?" he inquired.

"Do I believe in Heaven?" she answered earnestly. "The capacity of the human heart for love, I believe to be as large as its capacity for suffering, and *that* is awful!"

"And does he really care for her?" asked Mr. Gartmore, with slight irrelevancy to his former question.

"Yes: it is first love on both sides. They were to have been married long ago, only he dreaded dragging her down to poverty (he shall tell you the story himself in full); and then she grew jealous, as all loving natures will, on slight grounds, or, rather, on none at all—and left her home—and left him—and started out, like a foolish, perverse, little girl as she was, to make her way in the world alone. He, you must know, is very poor still; and there really seems no chance of his fortunes mending, unless," she added, laughingly, "you could get some fine, fanciful lady to 'take him up' and make him the fashion. You had better, however, not re commend him to Sir John Lestock's attention; as I feel quite sure he would poison the baronet and his daughter, if the chance were given him, without the slightest scruple of conscience."

" I have a great mind then to send him to prescribe for my brother's gouty leg," growled out Mr. Gartmore; " but stay, here he comes. Well, Doctor, how is your patient? I mean, Miss Crepton: there, there man, don't look so foolish—I see by your face all is as you could wish. Now, away up to Miss Crepton again, and say I want to see her here. An old fellow's privilege, you know," he added, seeing Charles did not altogether like his mode of address, " to order young ones about."

Very timidly Alice came in, followed closely by one, on whose shoulder she had wept out, poor little soul, an ocean of repentant tears. Very timidly she entered, with her heart throbbing violently, and a colour in her face, and a moisture in her eyes; but Mr. Gartmore, more kindly and considerately than was his wont, taking no notice of her embarrassment, introduced her, formally, to Miss Leake—motioned her to a seat on the sofa beside him, and began:

" I wanted to tell you, little one, I have disposed of your book."

" Already!" she cried, and a bright, earnest look of delight and surprise broke out over her face, like sunshine after a shower—" already!—"

" Yes, and here is the price; little enough, you will say—but we shall do better next time. Take it, child; don't you see what it is?"

" Fifty pounds—all mine?" she asked, doubtingly.

" Honestly earned," replied Mr. Gartmore, with a smile.

" And may I do what I like with it?" she demanded, still incredulous.

" Certainly, it is your own."

" My own!" she repeated; the words seeming to let in a sudden light on her comprehension: " My own!"—and, perfectly regardless of the presence of strangers, she sprang across the room to Charles, and thrusting the money into his hand, and looking beseechingly up at his pale, worn face, fell to crying violently.

"I wonder if you will give him your earnings as readily ten years hence, little lady!" said Mr. Gartmore, dashing down, with one worldly sentence, a whole goblet of sweet expectation, and love, and trust, and faith, and truth, and hope. For an instant Dr. Duvard looked reproachfully at him—and then, as careless of appearances as she had been, folded the girl to his breast, as though he would, by this simple action, have shielded her constancy and purity even from suspicion.

"There, there, don't be angry," said Mr. Gartmore, deprecatingly, "I did not mean to grieve you; only having had a hand in the getting of the money, I thought I had a sort of right to make what comments I chose on the way it was spent. What say you, Miss Leake?" added he, turning towards the chair she usually occupied, but it was empty.

Silently she had stolen from the room, and flinging herself across her bed, wept such scalding tears, as seemed as though they had been poured from some demon's cauldron, not wrung from any mortal heart. They scorched her cheeks as they streamed from her eyes; yet the paroxysm,

all vehement though it was, did not relieve
her.   It appeared, indeed, that the stream, unwholesome though it might be, had kept open
some beneficial channel within her frame, which
dried up the moment the torrent escaped, turning
everything in her soul into unprofitable dust and
ashes.   Dust and ashes!—love, happiness, fame,
wealth!   She had touched them all—and this
was what they crumbled to, under her fingers.

Dust and ashes!—it was the sum-total of her
life's experiences: she only fully comprehended
that truth then.   Jealousy, however, of the pale-
faced girl, whose fortune seemed dawning now so
brightly, had nothing to do with that wild burst of
uncontrollable grief.   There never lived a woman
so free from a taint of the sort as Judith Mazingford.   No—it was only the bitterness of the
contrast that struck home to her so forcibly and
suddenly, that she could not subdue the promptings of her rebellious heart, but felt herself constrained to lie there weeping, till the fit was over
and the fountain dry.

At last she arose, and bathed her eyes, and
re-entered the apartment.   As she crossed the
threshold, she heard Mr. Gartmore say, in a

somewhat excited tone, " It really strikes me, young people, you have waited far too long already; I insist upon its taking place at once."

And then Judith knew they were to be married immediately, and that Mr. Gartmore was going to help them on in the world.

CHAPTER IX.

ALICE and Charles went abroad for the honey-
moon, and during their absence Mr. Gartmore
amused himself in having a house " done up"
nicely for them, and by spreading amongst all
his acquaintance an account of Dr. Duvard's
extraordinary talents and abilities.

Two or three old dowagers, possessed of more
money than brains, aud more fancies than
ailments, were worked up by Mr. Gartmore to
such a pitch concerning his protegé, that they
counted the days until his return to town should
give them some fresh medicine to swallow—
some new medical pet to take up, pat, stroke,
and get wearied of.

Miss Lestock, too, hearing of the new doctor

whom her rich uncle thought fit to praise, enquired concerning him; but Mr. Gartmore put his veto on Charles being called in for her case, by declaring it was one only fit for a surgeon, and that he should recommend her to repair to the most eminent in London at once. In brief— between upholsterers and paperers, painters, and ladies afflicted with finger-aches, Mr. Gartmore's time was pretty fully occupied—so fully, indeed, that he should have had little leisure left to attend to Judith, even had she wanted his society, which she did not.

One day, however, he told her he had seen her husband, who was just starting off for Wales; and being subsequently informed of his arrival there, Judith ventured to stir out—to drive away miles and miles from London—and breathe once more the pure fresh air of heaven —to feel again, for a few brief minutes—free.

It seemed to give her fresh life that strange, unwonted holiday; and even whilst her disease was making greater strides than ever, she looked better than she had done for months previously. Her last book was out, and successful. In it she had put forth the best powers of her mind

—into it she had flung the best and richest treasures of her imagination—it was the dying song of the swan lying among the reedy borders of the lake of time—her farewell gift to a world she was leaving for ever—the noblest and finest utterance of a great authoress, who, had time been given her to finish her career, would have left a name behind her—a name, writ with a pen of iron on the imperishable rock of fame.

But as matters stood, it was "writ in water" on the waters—traced in the sand, for the next wave to wash away and obliterate for ever—it was a feather in the breeze—a star shooting down in the darkness of the night—a flower of the tropics blooming and dying in a day—a song of the wild bird, heard and forgotten—a great design unfinished—a tale half told—a life uncompleted.

The fragments she left behind her were wonderful, but could never be pieced together into a stupendous whole; still they were wonderful, and the last work, which she gave as a legacy, was one that stirred the hearts of thousands.

And yet the applause of the world, echoing back as it did into her desolate room, seemed to give her no pleasure. Adverse criticism could not touch her now—the riches and the praises, the censures and the vanities of this earth had power over her no longer—from all—from gold with its glittering splendour—from fame with its thousand tongues—from publicity with its adder-like stings—from sickness with its pains —from sorrow, fear, and memory she was fleeting away. The reviews were read and laid aside—the money was paid away to her old enemy—a last bribe to silence—the dream was past—the vision dispelled. No thought of temporal success or temporal failure disturbed her heart then, for she was looking out from the very shores of time to the calm boundless ocean of eternity.

It was something like this she once said to Mrs. Duvard, who, after her return to London, came gently forcing her presence on the invalid; all unconscious of the relationship existing between them, ignorant of the fact that the authoress, whose works were her ideal of perfection, was one with the beautiful woman who stood so solitary in the world—she poured out her admiration into ears that had never heard such words of genuine unaffected praise before. The great voice of the public was never so sweet or soothing to her vain woman's heart as the tones in which Alice spoke of "the love she felt for a woman she had never seen, of all the good her works had done her."

"And is it not a shame," said the young wife one day, "that her works should be so hacked up as they are in many papers? I declare I get quite angry—it must grieve and vex her to such a degree."

Judith laughed. "If the works had not been cut up in some of the reviews, it would have proved there was nothing in them. What is not worth pulling to pieces cannot be worth reading, and if you go on writing, you will find that the higher up you get on the literary ladder, so in precise proportion will be the apparently harsh, but really serviceable criticism you will have to put up with."

"Do you think so?" asked Alice, doubtfully. "It seems to me very hard, nevertheless. It sounds so unjust—so cruel!"

"My dear child," interrupted Judith, "what are these people to this woman? that you should get so indignant about the matter. Do you think that the worst review that ever was written could affect our sex, like a harsh or cutting sentence at home? Believe me, it is never through her vanity that a woman can be really touched —it must be through her love; and those authoresses who think that fame, or wealth, or the world's applause, can make up to them for the want of domestic ties—for the love of father and mother, brother, husband, sister, and children, are not women, dear Alice; but poor, weak, mockeries of men. Bring the case home to yourself—and you will see that your pity and your indignation are alike thrown away—that though favourable criticism might be pleasanter, the reverse is not so fearful an ordeal after all."

"But then she is so much cleverer than I could ever be—and her books are so beautiful."

"To your thinking, perhaps, but not to her own."

"Then you really believe that these reviews do not grieve her?" said Alice, earnestly.

"I know they do not," was the reply. "The woman who wrote these books has passed through such an ocean of suffering, that such things as these seem to her but as the white

spray that relieves the monotony of the breakers
on which she has long been drifting. In every
relation of life she has been unfortunate, and
when in solitude she reads these paragraphs,
they rouse her sometimes from a lethargy that,
at intervals, comes over her, and seems worse
than death—she knows that if these critics
could see the woman instead of the authoress,
that, for the sake of her struggles and her suf-
ferings—in consideration of all she has hitherto
endured, and of the short time she can remain in
this world—they would be more lenient; but
she does not want pity from any one; she has
lived without it, and she can die without it—of
a truth—yes."

And as Judith concluded, she rose and would
have walked over to the window, but a pair of
twining arms were around her, and Alice was
out—

"Oh! you know her, I am sure you do.
Are you she?   Are you Mrs. Spierson?"

"Not Mrs. Spierson, nor yet Miss Leake,
Alice," was the reply; "but your most wretched
cousin, Judith Mazingford.   I am the poor, frail
idol you have worshipped—crumbling into dust."

"Sit down, you look so pale," exclaimed Alice—and even as she spoke, Judith tottered to a chair. "I have talked too much—now leave me," she muttered.

"Never again—never—never again, you will come home with me, and I will nurse you well; you will be near Charles; and the very servants need scarcely know you are in the house. I won't listen to anything—you shall come away the minute you are better."

And the result of the matter was that Mrs. Duvard carried her point, and bore Judith off in triumph to her own house, where with care and attention, and skill, another pause was obtained in the march of the terrible disease which was stealing her away.

Then to weakness succeeded restlessness. She liked to be always out. She said remaining quietly within doors, as Dr. Duvard recommended, would kill her; and he, knowing that whether in or out made, in her case, very little difference, let her have her way in that, as in all other things.

Once she went out with a short tale which Alice wanted to get into print—for though she had done writing herself, yet still she liked the air of a publisher's office—she had memories, associated with literature, which were, probably, the calmest and happiest of her later life.

She told Alice afterwards it was a curious chance which led her to that place, at that particular hour, and so perhaps it might be called, only those events which we style "chances," are really nothing more extraordinary . than the meeting places of two roads, to which we must inevitably come if we pursue the path allotted unto us.

But call it by what name you will, the fact was undeniable, that coming out of the publisher's inner sanctum into his more public shop, she beheld an old man enter, and with an excited manner, address a few words to the assistant behind the counter.

Judith never could tell what impelled her to pause on the threshold and watch out the little play to the end. However, she did so, and saw a parcel which she knew by intuition contained manuscripts, handed back to the new comer without a word.

"Rejected," said the old man, tremulously.

"Won't do—not suitable," rejoined the other, and he was turning away, whistling, when, in a voice shrill with disappointment and emotion, the person whose appearance had interested Judith, cried out, as he flung the parcel down on the counter.

"But you *must* keep it, or on your head be his death—for I tell you the words that are traced on that paper, were written not with ink, but with blood."

Never before had such a speech been addressed to the unoffending youth, innocent as a child of the refusal of the MS., and totally taken aback by such an unexpected outbreak, he stood staring after the speaker, who rushed, like one distracted, out of the door, leaving the parcel behind him.

"Who is that gentleman?" Judith demanded.

"Don't know, ma'am—never saw him till the other day, when he called first about these papers," was the reply with which Judith had to content herself.

Perhaps it was a thought of her own father—of his disappointed life and fruitless endeavours, that induced Mrs. Mazingford to follow in the footsteps of the stranger, whom she overtook in St. Paul's Churchyard, just as he staggered up against the railings of the Cathedral.

"Will you excuse my addressing you, sir," she said, "but are you ill?"

"Madam!" He strove to raise his hat, but strength failed him, and he could not accomplish his object, or finish his sentence.

"I will see you home," Judith returned, quietly; despatching at the same moment a gaping lad to obtain a conveyance. "Just try to tell me where you live—there, that will do;" she added, as he muttered out two or three words, in a low tone. "Now, lean on me;" and, with the assistance of a policeman, she got him seated in the vehicle, and told the driver where to go.

"Number seven, I think you said?" she asked, as they stopped before the door of an apparently empty house—and he nodded in reply.

A pretty-looking young girl appeared, in answer to the driver's knock.

"Sick gentleman—says he lives here;" explained the latter individual, instructed by Judith; and at the words, Letitia Darwin, for it was she, sprang forward with a hurried exclamation of terror:

"Don't alarm yourself," said Judith, kindly; but the girl exclaimed — "Look, look," and pointed to her father, who, Judith for the first time perceived, had fainted.

"It is nothing," she answered. "Carry him in," she added to the man, "and then go for a doctor."

"Can you account for this at all?" asked that functionary, when he arrived.

Judith explained what she thought was the cause of the attack; but the man of medicine shook his head, and turned for further information to Letty, who either could not or would not impart any.

"I will tell you," she whispered to Mrs. Mazingford, after a pause; and bending down so near that the doctor could not hear what was said—the words "he was hungry," were spoken in her ear.

A silent pressure of the hand, and Judith was by the doctor's side again.

N

"It seems to me," she began, "that he must be weak rather than ill—perhaps he had walked far and fasted long. If you think there is any nourishment he might safely take, I will remain and see that he swallows it."

"You don't seem to me, madam, to be very strong yourself;" he retorted, brusquely; "and perhaps you may not be aware there is small pox in the house."

"Small pox," repeated Judith, "then is this—"

"No, this is not the commencement of it; but there is a youth lying at death's door, I believe, up stairs, at least so a friend of mine, who is attending him, told me."

"Not dying; oh! no, no, not that," cried Letitia, who had drawn close up to them, at the conclusion of the foregoing sentence, "He won't die! he must not—he cannot."

"Well, perhaps not," he answered, turning from her to Judith, for he was at the base of his profession, and worshipped, as all low natures do, the reality or the semblance of wealth. "As for my patient," he said, "a little weak tea, or mutton broth—or, or anything of that kind."

"I understand," replied Judith, placing the expected fee in his hand ; "and now, Sir, I think you may safely leave the case in my care."

With which brief dismissal she curtseyed him from the door; and then returning to Letitia, bade her get her father some wine and bread at once, and set about the work of recruiting his exhausted nature, as though her own cough had not been racking her frame.

"You are ill," said Letitia, anxiously; "You ought not to be here—I am so sorry."

"Sorry, that while life is spared me, I shall have strength given me to aid my fellow creatures ever so little. Ah! child, you don't know how happy it makes me to be here; years and years have passed away since I smoothed back grey hairs from any forehead — since a feeble man leant on my arm and clasped my hand. The sight of your father brings back the memory of my own; and I feel when I am thus tending him, that I am helping one over whom the green grass has long been springing."

"But the small pox—indeed you must go; I would not that for anything you caught it here."

" I am not afraid of contagion," Judith answered with a smile. " Is it your brother who is ill ?"

" No, not my brother ; though he is just like one," said the girl. And whether it was with bending over the fire, or with what she was saying, Judith could not tell, only she saw a flush come into the soft cheeks that spoke, she thought———

But no matter ; the girl's secret was her own, and she stooped her head close to the toast she was making, in a vain endeavour to hide the truth. Poor little soul ! it was the old story over again : love keeping watch below, and death standing sentinel above. Judith wondered which would prove triumphant — wondered about the daughter as she gave the father wine in spoonfuls, and coaxed him to swallow pieces of toast steeped in negus, and saw the colour coming back into his face—noble, self-denying creature as he was—who had starved himself to provide necessaries for the sick man, who lay above their heads dying.

At last he recovered his strength sufficiently to be able to sit up in an antique arm chair, and then Judith took her departure. "I will send a really good doctor to you at once," she said to Letitia, "who will save—your—brother if it be possible,"

In a minute the tears were streaming down Letty's cheeks—in a minute she was on her knees before Judith, kissing her hands, and even the skirt of her dress; and then, before the other could raise her, she was up again, fearful less such close contact might communicate the malady—should do her any harm.

"I quite forgot to ask your name," said Mrs. Mazingford, after a pause, which she employed to steady her voice. "Who shall I tell Dr. Duvard that I want him to attend?"

"Dr. Duvard!" cried Letitia; "oh! I wonder if that is the doctor Evan has wanted so much to see."

"Evan who?" demanded her visitor.

"Evan Crepton," was the reply. On hearing which, Judith hurried from the house, and finding Charles fortunately at home, despatched him forthwith on his mission without, however, informing Alice of its object.

For days and days, Evan hung between life

and death ; but at last the disease was subdued, and when it was, Letitia fell sick. But her's was a milder form, and with better treatment from the first, she speedily recovered. Not before, however, Alice and her brother met once again—not before he had told his own family of the kindness that the old Captain and his daughter had shewn him—not before Judith made the discovery, that whilst poor Letty was smitten, *he* was heart-whole—not before he had told, how falling, through ill-health, out of his situation, he had tried to help his income by translations and accounts of his travels—not before Mr. Gartmore had put him in the way of earning an independent livelihood, and made up friends with Captain Darwin, and began to feel that he could wish to have had a son like Evan, to take an interest in, and push on in the world, and leave his money to.

But then the old suspicion came across his mind again. Might not all these people be frank, and honest only in appearance—might not the respect and affection they shewed him be merely a silent way of asking for a favorable mention in his will ?—Was not human nature

just the same in Dr. Duvard's study and in
Miss Lestock's boudoir?—Was he not sowing
for himself the seeds of bitter disappointment,
ingratitude, and duplicity? If he were poor,
would these, his newly-found relatives, not be
the first to turn their backs upon him? Was
not poverty always fawning and always calculating? How could he, rich as he was, test
the truth or disinterestedness of any living
being?

Judith, indeed, he believed wanted nothing
from him—but then Alice, and Evan, and Miss
Ridsdale, were all her relations, and in Doctor
Duvard's welfare she took a deep interest; and
might not, therefore, her manner to him take
its color from the expectations she entertained,
that he would in due course make all her connexions something more than comfortable—
wealthy?

Might not they all be speculating concerning
his speedy death, and favourable testamentary
dispositions? Mr. Gartmore propounded these
questions to his own mind until he grew perfectly
morose and misanthropical again; but just
when he had arrived at this undesirable state of

feeling, the news of the failure of the firm of Moncton, Brabayar, Macdonald, and Company, fell with a sort of crash on the business-heart of London, bearing down with it many a happy home and haughty spirit into the dust.

They were an Indian firm, the largest at one time in the world—and as the size of the edifice had been vast, so the extent of its ruins was tremendous. Widows and orphans, men of business, and men possessed of private fortunes, all went down with the wreck together. There was not a class in the community, a person high or low, that was not affected in some way by the failure of a house which had been up to the very last considered far safer than a bank. There was a sound of weeping that spring throughout England. Ladies had to seek situations, and gentlemen clerkships—carriages were laid down, and arduous employments taken up, and from the hour the intelligence reached his ears, Mr. Gartmore sat down resolutely in an old arm chair, and putting all pity and sympathy from him, refused to be comforted.

Very possibly, even he could scarcely have credited how fast friends dropped away from him when once it became bruited abroad that he was actually beggared. Some, indeed, came to visit him from curiosity, and some for appearance sake, but most stayed away altogether.—— There are few in the world who care to come into close contact with a drowning man, and Mr. Gartmore himself stated that the waters had rolled over his head—that when he thought the heat and labour of the day was passed, he should have to go forth and toil for a new livelihood again.

"Good bye, England," he said one day in Dr. Duvard's drawing-room. "I must turn my back on the old country once more, and see whether India has still enough spare grounds left to support me while living, and bury me when dead."

"You shall never leave England so long as I have a home to share with you," exclaimed Dr. Duvard, "Do I not owe everything I have in the world to your generosity—is not everything here—furniture, practice, house, fees, patients, yours. Am I not young and strong, able with the help you have given me, to work for all, and will a treble blessing not fall on my labours?—

will fourfold strength not be given me to preserve
my profession if I am working for the man to
whom I am indebted for all the happiness
and comfort·that surround me? Come, Alice,
and persuade Mr. Gartmore that we are his
children, and that if he will only consent to try
our affection, we will do our best to make the
home he gave us a happy one to him. Now
we really must have our way in this, for I am
sure you would not wish to make us miserable,
and we should be so if you ever were to leave us
again."

And before the old man could answer, Evan
entered and commenced his appeal—he was in a
first-rate situation—if health were spared him
he could yet give Mr. Gartmore all he had been
accustomed to—all he should feel proud and
thankful to see him have in a home of Evan's
making. Was he not his father—had he not
been kind to him when near relations looked
cold—when, for all his mother or grandfather
cared, he might have died like a dog, and been
buried in a ditch? No, so long as Mr. Gartmore was rich he had no need of them, and
they could never dare to dictate his movements

to him; but now that he was a little poorer they had a perfect right to interfere with him as much as they liked, and if it were necessary, to bring him to Dr. Duvard's—*viat armis*—Evan, though not quite a Hercules, was ready and willing to execute the feat.

Then Millicent Ridsdale, too, came with the dear, kind pleading eyes, and soft earnest voice of old, to beg him let the " children have their own way,"—and as it was in vain for Mr. Gartmore to try single-handed to fight so many, he was forced to yield himself a captive on Doctor Duvard's hearth-rug; a conquest, which was celebrated like a national victory by Evan, and Alice, and Charles—Miss Ridsdale and Judith looking on quietly and thoughtfully.

" It won't last—it can't last," thought Mr. Gartmore—" they'll find out the difference when they have to keep me—when they feel the extra expense. It is the daily work which proves the strain. If they can stand that, they can stand anything; but they cannot—they will not. It is impossible."

It was not impossible, however, and so Mr. Gartmore found, such love and consideration had

never been shown him in the days of his wealth
as was now given him in the hour of his apparent poverty.   He found that it was quite
possible for him to believe in and like people,
and that taking it as a whole, it proved much
pleasanter to have some faith in his fellows, than
to be constantly accusing them of sinister
motives.

It was not merely among his own immediate
connexions either, that he found staunch friends.
Many an old acquaintance who had formerly
been afraid of even the semblance of toadyism,
now dropped often in to have a chat with him
about India, and the people they knew, and the
things they did there. True hearts, Mr. Gartmore
discovered beat under all sorts of covers ; and it
was during this period of feigned adversity, that
he winnowed out the wheat from the chaff;
that he placed men of the Sir John Lestock
stamp down under one head, and men like
Charles Duvard under another.   Then he
learned that all sweeping condemnation of
classes and parties are something worse than
foolish, and found that during the whole course
of his previous life, he had lived too much for

and in himself; that he had expected more
from his fellows than he gave back unto them
in kind: that the world he had so grievously
abused, was, when all that could be said against
it, had been said and done, far better than
himself. In brief, as much knowledge and
teaching came to his soul out of his sham
poverty, as comes to many a proud nature in
times of bitter trial and sore humiliation.

But best amongst all his new relatives, Mr.
Gartmore liked Judith Mazingford. There was
a something about her nature which accorded
with his own; and although her life had for
years past been but one long dreary effort at
concealment, though she was forced to appear in
the world as a hypocrite—a being with a score
of aliases and a list of sins—still, strange as it
may sound, there was not one in whose presence
he felt so keenly the deceit of the part he was
playing, as in hers.

And yet she never pitied him—never seemed
even to consider him a fit object of compassion.
She told him once, point blank, that she thought,
spite of the way in which his loss had effected
his spirits, " he was, and ought to be really

much happier than in his cold, formal lodgings in Emery Street."

She used to laugh at his lamentations, and compel him to laugh at them himself. She said he was moped for want of something to do, and offered to give "copying work," because, she added, "I am wearied of idleness, and believe I must take to my pen again, though I have vowed never to write another book."

And she did take up her pen again, as she had declared she would ; and while Dr. Duvard looked grave, and Alice anxious, she persisted in her determination. "That dreadful woman, Doctor," she exclaimed one day, "I find I must write on for her till I die."

So the great heart kept struggling on—struggling to preserve its secret, which was, however, gradually oozing out, though even to Evan, Alice never called her anything but "Miss Leake."

CHAPTER X.

AFTER Mr. Gartmore had been " playing at pauper" for about five weeks, he got tired of the character. It was such a bore to be always shamming—such a weariness to the flesh to sit desponding in an old arm-chair, when the happiest part of his life had just opened upon him. Such a nuisance to have to be double-faced, when for the first time for years he had met with people who were thoroughly honest and disinterested. Such a shame to have suspected those who had never shown half their love and friendship for him till he was deserted by every body else.

Altogether, Mr. Gartmore was tired. When money was wanted for any charity, he did not like to be forced to remain silent. When Dr.

Duvard came home, and told his wife about a whole family of fatherless children lying sick in fever, he longed to put his hand in his pocket, and give his son-in-law, as he called him, a five-pound note to spend for their relief. When Alice said, in answer to any remark of his, that they had better be economical till Charles had made a fortune, his tongue curled itself round in his mouth in the effort he made, not to deliver himself of a sentence commencing with " economy be—"

Further, he knew he was acting the part of a consummate hypocrite ; and then he saw many nice little things that Judith would have liked, and he would have bought, only he thought of his feigned poverty ; besides which, he wanted to settle a hundred a year on Captain Darvin, and bid that boy Evan marry, like a sensible rational being, and furnish a house for the young couple.

" Hang it, " he thought, " look what an amount of happiness I could bestow with four or five thousand pounds, which I have hitherto cut myself out from, because forsooth I must go and imagine every soul in creation was worse -

than myself. But I won't stand it any longer. I am determined I won't. Judith ought to go out of town, and I am wearied of London too, and I want to get away from the overgrown city, to purer air, and a quieter home, and I wish to do something besides. Yes, and I will do it if I can."

What was that something besides, think you, dear reader? To found an alms-house, or build a church, or endow an hospital, or rear an asylum? No, it was nothing so philanthropical, though, perhaps, far more common-place—he wanted to marry.

Do not laugh at the idea, do not even smile at it in your mind; for the man's heart was fresh then as at thirty—it was yearning as much or more for something to twine its loving tendrils around, as in the days when he was younger, happier and poorer.

If you have kept your affections unchanged for more than the third of a life-time—if, after years of absence, of change, of bitterness, you are still conscious that the woman you cared for once is dearer than any other unto your soul still—if you are thankful to God for the dear old wife who sits opposite to you, as you read these pages—seeming dearer, perhaps, after the long pilgrimage she has performed with you, than she did when, a blooming bride, she gave herself to you at the altar—if you have ever felt a pure, undivided, unalterable attachment for any one— if, in one word, you can say honestly and fairly, that the love of your youth is the love of your age—I leave the question to be decided by your judgment fearlessly; but if you are either so young, that you laugh at the idea of wooing and wedding, or so heartless, that you cannot comprehend the love that lives through time, and survives throughout eternity—then I say, scorn and mock not, because they who had been lovers in spring, wedded in autumn—because, when Millicent's brown hair was streaked with gray, and her husband's head silvered, they became man and wife, and entered into the holy state of matrimony, with greater faith and trust in one another than they could have felt in the first days of their early courtship: "We are not so young as we were once, Millicent," said Mr. Gartmore, as he took her work away from her one day, when she came over to Dr. Duvard's to keep Judith company, Charles and Alice being both from home—" but still that need not prevent our marrying now, if you care for me, as I really believe you did in the days before either of us had known sorrow, or found out what a cold, dreary world this is for unmarried folks to live in, when they get old and friendless. There is some hope of my saving enough for us to live on, out of the wreck of my fortune. Will you share the little I may have with me? There, there, don't speak; I know all you would say— that you have never thought of marriage for nearly thirty years past; that it would seem ridiculous for us to marry now; that we have each of us got on so far tolerably well alone, and can live apart to the end of the chapter. I know it all; and I know what is passing through your mind—but if you could only imagine what a desolate old creature I was in my solitary lodgings, if you would only consider that we might lead a cozy Darby and Joan sort of life, in some pretty part of the country, all the rest of our days—just as we might had we been married a quarter of a century since, I think you would not say me nay. Just answer me honestly one question, Millicent—Do you love me any less because I am old? Do you care for me less now than you did years ago?"

" I have never altered," she said, tremulously.

" Then what on earth should prevent our marrying?" he demanded; but Miss Ridsdale did not think fit to reply to his query.

" Dear aunt!" said a voice beside her, at the moment he was waiting for an answer, " say you will be his friend, companion, wife, during all the remaining days of his pilgrimage here below; do, to please your own Judith. It will be my last request to you, aunt. May I grant my own petition, and answer him for you—may I?"— And the wife, who had suffered in her own marriage so grievously, knelt down beside her aunt, and brought the altered face closer to her bosom, and kissed the forehead, so lined and crossed by sorrow, and wept. It was such a rare sight to see the dying woman shed tears, that Miss Ridsdale, with the ghosts of the past, and the sorrows of the present, and dreams of the future rising before her, flung her arms round her niece's neck, and sobbed aloud.

" Pray Madam, who sent for you?" demanded

Mr. Gartmore, gulping down something he felt rising in his throat—" I suppose you thought I could not get a wife for myself without your interference. I imagine you think you have managed in a minute what I could not have effected in a month."

"And have I not, uncle?" demanded Judith, looking up through her tears, and smiling, archly, in his face.

" Don't call me uncle, until your aunt gives you leave, you poor, broken-hearted, little soul. There now, don't cry, don't; we will go away to Madeira, and set you up again, and I will have a separation for you from that blackguard of a husband of yours, the moment I can claim a relative's right to meddle in your affairs. Millicent, just tell her when she may call me uncle, will you?"

Taking Judith to his heart with one hand, he held out the other to the true-souled woman, who had sat alone in Great Crowland Street, looking up at the evening sky, a long time ago— she placed hers in it, without a word, and in three days more they were married at the nearest church.

"And now, Judith," said Mr. Gartmore, "where shall we take you to—Madeira or Italy, which ?"

"Neither, thank you," she said, with a mournful smile, "I should like best of all things to go back to Wales. Take me to some sea-port, where I can look upon the great ocean, emblem of a mightier one, on which I shall soon set sail. Let my eyes rest once again on the hills, and the valleys, and the waterfalls of my native land, before I go home; and then, when I am dead, bury me beside Marcus Lansing, in Llandyl Churchyard. My heart has been lying with him for years—let my body rest there likewise."

"Judith," said Mr. Gartmore, severely, "I cannot tolerate such rubbish as this. You are not going to die—whenever you are free of that accursed tie matrimonial—"

"Only hear him !" interrupted the person so addressed, "and he not married four-and-twenty hours ! Well, uncle ?"

"I say, when you are clear of that scoundrel Mazingford, and when I have paid him out—as, with Heaven's help, I hope to do—you will get quite strong. You are much better latterly.

Your eyes are twice as bright as when I first saw you; and I declare, within the last three days you have got a colour like a rose; and bless my soul, child, you have never passed a week in bed, first or last; and you must never write another line of those confounded novels— that some way stir my blood within me, and that were nearly the death of you; for, to tell you the truth, I never was a penny the poorer by the failure of that bank; and I am rich enough for all—rich enough to start as landed proprietor, J.P., and so forth."

"So I suspected," said Judith, quietly, whilst Dr. Duvard and his wife looked at the new-made husband in blank amazement.

"And did you tell?" began Mr. Gartmore, a dark shade of distrust coming over his face, as he glanced doubtingly round at his connexions.

"I told nothing to any one," answered his niece. "In fact, I never suspected a fraud until you proposed to marry aunt Milly; and then I felt satisfied, putting little things together, that you had affected poverty for the purpose of testing our disinterestedness; and I hope that, on the whole, you have found us all you could desire."

"No, madam, I have not," he retorted; "for I have found you reading my thoughts like a book, and your aunt making difficulties about marrying me, and Dr. Duvard talking to you like a simpleton, and Alice—ah! indeed she is the only one that has come up to my ideas of perfection; for as for Evan—"

"Why, what has Evan done?" demanded Alice eagerly, whilst Judith fixed her eyes earnestly on Mr. Gartmore, who answered—

"Evan—ahem! will mend in time; but now, Judith, where are we to go? Should you like Madeira, or the south of France, or Torquay, or Italy, or where?"

"I should like to go to Wales," she persisted. "I want to get a glimpse of the blue mountains and the wandering rivers once again; and I wish to sit on the sea shore, and listen to the murmur of the waves. It cannot make much difference to me certainly, only I feel as if I should like to die at home."

"Judith," said Mr. Gartmore, passionately, "I cannot listen to such nonsense. You won't die—you must not—it is impossible."

And truly, looking into her face, and hearing

her usual style of conversation, it was hard to imagine it. For a long time previously, she had never spoken of her illness—never complained —borne pain and weakness in silence; for the unconquerable spirit battled almost to the last with the terrible power and strength of her insidious disease. She tried to keep death back from her, but it would not do. At last, she felt the first touch of his hand on her heart; and seeing how all her relatives were deluding themselves, she spoke.

"Doctor," she said, turning to her staunch friend, who was looking with troubled, anxious eyes out of the window—"Doctor;" and he turned and came close up beside the sofa where she was lying.

"Tell them," she continued, "fairly and truly what you know and what I know—that there is no hope, that Madeira, or Italy, or Wales, or London—it is all the same—that I am, in one word, dying."

There was an ominous silence for a moment. Then Mr. Gartmore, rising from his chair, cried nervously :—

"Speak out, man! Say you can cure her."

"It is beyond my skill," said Charles, in a low, hushed voice.

"Then let us have further advice at once," exclaimed her uncle, making a rush to the door.

"My dear sir—" remonstrated Dr. Duvard.

"Don't my dear sir me," exclaimed he, vehemently. "We ought to have called in some one else long ago. If you had done your duty, she might have been well ere now; but I will bring Dr. Threffman here in ten minutes. He is the first in his profession in London."

"For Heaven's sake, uncle—no!" entreated Judith, springing from the sofa, and seizing him, as he was about to descend the stairs. "Dr. Threffman knows me; and if Mr. Mazingford—"

"Curse Mr. Mazingford!" vociferated Mr. Gartmore. "Am I going to have your life sacrificed for a ruffian like that? Let me go, child!" and he broke away from her, and shot to the hall door.

"Oh! do wait!—please do!" cried Judith, running down the first flight after him; but as she reached the landing, she suddenly stopped, with a sort of cry.

"What is the matter?" asked Dr. Duvard, springing forward, just in time to catch her, as she fell heavily into his arms, with the blood spurting from her mouth.

She had burst a blood-vessel!

He carried her back into the drawing-room, and adopted such prompt measures as speedily stopped the hæmorrhage. By the time Mr. Gartmore came back with Dr. Threffman—whom he had had to hunt for half over London—she was sufficiently conscious to recognise, and even speak in a faint, weak voice to her old adviser.

"Well, Doctor, it has come to this at last," she murmured, stretching out a wasted hand.

"Mrs. Mazingford!" he exclaimed, and really for a physician he seemed wonderfully affected.

"You have done what was necessary, I suppose?" he said, turning to Dr. Duvard.

"Yes, you perceive she has burst a blood vessel within the last few hours."

"One of the larger ones?

"No."

"H—m!—that's well," said Dr. Threffman. "I will look in again to-night, if possible."

"But can't you do anything now?" demanded

Mr. Gartmore, impatiently—"what is the use of looking in, if you don't try to cure her?"

"Is the man a lunatic?" thought Dr. Threffman, while Judith moved her hand for her uncle to take, and said, faintly—

"It's just a question of time."

"Do you think so?" asked Dr. Threffman.

"Sure of it," she said.

"Then, sir, you may be so too," he remarked to Mr. Gartmore, bluntly, but not unkindly—and taking the old man by the arm he led him out of the room.

She lingered for more than a fortnight after that, and finally, to the astonishment of both her physicians, rallied so much as to be able to sit up supported by pillows in an easy chair.

"I never saw so hard a struggle," said Dr. Threffman to his medical brother; "I had no idea she could have lasted till this time: What a strength of will she must have."

"Do you think it that?"

"To be sure it is; one half, at all events. Why, she has carried the seeds of that disease about with her, to my certain knowledge, for years, but she would not give in then, and she won't now—she is fighting every inch of the way to her grave. She is a noble creature. I would give anything to have been able to save her."

"I have never heard a word of complaint from her, and no matter what pain she was in, she could hide it from every eye but mine. Yes, I have ever seen her, when the sound of her cough grieved my wife, smother and keep it back till she was almost suffocating."

With a hurried gesture and shake of his head, Dr. Threffman departed. "I should not like," he said, "to have all my patients interest me in a similar manner. It would soon cut up my practice."

And in truth the nearer Judith approached the tomb, the greater seemed her power of drawing all hearts unto her. Mr. Gartmore and his wife—Alice and Charles—hung about the invalid, and kept every painful or exciting topic from her knowledge. Thus, when news came of the dangerous illness of her brother, who had been injured in a descent to one of his own coal mines, the subject was never mentioned in her presence. Neither did Mr. Gartmore permit Mr. Mazingford to be named in the sick room, although reports were rife of his embarrassments and ceaseless efforts to find the woman he had rendered so wretched.

Judith, herself, appeared happier and more tranquil than she had ever been. Exhaustion of body frequently produces a quiescent state of mind, and standing on the very verge of the tomb, she enjoyed a peace and repose which she had never previously dreamt of.

Up to the last she never kept her bed; when she got too weak to walk, she was carried into the drawing-room, and placed in an easy chair, with all her friends gathered about her.

"I should have liked," she said, "a sight of the country again; and if it might have been, to have died beside the sea—but after all, it makes very little difference—only promise me I shall be buried at Llandyl: never let me be laid in Wavour vault—I could not rest there. I am sure I should rise up in my shroud and walk away from it."

"I promise!" answered Mr. Gartmore.

"And do not forget to tell the friends of those un_appy wretches who are confined at

Crafton, my experience there. Say it would be better to kill them at once. I wrote anonymously to all I could get the names of, but your representation will carry more weight with it."

"I shall rout out the big spider that rules there, I have sworn that," said he, savagely.

These, in fact, seemed to be Judith's only two desires; but, occasionally, she harped upon them with a pertinacity which would almost have conveyed the idea that the malady was affecting her mind.

Generally, however, she was calm and collected, talking as much as her strength permitted her about the plans and prospects of her relations, on subjects of general interest—but scarcely ever of herself.

She was very fond of Letitia Darvin, and had her frequently at the house, and once told the girl to be sure to send Evan—who was absent from town on business—to her the moment he returned to London.

"I want to see him particularly," she said, and Letitia remembered her message.

One day, when she was weaker than ordinary, and left by a rare chance alone for a few minutes,

Evan came in. He looked pale and careworn, and there was a look of anxiety in his face, which deepened into an expression of absolute agony as he beheld the ravages a few weeks had made.

She held out her hand to him, which he took and retained in his own. Judith felt that he was trembling like a frightened child, and the sight of his emotion caused her voice to quiver as she spoke.

"I wanted to bid you good bye. I was afraid you would not come back in time to see me before I went."

"Oh! you must not die—you shall not die— I cannot spare you. I have loved you as I never loved anything on earth before. I cannot live after you;" and he fell down on his knees beside her, and hid his face in her dress, and wept like a child.

For a moment she bent over him, toying with his hair, while the tears came into her eyes and checked her utterance.

"And so, poor boy," she said at last, "you have fancied yourself in love with me, and have rushed, as many before you have done, after a shadow, leaving the substance behind. Look up, Evan, and listen to me. I told Letitia I wanted to see you before I died, and it was to say this: you must crush out the feeling you have just expressed; you must think of me as a cousin or a sister lost, but never as of one who might have been your wife. Raise your head, and hear what I have to say. Were health restored to me to-morrow, I could never marry you. I am not what I may have seemed to you, a dying girl reluctant to leave this world, but a weary wife thankful at the prospect of release. You have cast the best gift of your soul before a woman without a heart, who could never be more to you than a wretched, unhallowed memory, unless you will crush the folly in your breast at once and for ever.

"Long ago," she continued after a pause, "I loved a man whose murderess I virtually was. I could never have cared for any one else. I was his wife before heaven and my conscience, and yet—don't turn from me—I married a man whom I hated—who had blighted my whole existence—who is living now. I am not Miss Leake, Evan, but your cousin, Judith Mazingford."

o 3

With a cry he sprang from the ground, and looked despairingly in her face.

"No love, no heart, no hand, poor child, could I ever have given you; and what was but folly before, would be criminal now, if you do not endeavour to battle with, and conquer it. I do not press the point upon you now Evan, but as I know there is a pure gentle girl who loves you, as you have fancied you loved me, I leave it a last injunction upon you to remember hereafter that my dying wish was, that you should make Letitia Darvin your wife. It is not death, recollect, that separates you and me, for eternity puts no gulf between those who could never be united in time."

He did not answer. He was back again in his old attitude, weeping beside her; and she let him vent his sorrow thus, whilst she tried to soothe and comfort him, as a mother might have done.

So they remained for some time, until at length a noise and bustle attracted Judith's attention. There was a sound as of remonstrance and expostulation; then she heard Mr. Gartmore's voice raised as if in anger; finally, a loud and imperious,—" I tell you I know she is in the house, and by ——— I won't be kept back by any one," caused Judith to start up, and cry to Evan.

" Don't let him see me. Don't, oh, don't let him come here. Go and prevent him."

He sprang across the room at her bidding, as a sound of scuffling commenced down stairs. He had not reached the door, however, when Judith, stretching out her arms, shrieked out the words, " I'm dying," and tottered back into her seat, her neck and dress dyed crimson with the blood that poured in torrents from her mouth.

" Help, help, Charles, help !" shrieked Evan, and in another moment the room was full. Drs. Duvard and Threffman were the first who entered ; then Mr. Mazingford, accompanied by two or three people that looked like officers of the law, rushed into the apartment, followed by Mr. Gartmore, red with passion, who made a spring at the intruder, and tried to drag him out again.

" Hush, gentlemen, hush," said Dr. Threff-man, solemnly raising his hand, " she is dead !'"

"I don't believe it," said her husband, furiously; but it was true for all that.

Tossed no longer by tempestuous billows—vexed no more by contrary currents—safe at last from wind, and wave, and weather; out of reach of the ceaseless spray of petty ills and trials; shielded for ever from the blasts of adversity—the roaring storms of sorrow—free from pursuit, secure from persecution, with no horror of detection, no sickening for a haven of earthly rest—no further feeling of earthly joy or pain, pleasure or regret, she lay there dead !

The poor frail bark, which had suffered so terribly, and battled so gallantly, had found a peaceful harbour of refuge at length.

Just in time she had reached it, and with an expression of impotent rage her enemy gazed upon the prize which had escaped him—when near enough to touch it, when absolutely within his grasp, a mightier than man had interfered to rescue her from him.

For she was indeed dead—a waif on life's ocean no longer—out into the broad, fathomless, trackless, mysterious ocean of eternity she had . floated :—

From life, across the sea of death—home.

"Bear witness to the fact," said Mr. Gartmore after a long silence, addressing those present, "that on the 25th of this month, Judith, wife of Lewis Mazingford, expired."

Without answering a syllable, Dr. Threffman having looked at his watch, took out a card, and made a memorandum of the day and hour.

CHAPTER X.

CONCLUSION.

IT was not without good reason that Mr. Gartmore had called such immediate attention to the hour and day of Judith's death, for within a fortnight from that period, legal enquiries began to be made, concerning the date of her decease.

"Why do they want to know?—Why do they come teazing here at such a time?" asked Alice with tearful eyes.

"Because if Judith had died a week later, my dear, Evan would not have been heir to Llandyl Hall, as he is unquestionably at present," answered Mr. Gartmore. "So you see by his brutality that wretch has done himself out of a snug fifteen thousand a year. Serve him right, too. He talks of legal proceedings. I only wish he would fulfil his threat, and I would drag him through every court in England. I have not done with Mr. Lewis Mazingford yet, however," added Mr. Gartmore, with a sort of tremor in his voice. "I have got a few accounts still to settle with the fellow who blasted the life of as noble a woman as ever went to her grave broken-hearted. A scoundrel who would not even let her be buried in the spot she had chosen, till I gave him a cheque for the permission. Selling his wife's corpse, in fact—Oh! Judith, if I could hang him I would!"—And the old man, whose heart had twined around the dead, and clung to her even in her grave—who could never think of her wrongs and her sorrows without a burst of indignation, lifted up his hands, as if he were addressing some invisible being, and broke out into one of those violent fits of rage and grief in which he had indulged himself ever since he came fully to understand how dear Judith was to him—and that there was no possibility of prolonging her life.

He said truly when he stated he had not yet done with Mr. Mazingford, and neither, had Mr. Mazingford's creditors. For a long time they had been kept quiet with promises, and for a shorter period they had waited patiently until the decease of Stephen—who was known to be incapable of making a will—should put the ex-member in possession of the Llandyl coal mines; but now that there was no chance of a solitary sixpence of the income ever reaching Mr. Mazingford—now that a perfect storm of public indignation, raised by Mr. Gartmore, abetted by Evan Crepton and Dr. Duvard, burst upon his head—now that the whole dreary story of domestic persecution and frightful tyranny was given to the world—every enemy he had on the earth fell upon him.

As to Crafton, the owner of it had to shut up his establishment, and before five years had passed away Mr. Gartmore read, much to his satisfaction, that the woman who after squeezing every shilling she could out of Judith, had told her secret, when at the very point of death, to her husband, was sentenced to transportation for life, for an attempted murder of an old lady, reported to be enormously rich, whom she was nursing.

And for the remainder of his career, Wavour Hall passed into the hands of Mr. Mazingford's creditors, who sold the antique furniture by public auction, and disposed of his stud, and got rid of the carriages, and let the house, and insured his life; and the last place where any of his former acquaintances caught sight of Judith's husband, was at a gaming table in Baden, where it is currently believed he cheated somebody once too often for his own personal safety.

Be this as it may, one thing is certain, that he never publicly appeared in England again, and that the select circle in which he once "lived, and moved, and had his being," from the hour of his wife's death knew him no more!

And as one wave swallows up another, so a very piquant little event, which occurred about a year after Judith's death, obliterated the memory of that branch of the Ridsdales from the polite recollection of fashionable society. People laughed till they were tired over the story of how Miss Lestock, making up friends with her dear uncle and aunt, " requested to know who those distingué-looking people were she had seen them speaking to, at the other end of the room ?"

" May I have the pleasure of presenting them to you, Adelaide?" said Mr. Gartmore ; and the lady was so delighted at the proposition, that accordingly, in the midst of a large circle of admiring friends, her uncle begged to introduce Mr. Evan Crepton and Mrs. Duvard, to their mother, and Miss Lestock to her children."

How the company tittered—for fashionable folks titter, reader, though not perhaps so often, or so loudly—just like Mrs. Owens, the greengrocer's wife, round the corner !   How red Miss Lestock grew—how haughtily Evan turned from her, without a word—how indignantly Alice looked in her face—how maliciously Mr. Gartmore surveyed the scene—how speedily Sir John Lestock left the room !

It was said he died of the shock ; but whether the attack of gout, which carried him off imme-

diately after, could possibly be ascribed to rage
and mortification, is a difficult question to decide.   He left his daughter all his personal property, on pain of forfeiture, however, if she ever
held any friendly intercourse with the Creptons,
by letter or otherwise.   " He need scarcely have
placed such a restriction on her," so his heir-at-
law said in a disappointed tone, and he said
right.

Amongst the Welsh mountains, amidst the
hills and the waterfalls, the valleys and the
streams of that wild and beautiful land, Mr.
Gartmore bought a property, from which he
could easily ride over to Llandyl Hall, and see,
as years rolled by, how Evan and his wife and
children prospered.   For young voices echoed
through the old pine plantations,—amongst the
woods that had caught the sound of Judith's
heart-rending recall, laughter, clear and joyous,
rang in the summer days—along the path she
had pursued, little feet went pattering.   The
house she had loved was beautified; and in the
still, twilight evenings, a happy group might
often have been noted, standing on the lawn of
the once dilapidated mansion—whilst far, far

below, where Llandyl spire pointed silently to Heaven—under the shadow of the church, beneath the spreading branches of an ancient elm, close to the quiet homes of her father, and mother, and Marcus Lansing, Judith Mazingford slept tranquilly at last—

> With her limbs at rest,
> In the green earth's breast,
> And her soul at home with God !

THE END.

J. Billing, Printer and Stereotyper, Guildford, Surrey.

CPSIA information can be obtained
at www.ICGtesting.com
Printed in the USA
LVOW10*1235110218
566112LV00011B/120/P